ALSO BY ANTHONY DeCURTIS

The Soundtrack of My Life by Clive Davis (coauthor)

*In Other Words: Artists Talk About
Life and Work*

*Rocking My Life Away: Writing About
Music and Other Matters*

LOU REED

A LIFE

ANTHONY DeCURTIS

LITTLE, BROWN AND COMPANY

LARGE PRINT EDITION

Little, Brown and Company
Hachette Book Group
1290 Avenue of the Americas, New York, NY 10104
littlebrown.com

First Edition: October 2017

Little, Brown and Company is a division of Hachette Book Group, Inc. The Little, Brown name and logo are trademarks of Hachette Book Group, Inc.

The publisher is not responsible for websites (or their content) that are not owned by the publisher.

The Hachette Speakers Bureau provides a wide range of authors for speaking events. To find out more, go to hachettespeakersbureau.com or call (866) 376-6591.

Library of Congress Cataloging-in-Publication Data
Names: DeCurtis, Anthony.
Title: Lou Reed: a life / Anthony DeCurtis.
Description: First edition. | New York: Little, Brown and Company, 2017. | Includes
    bibliographical references and index.
Identifiers: LCCN 2017008817 | ISBN 978-0-316-37655-6 (hardcover) /
    978-0-316-55242-4 (large print)
Subjects: LCSH: Reed, Lou. | Rock musicians—United States—Biography.
Classification: LCC ML420.R299 D43 2017 | DDC 782.42166092 [B]—dc23
LC record available at https://lccn.loc.gov/2017008817.

10 9 8 7 6 5 4 3 2 1

LSC-C

Printed in the United States of America

For Francesca, my mountaintop, my peak—
this, and everything

TABLE OF CONTENTS

TABLE OF CONTENTS

LOU REED

ANYTHING FOR YOU

P EOPLE ALWAYS SAY TO me, 'Why don't you get along with critics?'" Lou Reed told me one night in 2012. "I tell them, 'I get along fine with Anthony DeCurtis.' Shuts them right up." We were sitting in the dining room of the Kelly Writers House at the University of Pennsylvania, where I teach creative writing. I'd brought Lou down to do an interview with me in front of fifty or so invited guests and to have dinner with a dozen students, faculty members, musicians, and local media luminaries. As with so many things with Lou, it was touch-and-go until the very end.

Getting Lou to come to Penn, which is in Philadelphia, was complicated. Arrangements for his visit had been made months in advance with his manager, who assured me that Lou had approved them. The Kelly Writers House is an actual thirteen-room house in the heart of the Penn campus, and the interview would take place in the front room. Lou would be paid a modest fee, and the agenda was a brief reception, an hour-long interview, and a home-cooked meal served at the Writers House afterward. Patti Smith, Suzanne Vega, and Rufus Wainwright had all done it in previous years and had a great time. But Lou was different. I knew it was asking a lot of someone who didn't typically relish events of this kind, and I wanted to make sure in advance that he understood what the evening entailed. His manager assured me that he did.

But two days before the event, Lou's manager called and asked me if I would speak to Lou. Lou now wanted to do only the interview—not the reception, not the dinner. The intimacy of the event was the whole point, so that wasn't acceptable. But Lou was adamant. When I called the next day, Lou answered "Hello?" with a voice that sounded as if it was coming from inside a crypt. I explained the situation, and he matter-of-factly responded, "Well, we don't have to do any of it." The genial artist I had known for years had transformed into "Lou Reed." When we ended the conversation, I had no idea if he was going to show up or not.

He did show up. When he arrived, he greeted me warmly, as if nothing untoward had happened the day before, and we went into a faculty office that served as his greenroom. For his rider, Reed had requested kielbasa—which had caused great mirth for me and the Writers House staff. What would the fearsome Lou Reed insist on? Boys? Girls? Drugs? No, kielbasa. I later learned that kielbasa was necessary: it helped with his diabetes. A platter of meats and cheeses from Philadelphia's famed Di Bruno Bros. gourmet shop was brought to us, and Reed began chatting with me as if we had all the time in the world.

As we talked, I could hear the guests gathering downstairs for the reception. Reed, meanwhile, picked up a piece of prosciutto and, after tasting it, launched into an encomium to its excellence. It was, without question, the best prosciutto he had ever had. Could I please tell him where he could get some for himself? I introduced him to the woman who had ordered the food, and he peppered her with thanks and questions. In the meantime, the reception was now fully under way. People peeked into the room every few minutes to see if we would be coming out anytime soon. I decided the reception would have to be sacrificed. Lou was in a good mood, and if the interview went well, he might be willing to stay for dinner. We continued to enjoy the food, and finally I stood up and said, "We should probably go do our talk." He looked as if he had completely forgotten about it, but he stood up and followed me downstairs and into the front room.

When we emerged I could feel the audience's tense

energy. Lou, of course, seemed impervious. That kind of tension was the emotional sea he swam in, the air he breathed. The room was small, and it was packed. A number of people had traveled great distances to be there. Everyone had known that Lou was in the house, but his not emerging for the reception lent the gathering an edge. This was Lou Reed, after all. Maybe he would walk out. When we sat down in the two chairs set up in the front of the room, we adjusted our mics, and I thanked Reed for coming. "Anything for you," he said. Our conversation rambled on for an hour. We talked about writing, Andy Warhol, Delmore Schwartz, the Velvet Underground, and Laurie Anderson. We took questions from the audience, and then we were done.

Now Lou was in a great mood. He remained in his seat as people came by to say hello and brought memorabilia for him to sign. He was gracious to everyone, and looked over the rarities presented to him, mentioning that even he didn't have copies of some of them. Then, after about fifteen minutes, he joined us for dinner. Everyone got their Lou Reed story. And I got my compliment.

I'D GOTTEN TO KNOW Lou from writing about him in *Rolling Stone* and elsewhere, and over the course of more than fifteen years we'd regularly run into each other in New York—at clubs and concerts, at restaurants and parties. I always felt that one of the reasons Lou and I got along well was that we met socially before we ever met as artist and critic. In June of 1995 I got stuck at the airport in Cleveland, where I had gone to cover the concert celebrating the opening of the Rock and Roll Hall of Fame. Backed by Soul Asylum, Lou had turned in a roaring version of "Sweet Jane" as part of that show. My flight back to New York was delayed for hours and I was settling in for the wait when I ran into a record company friend, who introduced me to Lou and Laurie. There's nothing like an interminable flight delay to grease the gears of socialization.

"You reviewed *New York* for *Rolling Stone,* right?" Reed asked, referring to his classic 1989 album.

"Right."

"How many stars did you give it?"

"Four."

"Shoulda been five," he said. But he was smiling. The ice had been broken.

So we sat and chatted in the airport lounge. The subject of the Hall of Fame's list of the five hundred songs that shaped rock and roll came up, and Lou asked if "Walk on the Wild Side" was on it. It was, and he seemed pleased to be represented. Then, in a sweet gesture, he asked if Laurie's "O Superman" had been included. It had not, but at that moment I got a sense of how important she was to him. He didn't want to make the moment all about him.

Though I subsequently interviewed Lou a half dozen times or so, I remember those more casual moments with the most affection. I recall talking with him at length about Brian Wilson, whom he greatly admired, at a party for Amnesty International. Another time, I ran into him outside Trattoria Dell'Arte on Seventh Avenue when he and Laurie were heading to Carnegie Hall to see the Cuban musicians who had been part of the Buena Vista Social Club phenomenon. It was a warm summer night and Lou was wearing a light-colored short-sleeve shirt. He was in his late fifties at the time, and his hair was graying. In the fading sunlight, I could see the lines of aging on his face and neck. Rather than the daunting, leather-clad figure of Lou Reed, he looked like the man he had in a sense become: an aging Jewish New Yorker out for a night of entertainment with his arty, attractive girlfriend.

He also seemed to be in a terrific mood. He was excited to see the show and asked if I was going. When I explained that I didn't have tickets, he half-jokingly asked, "Do you think Laurie and I could get you in as some kind of" — he hesitated in order to come up with the exact right phrase — "celebrity perk?" We all laughed, but I was touched nonetheless.

Encountering him around the city that way always made me proud to be a New York native. An artist of incalculable significance, Lou was also, as one of his song titles put it, the ultimate "NYC Man," as inextricable a part of the city as, say, the Twin Towers. Now he and they are gone and the city still stands, however much diminished.

THOSE INTERACTIONS WITH LOU both spurred and complicated the writing of this book. I have been a Lou Reed fan for decades, since the Velvet Underground, and hold his work in the absolute highest regard. Other than Bob Dylan, the Beatles, and James Brown, no one has exerted as great an influence on popular music as he has. Particularly when we would run into each other unexpectedly, I would walk away feeling how extraordinary it was that I was on such familiar terms with Lou Reed.

I'm not unaware that I was useful to him. I wrote well and appreciatively about him. He always conceived of himself as a writer, and my having a PhD in American literature, writing for *Rolling Stone,* and teaching at a prestigious college all meant a great deal to him, though that's the sort of thing he would never admit. To borrow a phrase from one of Lou's close friends, the photographer Mick Rock, I saw Lou the way he wanted to see himself.

But I was always aware of his innumerable contradictions, and fascinated by them. Sometimes when I was interviewing him, I could see him tense up, watch his jaw tighten and his eyes grow cold, see him get ready to snap as he had famously done with so many writers so many times. See him about to become Lou Reed. Then he would remember that it was me, that it was okay, and he would calm down and simply answer the question. He would joke about how being insulted by Lou Reed had become something of a badge of honor in the music industry ("Kind of makes you hard, doesn't it?"), and how he'd used that persona to his benefit. "God forbid I should ever be nice to people: it would ruin everything," he told me. "The fact is, it works well, being thought to be difficult, because then people just won't ask you to do things you don't want to do. Being a nice guy? That's a disaster. You're just asking for trouble. People think, 'Oh, he's a nice guy, let's work him over.' As opposed to, 'Him? Forget it. He'll rip your throat out.'"

When Lou died I was as shocked as anyone who wasn't in his very closest circle. The opportunity to write this book emerged soon after, and I wondered about it. It's not something he would ever have wanted, and while he was alive I would not have written it. "Anything for you" would never have gone that far. No question: this book does not at all times see Lou the way he wanted to see himself. Aspects of his sex life, his drug use, and his cruelty that he came to be embarrassed about, and, in some sense, would have loved to erase, are discussed here in detail. As are his generosity and his kindness, his talent, his vision, and his genius. So if this book does not present him the way he wanted to see himself, to as great a degree as it was possible for me, it presents him as he was. And, I believe, as he knew himself to be. It is the full, intimate portrait, of an artist and a person, that he, like anyone of his stature, deserves.

Lou loved *Hamlet* and often would refer to it in conversation and interviews. Some lines from that play came to mind as I thought about what I wrote about him in here. At one point, when Hamlet is talking about his dead father, a monumental figure who literally haunts him, he says simply, "He was a man. Take him for all in all. I shall not look upon his like again." Lou Reed. All in all. Never again.

New York City
March 2017

1

FROM BROOKLYN TO THE CROTCH OF LONG ISLAND

NAMED AFTER HIS MOTHER's late grandfather, Lewis Allan Reed was born on March 2, 1942, at Beth El Hospital in Brooklyn, New York. His parents were Sidney Joseph and Toby Reed. Sidney was a smart, handsome, ambitious accountant and Toby a housewife whose beauty was remarked upon by all who knew her. Three years earlier, at the age of nineteen, she had been chosen "Queen of the Stenographers" at one of the many local beauty pageants in New York at that time. She had been nominated by the firm where she was working, United Lawyers Service, and it was characteristic of her reticence that she claimed the only reason she was selected was that "the really pretty stenographer was out sick that day." Her photo ran in the *Brooklyn Eagle,* and she was crowned queen at the Stenographers Ball held at the Manhattan Center on Thirty-Fourth Street in Manhattan, a run of subway stops and a world away from her life in Brooklyn.

The country was barely through the Depression and World War II was raging, but Brooklyn was a peaceful, if rough-hewn, place to live. The borough was overwhelmingly ethnic, with Italian, Irish, Jewish, and African American neighborhoods bordering one another and, in some instances, overlapping, with varying degrees of comfort. In contrast to the soaring towers and relentless modernity of Manhattan, Brooklyn was old-world and human-scale. The buildings were low and each neighborhood had everything its residents needed within a few blocks. The immigrant communities quavered on the tense balance of attempting to re-create the familiar comforts of their European homelands and embracing the fresh possibilities of life in the New World.

Both Toby's and Sidney's parents had emigrated from Europe in the early 1900s, her family from Poland, his from Russia. Sidney's father, Mendel Rabinowitz, established a successful printing business and settled in the Brooklyn neighborhood of Borough Park, a predominantly Italian and Jewish area. A recognizably Jewish name like Rabinowitz would do Sidney no good if he hoped to advance in the world beyond his neighborhood, so he legally changed his surname to Reed.

The Reeds were not religious and did not belong to a synagogue, although Lewis would eventually be bar mitzvahed. Sidney Reed, an opinionated man, despised organized religion. He was something of a loner, and the family did not have many close friends and did not belong to any neighborhood organizations. They lived in a small, walk-up apartment. Sidney was close to his younger brother Stan, who lived with the Reeds for a time, but for the most part the Reeds' family life was tight and enclosed. Lewis was the Reeds' first child, and, as the first and only son in a Jewish family, he was cherished.

Like so many men of his time, Sidney had struggled to find work in the wake of the Depression. A well-spoken man who prized the English language, he had dreamed of becoming a writer or a lawyer, but settled on being a certified public accountant, in accordance with his mother's wishes. Toby, whose given last name was Futterman, had left school to go to work and help support her family after her father died when she was in her teens.

The war was a frightening time for everyone, but particularly for Jews, as the Nazis swept across Europe and rumors and reports of the fate of that continent's Jewish population began to drift across the Atlantic to the United States. Personal disappointments were pushed aside, and a sense of tense, precarious gratitude became predominant. Simply to have a job and enough money to live and provide for a growing family—simply to be alive—seemed enough to be grateful for. Hoping for more was tempting the fates.

THE BROOKLYN THAT LOU Reed grew up in has been shrouded in a haze of nostalgia, perhaps deservedly. It sometimes seems as if the entire future of the music industry was forged by Brooklyn Jews of his approximate generation, Carole King, David Geffen, Neil Sedaka, Clive Davis, Neil Diamond, Gerry Goffin, Seymour Stein, and Barbra Streisand among them. Jewish families typically encouraged education and ambition in their children, and that manifested itself in both creative work and business. The practical business side derived from a sense that survival in post-Depression America required making sure you entered a profession that guaranteed the bills would always be paid. The creativity derived from an exactly opposite source, one out of the parents' control. As all immigrant groups tend to do, the Jews who came to New York attempted to reconstruct the homeland they had left behind. That provided a sense of comfort, and to contemporary eyes it looks romantic and charming. But these Brooklyn shtetls seemed restrictive and painfully old-world to the children and grandchildren of those immigrants. American music, radio, movies, and television all called to those young people with a wild sense of wide-open freedom that their neighborhoods and cramped apartments couldn't begin to rival. That generation would leave Europe behind and create a vision of America in the popular arts that, before long, would become the prism through which the entire world viewed the country.

For some, Brooklyn in the forties and early fifties was a world of egg creams and raucous, sunny afternoons at Ebbets Field, of men waiting at newsstands for the bull-dog editions of the next day's newspapers in order to get the sports scores and racing results, of women sitting outside on stoops to escape the heat, watching their kids and sharing gossip with neighbors. If Reed noted or participated in such routines, they only rarely penetrated his consciousness in later years, and he didn't share those reminiscences with others. He would repeatedly describe his upbringing in Brooklyn as a combination of familial oppression and neighborhood tension. As a songwriter, he would eventually exalt the grittiness of New York's streets, but as a young boy growing up, he found it off-putting—both frightening and a little beneath him. He couldn't even romanticize it in retrospect, though he described it in terms far worse than it likely was. Taking his imagination to the extreme was a habit that began early with him.

Reed attended P.S. 192 on Eighteenth Avenue, four

blocks from his parents' apartment. His mother would escort him to school, despite the short distance. Reed recalled that he didn't walk to school alone before the age of nine because "if you walked the streets, you'd get killed." As for the school itself, he said, "They lined you up in a school yard with wire fences, no grass to walk on. The playground was concrete and they had lunch monitors.... People were pissing in the streets. A kid had to go to the john, you raised your hand, got out of line, and pissed through the wire. It was like being in a concentration camp, I suppose." It's inconceivable, of course, that teachers, especially in a coeducational school at that time—or any other time, really—would call on boys to urinate through a fence rather than use the school's restroom. Perhaps the boys did it on their own when they were playing in the school yard and no teachers or oppressive "lunch monitors" were present, and Reed conflated the memories in order to enhance his anecdote. But then if, however ironically, you're comparing your elementary school to a concentration camp, anything is possible.

If Reed's contemporaries heard evocative street corner singing or the wonders of New York radio while growing up in Brooklyn, such charms were lost on or unperceivable to him. "I didn't hear nothin' in Brooklyn," he said. "The radio didn't exist." He concluded, "I couldn't have been unhappier than in the eight years I spent growing up in Brooklyn." Somewhat jokingly he later added, "Most of my childhood memories are not available to me. My childhood was so unpleasant that I absolutely don't remember anything before age thirty-one." Reed did attend Dodgers games with his father, though he would later disparage the experience, wryly claiming that the Dodgers' leaving Brooklyn — a source of never-ending heartbreak for, and much written about by, literary Brooklynites of those days — was the cause of his cynicism. He claimed to have cared about the Dodgers "very much," but their departure for Los Angeles in 1957 — ironically, long after Reed and his family had themselves left the borough — made it impossible for him to ever care about baseball again.

When Reed was five, his younger sister, Merrill, whose nickname was Bunny, was born. Now with two children, the Reeds, like so many other solvent families who lived in cities at around that time, began to think about moving to the suburbs. The war was over, and America was becoming the world's great economic engine. The baby boom was in full swing, and the crowded urban centers were beginning to seem indistinguishable from the cramped environments that so many of their ancestors had fled. The postwar era in America was characterized by a desire to establish a reassuring normalcy, to erase the Europe of wars and genocide, to lose the past and live in America's eternally bright future. No doubt the Cold War was coming into being, and the threat of nuclear annihilation lent a persistent undercurrent of dread to the era. But that whiff of mortality only fueled the desire for stability, a kind of submerged rage for order. The booming economy and the New Deal reforms that the Roosevelt administration had put in place to combat the Depression meant that social mobility was, for once, a true possibility in America. The dream of owning your own home was becoming a reality for millions of people. And when Sidney Reed was offered the job of treasurer at Cellu-Craft, a Long Island firm that, in the true spirit of *The Graduate,* manufactured plastics, it seemed as if the Reeds were finally getting their shot at that dream. So in 1952, the Reed family moved to Freeport, Long Island.

SIDNEY REED WANTED TO raise his kids on Long Island in part because he believed it would be safer, and he "thought that the opportunity on the island would be better," said Allan Hyman, one of Reed's close friends on Long Island, of Reed's father. "That was the way a lot of people felt." Freeport was one of the small towns along the south shore of Long Island that served as a bedroom community for New York. The Reeds moved there at a time when conformity was not merely desired or valued; it was an unquestioned good. The Reeds' home—an undistinguished three-bedroom ranch-style house at 35 Oakfield Avenue—cost $10,000, and it

had been built in 1951. Many of the families streaming to the island from the city were from Brooklyn,
and many of them were Jewish. Jews were a distinct, if
significant, minority, and Reed was enrolled in Hebrew
school at Congregation B'nai Israel, which he attended
three days a week—and loathed—in preparation for
his bar mitzvah. In stark contrast to the identity politics of today, assimilation was the order of the day in
the early fifties on Long Island, and none of Reed's
friends, Jewish or not, recall incidents of anti-Semitism
or bias. There was a black community in Freeport,
and students socialized across racial lines at the high
school level, though racial strife would erupt there later,
in the sixties. "It was a fantastic place to grow up," said
Doug Van Buskirk, who attended school with Reed.
"Probably anybody on the south shore of Long Island
would say that in the fifties. People could walk anywhere at any time of the day or night. We would return
late from a party and walk across town. It was a very
safe, almost totally a middle-class town."

While people identified with their local town, the
various spots along the shore—Freeport, Baldwin,
Oceanside, and Rockville Centre among them—all
bled into one another. Class distinctions blurred as
well. Professional families, like Reed's, lived on the
same street as blue-collar families who owned the local
shops or worked in service industries like plumbing
and heating. It was an era before McMansions and the

conspicuous display of wealth. Economic gradations existed, of course—a nicer car, a maid, ownership of a boat—but they were subtle and people didn't feel the need to make an issue of them. "I don't think any of us thought about someone's house not being as nice as someone else's," said Judy November, who was Reed's lab partner in high school, when her last name was Titus. "It was a different time; we were less materialistic about things. But all my friends, I thought, were economically comfortable."

If you weren't an old money family with the heritage and social cachet to show for it—and none of the families in Freeport were—your wealth or lack of it was a private matter. Even the competitive suburban ethic of "keeping up with the Joneses" was less about materialistic warfare than about maintaining the calm equilibrium of prosperous conformity that had brought everyone out there to begin with. Any sign of decay or indifference—an untended lawn, a battered car, a peeling paint job—evoked unsettling memories of the anonymous, teeming clamor and frightening disrepair of the city. In that regard, every family had to pull its weight in order to maintain the uniform and controlled demeanor that was the hallmark of suburban life. Anyone who could manage to scrape together $10,000 to buy a home in the area was likely to be "comfortable" or "middle class," to use two of the vague expressions Americans employed at that time—

and since that time—in order to blur class distinctions. And in the fifties, if you had arrived in a suburb like Freeport, you had planted your stake in the soil of the American dream. Even today, Freeport looks much as it did back then. The homes have been spruced up and expanded a bit, but not torn down for massive reconstructions. It's as if the houses themselves got the message: once you arrived in Freeport, you were there to stay. What was there needed to be maintained, but nothing more was required.

ACCORDING TO ALLAN HYMAN, Reed's father was "a quiet guy. Very reserved. I viewed him as fairly strict. He set up boundaries for his family and his son. He wouldn't tolerate people cursing in front of him. He had middle-class values and he wanted everybody to act appropriately. He wanted Lou to respect him and his mother. That's the way he was. My father was similar. They were very conservative. They expected that we would behave ourselves at the dinner table and we would dress a certain way.

"I had a lot of friends whose parents were very involved with their kids in sports and stuff. They were people you could go out and toss a ball with. My father and Lou's father were not like that. Lou's father was much more cerebral. He was also very penurious. Typically, when I went out to dinner with my friends' parents, they would always pay. But when I went with Lou and his parents, they would expect me to pay my share. Like, 'You had the hamburger. You owe a dollar fifty.'" As for Toby, Hyman said, "If you wanted to cast somebody as a fifties housewife living in the suburbs with an apron, taking care of her husband and children, that was Lou's mother. The ultimate wife. She was really attractive, gracious, friendly—a very nice person. She was one of those women who, when I was there, would always ask if I wanted anything to eat. She would bring me milk and cookies." Richard Sigal, another of Reed's Long Island friends, agreed. "I never got to know Lou's father very well," he said. "But Lou's mother—not only was she beautiful, but she was always very nice to me." Reed's sister, Bunny, described her mother as an "anxious individual through-out her life" who "took a traditional role with my father, always staying subservient to him."

Whatever its appeal for others, Freeport seemed like a jail to Reed. His parents did not have a large circle of friends. There were no cultural or entertainment trips to Manhattan for the family—no museum visits, no theater, no circus. It was a small, tight, protected world. Merely having arrived on Long Island seemed to be enough for his parents, particularly his father, who viewed the boring regularity of their lives as a virtue. Still, Sidney loved music and often played it at home—show tunes, Benny Goodman, big band jazz. He had a sizable record collection that was meticulously organized. But Reed would only describe Freeport and its environs in the most caustic terms throughout his life. "Hempstead's like the crotch of Long Island," he said in one memorable tirade. "It's one big bus terminal with faggots walking around saying, 'You in love?' Great Neck is the Jewish Towers. If you run into a diseased criminal mind, it's from Great Neck. Nobody goes to more great lengths to escape their upbringing than someone from Great Neck. Usually they become sadistic criminals who do senseless rape-murders on four-year-olds. You find a letter that says, 'I was raised in Great Neck, what'ya expect? Hi, Ma.'"

Reed's father and the desire for unperturbable respectability that he represented would become the central target of Reed's rebellion. "He would refer to my father as a horrible Republican," said Hyman, whose father was a successful lawyer. "And he would say that his father was a horrible, disgusting Republican accountant. I didn't get it at the time—I didn't know from Republicans. I just thought Lou was being Lou, trying to be outrageous and shocking, which he was starting to become. He would love to shock. That was his thing. It was probably one of the reasons I found him so interesting, because most of my friends were not like that at all."

For his secular education, Reed attended the Caroline G. Atkinson Elementary School, which he entered in the third grade. He had been nervous and frightened in Brooklyn, and those feelings persisted in Freeport. According to his sister, who would go on to become a psychotherapist, Reed "suffered from anxiety and panic attacks throughout his life....It was obvious that Lou was becoming increasingly anxious and avoidant and resistant to most socializing unless it was on his terms. He was possessed with a fragile temperament." However, as with many of the children who were transported by their families from New York City to the suburbs, the change in environment enabled Reed to adopt an air of urban swagger. While many Freeport families were city exiles, not all of them were, so Reed's experience on the mean streets of Brooklyn gave him something like street credibility, or enabled its pretense. Perhaps more important, his rude behavior in the well-behaved town of Freeport was unlikely to elicit the same harsh response that it would have in far more confrontational Brooklyn. In Freeport, Reed could be one of the tough kids, or posture as one, with little in the way of consequences. "He started being disrespectful early on," said Richard Bloom, who attended school with Reed, and that behavior would continue.

NOT LONG AFTER THE Reeds arrived in Freeport, fifties youth culture began to disrupt the seemingly tranquil surface of that decade in America. Along with the

early tremors of rock and roll came cinematic antihe-
roes like James Dean and Marlon Brando. They brought
along with them the specter of juvenile delinquency,
the apolitical rebellion of teens against the conformity
and blandness American society had come so whole-
heartedly to embrace. Reed walked both sides of the
line. "Lou was a good student," November recalled.
"He was a fairly serious student. He wasn't known as a
bookworm, but he applied himself. He was considered
a responsible member of our class, and he was quite
well-liked." Reed would later describe his life growing
up on Long Island as terrible, but, in November's view,
"my sense was that he did enjoy himself. I did not
sense hostilities from him. I did not sense negativity at
all." He was even well-behaved as November's lab partner. "He was diligent," she said. "He didn't blow up
any experiments while I was in the room!" Reed
indulged all the same pleasures of suburban Long Island
life as his friends: tennis, outings to Jones Beach, horseback riding, movies, occasional boating, frequent
socializing.

Reed was also a great reader. "Lou and I were always
reading," said Richard Sigal, who attended school with
Reed from the eighth grade and stayed friends with
him through college; that Sigal would eventually
become a professor of sociology with a specialty in
deviant behavior was a fact that Reed would enjoy
when the two men resumed their friendship as adults.

"We loved Ian Fleming—the James Bond novels," Sigal said. "It was almost one-upmanship: who could get his hands on the new book and finish it first, so we could tell the other guy about it." That competitiveness extended into other areas as well. "We played tennis when we were in high school and college," Sigal said, "and it was like Connors and McEnroe. We were exactly at the same level. He'd win a set, I'd win a set. It pissed him off. He tried so hard to beat me, and I tried so hard to beat him. He didn't like losing."

But there were areas in which it was impossible to compete with Reed. "Lou was always more advanced than the rest of us," Sigal said. "The drinking age was eighteen back then, so we all started drinking at around sixteen. We were drinking quarts of beer, but Lou was smoking joints. He didn't do that in front of many people, but I knew he was doing it. While we were looking at girls in *Playboy,* Lou was reading *Story of O.* He was reading the Marquis de Sade, stuff that I wouldn't even have thought about or known how to find."

In the late fifties and the sixties, magazines like *Evergreen Review* and publishing houses like Grove Press, both founded by Barney Rosset, began putting out work that consciously attempted to subvert the self-satisfied conservatism of postwar mainstream American culture. Sexuality was an important front in that battle. Rosset led the fight for the publication of unexpurgated versions of D. H. Lawrence's *Lady Chatterley's Lover* and Henry Miller's *Tropic of Cancer*. The lines between sexually charged literature and erotic provocation for its own sake began to blur. *Playboy* published its first issue in 1953, and, month after month, titillating photographs of the girl next door with her breasts exposed nestled against short stories by literary heavyweights and essays about the freedoms afforded by the First Amendment. Similarly, serious literary work with daring sexual content appeared in avant-garde magazines next to photographs and illustrations that skirted the lines of smut. Insulting the sexual conservatism of the times in any way was a shot across the cultural bow.

If depictions of heterosexuality represented a threat to the mainstream, homosexuality was perceived as explicitly dangerous. Allen Ginsberg, William Burroughs, Hubert Selby Jr., Gore Vidal, and John Rechy, among many other writers, began exploring homosexual themes in their work, and the love that dared not speak its name began to find its voice. While considered controversial, such writers were also praised by forward-looking critics, and the fact that their work was considered shocking only increased its allure for the generation of burgeoning rebels that included Lou Reed. Writers began chronicling the ways of a heretofore invisible American underground, a world that Rechy eventually called the city of night and that Reed would ultimately make his aesthetic—and, at times, his personal—home. Hustlers, transvestites, male and female hookers, and drug users populated a subterranean realm that Eisenhower America, with its manicured suburbs, either was entirely unaware of or pretended did not exist. That the realm of gay cruising largely existed, of necessity, in criminalized environments—Mafia-run bars; marginal, potentially violent sections of town; shabby rooming houses and hotels—only made it more seductive and subversive. Such a world must have seemed as much an imaginative creation as Shakespeare's Forest of Arden for young literary rebels remote from New York or Los Angeles. For Reed, the city of night packed the same emotional kick—and it was a relatively brief car or train ride away.

Even in high school, Reed led something of a double life. On the most superficial level, he attended classes, participated in athletics, and got passing grades. "I saw him practically every day in junior high and high school," said Allan Hyman, who was on the high school's track team with Reed and would go on to college with him. "He was regarded as kind of a quiet kid. He certainly wasn't in the so-called in crowd, and neither was I. That wasn't important to him. He didn't care." Along with his friend Richard Sigal, Reed took a summer job cleaning up the trash with a pointy stick at nearby Jones Beach. According to Sigal, Reed did not last long in that position.

What Reed did think was important was music, writing, and sex. Speaking of his discovery of doo-wop, R & B, and rock and roll on the radio as a teenager in the fifties, Reed rhapsodized about "the dusky, musky, mellifluous, liquid sounds of rock and roll. The sounds of another life. The sounds of freedom. As Alan Freed pounded a telephone book and the honking sax of Big Al Sears seared the airwaves with his theme song, 'Hand Clappin',' I sat staring at an indecipherable book on plane geometry, whose planes and angles would forever escape me. And I wanted to escape it, and the world of SAT tests, the College Boards, and leap immediately and eternally into the world of Shirley and Lee, the Diablos, the Paragons, the Jesters. Lillian Leach and the Mellows' 'Smoke from Your Cigarette.' Alicia and the Rockaways' 'Why Can't I Be Loved,' a question that certainly occupied my teenage time. The lyrics sat in my head like Shakespearean sonnets with all the power of tragedy. 'Gloria.' 'Why don't you write me, darling / Send me a letter'—the Jacks. And then there was Dion. That great opening to 'I Wonder Why' engraved in my skull forever. Dion, whose voice was unlike any other I had heard before. Dion could do all the turns, stretch those syllables so effortlessly, soar so high he could reach the sky and dance there among the stars forever. What a voice that had absorbed and transmogrified all these influences into his own soul as the wine turns into blood." His favorite doo-wop songs, Reed later said, "made me believe that I could write a song."

REED'S OBSESSION WITH ROCK and roll in high school led him to the guitar. He found a teacher and went for one lesson, during which he demanded to learn only four basic chords that would carry him through most of the songs that he wanted to play. He organized bands for school talent shows, and, along with friends like Richard Sigal, on guitar, and Allan Hyman, on drums, started playing local gigs. Reed drafted Judy Titus to join him, Sigal, and another Freeport High student for a performance at the school's talent show. "I was looking for an opportunity to be part of the variety show, so it just fell into place," Judy November said. "We rehearsed, and it went over pretty well. Lou was the orchestrator of our event, but he wasn't a dictator about it at all." Reed also performed at the school with a friend named Alan Walters and a singer named Phil Harris, who was one of Reed's classmates. "We were in many of the same classes together, and quite a few times we went over to his house to hang out," Harris recalled. "We were both interested in music and most of the 'in' bands and groups of the time." Reed, Walters, and Harris performed a Little Richard act, and Harris, who sang lead, remarked in 2008 that he was "still hoarse to this day." Reed and Walters sang backup and Reed played guitar. The performance was successful enough that the trio decided to see if they could come up with some material of their own. They got together at Reed's house and generated two midtempo doo-wop songs: "Leave Her for Me" and "So Blue." One inspiration for their songwriting was a neighbor who had heard their performance at Freeport High; he mentioned that he had a contact in the music industry and asked if they would mind performing some of their original songs for him. Once he heard the songs, he put Reed and his friends in touch with Bob Shad, who was an A&R man for Mercury Records and was about to launch his own label, called Time.

Shad liked what he heard and signed the group, which had been calling itself the Shades, to his label. It was an all-too-typical arrangement for young bands at that time. "I used to ask Bob Shad how we were going to get paid from record sales," Harris recalled, "and what I got for an answer was not to worry about the business end of the deal." As teenagers and high school students, they felt that they were in no position to push matters any further. Shad brought the group into the studio, and arranged for an additional singer to fill out the background vocals with Reed and Walters. Incredibly, Shad also lined up the torrid sax player

King Curtis and famed R & B guitarist Mickey Baker to play on the record. The songs are unremarkable by the standards of the radio hits of the time, but not bad at all for kids, and Curtis's playing is vivid at every moment. As for the songwriting, "Leave Her for Me" was credited to "Lewis Reed," and "So Blue" to Reed and Harris. In an early reflection of Reed's style sense, the group would perform in dark sunglasses—hence the Shades. Shad, however, was concerned that both the sunglasses and the name would get them confused with other bands, so, with inadvertent wit, the group renamed itself the Jades. They likely were thinking of the gem, though, as a budding litterateur, Reed might well have been aware of the word's historical use to describe sexually disreputable women, a usage that comes down to us in the term "jaded."

"Leave Her for Me" achieved its moment of glory when it was played on the Swingin' Soiree, a show hosted by the legendary New York disc jockey Murray Kaufman, universally known as Murray the K, on 1010 WINS, then one of the most important rock stations in the country. To Reed's immense disappointment, it was not Kaufman, who had taken that night off, but a substitute DJ who played it. (The band later lip-synched the song at a Long Island dance party at which Kaufman made a brief personal appearance.) The two-sided single also appeared in jukeboxes on Long Island. Reed would later claim that he received a royalty check for seventy-eight cents, prompting Phil Harris to joke that Reed owed him a third of that for his songwriting contribution. The Jades also took their show on the road. "We played openings of shopping malls and other events after the release of the 'So Blue' record," Harris said. "We played in bars and other such establishments and anywhere where people would listen. Sometimes they did, and sometimes not. The outfits we wore were classics of the fifties. Shades, peg pants, string ties, and jackets with glitter on them." After "So Blue," Shad invited Harris to record some other songs for him. Notably, the other Jades were not included in that invitation. Reed, however, recorded other tracks for Shad in 1962, including the teen-pop confections "Your Love" and "Merry Go Round," neither of which found much success. Reed's brush with exposure, however, encouraged him to continue to try to place his songs. "I used to go up to Harlem," he recalled. "I met this guy, Leroy Kirkland, who was the arranger for the orchestra at the Alan Freed rock-and-roll shows. I'd go with him to get the Harptones or somebody to record one of my little songs. Isn't that a thing of fantasy?"

Reed did not limit his performances to the Jades. "We started a garage band dubbed the Valets by Lou," Richard Sigal said. "I never liked the name, but Lou was the leader." Along with Sigal, whom Reed taught to play guitar, Allan Hyman played drums and Bobby

Futterman, a cousin of Lou's who lived in a nearby Long Island town, played bass and guitar. Jerry Jackson, an African American football star at Freeport High, also performed with the Valets, as a singer. "Jerry had a good voice, and he would sing lead on some songs," Sigal recalled. "Lou always said to me, 'You have the sweet voice,' so he wanted me to do the slow songs. I sang 'Castle in the Sky' by the Bop-Chords. I would do the doo-wop songs, and Lou would do the fast, gravelly ones. He always liked 'Bony Moronie.' We played parties, the beach clubs and bars along the strip on the south shore of Long Island. You never knew if you were going to get paid or not with the Valets; sometimes our pay was dinner, a plate of spaghetti. We played private birthday parties at people's houses, where the neighbors would call the cops, and they'd come and tell us to turn it down. We always played loud." The Valets followed a standard routine: "Three fast songs and one slow song, especially if you wanted to get people out dancing. Sometimes you'd go to a dance where the boys would be on one side of the room and the girls on the other. So we'd start with a slow song and they'd always dance to that. Then you'd lead in with a fast song. That was the format."

"Lou was starting to become enthusiastic about music," Allan Hyman said of his high school friend, "and he started taking it a lot more seriously than I did at the time." Sigal recalled Hyman missing Reed's cue to end a song one night. "Allan was banging away on his drums and he's looking up at the ceiling and he's got his eyes closed. Lou reached over and rapped Allan on the head with his knuckles hard enough for me to hear. Allan looked startled and Lou just gave him a glower and we wrapped up the song. I guess that's sort of indicative of how Lou dealt with a lot of people in his bands over the years."

IN ROCK AND ROLL, Reed discovered a yearning and lyricism that complemented the rawer truths he was encountering in the literature he was reading. Sex, of course, suffused both of those aesthetic pursuits. As Reed and his high school buddies began to explore their sexuality, as all adolescents do, he followed his own path. "As we got older in high school, we started to become interested in girls," Hyman recalled. "His view was always different from the view that most of us took toward girls. Completely different. I'm not aware that he ever dated anyone seriously in high school."

While it was typical for Hyman and the other boys in Reed's crowd to find girls to go steady with, Reed took another approach. "We all had long-term girl-friends. Like, for months on end, or a year, we would be going steady," Richard Sigal said. "Lou never did.

All of a sudden he would show up with these girls. They were all sluts. I had no idea where he found them. He didn't do traditional things, like take them to the movies and then to the ice-cream parlor. Lou once told me, 'I like girls with black hearts.' I think that's telling." Sigal recalled Reed recounting a visit from one such black-hearted girl. "Once I was over in the den at his house, and he was on the phone with some girl," Sigal said. "I guess his parents had gone away and he had had this girl over the night before. He started speaking angrily to her about the fact that she had given him a blow job and when he came in her mouth she ran into the kitchen and spit it into the sink. He said, 'You spit that all over my dishes!' That's classic Lou. I don't know if it was mock anger and he was trying to impress me. I was just shaking my head."

Allan Hyman had a sense of where Reed found some of his girls. "There was a radio station in Freeport called WGBB, and you could call in and make dedications," he said. "There were so many people trying to call that the line was always busy. But between busy signals you could actually have a conversation with the other people waiting. There may have been dozens of people waiting to get through, but you could speak to a girl and get her phone number. Lou met a girl in Merrick that way. This was before we could drive, so she eventually took a bus or train to Freeport, and Lou took her to the Grove Theater on Merrick

Road for an afternoon matinee. They sat in the balcony and Lou was making out with her with his hand under her sweater. I couldn't imagine anything more outrageous! But they had matrons with flashlights in theaters in those days, and one of them saw what was going on, and told them to knock it off. Lou told the matron to go fuck herself, and she called the manager, who escorted them out of the theater."

When Reed grew tired of his friend from Merrick, he passed her along to Hyman, an early manifestation of his fluid sexual boundaries. She was the first person who ever offered Hyman marijuana, which was still very much a forbidden drug in the fifties. ("Are you addicted to those?" he asked her when she fired up a joint. "She started laughing.") "I literally learned about sex from this girl, and Lou was the one who found her first," Hyman said. Hyman's prom date was another of Reed's finds from Merrick. In Hyman's senior yearbook, Reed wrote, "Let me know how you do with Gots," using a nickname they had come up with for the girl. On prom night, Hyman was driving and his date was in the front seat, while Reed was energetically making out with his date, a girl from East Meadow, in the back seat. When Gots expressed outrage at Reed's shenanigans with his date and refused Hyman's overtures, Hyman grew angry. They drove to the Rockville Center Oasis Diner after the prom. Afterward, Hyman drove away with Reed and his date, leaving

Gots at the diner. Reed, perhaps recalling his own escapades with Gots, halted his activities in the back seat to urge Hyman to reconsider. "You've got to go back and pick her up," Reed told him. "You can't leave her there." At three or four in the morning, Gots agreed to have sex with Hyman. "Finally," Reed remarked from the back seat. A Freeport policeman on patrol interrupted their tryst, however, so Hyman's plans were foiled. "Lou was in the back seat, hysterical," Hyman recalled.

By contemporary standards, such adventures seem relatively innocent—and they were. "We didn't get a lot of sex in the fifties," Hyman explained. "It was a different time. Most of the people I knew were fairly conservative in that regard." But Reed moved well beyond the adolescent boy-girl dramas that preoccupied his friends. "Lou's view started becoming increasingly bizarre," Hyman said. "It became more bizarre in his poetry, and his writing generally took on what would be described today as a gay tone, if you will. He started talking about having relationships with men, which I found amazingly rebellious at the time. That's the only way I could describe it. It wasn't that I viewed it as being bad. It just seemed so foreign."

Hyman noted that a number of boys in their school were overtly "effeminate"; they appeared gay—or "queer," in the nomenclature of that time (and, ironically, of our time as well) — and it eventually turned out that they were. Reed, however, was not one of them. "He was always interested in girls — always," Hyman said. "So when he started showing me the poetry and the writings, I found it confusing. And they were always bizarre stories. Like he would write about meeting a guy in a men's room and having sex with him in one of the stalls, describing it in great detail. Now, maybe he was doing that and just never talked about it, but this was in high school. I viewed it as Lou being outrageous, being provocative. Maybe he was taking it from books." Indeed, the men's room scene Hyman described was something of a trope in the literature Reed was likely reading, not to mention in some people's real lives. Walter Jenkins, a trusted aide of President Lyndon Johnson, and, in England, Brian Epstein, before he managed the Beatles, were just two of the prominent men who were arrested for sexual activity in public men's rooms in that era. In Greenwich Village, the men's room at, of all places, the Howard Johnson's at the corner of Eighth Street and Sixth Avenue was a noted cruising site, largely due to the diner's proximity to Christopher Street and Greenwich Avenue, both gay hot spots. When Hyman asked Reed about such scenes in his writing, Reed responded, "Haven't you ever had thoughts that were different? Didn't you ever think about stuff like this?

What about fantasies?" When Hyman said that in fact he hadn't indulged in such fantasies, Reed just shrugged. "This is life," he said. "This is what people think about."

But Reed may well have been doing more than reading about such activities. "We all knew everything about one another," said Richard Sigal about the group of male friends that he and Reed were part of, "but Lou had a secret life that I still don't know a lot about. One part of that was, he was buying weed somewhere. Where? I hadn't a clue. In those days, I wouldn't have known where to begin to find dope." Another part of that secret life took place at the Hay Loft, a gay bar in Baldwin, Long Island, not far from Freeport. The Hay Loft catered to a young gay and lesbian crowd. Hofstra College, for one thing, was not far away. (One habitué of the Hay Loft was James Slattery, a resident of Massapequa Park who would later transform into the Warhol film star Candy Darling and earn a prominent mention in "Walk on the Wild Side.") The bar featured music, and Reed would occasionally perform there. Richard Sigal remembered Reed describing the Hay Loft scene to him: "Lou said that sometimes the patrons there would grab his ass or his crotch. I asked him what he did when that happened, thinking that he would probably deck somebody. He said he just laughed. I was pretty naive at the time and it never occurred to me that he might have enjoyed or encouraged it."

Eventually, Reed started bringing his straight friends there, as he would do in later years with the after-hours clubs he frequented in downtown Manhattan. Allan Hyman was one such visitor. "It was very shocking," Hyman recalled. "I didn't really get it. The crowd was very young, just a little older than us. You only had to be eighteen to drink in those days, but you could get phony proof when you were fifteen and get served almost anywhere. Lou obviously knew some of the people there." Reed also brought Hyman to a gay bar he frequented in Oceanside.

Reed eventually began, in Hyman's terms, to "display an effeminate attitude. Instead of being an average teenage kid. It was almost as if he was putting it on, like it was just for shock value, but I don't think he acted that way around people he wasn't comfortable with. One of the things about my relationship with him is that he liked to shock me. He liked to say really provocative things and see what my reaction would be." Richard Sigal remarked, "Lou was an experimenter. He experimented with his sex life. He experimented with drugs and alcohol. He experimented with his music. There was a unique fabric that enveloped all those areas of his life, that tied him together, and made him a unique person."

When it came time to think about college, Reed and Hyman became fixated on Syracuse University, a private school in upstate New York with a solid academic reputation. But it wasn't the academics that attracted them to the school. Reed's father drove them to Syracuse for a weekend visit, and they had the time of their lives. "We thought we had landed in heaven," Hyman recalled. "Lou's father went to sleep, thankfully for us, and we met all these girls and were partying. I was thinking about what a party we were going to have when we got up there. When we were driving back, Lou said to me, 'This is going to be so cool. We're going to have the best time!' And I said, 'Yeah, I can hardly wait.'"

Reed's senior yearbook describes him as a "valuable participant" on the school's track team, and it states his interests as "basketball, music, and, naturally, girls." He had "no plans" after graduation but was prepared to "take life as it comes." Life, alas, would not prove so easy to take, however. When he graduated, Reed informed Hyman that he would not be going to Syracuse, although he had been accepted at the school. The pressure of his experimentations and the questions they raised about his identity had begun to get to Reed. He said that he had been feeling depressed, and that his parents thought it would be best for him to stay nearby. "He never shared it with me," Hyman said, "but I guess he was going through a period where he was questioning his sexuality. And I think his parents got caught up in it." Reed had also been accepted at New York University, which, along with its campus in Greenwich Village, had an additional campus in the Bronx, where he enrolled. Staying close to home did not relieve his depression, however, and Hyman's suspicion that Reed's parents got "caught up" in his problems proved all too true. Reed's mood swings, acerbity, and general rebelliousness had certainly caught their attention. He and his parents fought about his mysterious comings and goings, and the "effeminate" behavior that Hyman described could not have helped matters. Homosexuality was not merely regarded as a clinical psychiatric disorder at the time; its legal status was dubious at best in many parts of the United States. For parents like Sidney and Toby, for whom middle-class respectability was a paramount concern, the possibility of their son being homosexual would have been deeply disturbing. There is no question that Reed's parents loved him. He was their firstborn child and their only son—a special status in a Jewish family. His younger sister adored him. But his wild ways upset the orderly life the family had come to Freeport to enjoy, and now the seriousness of his depression called his mental stability into question. It's quite possible that Sidney and Toby were worried that their son might take his own life. One day, during Reed's freshman year at NYU, when he was seventeen, his parents picked him up at school and brought him home "limp and unresponsive," in Bunny's description, "dead-eyed" and "noncommunicative." At odd moments he would begin laughing maniacally. Sidney and Toby told Bunny that her brother had suffered a "nervous breakdown," and they kept the news from everyone else.

Sidney and Toby sought help for Lou, and doctors suggested that he might be schizophrenic. According to Bunny, their reasoning was that Lou may not have been picked up often enough as a baby and had been left to cry in his room—a ludicrous notion, needless to say, but a common idea at the time and one that would instill intense feelings of guilt in Toby, feelings from which she would never recover. Lou's condition exempted him from the draft, although, as was also common at the time, he might well have exaggerated his symptoms through drugs or other means. A psychiatrist wrote a letter that, according to Bunny, stated that Lou "suffered from delusions and hallucinations, saw spiders crawling on the walls and...might be schizophrenic." Lou framed the letter and hung it on the wall of his room.

The Reeds ended up agreeing to have their son undergo electroconvulsive therapy—electroshock therapy, as it was called at the time. Writing years later about that decision, Bunny explained, "My father, controlling and rigid, was attempting to solve a situation that was beyond him. My mother was terrified and certain of her own implicit guilt since they had told her that this was due to her poor mothering. Each of us suffered the loss of our dear sweet Lou in our own private hell, unhelped and undercut by the medical profession." As barbaric as the notion sounds—and, indeed, as barbaric as it often was in practice—ECT was a common treatment. Indeed, in much milder forms, it is still used today. Reed, however, was devastated by his treatments, which took place at Creedmoor Psychiatric Hospital in Queens, New York, in a series of outpatient visits on which his parents accompanied him. "I watched my brother as my parents assisted him coming back into our home afterwards, unable to walk, stupor-like," Bunny wrote. "It damaged his short-term memory horribly and throughout his life he struggled with memory retention, probably directly as a result of those treatments."

Whether or not Reed's alleged memory loss had anything to do with his ECT treatments—his subsequent prodigious drug and alcohol abuse could well have been factors—he came to regard his being subjected to them as an egregious family betrayal, a kind of Oedipal revenge. His feelings about his father, in particular, were irretrievably darkened. According to Bunny, Lou's bisexuality was not a reason for her parents' consenting to the treatment. That view is "simplistic and unrealistic," she wrote. "My parents were many things—anxious, controlling—but they were blazing liberals. Homophobic they were not. They were caught in a bewildering web of guilt, fear, and poor psychiatric care." Still, given their backgrounds and the mores of the time, they would have had to be cultural visionaries not to include Reed's potential gayness in the welter of issues that were factors in his problematic behavior. Reed's gay posturing in his parents' and others' presence was a defiant, conscious provocation, and, along with his mood swings and general recalcitrance, it elicited a crushing response, one that would ravage his family and poison his attitude toward it forever. Bunny expressed no doubt that her parents regretted their decision "every day until the day they died. But the family secret continued. We absolutely never spoke about the treatments, then or ever."

Reed, too, largely kept the story of his treatments to himself. Some of his closest friends would not learn about them until years later. Allan Hyman described Reed's affect during and immediately after the treatments. "When I saw him during the holidays, he was very withdrawn," he said. "He was never a friendly, outgoing type, but he was totally hostile and more sarcastic than ever. He was dark." Hyman saw no trace of his friend's former humor and liveliness. "He had always had this rebellious side to him, but that was kind of comical. It was fun." Now, "he had a nasty edge to him that he had never had before. Everything was fucked up. This person was ridiculous. That person was full of shit. Very cynical."

2

CORNER TABLE AT THE ORANGE

OU REED STAYED AT NYU for two semesters, and during that time he received follow-up treatments for his depression at the Payne Whitney Psychiatric Center on the Upper East Side of Manhattan. Eventually, his mood began to improve, and he revived the plan he had hatched with Allan Hyman for them to attend Syracuse University together. Located about 250 miles north of New York City, Syracuse, while geographically remote, was, and remains, a well-regarded private college, and at the time Reed attended, it was also a national football powerhouse led by fullback Ernie Davis, who, in 1961, became the first African American to win the Heisman Trophy. Reed was primarily interested in English and, ironically enough, given his relations later on with many practitioners in the field, journalism. Syracuse was strong in both areas.

Some of the more typical aspects of college life proved problematic for Reed. He enrolled in the campus's ROTC program, an option available to Syracuse students who wanted to opt out of the physical education requirement. In an oft-repeated story that most likely is apocryphal, exaggerated, or simply untrue, he was expelled for pointing an unloaded firearm at his commanding officer's head. That Reed mishandled his weapon in a way that was regarded as potentially dangerous — and that such an infraction proved the last straw in what no doubt was a checkered military career at best — is far more likely.

Hyman, meanwhile, made the mistake of inviting Reed to rush the fraternity he had joined. Hyman recalled, "He thought it was the stupidest idea he'd ever heard. He thought fraternities were ridiculous, the ultimate middle-class, sellout thing to do." Nonetheless, in characteristically contradictory fashion, Reed agreed to do it. "So he showed up one night during rush," Hyman said. "He walked in like he had just rolled out of the gutter, wearing a jacket that was stained and threadbare. He looked like a bum. Conversation stopped completely when he walked into the room." Of course, that was entirely Reed's intention. "He loved it," Hyman said. "One of the brothers walked over to him and said, 'You walk into a fraternity dressed like that?' Lou said, 'Fuck you. I wouldn't join this fucking asshole fraternity if you paid me.'" That was the end of the evening. As they were leaving, Hyman asked Reed, "Why did you even bother showing up?" "Because you asked me to," Reed replied.

Hyman had more success — up to a point — when he approached Reed about forming a band at Syracuse as they had back in Freeport. "I was anxious to do it, more than he was," Hyman recalled. "I thought we could make some money and have a lot of fun playing fraternity parties. And not just in Syracuse, but at Cornell, Colgate, and other nearby schools. So we got together and formed this band called L.A. and the Eldorados, which was pretty funny because the El Dorados were an existing group at the time. That didn't matter to us." As for the "L.A.," that stood for Lewis and Allan. Reed and Hyman recruited guitarist Lloyd Baskin and pianist Richard Mishkin, who eventually switched to bass. They arranged to buy a Fender amplifier from a music store in Syracuse on an installment plan, and they were ready to go. The only problem, Hyman pointed out, was "that we didn't anticipate how crazy Lou was. I would book a job at my fraternity, for example, for a hundred dollars — twenty-five dollars each for the night. But at the last minute, Lou would refuse to show up. He would just say, 'I'm not doing this.' I'd say, 'We made a commitment to play this job,' and we'd get into a huge screaming fight. He would eventually show up, but he'd be hostile. He'd turn his back to the crowd like Miles Davis and insist on playing his own music. We would always be escorted out."

Richard Mishkin was a fraternity brother of Allan Hyman's in Sigma Alpha Mu, a so-called Jewish fraternity because at the time Jews were not permitted in many other fraternities. Mishkin had attended the High School of Music and Art in Manhattan, and had considered attending Oberlin Conservatory but ultimately enrolled at Syracuse, where his father had gone to school. He was serious about music, and he and Reed formed a bond — to a degree. "Lou and I really hit it off right from the beginning," Mishkin said. "But when I say 'hit it off' — you don't hit it off with Lou. You find commonality and deal with his bullshit." One element of Reed's "bullshit" was his desire not to simply play the current songs that the band's audience wanted to hear. "He was always interested in making a statement — pushing people and shocking people," Mishkin said. "My attitude was that we were getting paid far more than we were worth to play the music these people wanted to hear so they could dance. They weren't listening to the words. But Lou, in his mind, was a poet, and he really wanted to put his poetry to music. That was fine. As long as it could be danced to, I was happy with it."

But making music that could be danced to was not

Reed's goal. Not long after arriving at Syracuse, he importuned Katharine Barr, the sorority girl who ran WAER, the university's radio station, about having his own show. The station primarily played classical music and show tunes, but Reed had other ideas. He explained that he wanted to do a jazz show, and Barr agreed, somewhat reluctantly. "I knew I was in trouble...when instead of it being *The Lou Reed Show* or *Lou Reed Jazz* or whatever, he called the program *Excursions on a Wobbly Rail,*" she later said. Reed borrowed the title from the closing track on pianist Cecil Taylor's 1958 album, *Looking Ahead!* Taylor was a boundary-breaking player who helped pave the way for free jazz, and looking ahead was exactly what Reed desired to do. That explosive tune was representative of what Reed wanted to play on his show. His avant-garde tastes and tendency to argue with friends who would crank call him on the air led to complaints from listeners. Syracuse wasn't ready for Reed, Barr said, and "it wasn't too long until the wrath of the faculty and administration rained down on me. And I had no choice but to let him go."

It was at Syracuse that Reed began to take himself seriously as a writer and formulated the idea that he would return to again and again in interviews: he believed that rock and roll could serve as a medium for lyrics that addressed the same themes addressed by writers like William Burroughs, Allen Ginsberg, and

Hubert Selby. From his love of doo-wop, Reed had learned that rock and roll could be as transporting and lyrical as any other art form, that it could speak directly to the heart with incandescent power. But the rebelliousness of rock and roll, its ability to get under the skin of adults generally and authority figures in particular, suggested that the music held the possibility for true subversion. Why waste that impact on lyrics that had nothing to say? If you were going to be attacked anyway, why not say something that truly unnerved the powers that be? That became and would remain Reed's project. "Lou fashioned himself a rebel because he didn't fit in society the way a lot of people do," Mishkin said. "That was who he was. He clearly enjoyed being offensive and he always understood exactly what he was doing. He used to sing this song called 'The Fuck Around Blues.' In nineteen sixty-one or sixty-two, people didn't stand up on a stage and do that. But Lou did. I thought it was perfectly okay until I realized that maybe the venue wasn't right. We'd lose gigs. People would get pissed off and throw beer at us. But we'd just change the name of the band and go back and play there again later."

One of those alternate names was Pasha and the Prophets, Pasha being one of Mishkin's nicknames. That version of the band sometimes included a black female singer and other black musicians. "Lou and I would go down to the bars in the black neighborhoods in Syracuse, and everybody would look at us like we were going to die," Mishkin said. "Most of these bars had pickup groups. I remember asking if we could sit in, and the musicians just laughed. They said, 'You white boys can't play this music.' But, in fact, that's the music we played. The musical influences that were strong for Lou and me were Jimmy Reed, John Lee Hooker, a lot of Mississippi blues players. When we did sit in on occasion, they were astounded. I mean, we weren't that good, but we were certainly as good as the guys that were playing there." Reed and Mishkin eventually won the musicians over, and they would hang out and have a good time. Then they would offer to return the favor. "We'd say, 'Listen, we have a band and once in a while we need guys who play like you,'" Mishkin recalled. "They'd say, 'How much do you pay?' Whatever we paid them was more than they usually got, because we got paid way more than we were worth." Indeed, both men were making quite good money for college kids. "We had a backup gig at a big beer hall, for townies, mostly, but a lot of college kids went there," Mishkin said. "That was for whenever we didn't have a frat gig on a Friday night. We'd get a hundred and twenty-five dollars—twenty-five dollars each. When we played fraternities, we'd get anywhere from two hundred and fifty to seven hundred and fifty dollars, which was a lot of money back then. We didn't play constantly, but we played often, and I never didn't have money in my pocket."

As time went on in Syracuse, Mishkin became one of the earliest in a long line of people whose job it became to look after Reed. "I became Lou's keeper," he said. "It was my job to get him up in the morning, to make sure he got to the gigs, to make sure we had the equipment we needed to play. I did a lot of the booking in the beginning." Mishkin also provided the band car for L.A. and the Eldorados, replacing Allan Hyman's Jaguar sedan, which had previously served that purpose. "It was a white, two-door Chrysler New Yorker with big fins on the back and a push-button transmission that my grandmother gave to me because she had bought a new car," he said. "A friend drew big red guitars on the fins, with 'L.A. and the Eldorados' across the front and across the trunk, with maybe G clefs or something. That was the car we used to go to gigs. It had a big trunk. Our equipment at that point was pretty minimal: two guitars and a bass, two amps. I had chains that I'd put on it to get around upstate in the winter."

As an extracurricular activity, Mishkin, who had grown up hunting pheasant, took Reed hunting, another obviously misguided idea. "I had a shotgun, but I don't think I gave him a gun," Mishkin said. "We shot some pheasant and gave them to our girlfriends to cook. But it was so not Lou Reed to go out into the woods. He bitched from the minute we left until the minute we got back: 'Who wants to walk around in the woods? Why would you do something as crazy as this?' But he was laughing, and he had a great time."

THE MOST SIGNIFICANT MUSICAL contact Reed made at Syracuse was with guitarist Sterling Morrison, who had also grown up on Long Island. Morrison had applied to and been accepted at Syracuse but initially chose to attend the University of Illinois. Reed and Morrison met when Morrison visited Syracuse to see his friend Jim Tucker, who was also from Long Island and who lived in the room beneath Reed's. Tucker and his sister Maureen had known Morrison from childhood. Morrison would eventually transfer to Syracuse for a time, and he and Reed would occasionally play together, both at school and on Long Island during breaks. They remained friendly, though their musical relationship in the Velvet Underground wouldn't blossom for several years.

At Syracuse, Reed characteristically turned what might have been thought of as a handicap to his own advantage. Given the treatments he had undergone for depression, Reed was able to get an off-campus apartment. "He claimed he had a mental illness so that he couldn't live in the dorm," Mishkin recalled. "I had a car as a sophomore, which was typically not permitted, but I claimed I needed it for work. The work I needed it for was the band, so that was legit. So we had a car to get around in, and an apartment where we could bring girls. Girls couldn't go to the boys' dorms, and vice versa, in those days." Not that Reed's apartment was exactly a luxurious love den. He shared it with Lincoln Swados, a gifted and highly eccentric writer and musician from Buffalo, with whom Reed would remain friends. "It was dirty, messy, pistachio nutshells all over the place, cigarette butts piled up," Mishkin recalled of Reed's digs. Indeed, Reed was so partial to pistachio nuts, which at the time were frequently dyed red, that his fingers were often stained by their coloring.

Richard Sigal, who attended Alfred University in upstate New York, had remained friends with Reed and visited him at Syracuse with his friend Tommy, whose sister went to the school. He remembered his first visit to Lou's room: "We knocked. No one answered. I tried the knob and the door opened. It was five p.m. and the room was dark. As our eyes grew accustomed to the lack of light, we noticed that it looked like a tornado had blown through the room. There was stuff piled on other stuff. Every chair was stacked with books, clothes, junk. The sheets were gray, which was not their actual color, but from never having seen the interior of a washing machine. His sheets were also covered with his writings. Apparently, when he'd get a thought while in bed, instead of looking for a piece of paper—an impossible task, given the state of his room—he just wrote the ideas on his sheets. That's probably why they were never washed. Finally, I noticed a hand and wrist poking out from the sheets. I peeled back the covers and there was Lou. He sat up, rubbing the sleep from his eyes. I asked why he was sleeping at five in the afternoon. He said he stayed up all night and slept during the day. God only knows how or when he went to his classes."

As Reed roused himself, Sigal could see that something was bothering him. "While he was sitting on the side of the bed clearing his head, he said, 'Swados!'" Sigal recalled. "He said it louder and then screamed, 'Swados!' I had no idea what he meant. It sounded like some sort of mantra. Then he said, 'Swados, stop playing that...'—I don't remember if it was a drum or a guitar. Neither Tommy nor I had heard a thing. But Lou, with his sensitive ear, had heard Swados playing an instrument. Enter Swados from another bedroom. Lou introduced us to him; he was an odd sort. He disappeared after the introduction." Sigal had an even more dramatic experience on another visit with Tommy. "Once again, the door was open, but no Lou. I was about to leave him a note, when a guy came bursting through the door, a large fire extinguisher in his hands, threatening to spray us because the CIA was chasing him. He kept threatening us, and I started eyeing a large cast-iron skillet in the kitchen that I thought might fit well against his head. Tommy and I could probably have taken him, but neither of us wanted to get sprayed with the extinguisher. This went on for a while, with the guy's paranoid delusions motivating his aggression. That's when I went to the window and looked out. I told the guy that the CIA guys were gone. He lowered his nozzle and slipped out the door, which I quickly locked behind him."

Relieved, Sigal later pondered the significance of that intrusion. "I don't think it was an accident that this guy ended up in Lou's apartment," he said. "He was probably one of Lou's druggie friends. When we later told Lou what had happened, he just laughed, but never explained who the person was or why he was there." The "druggie friends" theory reflects Sigal's assumption that Reed was an early participant in the drug culture that was just beginning to come to the fore in the early sixties. "I do remember him telling me that he sent to Arizona to buy some peyote," Sigal said. "When it arrived, he diced it into a fine pile, then swallowed a handful, chased by a glass of water. 'So what happened?' I asked. 'I threw up,' he said."

That was hardly Reed's only drug experience while at Syracuse. His sister, Bunny, was on a teen tour in California as a high school student when her parents called and informed her that she needed to see a doctor to get a gamma globulin shot, as they had done. It was a precautionary measure because Lou had contracted hepatitis from using a dirty needle, though this detail was never explicitly discussed. Richard Sigal recalled visiting Reed at his parents' home in Freeport during a college break. "God, he looked horrible," Sigal said. "He was yellow and he looked like a Biafran. He was just skin and bones. I asked his mother, 'What's wrong with Lou?' And she said, 'Oh, he has hepatitis.' I thought, 'Lou is fooling around with drugs,' but we never discussed it."

Given such events, Reed's reputation as a user began to spread. It was still the early sixties, and any sort of drug experimentation was far more of an underground experience than it would be in just a few years. Sigal recalled being home from college on break at his parents' house, hanging out with two friends from Freeport, when Reed dropped by to see him. "When he walked in the door, those two guys stood up and left. I didn't know why. Later I asked them, and they said, 'Hell, he could be carrying drugs.' It was almost like, if Lou walked in, you've got to pull the shades down. They didn't want any part of it." In the preprofessional world of suburban Jewish Long Island, drugs held little glamour. They were seen as part of the urban life that those families had moved to Long Island to escape.

*   *   *

REED'S ROMANTIC LIFE TOOK a dramatic turn for the better when he met Shelley Albin, an art student who had come to Syracuse from Highland Park, Illinois, a posh suburb north of Chicago. To this day, Reed's friends speak in rapturous tones about her beauty. It was a quality Reed appreciated. "When I would come into a room, I recognized that I would get attention," Albin said. "I never quite understood it, but Lou liked it." On one of Sigal's trips to Syracuse, Reed introduced him to Albin. "She was exquisite, a total knockout," he said. "Lou scored big-time having Shelley as a girlfriend. I think she was the first steady girlfriend he ever had." Allan Hyman remembered her in similar terms. "Lou ended up with this gorgeous, really nice girl in college," he said. "I knew Shelley well. She was great. I couldn't believe how terrific she was for him. It was the first time he had a girlfriend that I'm aware of. When he was seeing her, he actually started coming out of his shell a bit. She seemed very bright, and she was nuts about him. But they were polar opposites. As introspective as Lou was and how outrageous he would act toward others, she was just the opposite. She was very sweet and personable, somebody you would never expect would be interested in hanging out with him." Albin's friend Erin Clermont, who would later befriend Reed and become an occasional lover of his, recalled the first time she saw Reed and Albin together. "I was very struck by him," she said. "He seemed slightly smaller than she was, and there was something sexy about that. They used to be able to wear the same jeans."

Albin saw something beneath the veneer of hardness and sophistication that Reed affected. "It's a strange word to use about Lou, but he was pretty naive," she said. "I was tremendously naive. I didn't have that much experience when I came out of high school. This was the sixties. It wasn't a very slick world. I came from the Midwest." Highland Park, she said, was a suburb somewhat like Westport, Connecticut. "I grew up in the woods," she said. "There wasn't a lot to do besides ride your bike and run around in the back. College was a whole different world. Just being able to smoke was a big deal. Girls still routinely wore dresses and skirts to class." She added, "As a freshman I had a nine o'clock curfew that was really enforced. They would look to see if you were in your room. If you wanted to go away for the weekend, you had to have a note from your parents. They had alarms on all the doors, and boys couldn't get past the front desk. There were double doors and guards." Albin responded to both the sensitivity she detected in Reed and the larger world that his interests suggested. For college, she wanted, like Reed, to get away from home, so choices like the University of Illinois or the University of Wisconsin were out of the question, as far as she was concerned. Her parents showed little interest in where she went to school, believing that she would only be going to get her "Mrs." degree. "My girlfriends all got the same treatment," she said. "It was a completely different era. You were going to be a secretary or a teacher and that was it. It was never taken seriously that girls should study or be interested in books." She had hoped to attend the University of California at Berkeley, an adventurous choice for a Midwestern girl, but her parents vetoed that. A cousin who was an artist recommended Syracuse because of the quality of the school's art program and because he knew a dean there.

Albin met Reed when she was a freshman and he was a sophomore. "When we met he had the reputation of being kind of a rascal, that he was an evil guy and you had to be careful around him," she said. "Those fraternity boys he knew—Richie Mishkin and Allan Hyman—they didn't dare act out the way Lou did. So to know Lou sharpened their edge a bit—or so they thought." Despite his image-making, Albin did not initially find Reed a fearsome figure. "He was still more of a kid who would play basketball or tennis, and he played folk music and old fifties stuff," she said. "That's what that era was. They'd hang out on street corners and play banjos and guitars. It wasn't the same Lou as people think of as Lou Reed. It was a sweeter Lou." Albin herself played guitar, and she and

Reed would occasionally play together in private or for a few friends in somebody's kitchen. As for his reputation as a sexual player, that, too, was something of an image. "I got the impression that he never really had a girlfriend in high school," she said. "I didn't ask him. I think he put on an aura later of being a ladies' man. Hardly at all. That didn't fit with the guy I met. He didn't do as much in college as he pretended later. I met him after he'd been at college for a year. He was awkward. Boys I went out with in high school were smoother." What drew her to Reed was his sensibility. "I liked his brain," she said. "We could talk for hours and hours, days and days. We liked to read the same books. He would write a story and I would make a painting on the same subject. We just got along. We connected. He was the first person who thought like an artist and spoke like an artist, a writer, a creative person. He was an incredible romantic. So we connected on that level. It was very much a creative-mind thing. I was crazy about him. I was absolutely in love with him."

Reed's relative inexperience manifested itself when he brought Albin home to visit his parents in Freeport during school breaks. On her first visit, Albin said, Reed "opened the door to his bedroom and said, 'Wait here.' I waited for what seemed like an hour. I thought, 'This is bullshit. I'm going out there.' He had parked me in there for who knows what reason. I think it was because he didn't know how to bring a female home to his parents." As for Reed's parents, Albin said, "I was quite struck by how warm they were. Very outgoing and welcoming." In their eyes, it probably didn't hurt that "I was white. I was straight. I was a girl. I looked like Miss Midwestern, and I was at the time. I think his dad was a great guy. His father was just grateful to see a normal person." That she was an upper-middle-class Jewish girl no doubt helped as well.

Reed had not characterized his parents in any negative way beforehand. "He didn't think they were evil," she said. "He didn't say a word to me about how horrible they were or what a bully his dad was. He told me about his electroshock treatments, but he never said it was because he was supposedly gay. Back then, if a doctor told you to do something, you did it. That's the way our parents were brought up." Still, Reed was not above provoking his parents. "Lou made it difficult for his dad on purpose," Albin said. "He liked to pick scabs. That's who he was. He would flip his hand around and kind of wiggle his ass on purpose near his father or near people on campus. And it got to be so that he eventually walked like that more often. When I first met him he wasn't doing that. He would do that to get attention." Her impression of Reed from seeing him around his parents was that he was "overly catered to, like a lot of boys are, even when they grow into men. 'I don't eat those vegetables.' 'I don't do this, and

I don't want that.' He was repeating what he grew up with. I never thought anything of it because that was the way I grew up. Dad is the boss. Mom stays home, and doesn't have an opinion. Mom gives up her life. Lou was very insecure, and he needed a nurturer. Like many men are, Lou was basically looking for a replacement for his mother with a little sex thrown in." She even detected a strategy at work when he told her about his electroshock therapy. "He didn't seem to have a lot of anger about it, or at least he didn't express it," she said. "What he was using it for was to say, 'I'm not an average guy. I'm really special. I'm really different. I can't be counted on to be normal. I may do something a little weird. Aren't you a little afraid of me?'"

That impulse also came through in Reed's effort to keep Albin off-balance regarding his sexuality. "He was always trying to get your goat and poke at you, no matter who you were," she said. "He always thought it was cool to have a woman who looks like a guy. That had a lot of fantasy worked into it for him. I don't know if he was actively bisexual. I had a nine p.m. curfew at school, so I was not around at nighttime, and he had another life. I never asked, 'Where did you go, and what did you do?' I suspect he got involved with guys at some point here and there. And it's not as if he wasn't going to do it if I asked him. But Lou and I would look at a guy and discuss what he looked like, how cute he was." Later at Syracuse, Reed hung a poster for John Rechy's groundbreaking gay novel, *City of Night,* published in 1963, on the wall of his room. Albin took the ambiguity in stride. "You want to go screw a guy? Go ahead. It had nothing to do with me—I'm not a guy. I'm not jealous of that. He would screw a chipmunk if it felt good. That was his attitude." Like so many people in Reed's life, she ultimately abandoned the effort to define his sexuality. "Whether Lou was gay or bisexual, it doesn't really matter," she said. "I think he floated. I think by nature he was more driven to women because of his relationship with his mother. That's what he thought was normal. It was comfortable."

On one of their trips to Freeport during a college break, Reed took Albin to the Hay Loft. "It was a mixed gay bar, men and women," she said. "Lou liked to set up scenarios so he could write about them later. There was a woman there whom I found attractive, and we were dancing. Why not? He was trying to get this thing going where she and I would go out to the car. I didn't want to. 'Come on, you'll like it.' 'I don't want to.' So he gave up." What Reed had in mind, according to Albin, "was not a threesome—just me and her. Totally voyeuristic. He thought that would really shock me. The fact that I wasn't interested in it didn't occur to him."

Reed also had Albin accompany him on a trip to Harlem, presumably to buy drugs. "I don't know why else he would have gone there," she said. "It was a family apartment, and the guy was a nice guy. But it was a dark, stinky hallway and stairwell. I knew this was a place we were not supposed to be." The worst part, however, was driving there with Reed from Long Island. "He was a horrible driver, a scary, horrible driver," she said. "I had never driven with him on campus, but when we got on the highway, it was horrifying. I never would get in a car with him again, ever." That jaunt to Harlem was hardly the only time that Albin, who didn't drink or use drugs, experienced Reed's involvement with the drug culture in Syracuse and beyond. The various fraternities that his band played gave him "access to a world that he could sell drugs to," she said. "He had a good business selling heroin to the fraternities. That was before he had begun to use it. When I met him he really wasn't doing much drugs—weed, poppers, whatever." He also used Albin as a way to conceal his activities, rightly assuming that her innocent beauty, general rectitude, and Midwestern demeanor would shield her from suspicion. Albin's upbringing, very typical of the time, had taught her that a woman should do whatever was necessary to accommodate her man. "Any man's opinion is better than yours," is how she described the ethic of that era. Consequently, Reed's wishes were beyond questioning. "He would keep a grocery bag full of pot in my dorm room," she said. "'Okay, I'll keep it there.' He would say, 'Bring a handful to so-and-so and get the money.' 'Okay.' He said, 'I'm going to get some peyote from Arizona and have it sent to your address.' Now, I could have gotten booted out of school for all this. It didn't occur to me to say no. It never occurred to me that really what he was doing was protecting himself. He was a user, and I was susceptible."

At one point, during a period when she and Reed were on the outs, Albin dyed her brown hair blonde. "At the time it was considered trashy to bleach your hair," she recalled. "It became more orange from my natural reddish tint, fairly crass and ugly. As my mother said when I got off the plane at home, 'Why not carry a mattress on your back, too?'" Reed, of course, loved it, and insisted that Albin come visit his family on Long Island during a break. "He wanted to horrify his parents, to show how he had 'corrupted' and 'ruined' the girl his father and mother liked so much—the wholesome Midwesterner," she said. "I indulged him, and it was a strange trip."

Finally, Albin decided she had had enough. "The reason I left is he began being really crappy to me, and it was just nasty," she said. "It was stuff you would do if you were an overbearing, abusive husband. 'I'm going out for drinks with the guys. You stay home. Don't you dare let me catch you out.' That kind of thing. In my sophomore year, I lived in a small house—they called them cottages at Syracuse. There were maybe twelve rooms. You could go in and out when you wanted. I was mostly living with Lou, and he was just, 'I'm going out. I don't want you to come.' So I'd go back to my room. The next day the married couple that Lou shared an apartment with would tell me, 'Lou had some girl with him that night and he was really nasty to her. We could hear it. I thought you ought to know.' It bothered me and it didn't bother me. I just recognized he was more trouble than anything else."

One night, after Reed had been "doing that kind of stuff" for a couple of months, Albin was at a party where Reed was playing when "Richie Mishkin said to me, 'Lou is getting a blow job, and he wants to know if you want to come and watch.' I don't know if it was a guy or a girl, or if Lou was saying that or Richie made it up, trying to be risqué, letting some of Lou's evilness rub off on him. Who knows? But that was the end of it. I left and said, 'That's it. Goodbye.' You can push me for a long time and I'm very tolerant, but when I'm done, I'm done. You were supposed to be the girlfriend who was really his mother, and I wasn't interested in that. I was done."

That may have been it as far as Albin was concerned, but not Reed. "He kept trying to get me to come back to him," she said. "He couldn't imagine that he could be so offensive that somebody was going to say, 'That's enough.'" They would remain in touch even after Reed graduated from Syracuse and returned to New York, and Albin would loom for a long time as a symbolic figure for Reed, the metaphoric embodiment of everything he "had, but couldn't keep," as he put it in "Pale Blue Eyes," the gorgeous ballad he wrote about her, though Albin did not have blue eyes. Ever the writer, Reed was perfectly capable of altering the facts for the sake of a more effective image, one that, in fact, had a private meaning for the two of them. Indeed, Albin served as an inspiration and sounding board for Reed. "A song like 'I'll Be Your Mirror'—that's a conversation we had word for word," she said. "I know when he wrote it; I think it was my junior year in college. I got a lot of letters from him. A lot of them were lyrics. One of them was 'The Gift.' My mother met him and one of the reasons she hated him so much is because she read those letters. She didn't realize it was just a writer writing. Lou just thought out loud and he wrote. A lot of them were about the Hay Loft, and a lot of other things that your mother really should not know. I dumped them all into an incinerator when I was purging him from my life." As an artist herself, Albin summed up Reed's approach to life: "Everything you do, everything you look at, everybody you know, and every conversation you hear—it's fodder. To expect a writer not to use you is craziness." Reed, she said finally, was "a romantic. He could be very sweet. He's probably the only person who ever literally gave me a heart-shaped box of chocolates on

Valentine's Day. But he wasn't happy unless he made somebody more miserable than he was. That is exactly what he fed off as an artist, as a writer, as a songwriter. Misery made for his best work, whether it came from me or somebody else. So I'd call him a romantic and I'd call him sweet, but I'd also call him an incredible pain in the ass. He wasn't anybody I wanted to live with and put up with. It wasn't worth it. It was too much grief."

WHILE AT SYRACUSE, REED met and studied with the poet, essayist, and short-story writer Delmore Schwartz, who had a decisive impact on him. Schwartz achieved acclaim in 1938 with the publication of *In Dreams Begin Responsibilities,* a collection of stories and poems that established him as one of the leading voices of a new generation of American writers that would succeed such modernist giants as T. S. Eliot, Vladimir Nabokov, and Ezra Pound. Schwartz was just twenty-four when *In Dreams* came out, and his promise seemed unlimited. He was young, handsome, immensely talented, and spellbindingly articulate. Sadly, that promise was never entirely fulfilled. Haunted by his parents' divorce, Schwartz divorced twice himself, and the second breakup proved particularly devastating. He had begun to drift into paranoia, and at times he was convinced that his estranged wife was having an affair with Nelson Rockefeller, then a prominent political figure—and eventually governor of New York and vice president of the United States—whose family had amassed a fortune through its control of the Standard Oil company. The Rockefellers' immense wealth, political power, and international influence made them the relentless focus of conspiracy theories of all sorts, sometimes with good reason. Schwartz, however, saw the Rockefellers not merely as geopolitical power brokers but as specifically fixated on destroying his life and career. Unfortunately, he was doing a spectacular job of that himself and did not require their assistance.

Despite his precarious grip on his sanity and the erratic quality of his later work, Schwartz maintained his literary reputation into the sixties. In 1960 he was awarded Yale University's prestigious Bollingen Prize for Poetry (previous winners included Ezra Pound, Wallace Stevens, and W. H. Auden), and he was invited to John F. Kennedy's 1961 inauguration, though the invitation reached him four months late because he had no fixed place to live at the time. Schwartz was still able to captivate listeners in conversation, and he retained enough charisma to attract a seemingly endless series of young women. Nonetheless, his many loyal and influential friends feared for his well-being. His condition had reached the point where they regularly needed to bail him out of difficulties with landlords and other creditors. His alcoholism and paranoia raged at times, and he often rewarded his friends' efforts with anger, insults, and suspicion. Poet Robert Lowell and novelist Saul Bellow, both of whom would write about Schwartz in some of their best-known work, and other friends helped land him a position in the English department at Syracuse, which had recently formed a creative writing program. Administrators at Syracuse were aware that Schwartz was hardly functioning at the height of his powers, but his reputation carried the day and he joined the faculty in the fall of 1962.

Like many charismatic professors with few emotional boundaries, Schwartz tended to attract worshipful students. Indeed, a young woman, still in her teens, who had recently studied with him at the University of California joined him for an ill-fated few months at Syracuse. Schwartz introduced her as his fiancée and described their lovemaking as "like Grant taking Richmond." However, after he suggested that she was in danger of being killed by an unnamed assailant, she arranged to be shepherded out of town, never to return.

Nonetheless, Schwartz had little trouble finding acolytes at Syracuse, Reed primary among them. Along with the classes he taught, Schwartz daily occupied a corner table in the back of the Orange Bar on Crouse Avenue, just off campus. The legal drinking age was eighteen in those days, so socializing with professors in bars around campus was even more common than it is today. Shelley Albin spent so much time around

Schwartz while at Syracuse that it was difficult for her to recall if she had ever actually taken a course with him. The man Saul Bellow called the "Mozart of conversation" kept students spellbound with tales of the literary masters with whom he had rubbed shoulders. Schwartz taught a course devoted to James Joyce and carried around a copy of Joyce's *Finnegans Wake* that was covered in his own annotations. Simply displaying such fluency with that famously daunting novel would have been enough to excite admiration in English majors. Schwartz, a superb reader, would recite passages for his students' delectation, and his immense knowledge and deft comprehension of the intricate, highly musical rhythms of Joyce's prose would leave his disciples reeling. Schwartz was also a great admirer of Sigmund Freud, and his approach to literature embedded the written word squarely within the life of the author who had written it. That was a departure from the dominant critical approach at the time, which viewed literature as free of both history and individual psychology. Schwartz's discussions of literary titans like T. S. Eliot and James Joyce frequently included gossip and sexual speculation about their personal lives. In short, he treated his students with an easy familiarity, as if they were insiders, privy to the same knowing insights and sly observations that he was.

Reed found this irresistible. Through Schwartz he found entrée into a larger world, one where writers don't just sit in their rooms and conjure masterworks, but where they hold forth in public in compelling ways about matters both serious and trivial. In Reed's eyes, Schwartz was a rock star, a stature magnified by the relative obscurity of Syracuse—he was a genuinely big fish in a small pond. That he had achieved literary fame while still in his twenties only made him a more attractive figure for Reed; that was precisely the fate he desired for himself. Shelley Albin said that Reed was the first person she had met who "thought like an artist and spoke like an artist"; Schwartz fulfilled that role for Reed. That Schwartz took Reed seriously as a writer intensified the effect he had on him. "I'm not surprised by his friendship with Lou," said James Atlas, Schwartz's biographer. "Delmore was a powerful figure by that time and had friendships with a number of younger writers. Anybody with a serious interest in art and literature would have been someone Delmore responded to." Schwartz was a Brooklyn Jew who rose to important artistic heights, and in him Reed read his own destiny. Reed would speak rapturously of Schwartz for the rest of his life.

Reed's friends, however, were divided in their views on Schwartz. Lincoln Swados, who coedited a literary quarterly with Reed named *Lonely Woman* after an Ornette Coleman tune, shared Reed's admiration. Albin's friend Erin Clermont, who aspired to write fiction herself, was another of Schwartz's fans. "Those gatherings at the Orange Bar was really where I got to know Lou," she said. "Lou worshipped Delmore. There would be six or seven people around the table on any given night. I would sit there like a quiet chick at the table, but Lou would contribute to the conversation. I remember someone once said to Lou, 'You always speak in italics.' I love that. That was true to the end of his life. But to me, Delmore was at the Orange as a teacher — one of the best teachers I've ever had. He was a marvelous raconteur and he had so many stories." As was hardly uncommon at the time, Schwartz took Clermont's admiration as a sexual invitation. "He did stick his hand down the back of my pants one time," she recalled. "He was probably close to fifty by then. For me, he might as well have been eighty. I was not into that at all. I either just ignored it or pulled his hand out. Still, his voice was beautiful, and as a young man, he was very beautiful." Richard Mishkin, who would stop by the Orange occasionally, took a more jaundiced view. "Delmore was drunk all the time. He seemed like a has-been — and sad. He was past his peak because he put himself in that position by drinking. Like Lou, he was an egotist and thought whatever he said was gospel. What he did was important, but it wasn't that important."

Albin, of course, was another regular at Delmore's Orange Bar sessions. "I don't drink" were the first words she said to me when I asked her opinion about Schwartz.

"I'm not a fun drinking date, nor do I find people who are drunk or high fun. So Delmore was not half as interesting or magical to me as he was to the people who were drinking around him for four or five hours. I think he was overrated. Most often I was there for an hour and then I would leave." She had strong recollections of his conspiracy theories. "By the time we knew him, he was totally paranoid," she said. "He had the Rockefeller paranoia going—that's what you heard about all the time. He drank so much and became incoherent. He'd be spitting while he was talking, and if he ever ate anything it was all down his front. If I stayed four feet away, I was okay." In Delmore's view, Albin was the sort of mother-protector for Reed that he sought in his own wives and paramours. "He'd turn to me and say, 'Your job in life is to be sure that Lou is a writer—and not this crappy rock-and-roll stuff. I can get him into Harvard. He can get into Princeton. He's got to be a writer, and that's your job.' Then he signed a book to Lou, but gave it to me. It was like, 'I'm giving it to you, because it's your job to stay with Lou,' or whatever. Okeydokey. It was like, 'You'll be the mother and the adult here.' I don't have the book. I gave it to Lou. But Delmore was very impressed with Lou and wanted Lou to be like him. I do think he was sort of the father figure that Lou wanted."

Reed always said that Schwartz threatened to come back from the grave and haunt him if he ever sold out and betrayed his literary talent. Schwartz may well have seen rock and roll as such a betrayal, but Reed would later write to him about his efforts to get a music career going, and it's unlikely he would have dwelled on that if he believed that his mentor would have disapproved. Reed took the threat seriously, however, and held Schwartz up as a standard of artistic integrity. His version of Schwartz was, in part, his own invention, a version that omitted the writer's paranoia and alcoholism, perhaps because Reed sensed those qualities in himself. He could spare Schwartz his judgment— and spare himself as well.

3

FELLINI SQUARED

DESPITE A ROCKY CAREER at Syracuse — getting tossed off the student radio station and booted from ROTC, dealing drugs — Reed graduated with honors in June of 1964 with a BA in English. Along with his generally outrageous behavior and innate desire to shock, Reed displayed a characteristic savvy during his time at Syracuse. His rebelliousness aside, Reed took care to avoid getting kicked out of school. He pushed the college to the limits of its tolerance, but he also taught himself how to work the system to his advantage. "When all is said and done, there was no reason for Lou not to graduate," Richard Mishkin said. "He went to class and he was very smart. And he made sure he took classes, especially as a senior, that you couldn't fail unless you never showed up." Just as he had exploited his psychological problems to get off-campus housing, Reed deftly negotiated his course requirements so that he wouldn't have to take too many classes he didn't like. "Lou waited until senior year to take these nasty required courses," Erin Clermont said. "We wound up in the same botany class. I had to take biology and botany, but Lou made a deal with the dean, so he only had to take one required science course, and he copied my notes for that one. That was the first time it hit me: boy, he's very clever. He had an angle. Why didn't I do that?"

After graduating, Reed returned home to his parents' house on Long Island and promptly succumbed to a hepatitis attack that sidelined him for two months. He wrote to Delmore Schwartz and explained that he had set aside his application to Harvard because he wasn't sure if he wanted to go back to school, then or ever. He had not even looked at anything he'd written for six months, but when he finally did, he told Schwartz that he thought he had talent but needed to work hard. Primarily, however, he was trying to get his music career off the ground. He wrote about a "folk album" he had made that he hoped might elicit some interest from record companies, but they were having trouble with his lyrics, which they considered "offensive." Other musicians, including an unnamed English band, were considering recording his songs. To make money he planned to take a job with the welfare department in

New York, because he wouldn't have to wear formal office clothes and he might be able to help some suffering people. He also mentioned his attraction to the city's sexual underground, though he described those interests as deriving from a personal weakness. He talked about Park Avenue johns who were willing to pay hundreds of dollars—a significant amount of money in those days—to watch couples have sex. He said that he couldn't resist exploring that world, walking right up to the edges of it, and, occasionally, toppling into it.

Reed later wrote about this period, during which he also spent two weeks working as a copy editor for a divorce lawyer: "Much of my income came from selling envelopes of sugar to girls I met at clubs, claiming it was heroin. This led to hours of feigned stonedness with those more gullible than I, watching carefully to make sure they didn't OD on sweets. What happened to the original drugs is another story." The Vietnam War was beginning to escalate, and now that he was out of college, Reed lost his student deferment. However, because of his emotional and psychological problems, he received a 1-Y classification, meaning that he would be drafted only in case of a national emergency or an outbreak of war, which, technically, did not apply to Vietnam because Congress never officially declared war.

Most notably, however, Reed took a songwriting job with Pickwick Records, a budget label whose factory-style work-for-hire ethos made the sweat-equity, no-nonsense hit-making of the Brill Building seem like Mount Olympus. In those days, fly-by-night record companies would jump on any trend — a dance craze, a musical style that would catch fire on the radio, like surf music or teen-tragedy ballads — and cash in on it. "They would put us in a room and say, 'Write ten California songs, ten Detroit songs,'" depending on what was happening at the moment, Reed recalled about the situation he had found himself in with three other songwriters for hire: Terry Phillips, Jimmy Sims, and Jerry Vance. Musicians, including Reed, would be assembled to record the songs, and albums would be printed up with covers and newly minted — which is to say completely made-up — band names designed to trick young record buyers into believing they were getting songs by established bands, rather than hastily assembled copies or obvious attempts to monetize trends. This was a time well before rock audiences became sophisticated consumers of the music. These albums, sold in five-and-ten stores and down-market department stores and purchased by teenagers or their unwitting parents, were inexpensive to produce. If they sold even a few thousand copies, the profits were considerable. While Reed wasn't the most accomplished musician, he had ranging tastes and an ear—and deep fondness—for pop music. Suddenly, he had something like an outlet, albeit the most low-rent one possible.

Pickwick, located in Long Island City, a section of Queens not far from Manhattan, was something like a songwriting emergency room. Every problem, difficulty, or complexity that could present itself in a songwriting situation did, and the job became something like a laboratory for Reed's more serious songwriting. While there, Reed would demo songs like "Heroin" and "I'm Waiting for the Man," which he had begun working on at Syracuse. One wonders what his employers made of such efforts. For the songs that he cowrote for Pickwick—numbers like "Cycle Annie," which is credited to the Beachnuts and channels the surf duo Jan and Dean, and the rocking "You're Driving Me Insane," credited to the Roughnecks—Reed often sang and played guitar for the label's in-house band. To cite a perfect example of how the Pickwick method worked: Reed read in a newspaper one day that ostrich feathers were going to be a fashion trend. In order to exploit that unlikely development, Reed and his cowriters hastily came up with a song called "The Ostrich," which—whether sincerely or ironically, it's hard to tell—attempted to incite a dance craze. The song opens with a bruising bass line derived from the Crystals' 1963 hit "Then He Kissed Me," and Reed unleashes a searing guitar line. His vocal is a hoarse shout, a radio DJ's manic exhortations to the imagined dancers to put their heads between their knees and do whatever they please. While its lyrics and concept are ridiculous, the song, aptly credited to the Primitives, sounds like raw, rough-edged garage rock, a sound much cruder than what was on the radio at the time.

Which didn't prevent the powers that be at Pickwick from discerning commercial potential in the track, particularly when a local TV show invited the Primitives to perform for its on-air dance party. The problem was that the Primitives didn't exist. That was hardly insurmountable. Terry Phillips, one of Reed's cowriters, was charged with assembling a band to play the show and some other promotional dates. Phillips rounded up John Cale, a young, Welsh, avant-garde classical musician; the sculptor Walter De Maria; and Tony Conrad, who, like Cale, was a member of minimalist composer La Monte Young's Theatre of Eternal Music, which was also known as the Dream Syndicate because of the droning, trancelike music the ensemble created. Phillips evidently assumed that Cale was a pop musician because he had long hair—such were the times. Also in his favor: the Welsh lilt in Cale's speech could easily have been mistaken for an English accent, an inestimable attraction in those innocent days of the Beatles-led British Invasion.

By any measure, this was an unlikely quartet. Cale,

a classically trained musician, had come to the United States on a Leonard Bernstein scholarship in modern composition; he had been interviewed for the position by the composer Aaron Copland. Skilled at many instruments, including viola and keyboards, Cale played bass with the Primitives. For all that, Cale had little more than a passing familiarity with rock and roll. Moreover, Walter De Maria, on drums, and Conrad, who played guitar, were hardly rock musicians themselves. Up for a bit of fun regardless, the four young men did some rehearsals, played the TV show and some other promotional spots, and then disbanded. But the crucial bond between Reed and Cale had been forged.

Though they came from very different backgrounds and had very different styles and tastes, the two men soon discovered that they had much in common. Reed's long-standing desire was to combine the literary ambitions of writers like Allen Ginsberg and Hubert Selby with the energy and immediacy of rock and roll. Cale wanted to move beyond the insular world of the avant-garde and see what the possible impact of his forward-looking ideas might be on a larger audience. Both found themselves in the right place at the right time. The traditional boundaries between all art forms were beginning to crack, and new syntheses were emerging. As the source and center of so much of the country's aesthetic activity, New York was the ground zero of those new directions. "It was a period when a lot of new took place," said Bob Neuwirth, a musician, songwriter, and painter, about New York in the midsixties. "Different aesthetic energies all popped up at the same time. Painting changed. Sculpture changed. Dance changed. Theater changed. Classical music changed. Jazz changed. Folk music changed. Rock and roll changed. It was a typical New York cultural shifting of the ground beneath you."

Reed was impressed by Cale's tony credentials and by his avant-garde credibility. Cale was sharp enough to perceive the vulnerability beneath Reed's know-it-all posturing, as well as his unique talent: "My first impressions of Lou were of a high-strung, intelligent, fragile college kid in a polo-neck sweater, rumpled jeans, and loafers. He had been around and was bruised, trembling, quiet, and insecure." Reed played Cale some of the songs he was working on, including "I'm Waiting for the Man" and "Heroin." Because Bob Dylan was the rare model for someone with Reed's aspirations, some of the songs Cale heard initially sounded like folk music to him, a genre whose plainspoken earnestness and relative musical simplicity held little appeal for him. It did not take long, however, for him to comprehend that Reed's ambitions ran in a different direction. "I missed the point," Cale said about his initial response to Reed's songs, "because I hated folk songs, and it was not until he forced me to read the lyrics that I realized these were not Joan Baez songs. He was writing about things other people weren't. These lyrics were literate, well-expressed, tough, novelistic impressions of life. I recognized a tremendous literary quality in his songs, which fascinated me — he had a careful ear and was cautious with his words. I had no real knowledge of rock music at that time, so I focused on the literary aspect."

The complicated dynamic of Reed and Cale's relationship began to take shape as Reed was struggling to move his career forward. Cale encouraged Reed not to see himself as frail and damaged. Reed, Cale recalled, was "seeing a psychiatrist who prescribed a tranquilizer called Placidyl. When I asked why, he said, 'I think I'm crazy.' I told him, 'Fuck, you're not crazy.' I didn't believe in schizophrenia. All I saw in it was a different way of seeing things. Anyway, I could not believe somebody who was writing those songs could be crazy." Cale began to withdraw somewhat from the downtown avant-garde world he was moving in to concentrate on working with Reed. He became determined to demonstrate to Reed exactly what they could do with his songs by combining Reed's groundbreaking lyrics and intense knowledge of rock and roll with his own avant-garde approach to sonics. "I would fit the things Lou played right into my world," Cale wrote.

"He was from the other world of music and he fitted me perfectly. We were made for each other. It was so natural. I'd show him something that he could do and he seemed constantly astounded by my ability to bring these things out in him. I felt a little taken aback, but when I first met him he had a great deal of ability that was waiting to get tapped. I tried to be supportive and show him what he was capable of doing. Lou was really low on energy at the time. It was a challenge to help somebody who was depressed by the lack of response he was getting, yet showing a determination to go on. So I found myself in a Svengalian position from the point of view of effort."

Certainly, Cale's educational pedigree and musical sophistication meant that Reed would have taken his encouragement seriously. Cale's intense interest in what Reed was trying to do was a counterbalance to the insecurity and depression that afflicted him. But Reed also served as a mentor to Cale, who was exactly Reed's age and had just moved to New York from London, where he'd attended Goldsmiths College. New York was not as daunting an environment as it would later become, but it still could be intimidating to outsiders, and Cale had been moving in hip downtown circles, an isolated world. Unsteady as he may have been at the time, Reed was a streetwise native who knew the local terrain. He was ambitious and willing to hustle to get where he wanted to go. Cale recognized those qualities in his new friend, and valued them. "There were certain characters I had in mind all along who I thought would be able to succeed in New York," Cale later wrote. "In Lou Reed I found one of these characters. To me, he was the kind of person who would survive in New York, and I wanted to learn from him. You might even say that learning was what I really wanted to do, more than achieve. Lou Reed was the first person in America with whom I connected both by example and shared experience.... At first it was mainly about literature and classical archetypes. Lou turned me on to the novel *Last Exit to Brooklyn* by Hubert Selby. Lou's thing was going straight to the unconscious. He was able to talk about a variety of things that were very fresh and original, and he loved conversation." Before long, Cale stopped working with La Monte Young and "dove into working with Lou. I was terrifically excited by the possibility of combining what I had been doing with La Monte with what I was doing with Lou and finding a commercial outlet. My collaboration with Lou simply overtook my community of interests with La Monte."

While he continued to live with his parents, Reed began spending more and more time at Cale's apartment at 56 Ludlow Street on the Lower East Side. The area consisted of tenement buildings and loft spaces that were increasingly becoming available, legally or illegally, as manufacturing businesses abandoned Manhattan. Rents in the area were cheap, and artists willing to live with few amenities, improvised utilities that skirted safety codes, and often rats, took over these spaces as they became available. Filmmakers, musicians, painters, sculptors, and actors could live and work in the large flats, and would stage performances there as well. The neighborhood was gritty, but, as was so often the case in New York, that rawness mingled with lyricism and glamour. "I had a loft on Spring Street with a little greasy spoon below that I think is a Prada store now," recalled Eric Andersen, a singer-songwriter who lived in New York at the time. "Jackie Kennedy popped by one day to visit the printing factory upstairs that did art books. And this friend of William Burroughs lived on the top floor. He played sax, so he'd go up on the roof near the alley, and you'd hear this beautiful sax playing at night."

Reed and Cale began working on songs at Cale's apartment. As their friendship developed, they realized that they shared interests beyond music and literature, not all of them so high-minded. Reed's consumption of drugs continued, while Cale recalled that "before I met Lou, I had snorted, smoked, and swallowed the best drugs in New York, courtesy of La Monte, but I had never injected anything. We smoked pot, took acid and other pills, mostly downs or Benzedrine. Now dime and nickel bags of heroin were added to the menu." Reed injected Cale with heroin for the first time, an intimate initiation into the ninth circle of illicit drug use that bound the two men more closely together. It also led to them being stricken by hepatitis. And Cale became familiar with Reed's perverse desire to provoke. Reed, he wrote, "enjoyed taking situations to extremes you couldn't imagine until you'd been there with him. He would befriend a drunk in a bar and, after drawing him out with friendly conversation, suddenly ask, 'Would you like to fuck your mother?' I thought I was reckless, but I'd stop at goading a drunk. That's where Lou would start." They would travel to Harlem and busk on the streets together, Reed on guitar, Cale on viola.

Various members moved in and out of the group, including a couple of female singers, as Reed and Cale sought to define the music they wanted to create. They named the group the Warlocks, though the possibility of the Falling Spikes—an allusion to the slang use of "spike" for a syringe—seems to have been at least jokingly considered and casually used in some instances. Tony Conrad moved out of Cale's Ludlow Street apartment and returned to filmmaking, and Walter De Maria, while attracted to the music Reed and Cale were developing, decided to concentrate on his own artistic projects. Cale recruited Angus MacLise, another member of La Monte Young's Theatre of Eternal Music, to be the group's percussionist. Reed, meanwhile, encountered Sterling Morrison, his old guitar-playing acquaintance from Syracuse, on the subway, and he and Cale invited him to play with them. Morrison agreed and soon became a member of the group.

The band decided to call itself the Velvet Underground after seeing a copy of a paperback book by that name that Tony Conrad had found in the street. (As with all origin stories, this one is somewhat in dispute: Angus MacLise's wife later claimed that he had purchased the book and that the others had seen his copy.) Written by journalist Michael Leigh, whose daughter the Velvets would later meet in a Philadelphia club, and published in 1963, *The Velvet Underground* was very much a product of its time. It purports to explore the subterranean worlds of fetishism, consensual extramarital sex, and S and M, subjects that were far beyond the pale of mainstream publishing at that time. To avoid censorship, the book couldn't simply be smut; it needed to display an element of "redeeming social value." Consequently, the book combines a portentous tone of disapproval, an obsessive historical scope dating back to the erotic shenanigans of the ancient Greeks and Romans, and a lurid fascination with the lubricious details of the present-day acts and impulses it describes. The title appealed to the band because the term "underground" was already being used to describe the experimental film scene taking shape in downtown New York, a scene in which the band members had many friends. Applying that same subversive impulse to music could easily stand as a statement of intent for Reed and Cale's artistic goals. That Reed, who actually read the book, was fascinated, both personally and as a songwriter, with what would at the time have been termed sexual deviance only made the reference, obscure as it would have been to most people, all the more fitting.

No infrastructure existed for rock bands at the time, even at the most commercial level, let alone along the fringes the Velvet Underground inhabited. The band played at clubs around the city for little more than meals, and also performed at happenings staged in their friends' lofts in which films, visual artwork, and music all combined in a swirling phantasmagoria that presaged both aesthetic trends and the emerging spirit of the times. Tapes of the band's performances at these events began to circulate, even in Europe, where film-maker Piero Heliczer, who occasionally played sax with the Velvets and who had them play along with his films in his loft, frequently traveled. In July of 1965, the band recorded demos of six songs—including "Heroin," "I'm Waiting for the Man," "All Tomorrow's Parties," and "Venus in Furs"—at the Ludlow Street apartment. Versions of that tape, too, began to make the rounds—along, possibly, with others that may not have survived—as the band sought increased visibility and a record deal. John Cale brought a version of the tape to England and got a copy to Marianne Faithfull in the hope that she would pass it along to her boyfriend, Mick Jagger, or the Rolling Stones' producer and manager, Andrew Loog Oldham. As inevitably happens, the tape began circulating beyond its intended recipients, and an English band aptly named the Deviants began performing "Prominent Men," a mild protest song—complete with Reed mimicking Dylan's phrasing and, unbelievably, harmonica accompaniment—that appeared on the tape.

Barbara Rubin, whose films the band also occasionally accompanied, introduced the group to Al Aronowitz, an influential New York journalist and scenester. In those relatively early days of rock and roll—and for decades after—there was essentially no such thing as conflict of interest on the music scene. Journalists promoted bands they liked in their writing, and often helped those bands get signed to labels. They served as managers and consultants, publicists and critics, friends and lovers. The established worlds of journalism and the music business were, for the most part, equally clueless about the new cultural changes taking shape, so if you were young, in the know, and at all ambitious, there were plenty of gaps to fill. Aronowitz, who wrote for the *New York Post* and was sufficiently well positioned to introduce the Beatles to Bob Dylan in a New York hotel in 1964, knew everyone on the scene and liked to make things happen. He wasn't precisely a fan of the Velvet Underground, and when he took his friend Robbie Robertson of the Band to hear them, Robertson was completely dismissive. But Aronowitz was sufficiently intrigued to visit with the group while Brian Jones of the Rolling Stones and songwriter Carole King waited in a limousine for him to finish. Whether in an official capacity or not, he became something like the Velvets' manager for a brief time.

Aronowitz, who lived in New Jersey, also managed a folk-rock band named the Myddle Class, which was based in Berkeley Heights. He arranged for the band to sign to a label run by fellow New Jersey residents Carole King and Gerry Goffin—hence King's presence in the waiting limousine. Aronowitz had booked the Myddle Class for something like a hometown gig at Summit High School in Summit, New Jersey, and he lined up the Velvet Underground as an opening act. It was to be the Velvets' first paying job: seventy-five dollars, the equivalent of a month's rent for many people in those days, but still not much given the four-way split. The prospect of a paying gig, however, was enough to drive Angus MacLise out of the band. The Velvets' pop aspirations would always be in conflict with their avant-garde urges, and that struggle was particularly acute for MacLise. Reed would later joke that MacLise could not accept the notion that the band would be expected to begin playing at a certain time and end at another time—a notion that, given MacLise's relationship with the open-ended, time-bending performances of La Monte Young, apparently seemed impossibly restrictive to him. As a result, he quit the Velvets shortly before the Summit High gig, plunging the band into temporary crisis.

Reed, Cale, and Morrison needed to find a replacement fast. One name that came up was Maureen Tucker, the younger sister of Jim Tucker, Morrison's friend from Syracuse University whom Reed had also met. Going from a drummer who had been playing with one of the leading minimalist visionaries of the era to a college friend's kid sister from Long Island who had never performed live might initially seem like a step down, but, rushed and unconsidered though the decision was, the choice of Maureen Tucker proved inspired. A rock band with a female drummer was simply unheard of at the time. It could have been seen as a gimmick, except that Tucker's looks didn't at all correspond to the eye candy criteria that might have made that notion credible. She was slight, cute rather than conventionally pretty, and boyish-looking. Her drumming, too, was a significant departure from most rock drumming. Though far from a virtuoso, she was an admirer of the Nigerian drummer Babatunde Olatunji, the relentless tribal jams of Bo Diddley, and the minimalist swing of the Rolling Stones' Charlie Watts—hardly the presumed influences of, in the parlance of the times, a "chick drummer." She played standing up, didn't use a high hat, never rode her cymbals, and emphasized her tom-toms over her snare. The result was a sound that brought a raw primitivism to the Velvets' more experimental moments, and added an off-kilter touch to their more conventional pop-sounding songs. That Tucker had a car and an amp, both of which the band sorely needed, didn't hurt. Reed traveled to Levittown, the Long Island suburb where Tucker was living with her parents, and auditioned her. On the strength of that one afternoon's performance, she was in.

The Summit High School gig has become the stuff of legend, the unlikely place where the classic lineup of the Velvet Underground made its public debut. That the Velvet Underground—or the Myddle Class, for that matter—were playing a gig at a high school was another example of the nonexistent infrastructure of the day for rock music. High schools held dances and had at least modest budgets; some hired bands to perform. Back then it was as simple as that. A hustler like Al Aronowitz would be quick to take advantage of whatever possibilities lay nearby, and this was one of them. Admission was two dollars and fifty cents, and another band, the Forty Fingers, played along with the Velvets and the Myddle Class. By most accounts the Velvets' three-song set — "There She Goes Again," "Venus in Furs," and "Heroin" — caused half the crowd in the school's auditorium that night to exit. It's unlikely that anyone who went to that performance to see the Myddle Class was at all prepared for anything like the Velvet Underground. Aronowitz was intrigued, wryly telling Sterling Morrison afterward that he was struck by the band's "polarizing" effect on its audience. Cale recalled apologizing to the Myddle Class for driving people out of the room, but "secretly I was exhilarated." And already, the Velvets began to exert the influence that is so much a part of their legacy. Clint Conley, who would later play in Mission of Burma, and Rob Norris, who would play bass in the Bongos, were both in attendance that night. "I think it was one of the most important nights of my life," Norris said. "I felt like someone turned a blender on inside my head."

Aronowitz's next effort on the Velvets' behalf was to arrange a residency for the group at the Café Bizarre on West Third Street in Greenwich Village. When it opened in the late fifties, the Bizarre was one of a number of significant Village clubs in the folk music revival. By the time the Velvets began playing there in December 1965, however, the place had become a tourist trap with a corny horror theme, something like a haunted house. Its very name suggests the degree to which the club attempted to trade on the exoticism of Greenwich Village to attract outsiders looking for a cheap thrill. Inside, the club wasn't especially large and did not even have a raised stage. Maureen Tucker did not have enough room for her drum kit, so she played tambourine. Tables were set up for audience members, whatever few there were. The Velvets played multiple sets six nights a week for meals and virtually no money—grueling terms even by the standards of the day. They interspersed their own material with covers of rock and R & B tunes. The audience, at least at first, hardly consisted of potential Velvets acolytes. They barely paid enough attention to be offended by what they were hearing, let alone won over by it. However, the steady gig did provide the band with something like a showcase venue where friends, fans, and supporters could come see them and invite other guests. Barbara Rubin brought Ed Sanders, a poet and member of the Fugs, and, eventually, another notable friend: Andy Warhol.

The midsixties were a time when mainstream culture seemed open to new ideas, and artists who worked in rarefied fields saw the possibility of reaching larger audiences. As a pop artist, Warhol was a renegade. If the press had fun with the abstract expressionists—is that a painting or a drop cloth?—Warhol's insistence that soup cans and Brillo boxes could be art made him a darling of the tabloids. A keen student of the media and a firm believer that all publicity was good publicity, Warhol encouraged the coverage, as condescending and sarcastic as it could occasionally be. He also saw the possibility of diversifying his fame portfolio beyond the world of visual art. He had already begun making films, and musicians like Bob Dylan and Brian Jones of the Rolling Stones had visited the Factory, the work space he occupied at 231 East Forty-Seventh Street, exciting his interest in rock and roll. Dylan and the Beatles had transformed rock music into something that adults could care about. Warhol was fascinated by celebrities of all kinds, and he could see that rock "artists" — a notion that was just beginning to be taken seriously — were becoming something like a new aristocracy. He began to be curious about how he might enter that realm of the popular arts as well.

Filmmaker Paul Morrissey served as something like Warhol's alter ego at the Factory. If Warhol was shy, silent, and passive, Morrissey, a scrappy Irish Catholic graduate of Fordham University and a military veteran, was aggressive, confrontational, and outspoken. Warhol had been approached about becoming involved with a discotheque in Queens, a ludicrous idea until Morrissey suggested that Warhol sponsor a band that could play there, simultaneously drawing attention to the club and presumably making money for the Factory. Barbara Rubin approached the poet, photographer, and Factory stalwart Gerard Malanga to take pictures of the Velvet Underground at the Café Bizarre, and Malanga asked Morrissey to come along with him to help him get the lighting right. Thinking that the Velvets might possibly be the band he was looking for, Morrissey consented to go. He liked the look and sound of the band and recognized how distinctive it was. He talked to the Velvets about Warhol managing them—the band apparently did not even mention Al Aronowitz—and the next night Morrissey and Malanga returned, bringing Warhol and Edie Sedgwick with them. According to Morrissey, Warhol was reluctant to get involved with a band, but the filmmaker persuaded him, and the Velvet Underground entered a decisive new phase in its development.

Whatever his initial reluctance, Warhol soon embraced the Velvets, and they entered the life of the Factory, an environment to which Reed, in particular, adapted with ease and enthusiasm. Most important, he quickly saw how an affiliation with Warhol would increase the band's profile, while adding to the allure of its hipness. The environment of the Factory, where gender lines blurred and methedrine was the drug of choice, could not have suited him better. "At first, before they got to know him, everybody at the Factory adored Lou," Cale later wrote. "In many ways it was the best home he ever had, the first institution where he was understood, welcomed, encouraged, and rewarded for being a twisted, scary monster. Lou, for his part, gave them what they wanted, parading his whole catalog of queeny, limp-wristed poses and ambitions. Lou took to the Factory water like the proverbial duck. I was a little less enthusiastic about the heavy gay scene that dominated the Factory, and the hierarchy by which the inhabitants appeared to live or die."

Warhol was something like the vacant center around which everything at the Factory revolved. He was the force that attracted glamorous figures, exclusive party invitations, and media attention, but his passivity allowed anyone around him with a more assertive personality to shape the environment in his own image. As Warhol's right-hand man, Paul Morrissey made the most of that dynamic. He directed Warhol's films and filled in the conceptual spaces between Warhol's cryptic utterings, turning Warhol's idle thoughts into creative action. But for all his talent and energy, Morrissey was no less dependent on Warhol than were any of the other Factory scenesters. A new Warhol movie was an event. A Paul Morrissey movie? Not so much. Because Morrissey and Reed both harbored ambitions beyond being Warhol acolytes — not to mention the abrasiveness of each of their personalities — the two never got along. Morrissey admired Reed's talent but ultimately had little interest in rock and roll. He also quickly spotted Reed's hustle and controlling tendencies. Running things at the Factory was Morrissey's job, and he had no interest in the lead singer of a no-name band making it more difficult. Everyone at the Factory was a rival with everyone else there for Warhol's attention and approval, so tensions always bristled beneath the veneer of merry speed-freak hijinks.

Reed found the environment of the Factory heady. His time as part of Delmore Schwartz's circle at Syracuse had introduced him to the idea of being around someone whose influence extended far beyond the classroom, the bar, or the campus. But Warhol was operating on an entirely different level. Schwartz's best days were behind him, whereas Warhol was rising in terms of his visibility, impact, and success. Schwartz was the past, Warhol the future. Reed had enormous respect for Schwartz's literary triumphs, but that was part of a far more rarefied world than the one he was moving in now. Warhol was not simply attuned to the media world that was taking shape in the sixties; he was helping to create and define it. If Schwartz disapproved of rock and roll, Warhol was fine with it, as he was with almost anything as long as it was "fun." The Factory wasn't exactly packed with readers, though someone like Danny Fields, who had graduated from the University of Pennsylvania and briefly attended Harvard Law School, was smart and informed, and Gerard Malanga was a poet. But the mixture of pop art, movies, photography, and music seemed up-to-the-minute and exciting. Not yet forty, Warhol was fifteen years younger than Delmore Schwartz, but still old enough to occupy the fatherly role that Reed required of his mentors. Warhol would surround himself with admirers as Schwartz did, but his quietness and passivity were more to Reed's liking. Reed had more room to exert his own power while still learning from a master. He studied Warhol carefully and, even in his moments of greatest excess, he observed everything that was going on around him. Indeed, it was at the Factory that Reed truly refined his voyeuristic writer's eye.

Warhol was taken with Reed from the start. "I think Andy was afraid of him because he was so cute," Danny Fields said. "Andy was a big old queen and Lou was adorable." And Reed found much to observe in the characters who wandered in and out of the Factory. "I was sitting there one afternoon, and Judy Garland was sitting next to me," Fields said. "Rudolf Nureyev is getting off the elevator. Tennessee Williams would be there. We were awestruck." The band would rehearse there. Warhol would do his printmaking, and Morrissey would be shooting. Everyone would be socializing, though with an edge. Reed and Cale got a charge from the scene, but not everyone in the Velvets camp took to it so easily. "Moe and I were pretty young and from Levittown," said Martha Morrison, who was Sterling's girlfriend at the time (she would become his wife) and Maureen Tucker's best friend. "The stuff that people did for shock value or just because they were creeps—that part of the Factory was hard for me. A lot of drugs, of course—not that I noticed anybody doing it, but they certainly looked like they had. The women, the girls, were really trying their best to be shocking and get some attention, maybe be in a movie. We were constantly shocked. Moe and I did a lot of hiding in the bathroom. Unfortunately, the bathroom was worse than whatever was going on outside, because there were all these drawings in there—essentially pornography."

Richard Mishkin, who had played with Reed in earlier bands, had also moved to New York after college, and the two reconnected. Reed was staying at the Ludlow Street apartment with Cale some of the time, and of that situation Mishkin said, "I couldn't believe what he was living in. It was so out of character for Lou, a Jewish boy from Freeport, living in a walk-up." Reed invited him to hang at the Factory and play occasionally, just the two of them or with the Velvets, for whom Mishkin would sometimes play bass. "We had worked on songs like 'Heroin' and 'Walk on the Wild Side'—the music, not the words—at Syracuse, so we picked up on that," Mishkin said. He and Reed would occasionally play together on the top floor of a Brooklyn brownstone that Mishkin's father and grandfather, who were sponsoring a housing project in the area, were using as a real estate office. "The building was standing alone in the middle of nowhere, because the rest of the buildings around it had been demolished," Mishkin said. "It was not that inconvenient; it was right across the Brooklyn Bridge.... We could play anytime, as loud as we wanted, because nobody was around. And Lou rehearsed. He was never one of those people who would pretend you could just get up onstage with other people and make a cohesive sound. He understood that you had to practice."

Along with the material Reed had worked up with the Velvets, they also played some of the covers they had done as L.A. and the Eldorados. But Reed, in collaboration with Cale, had already set his sights beyond whatever they had done before. "There was this whole genre that was just noise that I really didn't like," Mishkin said. "I was never into heavy metal, and this almost felt like a precursor to that. In college we never played loud, because we didn't have the amplification, but now the music started to get really loud. Also, I always liked repetition in improvisation, but constant repetition was just not comfortable for me. I felt that Lou wanted to do something that would antagonize the audience, in the way that only Lou could do. John Cale and I had some kind of understanding as musicians. I'm classically trained, and he's classically trained. But I was not into John Cage. I liked modern music, but Stravinsky and stuff like that. Atonal was not what I loved. It was almost like they were combining what I would have considered 'insult music' with rock and roll. If you couldn't appreciate it, that was too bad. You had to intellectualize to become sensitive to it. That's where Lou was heading. I don't know that he was doing it to be offensive. He was doing it to find wherever it was he was going."

Where he was going, in Mishkin's view, was toward a role that had just begun to exert genuine cultural influence. "Lou thought of himself as a rock star," Mishkin said. "As much as he wanted to be a poet, he wanted to be a rock star. Whereas Dylan was a songwriter, that wasn't what Lou was striving for. Lou was striving to become a rock star, which happened to include writing music. But it also included something different that would set him apart. He was trying to develop the personality and the aloofness that, in his mind, he thought a rock star should have. I think he wanted to do that from the time he first started singing and playing in front of people. Lou knew in his heart that he was unique, and he was taking this noise and trying to translate it into something that would make him stand apart. That's where we parted ways musically."

Mishkin had the opportunity to observe Reed at the Factory. "Andy was like a master puppeteer," he said. "He was privy to things because of who he was. One day, he pulled everybody together and said, 'I just got this, and this is going to be the next big thing,' and he pulled out a film of the Who. Nobody had heard of them, but they were breaking guitars and Keith Moon was wild.

"If Andy was the general, Lou was one of the lieutenants. People looked up to him because Andy respected him. It was like he was a project of Andy's, a work of art. All the hangers-on there were in awe of people like Lou and Paul Morrissey. I don't know how it changed when Lou started to gain fame on his own, but Lou was really in awe of Andy, and he should have been. Andy was mentoring Lou."

Mishkin had his own run-in with Warhol, during the shooting of one of Warhol's films in an empty apartment in a dilapidated building on the Lower East Side, not far from the Velvets' Ludlow Street apartment. Mishkin had moved back into his parents' apartment after dropping out of St. John's University Law School, and on this particular day, his mother needed to locate him. "My mother was a little Jewish lady, and she was going crazy trying to find me," Mishkin said. "So she walks into this abandoned apartment in the middle of Warhol making one of his films and says, 'Where is my son Richard?' It was so funny. Lou couldn't stop laughing."

In the evenings, Warhol, who, like Reed, hated to be alone, took advantage of the dozens of invitations he received to parties and openings, and he would bring along a crew from the Factory, including the Velvets and their friends. Class distinctions are not supposed to exist in America, so they remain hidden. Of course, they were always in place, but the sixties marked a time of class realignment. When Warhol would attend a Park Avenue soiree with a group of his followers, hierarchies shifted. The Warhol crowd may not have been wealthy or well-bred, though in some instances—Edie Sedgwick being one example—they were. But they were young, good-looking, creative, sexually daring, and brash, and they carried Warhol's imprimatur, which had its own social weight. "We were definitely observed and watched, and we were aware of that," Martha Morrison said. "Even just walking down the street or walking into a place like Elaine's or Ondine, you did feel like you were ultracool and being looked at."

"You just felt like you were at the center of things, and Lou had to feel that, too," said Danny Fields. "Nobody was saying you must or you can't. It was like, 'What is this world we're in?' We'd open the paper and read about ourselves: 'Oh, my God, that's us!' Was it weird and drug-ridden and depraved? I don't know. It was just us. And Lou was going through exactly the same thing. From their dump of an apartment to any-one in the world you wanted to meet. No one knew how to cope with that. We were at the center of some cyclone. And Andy was just getting bigger and bigger."

*   *   *

VERY SHORTLY AFTER WARHOL took the Velvet Underground under his wing, he and Paul Morrissey decided that the band needed a touch of glamour and mystique. To provide those virtues, they insisted that Nico, a German actress and model who had drifted into the Factory scene, be added to the group as its "chanteuse," or lead singer. Born Christa Paffgen in Cologne in 1938, Nico—a name given to her by a fashion photographer in Berlin—began modeling as a teenager. She was five foot ten, strikingly blonde, and strikingly beautiful, with porcelain skin and perfectly sculpted cheekbones. By the midsixties, she had spent a decade or so on the verge of a major breakthrough that never quite seemed to arrive. She had a bit part in Federico Fellini's classic 1960 film, *La Dolce Vita,* and a lusciously erotic portrait of her appeared on the cover of Bill Evans's 1962 album, *Moon Beams.* While her modeling career was successful, she never rose to the level of the kicky, childlike women who were beginning to define the feminine look of the sixties. Part of the reason was that, unlike the models who embodied the period's carefree flirtatiousness, Nico exuded an icy distance. In that, she was an apt fit for the Velvets, whose brooding, droning songs defied the optimism of so much pop culture at that time. Also, despite her great beauty, there were elements of androgyny to

Nico: her low-pitched voice, her thick German accent, her haughty remove. Without doing much of anything, she communicated drama. It was hard not to look at her, and Warhol and Morrissey understood the appeal of that—they were visual artists, after all, not musical ones. And Nico's visual qualities, far more than anything to do with music, were the reason they installed her as the Velvets' lead singer.

Nonetheless, Nico had already attracted notable attention on the music scene. Brian Jones of the Rolling Stones had introduced her to Andrew Loog Oldham, the band's manager and producer, who wanted to sign and record her for the label he had recently launched. Bob Dylan met her and offered her the song "I'll Keep It with Mine," and his manager, Albert Grossman, persuaded her to move to New York with promises to help with her music career. That Nico wasn't much of a singer was beside the point. She had a look and an aura, and that was quite enough.

Of course, the notion of Warhol and Morrissey unilaterally deciding that Nico would be the Velvets' lead singer was an outrageous affront, and Reed felt it. "Can you imagine doing that to a band?" Danny Fields asked. "This is a legitimate, fabulous, unique, magnificent band, and because their management thinks they're boring, they put a German model in front of them? 'Oh, there's nothing to look at. People need something to look at.' And here's this beautiful woman who drifted into their orbit, so let's make her the lead singer." Reed certainly made his feelings known, but he was savvy enough not to rock the lifeboat he had just climbed into. Working with Warhol still had plenty of advantages that were yet to be realized. Reed's strategy was to minimize Nico's role: despite her desire to, she would not be singing every one of the band's songs—just a handful that Reed deemed appropriate for her. He also undertook an affair with her, an effort he would employ many times later in his life: sex as a means of control. Outside the context of the band's music, however, Nico would find her own form of rebellion, her way of getting under Reed's skin. She took to publicly attributing his hostility toward her to resentment about what Germany had done to the Jews, or what, as she put it, her "people" had done to "his people." At a band rehearsal at the Factory, Nico idly responded to a cool hello from Reed after she'd arrived late by saying, "I cannot make love to Jews anymore." Given Nico's imperious air and Reed's self-consciousness about his stature at the Factory—and about being a suburban Jew—her brush-off seared him. Nico's ongoing fascination with Bob Dylan, meanwhile, may well have been the reason for Reed's many caustic—and sometimes anti-Semitic—remarks about him over the years. Reed would insist that the group be referred to as the Velvet Underground and Nico, giving her second billing and making it clear that she was not officially a member of the band.

While all this was going on, Reed maintained contact with Shelley Albin. As he would with many people, particularly women, throughout his life, Reed would call her when he felt frightened and alone. "I remember him saying to me when he was first in New York, 'You don't understand how lonely it is,'" she said. "I would say, 'You're getting somewhere, you're doing this and that,' but he would say, 'No, it's so lonely.' It didn't matter who he was with. He was always looking for nurturing. He was really desperately lonely. He kept trying to get me to come back to him."

ANDY WARHOL IMMEDIATELY PROVED his value to the Velvet Underground beyond buying the band equipment and providing rent money and a rehearsal space. He arranged for them to perform at a psychiatrists' convention at Delmonico's Hotel, a classic New York locale. The scene was a prototypical midsixties clash of cultures, the arbiters of normalcy meeting the emerging hordes who were in the process of redefining—if not shattering—the very concept of normality. Psychoanalysis was still the rage, the province of creative types interested in exploring every aspect of their psyche to discover new, subversive sources of vision. But in

many ways psychiatry remained a conservative field—
for one thing, homosexuality was still regarded as a
form of mental illness. It would not have been lost on
Reed for one second that his audience on the night of
January 13, 1966, consisted of practitioners of the profession that had recommended his devastating electroshock treatments. The event was the annual dinner
of the New York Society for Clinical Psychiatry, and
the organization had invited Warhol to speak under
the billing "The Chic Mystique of Andy Warhol."

Warhol no doubt accepted the invitation for the
sake of a paycheck and a laugh, but, being cripplingly
shy, there was no way he would deliver a typical dinner speech to the tables of "black-tied psychiatrists and
their formally gowned wives." Instead, he showed films,
and then the Velvets performed "Heroin" at deafening
volume. Gerard Malanga brought along a bullwhip,
Edie Sedgwick danced seductively, and Barbara Rubin
and underground filmmaker Jonas Mekas ran through
the crowd with cameras as Rubin peppered the psychiatrists with lurid sexual questions. Most important
of all, the event was widely covered, with the *New
York Times* and the *New York Herald Tribune* both
running sizable stories, and mentions turning up in
Newsweek and other publications. It was the sort of
publicity that an essentially unknown band could never
have gotten on its own, as Reed certainly realized.
Nonetheless, it could not have sat well with Reed that

the *Times* described Cale as the "leader" of the Velvets and that Warhol talked about Nico as "a famous fashion model and now a singer." Reed himself went unmentioned. He would have noted the slight, but he kept his eyes on the prize. The Warhol gambit was clearly working.

Things moved quickly from that point. In January of 1966, Warhol filmed the Velvets rehearsing at the Factory for an hour and called the movie *The Velvet Underground and Nico: A Symphony of Sound*. In the film, the band does not play any songs, and while it's extraordinary to see the group at work at this stage of its career, the formless playing is not especially inspired. As one might expect, the last thing Warhol would have wanted to film was a conventional performance by a rock band, so the camera arbitrarily goes in and out of focus and almost completely ignores the standard strategy of concentrating on whoever might be playing the most important part at any particular moment. The camera does occasionally lavish attention on Nico, yet another indication of her significance in Warhol and Morrissey's estimation.

In early February, the Velvets played a week of shows at the Film-Makers' Cinematheque, which had been founded by Jonas Mekas and was located, at the time, at 125 West Forty-First Street. As usual, these were not typical concert performances. The band played as part of a multimedia event billed as Andy Warhol

Up-Tight. At the time, the term "uptight" had a double meaning: there was its contemporary sense of nervous and restricted, as well as a sense of cool and exactly in its place, as in the raucous Stevie Wonder single of the period "Uptight (Everything's Alright)." At the Up-Tight event, Warhol screened some of his films (*Vinyl, Empire, Eat, A Symphony of Sound*) while the Velvets played. A light show, photographs, dancing by Edie Sedgwick and Gerard Malanga, and filming by Barbara Rubin were also aspects of the happening. Such events were part of the zeitgeist as well as part of Warhol's improvisatory search for new directions: put everything out there and see what people respond to. The band did two performances a night, along with, hilariously, matinees on Saturday and Sunday. At these performances, the band, finally worn out by Nico's relentless insistence, performed Dylan's "I'll Keep It with Mine," on which she sang lead. No one else liked the song and the band eventually dropped it, an early sign of Reed's frustration with Nico's presence. On the handbills for the Up-Tight event, Nico was billed entirely separately from the band.

Warhol then sought to take Up-Tight on the road, which, given the limitations of the time, meant a tour of colleges. Because Warhol's presence was the primary attraction, the events were mostly attended by art students and faculty, along with fun-seekers who took their cultural cues from that crowd. The troupe ventured out to New Brunswick, New Jersey, to appear at Rutgers University on March 9 (a gig for which Nico was paid a hundred dollars, the amount the rest of the band had to share), and then piled into a van to appear at the University of Michigan Film Festival in Ann Arbor on March 12. If New Jersey was a stretch, the Midwest was really pushing it for the Warhol crowd. But as such events tend to do, the Michigan performance attracted an audience of people who would continue to support the band in various ways — as fans, club bookers, and writers. As always, the Velvets proved to be divisive. Students who could feel the cultural changes taking place in the midsixties were energized by the rawness of their sound and the fever-dream swirl of the films and light shows. For more casual thrill-seekers, the deafening volume and the sheer strangeness of this crowd of New York freaks proved off-putting, to say the least.

BACK IN NEW YORK, by mid-March the time had finally arrived for the Velvet Underground to begin the residency at the Queens discotheque that had sparked Warhol and Morrissey's interest in the band in the first place. The deal fell apart when the venue's owner decided just four days before the Velvets' start date to book the Young Rascals instead, probably a better move than staging a Warhol-style Up-Tight happening in an outer borough. It was extremely unlikely that Warhol's fans would have ventured to Queens from Manhattan, where the vast majority of them lived. Meanwhile, the Rascals (led, as it happens, by keyboardist Felix Cavaliere, who had attended Syracuse University with Reed) had a number one hit with "Good Lovin'," and would have a much stronger draw. As it turned out, the club was closed down on its opening night for liquor law violations and later burned to the ground under suspicious circumstances.

So, what to do with the Velvet Underground, whom Warhol was continuing to support? Entirely by coincidence, Morrissey learned that a Polish meeting hall on St. Marks Place had become available to rent. St. Marks was the main drag of what would soon be dubbed the East Village because of its proximity to Greenwich Village. The area had historically been dominated by Eastern European Jewish immigrants and, farther east, by Puerto Ricans who had moved to New York in the fifties and early sixties. The Jewish population was in the process of dying off, moving to the suburbs with their children, and being driven away by crime and clashes with the younger Puerto Rican newcomers. The West Village was relatively settled terrain, so counterculture types headed for the cheaper rents a few blocks east. Second Avenue, which intersected St. Marks, had been a hotbed of Yiddish theater, and those abandoned venues began to be used for rock shows. (One of them, just two blocks south of St. Marks, would eventually become the Fillmore East.) The shrinking Polish community had limited need for its meeting hall, so Morrissey snapped it up for a month, dubbed it the Dom (an abbreviated version of its Polish name), and quickly readied it for the Velvets' residency.

It was a perfect example of a virtue made of necessity. St. Marks was an ideal setting for Warhol and the Velvet Underground. Putting aside the lovely coincidence that Warhol (whose family name was Warhola) was himself the child of Polish immigrants, St. Marks was hip, on the verge, and conveniently located for all the Factory crowd's friends in the city's various underground scenes. Renting the place for a month allowed for media coverage and word of mouth to build, and also enabled Warhol and the band to get the event's various elements in order — though, given Warhol's raw aesthetic, the performances were far from buttoned-down. Strobe lights, a glittering silver mirror ball off which lights were projected (soon to be known as a disco ball), spotlights, flashlights, Gerard Malanga's whip dancing with Factory scenester Mary Woronov, Barbara Rubin's guerrilla filmmaking, a psychedelic light show that made use of colored gels, screenings of Warhol's movies — all accompanied performances by the Velvets. Nico wore white, and the rest of the band wore black—because, Reed said, it made it easier to see the films and light shows being projected onto them. Like Reed's high school bands, the Velvets wore sunglasses—in this case, he said, to protect their eyes from all the lighting effects. It was groundbreaking stuff—a full-on sensual assault, intensified by the band's characteristic earsplitting volume. Morrissey decided to call the event the Exploding Plastic Inevitable. He claimed to have taken those three words from the liner notes on a Dylan album, but more likely they were inspired by Dylan's Beat-oriented, hallucinogenic wordplay.

In the course of the month of shows, the Velvets gained a significant reputation. The shows at the Dom were widely covered and became hip to attend for both the city's art crowd and celebrities who aspired to chicness. "I don't think we would have been anything without the fascination Warhol created," Cale said. "Walter Cronkite and Jackie Kennedy would come down and dance in front of us on the floor. TV would cover it. This was a huge party for everybody, and everybody made money and everybody was satisfied." As a performing band, the Velvets began to experience the true explosive force of the music they had created. It was one thing to demo a few songs, however visionary, in Cale's apartment. Staging performances that galvanized audiences was quite another. "Lou and I had an almost religious fervor about what we were doing—and it worked," Cale said. "Coming offstage after a set, I felt exhilarated because I knew that nobody knew what the hell was going on, and I felt in control."

Reed's friend Richard Mishkin occasionally played bass for the Velvets during their stint at the Dom, and he recalled, "I had never been in an environment like that, a claustrophobic space with a lot of people and strobe lights that after a while were just blinding. I don't know that many places like that existed at the time. I sat on the bass amplifier, so the noise was over-bearing for me. It was not acoustically a good room, and our equipment was terrible. During breaks I would walk around just to get a feeling for what was going on, and there were plenty of people who you just didn't know what they were, but they were defi-nitely stoned. It wasn't really an audience. I don't think there was a straight person—meaning some-body who wasn't high—in the entire place. People were constantly moving around, dancing, like this fluid, hallucinatory mass of people. It was brand-new, leading edge. It was way out there. It was like a Fellini movie—but squared."

Painter and musician Bob Neuwirth, who was one of Edie Sedgwick's lovers, saw the Velvets at the Dom. "It wasn't really rock; it was drug music," he said. "The lyrics were interesting. The most impressive thing about Lou as an artist was that he was so authentic. He never sang about suffering that he didn't have experience with. All those great, decadent songs that he wrote at that time were all about personal experience. I always found that admirable."

4

THE DESTRUCTIVE ELEMENT

A S THE VELVET UNDERGROUND began to gain a reputation, the next phase in Warhol and Morrissey's business plan came into focus: finding the group a record deal. In their manner of doing things as made sense to them rather than researching the process or consulting with others, the two men arranged for the Velvets to go into a recording studio with Norman Dolph, an executive in the sales department at Columbia Records who was also an art collector. Warhol had casually mentioned to Dolph that he wanted to make an album with the Velvet Underground. Dolph suggested that he could make it happen, and Warhol essentially turned the project over to him. The two men split the cost — estimated to be roughly $1,500 — of what turned out to be something like four days in the studio in the middle of April of 1966.

Dolph arranged for the band to work at Scepter Records, the studio of a label primarily known for such pop R & B artists as Dionne Warwick and the Shirelles. On their limited budget, the Velvets had to work not only quickly but at odd hours. They were likely to get bumped if Scepter needed the studio for one of the label's more commercial acts. Warhol ultimately would be credited as the producer of these sessions, though he was, at most, an intermittent presence and, of course, had no experience whatsoever in producing records. Neither, for that matter, did Norman Dolph, who did attend the sessions. But in both music and film, where Warhol was far more experienced, the title of "producer" can mean many different things. Sterling Morrison said that Warhol gave the band "confidence," and Reed always insisted that Warhol encouraged them to record their songs exactly as they wanted to, not to yield to any notions, their own or anyone else's, about what might be commercial or inoffensive. The sound should be raw, and Reed's "dirty words" and taboo subjects needed to remain unchanged. That was excellent advice and a crucial contribution, even if it simply strengthened the band members' resolve to do what they might have done anyway. Many producers have received far more lucrative credits for doing far less.

The Velvets were not entirely lacking in studio

experience. Reed had his boot camp at Pickwick Records, Nico had done some recording in England, and Cale had recorded with La Monte Young and others on the avant-garde scene. If they didn't have technical expertise, they had something far more important: a vision. Still, someone needed to make sure the songs got recorded. John Licata, Scepter's in-house engineer, helped out in that regard. Dolph, whom Cale would dismiss as a "shoe salesman," kept things moving because in the studio time is money and he was paying the bill. Reed and Cale knew what they wanted the band to achieve: primarily, the excitement and immediacy of what the group could do onstage.

As always, Nico became an issue. At first there was an impasse. She wanted to sing all the songs, and Reed did not want her to sing any. Finally, in line with the concept of replicating the live show, she got to sing the three songs she sang onstage: "All Tomorrow's Parties," "I'll Be Your Mirror," and "Femme Fatale." The sessions were serious, focused, and, by the Velvets' standards, professional. For example, despite the tension between Nico and Reed, when it came time for her to do her vocals, the band made sure that she was as comfortable as possible. Still, as Reed desired, she was scarce around the studio other than when she had to sing her parts. "We were really excited," Cale said. "We had this opportunity to do something revolutionary —

to combine the avant-garde and rock and roll, to do something symphonic. No matter how borderline destructive everything was, there was real excitement there for all of us. We just started playing and held it to the wall." For his part, Reed was as intent as could be. " 'Heroin' was an incredible thing when he did it," Dolph said. "It was not dizzy or out of control or as you might expect it to be if sung by an addict. It was delivered as an actor, familiar with the role, might portray it. It was a very emotional delivery."

When the sessions were done, Dolph made an acetate of the material they had recorded, which included nearly all the songs that would appear on the band's debut album. He and Morrissey then attempted to interest record companies in signing the band. It's hard to describe how different the Velvets sounded from what most bands were doing at the time. Nineteen sixty-six was a year in which some of the most adventurous music in the history of rock and roll came out, including Bob Dylan's *Blonde on Blonde,* the Beatles' *Revolver,* the Rolling Stones' *Aftermath,* and the Beach Boys' *Pet Sounds.* However, none of those albums were remotely as daring as what the Velvet Underground was doing. The drones of Reed's guitar and Cale's viola; Reed's fuck-you, deadpan vocals and Nico's Teutonic incantations; the songs' steely depictions of hard drug use and outré sexuality — none of those qualities were anywhere to be found in any other popular music.

Consequently, record companies' universal response to the Velvets' music, even with Warhol's endorsement, ranged from no interest to outrage.

One executive was intrigued, however. Tom Wilson had helped define the folk-rock sound that took Simon and Garfunkel to the top of the charts, and he had produced Bob Dylan's breakthrough hit, "Like a Rolling Stone," on Dylan's groundbreaking 1965 album, *Highway 61 Revisited*. Wilson had a background in jazz, was Harvard-educated, and was the only staff producer at Columbia Records who was African American. He could hear possibilities in the music that less adventurous ears missed. He also thought that Nico could be a major star, an observation that did little to endear him to Reed. Wilson had recently left Columbia to move to Verve/MGM, and he wanted to sign the Velvets to his new label, though it's doubtful he would have wanted the band without Nico, which speaks well of Warhol and Morrissey's instinct to bring her on board.

The band signed to the label in early May of 1966. Reed, however, refused to sign the original version of the contract, which stipulated that the band's earnings be delivered to Warhol and Morrissey. Reed insisted that the band be paid directly, and Warhol and Morrissey would be paid a management percentage out of the group's earnings. That was and is a far more typical arrangement, and it was a smart business move on

Reed's part. But it also revealed an early crack in his relationship with Warhol, whose feelings about money were complex: he was obsessed with it, but he didn't like to deal with it. Everything at the Factory revolved around Warhol, and in that boundaryless environment, money took on an emotional meaning that it might not have in a more conventional business situation. Reed clearly saw the Velvets as beginning to launch their career and wanted a professional arrangement, not a feudal one. Warhol worried about money constantly but avoided talking about it. He would not have seen Reed's move simply in business terms. He took it personally and resented it. Not long afterward, Reed would have the other members of the Velvet Underground sign an agreement that he would receive all songwriting royalties unless otherwise indicated. Feelings were ruffled there as well, but Reed was making his move.

In a continuing effort to expand the appeal of Warhol, the Velvets, and the Exploding Plastic Inevitable (EPI), the entire troupe scheduled a two-week engagement at the Trip, a club on Sunset Boulevard in Los Angeles that catered to the city's burgeoning hippie scene. If New Jersey and Michigan were stretches for the EPI, L.A. was beyond anything attempted before. Because it was America's entertainment capital, L.A. was, well, an inevitable stop for the EPI. But despite Warhol's fascination with classic Hollywood, everything the Velvets represented ran counter to L.A., particularly at that time. If Hollywood was America's dream factory, the Velvets represented uncut urban realism. If L.A. was all sunshine and pastel colors, the Velvets were nocturnal, dark, and dressed in black. As the club's name indicated, L.A. was undergoing a psychedelic surge, and the Velvets, of course, preferred speed and heroin. But perhaps the primary distinctions were simply geographical and attitudinal. The Warhol crowd—and the Velvets, in particular—brought every iota of their New York condescension to L.A. And L.A., ever intimidated by and resentful of that stance, responded in its own passive-aggressive way: it was eager to embrace this cool new happening from New York but equally eager to resist the implication that New York was the only conceivable source of such edgy revelations.

The poster for the two-week run gave top billing, as usual, to Warhol, and on opening night, musicians and actors turned out in force—as everyone had hoped, the word had gotten out. David Crosby of the Byrds, Ryan O'Neal, Sonny and Cher, Jim Morrison of the as-yet-unsigned Doors, John Phillips and Cass Elliot of the Mamas and the Papas, Tony Hicks of the Hollies—all were in attendance. The EPI put on its standard multimedia extravaganza, and the Velvets played at deafening volume. The L.A. media covered the event extensively and pondered its meaning with predictably little success. Responses from attendees were mixed at best. Cher, who was nineteen at the time, walked out in the middle of the show, and got off the best line about the event. The Exploding Plastic Inevitable would not be the next big thing, she asserted: "It will replace nothing, except maybe suicide." Warhol, of course, loved that line and wanted to use it in future promotions. The EPI caused enough of a ruckus that the Trip was temporarily closed by the L.A. police for mysterious reasons on the third night of the EPI's residency. According to the rules of the musicians union, the Velvets could be paid their full fee for the three-week stint only if they remained in town, so the group holed up in a Hollywood Hills mansion known as the Castle that had previously housed Bob Dylan and other rock luminaries. While in Los Angeles with little else to do, the band went into the studio with Tom Wilson to work on "Heroin," "I'm Waiting for the Man," and "Venus in Furs," and possibly to do some work on the tracks they had recorded at Scepter in New York.

At the end of the month, the Velvets and the EPI traveled north to San Francisco to perform for three nights at Bill Graham's Fillmore Auditorium, resulting in another epic culture clash. San Francisco was in the process of becoming the ground zero of the hippie counterculture, and it lacked the underbelly of cynicism that complicates L.A.'s cheeriness. Graham's gruffness bruised Warhol's passivity, and the former's sense of San Francisco as the center of the musical universe abraded the Velvets' New York arrogance. "We were pretty much appalled by what was going on on the West Coast," John Cale said. "The hippie scene was not for us. They were scruffy, dirty people." The Velvets rolled their eyes at what they felt was the amateurishness of Graham's light show in comparison with what the EPI was doing, and the band's ear-bleeding feedback and New York posturing offended the locals. *San Francisco Chronicle* critic Ralph J. Gleason, who would go on to cofound *Rolling Stone* a year later, attacked Warhol, the Velvets, and their crowd as "all very campy and very Greenwich Village sick." That he could write a line like that in San Francisco, of all cities, which even then was a gay mecca, is indicative of the kind of horror the Velvets inspired. "I really didn't need Ralph Gleason landing on me, although I guess it was kind of cool," Reed said. "Why would people write these incredibly vitriolic attacks against us? *Naked Lunch* was out there. Allen Ginsberg was out there with *Howl*. Hubert Selby was out there with *Last Exit to Brooklyn*. What could the Velvet Underground possibly add to that? It's that music does something way past what a book could do in the same amount of time."

WHEN THE VELVET UNDERGROUND returned from the West Coast, the band's momentum slowed. Perhaps because of the contract revision Reed had insisted on, Warhol focused his interest elsewhere. Reed then suffered another bout of hepatitis. The Velvets and a skeleton crew of EPI regulars traveled to Chicago without him for what turned out to be a well-received two-week residency at Poor Richard's in the city's Old Town district. Reed didn't make the trip because of his illness, and Nico was off in Ibiza. Consequently, Cale handled the vocals, Maureen Tucker switched to bass, and Angus MacLise rejoined the group on percussion. The shows went so well that the band was held over for a week beyond its initial booking. While in Chicago, the band also played a daytime show at the Playboy Mansion, a mind-boggling notion. For unknown reasons, Verve did not seem in any particular hurry to release *The Velvet Underground and Nico,* though in July it put out the single "All Tomorrow's Parties" backed with "I'll Be Your Mirror." The release made no impact whatsoever, commercial or otherwise, but the fact that both songs feature Nico on lead vocals suggests that the label saw her as the band's star.

While Reed was recovering from hepatitis, he learned that Delmore Schwartz had died of a heart attack while living at the Columbia Hotel near Times Square. Schwartz's circumstances had deteriorated sufficiently that his body had lain unclaimed at Bellevue Hospital for two days after his death. Reed had maintained a correspondence with Schwartz and tried to visit him after he returned to New York, but Schwartz refused to see him. The poet's paranoia had deepened to the degree that virtually everyone he had known at Syracuse was now somehow implicated in the universal conspiracy to destroy him. Reed released himself from the hospital in order to attend Schwartz's wake with Gerard Malanga. Reed also attended the burial of his late mentor. Later Reed would write, "I was one of the first Medicare patients. A drug I shot in San Francisco froze all my joints. The doctors suspected terminal lupus but this turned out to be untrue. Anyway, it didn't matter since I checked myself out of the hospital to go to Delmore's funeral and never went back."

"Into the destructive element…that is the way," Schwartz had written on a bank deposit envelope found in his hotel room. It proved to be an instruction his former student would live by for many years.

As 1966 DRAGGED ON, the Velvets were in something of a holding pattern as they awaited the release of their debut album. To this day, the reasons for the delay are debated. The album had essentially been completed while the band was in California in May, and acetates had been done by November, when Warhol passed one along to English rock manager Kenneth Pitt, who, fatefully, gave it to his then-unknown young client David Bowie, who was overwhelmed by it.

The likelihood is that no single, specific reason predominated, but a number of factors conspired against the album's coming out. Tom Wilson, who signed the band because of Nico, believed that the album needed more of her vocals. Consequently, Reed wrote "Sunday Morning" for her—as well as to accommodate Warhol's request that he write a song about paranoia. However, when Reed learned that the song would be released as a single, he decided to sing it himself and made that clear to Wilson in no uncertain terms. Perhaps Reed felt protected by Warhol, but rudely blowing off a request from the label executive who signed you was not a strategy designed to make your album a priority in his eyes. Reed's decision was right, though: his vocal has a gentleness and subtlety that Nico would never have been able to approach. Perhaps he might have found a better way to handle the situation—but then he would have had to be a different person. He may well have wanted to sing the song simply *because* Wilson—and Paul Morrissey—wanted Nico to sing it. Regardless, he would speak of Wilson only with enormous condescension for the rest of his life. The single, "Sunday Morning" backed with "Femme Fatale," was released in November to little response. It's notable that all three of the songs on which Nico sings lead were released on the band's first two singles.

Another possible reason for the delay was that Wilson had also signed the Mothers of Invention, with whom the Velvets had had several run-ins during their recent stay in California. Though the bands could not be more different, at the time they were both ground-breaking groups attempting to blend rock and roll with elements of the avant-garde. At least conceptually, the Mothers' *Freak Out!*—the title of their first album— was similar to the Exploding Plastic Inevitable. But the Velvets' association with Warhol put them at a disadvantage. As outrageous as they seemed, the Mothers of Invention were a recognizable band, while the Velvets were still perceived as part of Warhol's multi-media circus. Being associated with Warhol was an attention-grabber but also made the Velvets seem not quite serious—or no more serious than Gerard Malanga and Mary Woronov doing a whip dance. Warhol had no experience dealing with a record company, while the Mothers had a seasoned manager. With the two records ready for release at approximately the same time, it makes sense that Wilson, who produced *Freak Out!,* would opt to put out that album first, as he did in June of 1966. Pushing the Velvets release into 1967 would help prevent the two albums from competing with each other.

What's more, the artwork that Warhol conceived for the cover of *The Velvet Underground and Nico* might have caused delays as well. The cover was a gatefold, which was still a rarity at that time. More important, Warhol wanted a banana on the album's white cover that would peel off to reveal a pinkish phallic fruit underneath. Perhaps the most artistically adventurous cover concept for a rock album to date, it was expensive and complicated to produce, possibly leading to further delays.

FINALLY, VERVE RELEASED *THE Velvet Underground and Nico* in March of 1967, one of the most important years in the history of rock and roll. With the prominence of Bob Dylan and the Beatles, the notion that popular music could be taken seriously as art had begun to take hold. The release of the Beatles' *Sgt. Pepper's Lonely Hearts Club Band* just a few months later would enshrine that idea. That wasn't an album that meant very much to the Velvets — "*Sgt. Pepper* was a theatrical statement," Cale said, somewhat dismissively. But the notion that rock musicians deserved the same level of critical appreciation as artists in any other form was very much in the air. And it was perhaps the primary ambition of Lou Reed's career. In 1966 he had published an essay titled "The View from the Bandstand: Life Among the Poo-bahs" in which he dismissed the literary poetry of the time (notably exempting by omission his beloved Delmore Schwartz, who loathed rock lyrics) and lauded the words in rock songs. He savaged "Robert Lowell, up for a poetry prize without a decent word ever written. The only decent poetry of this century was that recorded on rock-and-roll records. Everybody knew that. Who you going to rap with. Little Bobby Lowell or Richard Penniman alias Little Richard, our thrice-retired preacher. The incomparable E. McDaniels [*sic*], otherwise known as Bo Diddley. Giving Robert Lowell any kind of poetry prize is obscene. Ditto worrying about Ezra Pound. And the Yale Poetry Series. The colleges are meant to kill you." (Ironically, Lowell's groundbreaking 1959 collection, *Life Studies,* can be viewed as an important precursor to Reed's own writing in its explorations of madness and psychosexual family turmoil.)

With their album out in the world, ready and eager for critical accolades, the Velvet Underground found itself in the odd position of being held back by the same force that was propelling the band into media prominence. Inevitably, the band was perceived as Andy Warhol's latest gambit. His name prominently appeared on the album's cover, and his production credit was nearly as large as the band's own. The back cover depicts the band onstage in front of a light show, and the small, individual portraits are partly covered by polka dots and other "psychedelic" lighting effects. Brilliant as the cover concept was, it somewhat overwhelmed the music. To this day, the Velvet Underground's debut is referred to as the banana album. Warhol denied it, but it's beyond a doubt that the cover was a reference to the weird notion spreading through the media at the time that young people had begun to bake banana peels and smoke them in order to get high. It was just the sort of tweaking of hippie earnestness that Warhol would have loved—it just happened to come along at the absolute apex of hippie earnestness. That meant that potential record buyers would perceive the album as a joke, another Warhol put-on. Cultural theorists could debate whether Brillo boxes, Coca-Cola bottles, or Campbell's soup cans were works of art, as Warhol's paintings suggested. But for the general public, Warhol was perceived as something like an aesthetic hustler—either a zany provocateur or an absolute fraud, depending on your degree of cultural tolerance.

Neither of those categories has anything to do with rock and roll. The clearly phallic—and undeniably gay and campy—implications of the full-size banana, which curves upward like an erection, not to mention the pinkish, fleshy fruit underneath the peel-off sticker (a tiny arrow and small type on the cover suggested "Peel slowly and see"), did not help matters. History would eventually catch up to Warhol—as it would to the Velvet Underground. Both would deservedly be hailed as geniuses, and the banana cover would be recognized as among the greatest album covers of all time. But at the moment, the association with Warhol and everything he represented seemed to be holding the band back.

This attention to the album cover is warranted not

merely because of the issues it created for the band and its ultimate historical significance; in the case of the Velvet Underground, the cover was an essential aspect of the marketing of the album. Brilliant as the album is, AM radio, the primary means of exposure for music at the time, would never play it. The music was far too daring. Even the more adventurous FM stations that were just beginning to redefine the air-waves would be unlikely to go so far as to play songs about heroin or kinky sex. Television appearances were out of the question. Print advertising — all based on the slogan "So Far 'Underground,' You Get the Bends" — typically emphasized the band's Warhol connections, declaring the album to be "What Happens When the Daddy of 'Pop Art' Goes 'Pop Music.'" The album's only commercial hope was word-of-mouth excitement, which is a slow build at best, or people being intrigued by the album cover in record stores. The vinyl format allowed for significant display opportunities. Record stores could place the covers in their windows or show them on their walls. In those days, music fans would flip through record bins and often were intrigued by distinctive album art. Warhol, however, would not speak to such fans in any but a parodic way, so those opportunities were lost. And when Factory scenester Eric Emerson threatened to sue the Velvets' label because his image was displayed without his permission on the album's back cover, the record had to be recalled and the cover redone, destroying any market momentum it might conceivably have built. The album ended up peaking at number 171, hardly an impressive showing but the highest any Velvet Underground album would reach while the original band was active.

To whoever managed to hear it, however, the album's music spoke definitively for itself. Side one opens with "Sunday Morning," Reed's answer to Warhol's suggestion that he write about paranoia. It features perhaps the Velvets' most delicate arrangement—a tinkling celeste, viola, and piano, all played by Cale—and Reed's most self-consciously sweet vocal. In what would become a consistent Velvets strategy, those sonic elements existed in tense opposition to the underlying dread of the lyrics. The song captured the mood that Kris Kristofferson would later distill in "Sunday Morning Coming Down," a sense that at a quiet moment that evokes spirituality and peace, your own life is nowhere near serenity. The song may be about paranoia, but the fear in it seems generated not so much by the outside world but by something perverse inside the singer himself, a "restless feeling" whose disturbing sources he doesn't "want to know." His inability to share the peacefulness of a Sunday morning is the result of his own habits and actions ("all those streets you've crossed not so long ago")—or perhaps both result from a kind of original sin that damns him to the intense isolation he feels.

"I'm Waiting for the Man," the album's second track, is the first iconic Velvets moment on record. It's about scoring heroin in Harlem, and the guitar, piano, and drums rattle like the Lexington Avenue local barreling uptown to 125th Street. In its gleeful, if cold-eyed, details it offers a vision that is precisely the opposite of the psychedelic Summer of Love just on the horizon. Reed amends the title line to "waiting for my man," which gives the song a sexy, homoerotic feel, as does the singer's hasty assurance to the locals that he's not in Harlem to chase black women around. Again, as in "Sunday Morning," the contrast between the music and the lyrics is compelling. Reed describes his character as "sick and dirty," and the wait for his connection is nearly unendurable. But the exuberance of the playing and the exquisite cool of Reed's vocal led to the charge that he was glamorizing addiction—an allegation that would follow him his entire life. But by the end of the song, even when the singer describes himself as feeling "so fine," he knows that he's a kind of Sisyphus who will be back tomorrow, desperate once again to score.

Nico makes her first appearance on the album with her lead vocal on "Femme Fatale," which Reed composed in response to Warhol's suggestion that he write a song about Edie Sedgwick, the Factory It Girl of the moment. The term suited Nico as well, though while the song describes a siren-like figure with whom men get involved at their peril, both Sedgwick and Nico proved to be damaged at their core, a painful vulnerability that Nico's voice brings to the fore, in stark contrast to Reed's deadpan background vocal. A woman singing about another woman being a femme fatale, a "little tease," and describing how she walks and talks lends the song a homoerotic charge as well.

The sexual power in "Femme Fatale" finds darker expression in "Venus in Furs," which takes its title from a novella by the nineteenth-century Austrian writer Leopold von Sacher-Masoch, whose name gives us the term "masochism." If the woman in "Femme Fatale" has to resort to teasing and pleasing to exert her power, Venus enslaves her lover Severin by virtue of her sexual dominance, the leather boots that he worshipfully kisses, the whip that "cures" the emptiness in his heart, which is the same desperate loneliness that afflicts the singer in "Sunday Morning." The song floats on a hypnotic drone created by Reed's guitar and Cale's viola, while Reed's vocal is a seductive incantation that summons the hothouse eroticism of Severin's submissive devotion. Unlike any other music at that time, "Venus in Furs" evokes a mesmerizing inner world of forbidden desires. That Venus is the Roman goddess of love intimates that love itself nurses a kind of corruption, a triumph of power over sweetness.

The album's next song, "Run Run Run," breaks that internal mood with raw guitar rock that, in its evocation of street characters (Teenage Mary, Margarita Passion) in ardent search of drugs, echoes the episodic storytelling of Dylan's "Highway 61 Revisited." In its presentation of specific characters and specific New York neighborhoods like Union Square, the song is also something of a precursor to "Walk on the Wild Side." Reed's strangulated guitar solos on the track also distinguish it from virtually all other popular music of the time.

The album's first side concludes with "All Tomorrow's Parties," Reed's preemptive eulogy for the Warhol crowd and, ironically, Warhol's favorite of the Velvets' songs. Cale's piano and viola and Reed's sitar-like phrases on guitar create a dirgelike setting for Nico's sepulchral vocal. The song beautifully taps into the loneliness and emptiness underlying the blithe party-going of the Factory crowd. All tomorrow's parties are finally no different from yesterday's, as unchanging as the song's portentous drone.

"Heroin," one of Reed's greatest masterpieces, is a bold, successful attempt to re-create both the appeal and the experience of shooting that drug. Like all of Reed's best work, the song takes no moral position on drug use; it simply attempts to render the experience from the standpoint of the user. More than seven minutes long, the song backs away from neither gritty details, like the blood that shoots back up the dropper as the user injects it, nor the eroticism that is so much of the allure, however unconsciously, for addicts. As in "Venus in Furs," the ritual of shooting up offers an escape from the daily agonies of the quotidian world; the drug, the singer declares, is his "wife" and his "life." The delicate guitar melody that begins the song evokes the drug's calm, while the rush of getting high comes through as Reed and Morrison on guitars, Cale on viola, and Tucker on drums whip up the tempo. The song is an extraordinary journey, and Reed would forever after mention how people would tell him that they first shot up as a result of listening to it, which made him stop performing it at various times.

"There She Goes Again" lifts its stuttering opening riff from Marvin Gaye's 1963 Top 40 hit "Hitch Hike." Reed would routinely quote soul and R & B songs throughout his career—and equally often pervert their intent, as he did here. While "Hitch Hike" is an amusing chronicle of erotic obsession, "There She Goes Again" finds the singer infuriated by a woman who, addled by drugs, rejects him but is perfectly willing to get "down on her knees" for other men, including his friends. The singer's recommendation—"You better hit her"—unsettled listeners even at a time when the likes of Carole King and Gerry Goffin could write a song called "He Hit Me (and It Felt Like a Kiss)." Still, the theme of sexual violence hardly felt out of place in the dark world the Velvets evoked, and it was not one that Reed would shy away from in his future songwriting.

"I'll Be Your Mirror," one of Reed's most delicate ballads and one that his Syracuse girlfriend Shelley Albin recalled that he began to work on in college, shifts the album's mood again. Sung by Nico, the song is a sweet reassurance to a lover beset by lacerating insecurities, a grimness, once again, underlying the song's gentle surface. "The Black Angel's Death Song," which Reed cowrote with Cale, shatters the idyll of "I'll Be Your Mirror." As Cale blasts angular phrases on his viola, Reed seems to be free-associating lyrics that focus on violence and mortality. Performing this song had caused the Velvets to lose their gig at the Café Bizarre, the owner had so hated it. Reed later wrote, "The idea here was to string words together for the sheer fun of their sound, not any particular meaning. I loved the title."

The Velvet Underground and Nico closes with its longest and most challenging track. "European Son" runs more than seven and a half minutes and is predominantly a raucous improvised jam. The songwriting is credited to Reed, Cale, Morrison, and Tucker, and the song is dedicated to Delmore Schwartz, a child of European immigrants. For all its length, the song has only eight lines of lyrics, which read as an oblique indictment of a culture that would "kill" an artist of Schwartz's gifts. Reed, of course, was well aware of Schwartz's hatred of most rock lyrics, but he had kept his mentor apprised of his progress as a musician nonetheless. It's tempting to think that Reed dedicated the closing song on *The Velvet Underground and Nico* to Schwartz at least in part because he believed, hoped, or perhaps even knew that on the strength of this album alone, he had already met the high expectations that Schwartz had set for him and inspired him to achieve.

5

AGGRESSIVE, GOING TO GOD

AFTER SUCH A LONG buildup, it was obviously disappointing to everyone involved that *The Velvet Underground and Nico* failed to make a significant impact. It was not even a critical success; for the most part, beyond a certain curiosity about Warhol's involvement and the album's loopy cover, it was simply ignored. But it did immediately begin to make its way, however slowly, out into the culture. Fifteen years later, Brian Eno would remark that he "was talking to Lou Reed the other day and he said that the first Velvet Underground record sold thirty thousand copies in the first five years. . . . I mean, that record was such an important record for so many people. I think everyone who bought one of those thirty thousand copies started a band!" The album's sales were actually not quite that dismal. In fact, in its first two years of release, *The Velvet Underground and Nico* sold nearly sixty thousand copies. Those are hardly blockbuster sales, but they do approach respectability. Eno's larger point is true, though, and it's why the album has provided inspiration for the countless alternative artists who followed the Velvet Underground. Before *The Velvet Underground and Nico,* there was no such thing as underground or alternative rock. You either had hits or you didn't. There was no other code to live by. The Velvet Underground made it possible for rock musicians to make the same appeal to posterity that poets, novelists, playwrights, and painters made before them. If their contemporaries didn't like or understand—or, in this case, even know about—their work, it was possible to imagine recognition sometime down the road.

In the short term, David Bowie had already begun to perform "I'm Waiting for the Man," and Brian Epstein, who managed the Beatles, met with Reed in New York and, at least briefly, considered managing the Velvets. Epstein died a few months later, but, given his concern for social propriety and his closeted gay life, it's hard to imagine that he would have taken on a band as unruly as the Velvets. That he was aware of the band at all, however, was significant. Mick Jagger said that the song "Stray Cat Blues" on the Stones' 1968 album *Beggars Banquet* was influenced by "Heroin."

Few bands whose work had sold so few copies had made an impression so high up the rock hierarchy.

Along with the Factory, one of the places where the Velvets were coming into contact with the hip cultural elite was Max's Kansas City, a kind of sanctuary of cool founded by club owner Mickey Ruskin in late 1965. Located near Union Square, an area deserted at night and entirely lacking social cachet at the time, Max's first became a hangout for visual artists. That provided a natural point of entry for Warhol, who then introduced his extended world of musicians, filmmakers, and "superstars," the motley collection of young women and transsexuals who, in a manner that proved astonishingly prescient, became famous because Warhol declared them to be. Max's became a kind of clubhouse for in-the-know people. Warhol took over the back room, held court there, and often picked up the check, a definite attraction for his frequently impoverished retinue, most especially the Velvets. As he had at the Factory, Reed became a significant presence at Max's. It was a rarefied world, one of the few places in which the Velvets would be perceived as important artists, and Reed carried himself accordingly. "Max's at that time was kind of a metaphor for what New York was becoming, and what would soon be impossible to sustain," said Danny Fields, who would sign such bands as the Stooges and the MC5 to Elektra Records.

"It was the place for abstract expressionist artists, bands who were playing the Fillmore, the Warhol crowd, poets, models. I introduced Jackie Curtis to Sargent Shriver there! After a while you couldn't fit fashion, poetry, rock and roll, art, and movies in one place. It was inevitable that Max's eventually had to give way to a place like Studio 54. But the big difference was that to get into Max's, you had to be fabulous. To get into Studio 54, you just had to look fabulous."

The Warhol crowd got up to their usual shenanigans at Max's—Martha Morrison recalled Brigid Berlin (dubbed Brigid Polk for her inclination to poke you with a methedrine-laced vitamin B shot) shooting speed while sitting next to her in the back room. But Reed was much more restrained. "'Lou Reed' was a character, too, you know," said Bob Neuwirth, who ran into Reed at Max's a number of times. "There was Lou the kid from Long Island, and then there was the public persona, the professional Lou Reed. But he was very casual. He wasn't really an attention junkie. He wasn't one of those guys who wanted to dance on tables, much less so than people like Bowie and Iggy, who were eventually around that backroom scene. Lou was much more dignified. I never found him to be in competition with anybody else. I never felt he was comparing his music to anybody else's. In his depravity, Lou was dignified. Dignified depravity."

*   *   *

BUT EVEN AS REED remained part of the Factory scene, the Velvet Underground's role in the solar system that revolved around Warhol was shifting. With the Velvets not earning money and his films starting to attract more attention, Warhol began to lose interest in the music scene. Meanwhile, now that the Velvets had an album out, even one that had underperformed in every regard except artistic achievement, Reed began to envision a career that involved more than being a satellite of someone else, however famous. Although Nico was the primary focus of the band in many people's eyes, Reed had succeeded in both limiting her role on the album and making her feel sufficiently uncomfortable that her leaving the group seemed inevitable. Like a Mafia killing, the excision of Nico from the Velvets wasn't personal for Reed—just business. Reed played guitar and wrote or cowrote a number of songs on Nico's 1967 debut solo album, *Chelsea Girl*, including the title track, and he accompanied her during a few of her solo shows. Toward the end of May, she turned up late for a Velvets gig at the Boston Tea Party in Boston, and the band refused to let her take the stage. After that, she was out of what Reed was increasingly coming to think of as his band.

Warhol was the next to go. Reed would sentimentalize his relationship with Warhol for the rest of his life, perhaps out of a natural desire to focus on the good in someone who had been so instrumental in his life and career. But at the time, Reed was convinced that Warhol had done as much as he was going to be able to do for the Velvets, and he had even come to resent the ineptitude of Warhol and Morrissey as managers. The band's music had progressed beyond Warhol's traveling circus. As a business, rock and roll was maturing, and the Velvets needed a manager who could help guide them through the new world taking shape. In later years, Reed would claim that Warhol asked him if he wanted to continue playing art venues or branch out and play music venues. Perhaps a conversation like that took place, but it seems unlikely, given how Warhol determinedly avoided conflicts of any kind. The conversation Reed described was more like something a father would say to his son, encouraging his independence, as if Warhol had assumed the caring paternal role that Reed had longed for his own father to fill. More likely, Reed had already seen opportunities he wanted to take advantage of, and Warhol had grown bored with playing the role of band manager. In any event, Reed "fired" Warhol, who was "furious" about it and called him a "rat." "That was the worst thing he could think of," Reed said, the childlike quality of the insult having obviously made an impression on him.

DURING THIS TIME, THE Velvets had begun playing regular gigs at the Boston Tea Party on Berkeley Street in Boston, as well as at other spots in New England. Boston, in particular, became a second home for the band. It's easy to understand the appeal. Boston is a sophisticated city, but it lacked the relentless media concentration of New York. The local papers would not be running daily updates on the doings of Andy Warhol and his entourage, so the Velvets would be free of that association. Because of all the colleges nearby, the town has always been a music hot spot, and the Velvets could build an audience there on nothing beyond their records and the power of their live shows, which were consistently getting stronger. No Nico. No bullwhips. No Warhol-style theatrical extravaganzas. Just great songs played with brilliance and ferocity for an audience that was, far from being jaded, excited to hear a compelling new band. It was a formula that worked beautifully.

Outside the media spotlight, the band members were relaxed and able to enjoy themselves both onstage and off. Martha Morrison described going to Martha's Vineyard with Reed and Sterling. She saw her role as helping them get along, though Reed could be difficult, and Sterling tried to avoid him when he could. "I was always inviting Louie, as I called him, trying to get them to be nice," she said. "One time, Sterling and I rented bicycles to go swimming—us Long Islanders love to surf. I invited Lou because he always wanted to come along, whatever we were doing, and I wanted to include him. On the way back, Lou got off his bicycle and went behind a car and took off his bathing suit and put his shorts back on. I was aghast that he would do that! But, you know, it's hard riding with sand in your bathing suit!"

Around this time, Reed started to show an interest in spirituality, an unlikely aspect of his personality that would find various expressions throughout his life: in tai chi and other martial arts; in meditation; in diets of different kinds; in his obsession with the chemical properties of amphetamine and its relationship to his health; in Buddhism; in the avant-garde jazz of John Coltrane, Cecil Taylor, and Ornette Coleman; and in the erasure of self that the S and M sex in "Venus in Furs" and drug delirium in "Heroin" evoke. Reed and the Velvet Underground are often rightly perceived as representing a kind of anti-sixties, a tough, streetwise corrective to the era's psychedelic utopianism. As always with Reed, however, that impulse in him was counterbalanced by its nearly direct opposite, an intense interest in transcendence. He attended the Easter Sunday Central Park Be-In in late March of 1967, and even his most debased activities seemed like necessary stops on a highly individual journey to redemption and salvation.

Rob Norris, who would later join the Bongos, met Reed around this time at the Boston Tea Party; Norris was then in his teens. "Every time I'd go there, we'd all hang out in the back room, and Lou would hold court," Norris said. "Different people would come back. It was very social; people would just wander in and out. Jonathan Richman was almost always there—he was very quiet.... People would ask Lou stuff like, 'How's Nico?' or 'What's Jackson Browne [who performed with Nico and played on her *Chelsea Girl* album] doing now?' He'd just say, 'What do I look like, a billboard?' I remember this one woman was so crazy about him. She said, 'You make me so crazy, I just want to kill you!' Lou just looked at her very kindly and said, 'Why don't you just bake me a cake instead?' It was the sweetest thing."

Norris had recently journeyed to Haight-Ashbury to experience the good vibrations firsthand (1967 was, after all, the year of the Summer of Love), and he saw connections between what was happening out there and what the Velvets were up to. "The most fascinating time was after the Tea Party moved over to Lansdowne Street, and my friend said, 'I'm going upstairs to have a conversation with Lou, and I think you might be interested in it.' I just sat there while those guys talked about the deepest stuff. Lou was interested in the Church of Light. He was interested in astrology, energy healing. He talked about levitation. It was amazing to me." It's hardly unusual for people using amphetamine to engage in long, rambling, abstruse conversations. But even back then—and however high he may have been—Reed had little patience for people or subjects he wasn't interested in, so his discussing those topics at such length and with such enthusiasm is telling. Like many users, who regard their compulsion as a kind of hell to which they've been condemned, Reed discouraged Norris from drug use. "The first time I met him, when there was no one else in the room, Lou very sharply looked me up and down," Norris said. "I was eighteen or nineteen, and really nervous. He looked at me and said, 'Are you on speed?' I said, 'No. I'm just nervous to meet you.' He said, 'Good. Because drugs are shit. They'll just pollute you and ruin your life.' He was eating some kind of brewer's yeast. I was thinking, 'What the fuck have I walked into here?'"

Tony Lioce, a rabid music fan who lived in Providence, Rhode Island, and hung around the Tea Party, recalled similar experiences with Reed and the Velvets. "You'd pay three bucks and hear them play two long sets," he wrote. "And almost no one came. There'd be maybe forty people on a good night. And generally the same forty people night after night, including one girl who always showed up in a wedding dress." Reed, Lioce wrote, was typically "gracious and kind, talking about everything from a weird diet he was thinking about—eating nothing but lettuce—to his love of Dion and his total dislike of Frank Zappa." But Lioce also caught a glimpse of Reed's harder edge. Reed, he wrote, would "go from sharing a joint with us one night to making it very clear on the next that he had no interest in talking to anyone, us especially. One time, we brought him a bottle of Clan MacGregor Scotch, real bottom-shelf stuff but his favorite, and he was flat-out rude, didn't want to let us into the room to give it to him."

One of the reasons for the Velvets' extended stays in Boston was the manager Reed chose to replace Warhol: Steve Sesnick. Warhol was, needless to say, a hard act to follow, an internationally known artist. Sesnick was just a guy in Boston eager to step onto a bigger stage. He didn't know much more than Warhol about how the music business worked, and however cultured a town Boston was, it was hardly the entertainment center that New York was. But as far as Reed was concerned, Sesnick's lack of a public profile was part of his appeal. Reed got rid of Warhol in an effort to step out of his shadow, so what would be the use of working with another imposing figure who would be hard to control? Besides that, Reed was increasingly coming to see the Velvets as his band, and Sesnick conveniently shared that view.

"I don't know how Sesnick ended up managing the Velvets, because he really didn't know anything about how to do it," said Norris, who got to know Sesnick when he asked Norris, who played guitar, to join the Boston band the Rockets. "I think he just talked his way into it. He had the gift of gab. He was an odd man, quite a piece of work. He lived on alcohol and meat—he never ate anything else. That was his philosophy. He was domineering, even a bit dark and scary. He would play people off each other, try to keep people on edge. But he was silver-tongued, could charm anybody into anything."

That the Velvets spent so much time in Boston and essentially stopped playing in New York was, at least in part, a result of Sesnick's strategy. No doubt Reed perceived New York as Warhol's turf. Performing there regularly would make it much more difficult to move out of his sphere of influence. Some speculated that the Velvets were angry that New York radio didn't play their debut album, which doesn't make much sense since almost no stations played it. It's not unusual for a band, once it has achieved a certain stature, as the Velvets had with *The Velvet Underground and Nico,* to limit its exposure in its hometown and concentrate on building a national following. But that strategy makes much more sense for regional bands than it does for one from New York; if you have an enthusiastic following there, you pretty much already are a national band. Pulling back a bit from the New York scene may have been a smart move temporarily, but as the sixties were drawing to a close, some people were beginning to think of the Velvets as a Boston band. By any measure, that was a step backward.

*   *   *

IN SEPTEMBER OF 1967, the Velvets entered Mayfair Sound Studios in New York to record the follow-up to *The Velvet Underground and Nico.* Tom Wilson produced the album to the usual discontented mutterings of Reed and Cale, and Gary Kellgran and Val Valentin handled the engineering. In part because the Velvets had been performing live with such regularity, they'd worked up a fair amount of new material. But when it came time to choose the songs for the album that would be called *White Light/White Heat,* they concentrated on the most raucous and wildest of their repertoire. Perhaps Reed's inclination to write softer ballads like "Femme Fatale" and "I'll Be Your Mirror" had left the band with Nico, although a semblance of that type of song survives on the delicate "Here She Comes Now," which closes the first side. The album's aggressiveness might also be an expression of all the changes in the band's world. Nico was gone. Warhol was gone. Sesnick was in. The band was spending less time in its hometown, performing onstage more, and Reed and Cale's drug and alcohol abuse continued apace. "Our lives were in chaos. That's what's reflected in that record," Morrison said about *White Light/White Heat.* "Things were insane, day in and day out: the people we knew, the excesses of all sorts. For a long time, we were living in various places, afraid of the police. At the height of my musical career, I had no permanent address. I see that reflected in there."

For better or worse, the album made not the slightest effort to build on the momentum of *The Velvet Underground and Nico*. Cale described *White Light/White Heat* as a "very rabid record. The first one had some gentility, some beauty. The second one was consciously anti-beauty." Even underground FM stations had been reluctant to play songs from the first album; what were they supposed to do with *White Light*'s title track, a roaring hymn to amphetamine, or "Sister Ray," a rollicking, seventeen-and-a-half-minute epic that features murder, oral sex, and a main character who's so fucked up that he can't properly locate a vein to shoot up in? "Sister Ray," of course, was another of Warhol's favorites; he had encouraged Reed to resist any pressure to remove the line about a girl "sucking on my ding-dong." "The Gift" combines a short story that Reed wrote while at Syracuse with a variation on "Booker T.," an instrumental the band often performed live and named after the great Stax organist, Booker T. Jones. Cale suggested doing a spoken-word reading of the story, which centers on the sexual paranoia Reed felt when separated during the summer from his girlfriend Shelley Albin, over the instrumental. Presumably in order to take advantage of the ironic possibilities of his elegant Welsh lilt, Cale handled that reading, as well as the sung speech of "Lady Godiva's Operation," a song so erotically twisted in its medical torture that Reed wryly explained it by stating, "I had twenty-four shock treatments when I was seventeen years old. I suppose it caused me to write things like this." The album's most explosive track is "I Heard Her Call My Name," four and a half minutes of blasting distortion and feedback that features Reed's most savage guitar playing. At a time when most mainstream rock bands were becoming increasingly polished in their playing, as rock and roll transformed into the more grown-up and sophisticated "rock," the Velvets brutally serrated every edge of their sound.

The Velvets had a propensity to feel slighted, which should be taken into account alongside Reed and Cale's relentless complaints about what they perceived as Tom Wilson's, his engineers', and Verve's lack of interest, at best, and outright hostility, at worst. "It finally got to the point that the record company hated our music so much, they wouldn't even listen to it," Reed said. "When we recorded 'Sister Ray,' the engineer stood up and said, 'Listen, I'm leaving. You can't pay me enough to listen to this crap. I'll be down in the commissary getting coffee. When you're done, hit that button and come get me.' That's completely true." Cale frequently remarked about the attention Wilson lavished on the gorgeous women he brought to the studio while working with the band. Unlike Reed, however, who was consolidating his power, Cale would have valued a smart, outside perspective. "When I think of the many wonderful producers who would have been available to us, it boggles the mind that we did not use them," he said.

The Velvets were really enjoying playing live at this time, and they wanted *White Light/White Heat* to reflect the energy of those performances. Speaking about the band's live shows, Maureen Tucker said, "We used to rehearse, basically, onstage. Lou would come in with a new song, and the guys would practice it, so they would know the chord changes. But after that, the song would evolve onstage. The third time, or maybe the tenth time we played it, we decided it was right." Onstage, Norris said, the band was "like a finely tuned British racing car. I mean, they were just so together and tight and playful, too. They would do stuff like play their songs at different speeds, just to see what would happen. And Lou, I just never saw anybody play the guitar like that. That was a period where he was really going berserk, playing songs like 'I Heard Her Call My Name.' I couldn't believe how great it was." That song, yet another celebration of speed, evidently had a spiritual aspect as well, according to Norris, as does the title track, possibly a reference to Alice Bailey's *A Treatise on White Magic,* which Reed read and mentioned in interviews. Reed also spoke about white light as a kind of healing power. Norris said, "I had a completely different experience of Lou than so many other people. He would talk about light a lot. He said 'I Heard Her Call My Name' is about enlightenment. He always spoke of the feminine divine, and that's what the solo in that song is supposed to be. You know that line 'My mind split open'? That was supposed to be the feeling of being enlightened."

Writing about the Velvets' Boston Tea Party sets at around this time, Tony Lioce recalled, "Live, they were like nothing we'd ever heard. Propulsive and explosive, totally engulfing, so dark as to be almost scary. My kid brother joined us one night, couldn't handle it, and ended up taking a bus back home. Compared with the flower power marijuana we'd smoke in a parking lot before the show, this stuff was heroin.... The first set might include a dozen numbers. The second usually was just two: a black magic chant called 'Sweet Rock and Roll' that segued into 'Sister Ray,' still, to my ears, the most deeply disturbing piece of music ever written." Reed himself said about *White Light/White Heat,* "They say rock is life-affirming music. You feel bad, you put on two minutes of this — *boom.* There's something implicit in it. And we were the best, the real thing. You listen to ... this album — there is the real stuff. It's aggressive, yes. But it's not aggressive bad. This is aggressive, going to God."

As he did with the banana album, Warhol designed the cover for *White Light/White Heat.* Perhaps because the backdrop of the banana album is pure white, the cover for the follow-up is black, with a photograph of a skull tattoo on a Warhol actor's bicep layered on it, also in black. The black-on-black imagery also pulls against the twice-repeated "white" in the album's name, as well as against its reference to "light." Drawn to black-and-white in his own films and having been raised Catholic—he still regularly attended Sunday Mass with this mother—Warhol understood such oppositions well. Like the banana image and like *White Light*'s abrasive music, this cover was a rebuke to the brightly colored hippie optimism of the times.

Still, however smart and original, the cover was hardly inviting. The album was released in January of 1968 and, even more than its predecessor, fell flat. Without the Warhol hype machine or a sexpot lead singer, the Velvets had little beyond the quality of their music—intentionally off-putting and assaultive, in this instance—to gain attention for them. The label did release to radio stations a brief and strangely relaxed interview with Reed and Cale conducted by Tom Wilson, along with a photo of a bemused Reed being slapped five by Wilson. Oddly, Verve's advertising for the album mimicked the mystical-good-vibes ethos of the era that the album itself soundly rejected. "Come. Step softly into the inevitable world of the Velvet Underground," the ad copy read. "Where there is no now. Where yawning yesterdays fade out on timeless tomorrows. Where sounds reflect from plastic people....Come. To where vinyl virgins devour the macabre mind." Alas, there was definitely "no now" for *White Light/White Heat.* Reed summed up the album's fate: "No one listened to it. But there it is, forever—the quintessence of articulated punk. And no one goes near it."

WITHIN A COUPLE OF weeks of the release of *White Light/White Heat,* the Velvets went into A&R Studios in New York with engineer Val Valentin to record two new songs, "Stephanie Says" and "Temptation Inside Your Heart," each of which, in different ways, is a radical departure from the material on the album. Tom Wilson had left MGM by this point, so essentially the band produced itself, with Valentin's assistance. "Stephanie Says" is the first of four songs Reed would write in the voice of a female character chronicling her experiences; each song would be titled with the woman's name and the verb "says." (Reed later adapted "Stephanie Says" into "Caroline Says" on his solo album *Berlin.*) The gender play in the songs is intriguing, as Reed sings as if transcribing the thoughts of these women (or, in the case of "Candy Says," a transsexual) and their struggles; all are damaged in some way. "Stephanie Says" features a vocal that rivals Reed's performance on "Sunday Morning" in its delicacy. If, as Cale said, the songs on *White Light/White Heat* are rabid, "Stephanie Says" explores an entirely different emotional terrain. In Cale's view, "Stephanie Says" was about Steve Sesnick. "To Lou," Cale wrote, "everybody's gay."

"Temptation Inside Your Heart," meanwhile, is a relaxed, soulful rocker that also stands in marked contrast to the distortion-laden assaults on *White Light/White Heat*. Reed, Cale, and Morrison joked around while recording their background vocals, and it's almost moving to hear their banter, which they didn't erase from the track. The Velvets have become so enshrined in rock history that it's stunning simply to hear them interact as a band, enjoying themselves. It's possible that the two songs were done as a potential single, given the decided lack of commercial material on *White Light/White Heat*. In any event, no such single was ever released, and the songs would not officially come out until the mideighties.

The Velvets went back into the studio in Los Angeles toward the end of May and recorded versions of "Hey Mr. Rain," a song they had been performing live, but it would also not see official release until two decades later. This session would represent the last time John Cale worked in the studio with the band during its original lifetime.

ON MONDAY, JUNE 3, 1968, Valerie Solanas, a disgruntled writer and would-be radical feminist, shot

Andy Warhol point-blank in the chest as he was speaking on the telephone at the Factory. Solanas had wanted Warhol to produce her play, *Up Your Ass,* which he was not interested in doing. Solanas believed that Warhol and other male media figures had taken control of her life, and shooting Warhol was an attempt to free herself. She also shot and wounded Mario Amaya, an art critic who was at the Factory at the time, and she attempted to shoot Warhol's manager, Fred Hughes, but her gun jammed. It took a five-hour operation to save Warhol's life, and he was never the same again. Always an isolated figure even at his most social, he became more reclusive and much less trusting, and the Factory, which had moved from Forty-Seventh Street to Union Square West, close to Max's Kansas City, became much more security-conscious. The Velvet Underground was in Los Angeles when the news of the shooting broke, and Reed waited several weeks before calling Warhol in the hospital, a slight, however unintentional, that neither man would ever forget.

It was a violent moment in what was increasingly becoming a violent era. Three days after Warhol was shot, Robert F. Kennedy was assassinated in California after winning the Democratic presidential primary there. Two months earlier, Martin Luther King Jr. had been assassinated in Memphis. The war in Vietnam was escalating, and demonstrations and campus protests were growing heated. The optimism of the Summer of Love had faded, and generational warfare grew far more confrontational. While the Velvets always seemed studiously nonpolitical, the firestorm aggression of *White Light/White Heat* can certainly be heard as an early expression of the traumas of its time. Solanas, meanwhile, was determined to be schizophrenic and spent just two years in prison before being released, a sentence that outraged Reed and terrified Warhol, who lived in fear that she would again try to kill him.

AFTER THE RELEASE OF *White Light/White Heat,* the Velvets continued the approach to live performance that they had adopted—that is, they avoided New York and concentrated on cities like Boston, Philadelphia, Cleveland, and San Francisco, playing venues where they had developed a loyal, knowledgeable following. "We never had a booking agent who put together three-month tours and so forth," Sterling Morrison said. "We just wanted to go back to the cities and clubs that we liked.... We didn't especially want to play for people who didn't know us from Adam. We thought that was futile." Reed, however, had not yet completed his consolidation of power in the band. In September of 1968, he met with Sterling Morrison and Maureen Tucker at the Riviera Café near Sheridan

Square in Greenwich Village and told them that he wanted John Cale out of the band. Morrison and Tucker were not only shocked, but opposed Reed's decision. Reed was adamant. His position was that either Cale was gone or he himself would quit the band. It was a bold gesture, one that Morrison and Tucker ultimately had no way of resisting, since Reed was the band's primary songwriter. As a further insult, Reed demanded that Morrison deliver the news to Cale.

On the most obvious level, Reed's removal of Cale was his final gesture of taking control. Cale's background, temperament, virtuosity, and sophistication ultimately made him, in Reed's eyes, a rival, not a collaborator. After two albums failed commercially, Reed may well have believed that the Velvets needed to move more toward the mainstream, a direction that would have held little appeal for Cale. Cale believed that Steve Sesnick had been encouraging Reed in his belief that the Velvets were Reed's band; it's always easier for a manager to deal with one primary artist than with two or more. Cale had not only established his own artistic reputation; he had married the fashion designer Betsey Johnson, who, even at that early stage in her career, had earned a name of her own in the hipper precincts of Manhattan. She was a hard-charger and encouraged Cale to stand up for himself; she also brought him a significant level of visibility beyond the band, a development that would not have sat well with

Reed. Most simply, Reed likely believed that, as with Warhol, he had already gotten whatever he was going to get from Cale. He had grown more confident in his own songwriting and, after making two albums, had a clear idea of what he wanted to achieve. He had a manager who believed in his vision. Having to run every decision by an artist who was as talented and accomplished as himself came to seem like a chore. Without question, Cale's contributions to the first two Velvet Underground albums were as important as Reed's. Perhaps that was a virtue at one point. For Reed, it had become a problem.

Reed selected Doug Yule, who at the time was playing with the Boston band the Grass Menagerie, to replace Cale. Like Reed, Morrison, and Tucker—and, notably, unlike Cale—Yule was a native of Long Island. He had been a student at Boston University and a musician in local bands. Though Yule had seen the Velvets perform only once, Reed and the other band members would occasionally stay in the apartment he shared with other musicians on their frequent visits to Boston. Sesnick was familiar with Yule as well. Yule claimed that his astrological sign of Pisces—the same as Reed's—played a role in his selection, too: Tucker and Morrison were Libras, so two Pisces evened out the pull between balance and intuition. Given some of Reed's interests at the time, it's impossible to rule out that notion.

Cale was such a distinctive musician that it's hard to think of anyone replacing him, but that wasn't Yule's job. Yule was a multi-instrumentalist who could comfortably play bass, guitar, and keyboards and sing, as necessary. He was just twenty-one at the time and delighted to join a band as accomplished and highly regarded as the Velvet Underground. There was no way he was going to create problems for Reed; he had neither the standing nor, by temperament, the desire to do so. The band ran through the Velvets catalog with him, and in a matter of weeks, Yule was on the road with the group. "I knew it would make some difference," Tucker said about Cale's departure and Yule's entry, "but not as much as it did. Lou couldn't tell John some of the things he could say to Doug." As he sometimes did with younger musicians, Reed occasionally took on a mentor-like role with Yule, even jokingly introducing him onstage as his "brother," in part because of their similarly curly hair.

Onstage, the band gained in focus what it lost in range. The Velvets were now a conventional rock-and-roll band in the best sense of that term, and their playing was at once looser, more relaxed, and, in some sense, wilder. Even the band's most explosive playing—the versions of "Sister Ray" that ran close to forty minutes, for example—amounted to recognizable, rhythmically intense jams, an element that was becoming common in rock shows generally, as the terse concision of rock and roll yielded to expansiveness and virtuosity. The Velvets, needless to say, were not battling soloists like the members of Cream or hippie dreamers like the Grateful Dead. Reed's guitar playing was primitive and idiosyncratic, while Morrison's was soulful and cleanly articulated. As a rhythm section, Yule and Tucker deftly complemented each other, her playing irreducibly tribal and her sense of time unerring, and his bass lines melodic and precise. When Yule switched to organ, he often used the instrument as a sustained drone, a simpler but still compelling version of the effect that Cale liked to get on viola. Reed called it "this all-enveloping cloud of heaven music." The new lineup quickly found its groove, and its live shows became word-of-mouth sensations. "The greatest thing about the Velvets was the holes in the music," Yule said. "The holes were the music. The space was vast and fun. Maureen was so straightforward— that left a lot of freedom for the bass. And Sterling was a 'part' guitar player. He would create something almost like a horn line on the guitar, then hold that for long periods of time."

In November, the Velvets went into the studio to record what would become their third album, titled simply *The Velvet Underground,* a gesture that is hard not to read as a slap at Cale. Perhaps as a means of emphasizing their new identity, the Velvets recorded the album in Los Angeles in the midst of doing gigs up and down the West Coast. The album represents a dramatic departure from *White Light/White Heat.* "I thought we had to demonstrate the other side of us," Reed said. "Otherwise, we would become this one-dimensional thing, and that had to be avoided at all costs." Released in March of 1969, the album displays both a delicacy and a straight-ahead rock-and-roll feel that distinguish it not just from the Velvets' previous work but from the louder, more bombastic sounds typical of rock music at the time. Intriguingly, while Reed had essentially taken over the band, the album opens and closes with songs sung by other band members.

The moving ballad "Candy Says," one of Reed's greatest songwriting moments, begins the album with an exploration of transsexual Candy Darling's desire to escape her birth gender. Few albums open with lyrics as chilling as these: "Candy says, 'I've come to hate my body / And all that it requires in this world.'" The song returns Reed to the world of the Factory, where Candy was perhaps the most beautiful of Warhol's superstars. As a means of establishing some distance from that world, Reed insisted that Yule take the lead vocal on the song, and he delivers it with gentleness and grace. Reed would explain his reasons for that decision in ways that alternatively flattered and condescended to Yule. Since Yule had never been part of the Factory scene and did not know Candy, his reading of the song would inevitably broaden its meaning. "Yeah, it's about Candy Darling—and trying to see things from that point of view," Reed said. "But it's also about something more profound and universal, a universal feeling I think all of us have at some point. We look in the mirror and we don't like what we see.... I don't know a person alive who doesn't feel that way." At other times, he suggested that Yule simply didn't understand the song and that this incomprehension mimicked Candy's own confusion about who she was. In any event, that track provides a memorable introduction to the band's new member.

As for "After Hours," which is almost like a music hall fare-thee-well to end the night, Reed wrote the song specifically for Tucker's voice. She sings with the unselfconsciousness of a young woman yearning for love, and she wraps up the album on a note of stubborn hopefulness. "You still don't hear that kind of purity in vocals," Reed said. "It has nothing to do with singing. It has everything to do with being. It's completely honest. Guileless. And always was. I couldn't sing that song. Maureen could sing it, and believe it, and feel much more. Because it's about loneliness. 'Someday I know someone will look into my eyes'— it can be so sappy and trite. But with Maureen doing it, especially being just a little off-key, it has its own strength and beauty and truth to it."

Reed wrote another of his great ballads, "Pale Blue Eyes," about Albin, whom he "missed very much" and still saw occasionally when she came to New York. She had married someone else, and in "Pale Blue Eyes," Reed calls her his "mountaintop" and his "peak," as well as, heartbreakingly, the epitome of "everything / I've had but couldn't keep." That song, along with "I Can't Stand It," which is not on *The Velvet Underground* but which Reed wrote at around this time, made it difficult for Albin to listen to his music for quite a while. "If Shelley would just come back / It would be all right," Reed sings on a version of "I Can't Stand It," mentioning his former lover by name. He regularly pleaded with her to leave her husband and come back to him, a move she did not want to make. "I didn't want to hear any of those songs, like 'I Can't Stand It,'" she said. "I might have been more susceptible and felt more sorry for him. But there was no divorce in my family. People didn't leave their husbands. I remember being very depressed at twenty-four: 'I got married at twenty-three. I've ruined my life.' But never a thought of divorce. You just made the best of it."

As much of a sonic departure as *The Velvet Underground* represented, its themes are entirely in keeping with the rest of the band's work. Three songs on the album — "Jesus," "Beginning to See the Light," and "I'm Set Free" — are spiritual in their desire for deliverance from the struggles of this world. There is a simple answer to the famous question that critic Lester Bangs raised in his *Rolling Stone* review of *The Velvet Underground,* the first review the band received in that magazine: "How do you define a group like this, who moved from 'Heroin' to 'Jesus' in two short years?" First, you don't need to define the band. Second, different as they are musically, those two songs are both prayers for escape and redemption. Even in his most optimistic moments, Reed would always regard himself as among the damned — the addicted, the deviant, the impulsively cruel, the mad. Rising above that condition is a central theme of all his work, including both "Heroin" and "Jesus."

The most experimental — and disappointing — song on *The Velvet Underground* is "The Murder Mystery," a nearly nine-minute verbal landslide that never coheres in any meaningful way. Commenting on the song years later, Reed suggested that he may have been trying to prove that the Velvets could still be an experimental band without John Cale: "I was having fun with words and wondering if you could cause two opposing emotions to occur at the same time. I'd fired John Cale from the VU."

For the cover of *The Velvet Underground,* the band chose a black-and-white image by Factory photographer Billy Name, who was a friend and lover of both Reed and Andy Warhol. As befits the album's stripped-down songs, the shot is simple and spare: the four band members relaxing on a couch at the Factory. In its own small way, an album cover once again proved influential for the Velvets. Dozens of indie bands in the late seventies and eighties would mimic its studied casualness, its refusal to pander to anyone's conception of what a band portrait on an album cover should look like. Album art was growing increasingly elaborate at the time. Even *The Beatles,* the 1968 release that became known as *The White Album,* was something of a grand statement, minimalist as it was. (The Velvets somewhat jokingly referred to their own release as *The Gray Album,* and borrowed the Beatles' eponymous title concept.) In the cover shot, only Reed, who is half in profile, is looking at the camera. The other band members are looking down or looking at him. Reed is holding a copy of *Harper's Bazaar,* and all four band members are dressed down. Reed looks preppy in a round-collared sweater with his shirt collar outside. It's an image that, without making a fuss at all, rejects everything about its time and its purpose—which is why bands who later wanted no part of the self-conscious, corporate merchandising of rock and roll gravitated to it.

When the album came out, critics praised it; Bangs's *Rolling Stone* review was gushing, an early manifestation of what would be the critic's lifelong manic-depressive relationship with Reed. Bangs's enthusiasm was typical of the coverage, but the album, once again, failed to gain any commercial traction. Beyond the clutch of positive reviews, the record was virtually invisible; for a long time it was certainly the least well-known of the original Velvets albums, and it may remain so to this day. The print ads MGM took out dropped the inappropriate hippie garble of their earlier media buys, but this time, along with mentioning the band members' astrological signs, the copy lurched into rock-crit gravitas. "Their music is just impure enough," the ad read, "so nervously energetic at times that you can't help but dance, at others so quiescently balladic that it requires mesmeric attention until you've deciphered every single nuance of the lyrics." That pitch, it seems safe to assume, generated very few sales. But the band persisted in touring, gradually building its word-of-mouth following gig by galvanizing gig.

As they had after *White Light/White Heat,* when they did a studio session to record "Stephanie Says" and "Temptation Inside Your Heart," the Velvets again went into the studio in New York, in May of 1969, just two months after the release of *The Velvet Underground.* For years, the songs the band recorded at this time and intermittently over the next few months — "I'm Sticking with You," "Foggy Notion," "Ferryboat Bill," "Andy's Chest," "Ocean," "She's My Best Friend," "Rock and Roll," "I Can't Stand It," "Ride Into the Sun," "I'm Gonna Move Right In," "We're Gonna Have a Real Good Time Together," "Lisa Says," and "I Found a Reason" among them—were rumored to be part of a "lost" fourth album for MGM, or at least demos for one. It's also possible that Steve Sesnick desired some material to play for other labels, since he wanted the band off MGM, which was hardly desperate to hold on to the Velvets in any case. Regardless, none of those songs, other than "Rock and Roll" and "I Found a Reason," would appear on a Velvets studio album, though the band was playing some of them onstage. And by April of 1970, the Velvets would be recording their fourth album for Atlantic Records.

EXACTLY HOW THE VELVETS made the transition from Verve/MGM, a label that, apart from having the bravery to sign them in the first place, barely understood them and certainly didn't know what to do with them, to an industry giant like Atlantic is unknown. Even with Warhol's support, Atlantic had passed on the Velvets when they were initially looking for a label without giving them more than a glance. Still, in New York circles, at least, Warhol's glow still meant something. "I think he thought they were Warhol-esque," Danny Fields said about Ahmet Ertegun, the cofounder of Atlantic. "He was working on signing the Rolling Stones; he was working on getting Andy to do the first Stones album cover for Atlantic. There was that connection. And although the Velvet Underground were no longer connected with Andy, they had that aura." Since then, the Velvets had made three albums and gained something like a cult following, but Atlantic was not the sort of label that went in for niche bands. The label had launched in the fifties as an R & B powerhouse and, on the strength of hits by the likes of Aretha Franklin, Cream, Led Zeppelin, and Crosby, Stills, and Nash, had helped define the sound of the sixties. Perhaps Sesnick exerted his charm, or someone at the label understood the band's importance and imagined the possibility of a commercial breakthrough. Whatever happened, the Velvets now had the opportunity to play on a much bigger stage—even if, strangely, their album would be released on Cotillion, a relatively new Atlantic subsidiary best known for hard-core Southern R & B.

When the Velvets entered Atlantic Recording Studios in New York in mid-April to begin work in earnest on their fourth album, they did so with a big handicap. Maureen Tucker had become pregnant with her first child and was unable to play at the sessions. Tucker's absence is crucial for a number of reasons, not all of them musical. Most significant, even as the band's sound grew increasingly conventional, her idiosyncrasies as a drummer fought that tendency. Once more-standard rock drummers—and the band used four of them in the studio — became part of the mix, the Velvets lost a rhythmic touchstone of their distinctive, off-kilter sound. Maureen's absence also diminished the Velvets' sense of themselves as a band. The new drummers were essentially session players, and Yule, who drummed on some tracks, had not been with the band very long. That left Reed and Morrison as the last remnants of the band's original lineup. If Reed had been at the height of his powers, he might have been able to firmly take the reins and make the band, and its sound, fully his own, but his insecurities crept up on him. Three albums had now failed to deliver on the hopes he held for himself and the group, and, spotting an opening, Sesnick began whispering in Yule's ear just as he had done with Reed. What might have been an opportunity for the band to build on its cult reputation instead became a power struggle, both within the band and within Reed himself.

Every band that manages to stay together for any length of time has a member who serves as its glue, and Tucker played that role in the Velvets. Her talent aside, she lacked any agenda other than wanting the band to succeed and wanting everyone to get along. She was the most down-to-earth member, the one everybody liked. The ambitions that created tension between Reed and Cale, and eventually between Reed and Yule, did not at all come into play with her. Most important, Reed regarded Tucker as a sister. He did not feel threatened by her, and he was tolerant, even protective, of her. Her absence created a void that negative feelings rushed in to fill.

THE SESSIONS FOR *LOADED,* as the Velvets' fourth and final studio album would be called, ran intermittently through the spring and early summer of 1970. Along with the ten tracks on the album, the band recorded versions of many other songs that, sometimes under altered titles, Reed would later include on his solo albums. To impress the band's new label and bring an end to the Velvets' five-year journey in the commercial wilderness, Reed was under pressure to write hits. Indeed, the album's title refers, however ironically, to Reed's apparent belief that the album was "loaded with hits," although a nod to Reed's continued drug and alcohol intake is also likely. Three Atlantic staff producers—Geoffrey Haslam, Shel Kagan, and Adrian Barber—worked on the recording of the album, which contributed to the feeling that it was far from a focused band effort. Steve Sesnick was also making his presence felt—to the extent of contributing off-tempo cowbell to an early take on "Sweet Jane." ("The guy couldn't dance either," Yule remarked.)

As the weeks went by and Reed seemed less and less manageable, Sesnick turned his attention to Yule, who was far more upbeat and malleable. As he had done with Reed in relation to Cale, Sesnick encouraged Yule, whose musical instincts were far more conventional than Reed's, to assert himself in the sessions. Sesnick also went so far as to ask Cale to come to the studio to record an organ part on one version of "Ocean." Cale was mystified but nonetheless agreed, though none of the other musicians were there when he played. "It may seem astounding in retrospect, but I instantly agreed to go and help them," Cale wrote. "During the 'Ocean' sessions all I could see was that everything had become more fragrant, the playing had become much gentler, there was an almost overwhelming emphasis on not playing loud. Lou wanted to go into the pretty stuff."

Reed began to lose interest in the sessions for a variety of reasons. While he wanted the band to have hits as much as, if not more than, anyone else, he did not respond well to pressure. Tucker's absence was a factor as well, and even Morrison began looking at the prospect of life beyond the band. He enrolled in courses at City College to complete his degree, with an eye to pursuing graduate studies in English.

Early in the summer, the band began a months-long residency in the upstairs room at Max's Kansas City, with Doug Yule's younger brother Billy, who was still in high school, filling in for Tucker on drums. Those shows went a long way toward reestablishing the Velvets in their hometown. Local supporters finally had a regular spot where they could see the band, and the shows were written about widely and favorably. While the room, which was small, was not always filled, word spread that it was a show to see. "The Velvets played there all summer for no apparent reason," said Lenny Kaye, who was there many nights. "It kind of became an upstairs hangout. There weren't a lot of people there, maybe fifty by the end of the night. It was interesting to hear the songs that would be on *Loaded* played every night. They weren't in their noisy-noisy period. They would play two sets. The first would be more formal. The second, people would dance to — a concept I find amazing. It was loose, almost like a fraternity party."

Reed was comfortable at Max's, mingling easily with the crowd of musicians, writers, publicists, record company execs, and artists, all of them fans of the band. But it was still a lot of work. The band played two sets a night, five nights a week, sometimes while working on *Loaded* in the studio during the day. Indeed, the wear on Reed's voice, never the strongest instrument, from singing at Max's is often cited as the reason Doug Yule assumed lead vocals on four of *Loaded*'s ten songs: its opening number ("Who Loves the Sun"), its closer ("Oh! Sweet Nuthin'"), "New Age," and "Lonesome Cowboy Bill." Reed particularly regretted not doing the vocal on "New Age," a song, tellingly, about faded promises and lost glory. "No slur on Doug, but he didn't understand the lyrics for a second," Reed later said. For Reed, who valued intelligence over any other virtue, that was a grave insult. But Reed, of all people, understood the difference between singing in front of fifty of your friends at a club and doing a vocal on an album that, at least potentially, people would be listening to for many years to come. So why didn't he simply let Yule sing at Max's and save his own voice for the studio? Maybe the live shows lifted his spirits and he didn't want to hold back there. In the studio, however, it's possible that he emotionally checked out and just didn't care. He was the type of person who, if he felt the tide turning in Yule's direction, would be simultaneously too depressed and too proud to fight it. Later he would simply say of *Loaded,* which was released in November of 1970, "It's still called a Velvet Underground record. But what it really is is something else."

LOADED'S REPUTATION, SUCH AS it is, rests primarily on two iconic songs, "Sweet Jane" and "Rock and Roll," songs that are not merely among Reed's absolute best but also undeniable rock classics. Each expresses a wistful idealism, a belief that love and rock and roll can save even the most damaged lives. Reed would often treat gender-bending as a pointed insult to conventional sexuality, but in "Sweet Jane," the couple's cross-dressing—"Jack is in his corset, Jane is in her vest"—seems more like a sweet kink, a sexy gesture to liven things up a bit in the bedroom. Indeed, the song exalts tradition—the days when poets "studied rules of verse" and women flirtatiously "rolled their eyes." The song indicts easy cynicism—the belief that "life is just to die," the sort of self-congratulating knowingness of many of the ultra-hipsters that, from the Factory to Max's, often surrounded the Velvets. The innocence of "Sweet Jane"—both in the character and in the song—is redeeming, a repository of hope, part of why the song remains so popular and so loved. That, and the indelible four-chord guitar riff that is one of the most identifiable moments in the history of rock and roll.

"Rock and Roll," meanwhile, is one of the genre's greatest songs about itself. In it, five-year-old suburban Jenny is rescued from an existence of pointless materialism ("two TV sets and two Cadillac cars") when she turns on a New York radio station and hears the sounds that save her life. The scene recalls the one Reed described about doing the math homework he detested ("despite all the computations") in his Long Island home and being transported by the sound of Dion's voice on the radio to a realm of infinite possibility. "'Rock and Roll' is about me," Reed said. "If I hadn't heard rock and roll on the radio, I would have had no idea there was life on this planet." The song's reference to "amputations" (as well as the "disfigured" parents in the album's "Head Held High") may well be allusions to the grisly fate of Lincoln Swados, Reed's roommate for a time at Syracuse, who moved to New York and attempted suicide by hurling himself in front of a subway train. He lived but lost an arm and a leg. Reed loved and identified with Swados, who was a talented writer, musician, and cartoonist, but whose psychological problems—he was diagnosed schizophrenic—left him crippled. As he often did, Reed manifested his affection in troubling ways. His friend Ed McCormack remembered Reed and Swados visiting McCormack's apartment, and Reed saying, "This schmuck, he tried to kill himself by throwing himself under a train, and he even fucked that up. He couldn't even do that right." But McCormack understood the deep feeling beneath the grim joking, as did Swados. "Lincoln seemed to take it in good humor," McCormack said. "I mean, you have to be pretty close to someone to be able to joke with them that way."

In the song, Reed insists on his conviction that "despite all the amputations," rock and roll could still save your life—and your soul. He admired Swados for going on in his own troubled way, and he may well have been thinking about himself as he felt the band he had formed and believed in slipping away from him. All the songs on *Loaded,* but most especially "Sweet

Jane" and "Rock and Roll," are songs about a kind of desperate encouragement, a call to believe that there is a future beyond even the most devastating breakages. They were songs to himself about himself, prayers that somehow, whatever happened, it would ultimately be possible to survive, to be "all right."

6

ALL THE THINGS THAT ARE MISSING

ON AUGUST 23, 1970, a Sunday night, the Velvet Underground showed up at Max's for the standing gig the band had held all summer. As usual, Billy Yule filled in for Maureen Tucker on drums, and the band's first set, kicking off with "I'm Waiting for the Man," consisted of seven songs from the Velvets' three previous albums and the forthcoming *Loaded*. But for the second set, which typically would turn into a dance party, Reed emphasized the softer, more contemplative side of his catalog; "I'll Be Your Mirror," "Pale Blue Eyes," "Candy Says," "Sunday Morning," and "Femme Fatale" were among those chosen. Reed regarded such songs as indisputable proof of his skills as a songwriter, and particularly as a lyricist. They were not the noise fests for which the Velvets had become known. They reflected and appealed to the romantic side of him.

No one in the band knew that Reed would quit the Velvet Underground after that night's show. That second set stands as both Reed's declaration of his talents and his wistful farewell to all that. He did not want to go out with a bang, but with a graceful goodbye. Danny Fields said good night to Reed as the musician was leaving, and Reed just walked by him. Fields later learned that Reed had quit the band, and he, in turn, told fellow Factory habitué Donald Lyons. "Oh, I guess they're going to be the Velveteen Underground from now on," Lyons said, which is essentially what happened. Fields, who was working for Atlantic at the time, immediately approached Brigid Berlin, who had taped the show that night while sitting in the audience with poet Jim Carroll. Fields brought Berlin's tape to Atlantic, and the label purchased it for $10,000, which Fields and Berlin split. *The Velvet Underground Live at Max's Kansas City,* an album consisting of songs from that tape, was released in 1972.

Reed had confessed to Tucker that he was leaving the band when she attended one of the Velvets' shows at Max's a few weeks earlier. He also spoke to Sesnick about it, though possibly not until after his last gig. The degree of Reed's forced alienation from the band he had cofounded, and of Doug Yule's elevation within it, became apparent with the release of *Loaded* several months after that final Max's gig. The entire project was presented in such a way as to diminish Reed's participation in it. The album's front cover did not feature any of the band members, but a mystifying and not especially inspiring illustration of smoke or fumes rising out of a New York subway station. "I was still very foreign in terms of my experiences in New York," said Stanislaw Zagorski, the Polish designer who created the image. "I thought of 'underground' in terms of the subway." The songwriting credits read "All selections are by the Velvet Underground," and Yule and Morrison are given specific credits, along with Reed. The only band member depicted on the back cover is Yule, shown seated and playing guitar amid the band's equipment in the studio. The band members' names are listed vertically on the back cover, and Reed's name appears third, after Yule and Sterling Morrison. Clearly, Reed was being punished, put in his place. Wresting back those songwriting credits would be another battle, with Reed ultimately ceding rights to the band's name to Sesnick in exchange.

REED'S MOTHER HAD ADVISED him to develop a skill that he could use to fall back on, and typing was it. Once he was out of the band, Reed took up residence in his old room at his parents' house, and worked for forty dollars a week as a typist in his father's accounting firm. When he actually did it, he found the work relaxing, though it was perhaps a form of relaxation indistinguishable from depression. Despite Reed's frequent portrayal of his father as a tyrant, the older man was likely pleased to have his prodigal son near at hand; he may not yet have abandoned the notion that Reed would come work for the firm, especially now that he seemed to be putting his music career behind him. As the boss's son, Reed came and went as he pleased. With music on the back burner, Reed was determined to focus on his career as a writer, so the typing came in handy in that regard as well. His "work" time could be devoted to his manuscripts.

Remarkably, once *Loaded* came out, it actually began to attract attention. Both "Sweet Jane" and "Rock and Roll" got played on FM stations in New York and other major markets, and the album was widely and favorably reviewed. Lenny Kaye wrote a lengthy review in *Rolling Stone* that described *Loaded* as "easily one of the best albums to show up this or any year." Had Reed not left the band, one could imagine a scenario in which the album became an underground phenomenon and, building on the momentum of the Max's shows, the band hit the road on an extensive and well-organized tour, with Tucker back on drums. The Velvets would have been profiled in the burgeoning underground press and in local newspapers in the towns they visited. *Loaded* would likely never have achieved massive sales, but it certainly could have done well enough to ensure the band an ongoing career and solidify Reed's place among significant rock songwriters.

Sadly, nothing like that was to be. Toward the end of his *Rolling Stone* review, Lenny Kaye noted, "Due to a near-textbook case of management hassles, Lou Reed left the group toward the end of the Max's engagement, and though there is a possibility of a reconciliation at some future date, the present situation doesn't look promising." That admission took the wind out of the otherwise positive review's sails. It stands to reason that Atlantic would have been similarly discouraged. The label likely did not have significant promotion plans for *Loaded* anyway, but how much support can you provide for a cult band whose founder, lead singer, and songwriter quit before the album even came out?

Sesnick's plan was to install Yule as the new leader of the Velvet Underground. He did not share that plan with Yule until Reed quit, but Yule became a willing participant once he learned of it. After Reed left, Yule recruited Walter Powers, a bass player from Boston who had also been in the Grass Menagerie, to join the Velvets, and he moved over to a more prominent role on guitar and lead vocals. Morrison and Tucker stayed with the new lineup, and, with Yule at the helm, the band began to play shows once again. Later, Morrison turned down Reed's offer to start a new band together and, in the summer of 1971, quit the Velvets to attend graduate school in English at the University of Texas at Austin.

With Tucker now the only remaining original member of the Velvet Underground, Yule and the band continued to tour in both the United States and Europe. Sesnick even arranged a record deal with Polydor for a Yule-led version of the band. Yule recorded an album called *Squeeze,* which came out in early 1973, working with only Deep Purple drummer Ian Paice and some session musicians. Its eleven songs, written by Yule, are harmless power pop, and history might have treated the album more kindly had it been released under Yule's name rather than the Velvet Underground's. (Interestingly, the English band Squeeze, whose debut album was primarily produced by John Cale, took its name from the album.) When it became apparent that Yule was not going to be able to lead a makeshift version of the Velvet Underground to commercial glory, Sesnick abandoned the band, and it broke up soon after.

BY THE TIME REED quit the Velvet Underground, he had become seriously involved with a young Columbia University student named Bettye Kronstad—five foot ten, blonde, quite beautiful, and nineteen years old. Having grown up in rural western Pennsylvania, she had moved to New York in 1967. She and Reed met in 1968 through Lincoln Swados, Reed's former Syracuse roommate who would soon begin taking classes at Columbia himself. Reed was sufficiently attracted to Kronstad that, after meeting her for the first time, he told her to ask Swados for a character reference since she had no idea who he was. Then, as he was leaving, he slapped her ass, smiled, and took off. She was shocked, but Reed stayed on her mind. "He didn't make the most positive impression," Kronstad recalled, but Swados told her, "Ignore it. He just acts like that sometimes.... He's a nice guy."

At first Kronstad ignored Reed's many calls. But she had heard of the Velvet Underground and was about to leave the country to travel in Europe for six months, so she figured, why not? For their first date, they went to the West End Bar, the legendary hangout of the Beats up near Columbia, and Reed proceeded to get seriously drunk. "He could barely walk, but he insisted on walking me home," Kronstad recalled. "And he didn't try to come up. He was a gentleman." She had two weeks left in town before her trip abroad, and Reed continued to call. Again, she initially thought it best not to respond. "I didn't really know what to think," she said. "First he smacks me on my bottom. Then he's totally drunk. I had a lot on my mind. I wanted to pack and go to Europe."

As always when it came to Reed and women, Kronstad's resistance to his pursuit only intensified his desire. He kept calling, and finally she called him back. "He said, 'Look, I want to see you before you leave,'" she said. "He assumed that, out of everybody else I knew, I would want to see him. The arrogance of that guy! Now, from a woman's point of view, there is a kind of charm to that kind of audacity. It's almost humorous." Still, she decided not to see him. But while she was in Paris, she picked up an English-language newspaper that happened to include an article about the Velvet Underground that praised Reed for his groundbreaking writing. "I was thinking, 'This is that guy I met—that's Lou,'" she recalled. "I'm trying to put this together with the drunk guy who smacked my ass." They began dating when she returned to the United States.

After Reed moved back in with his parents, he spent many weekends with Kronstad at her student apartment near Columbia, but at least one weekend a month she would come out and stay with him and his parents in Freeport, spending time at the private club they belonged to. Reed had equipment set up in his room, and he would work on his songs, often asking Kronstad, who he said had the voice of a "choirboy," to sing for him. When they were on Long Island, Kronstad fell in easily with his family life, more easily than Reed did himself. "His parents loved me," she said. "Minimum requirement: I was a girl. I was not a boy. They were a little concerned about that."

Kronstad said that Reed "hated working with his father" and that the relationship between the two men was strained. "There was a distance, a kind of formality to it," she said. "I know Lou felt like he disappointed his father because he wasn't going to take over his father's accounting firm. I actually think the conflict was more with Lou than it was with Sid. Sid clearly loved his son." Reed had told Kronstad about the electric shock treatments, and she gave his parents the benefit of the doubt: "I'm sure they did it because they were told it was the right thing to do, that it was in his best interests. These are not people who in any way whatsoever were trying to hurt him." Still, she saw that the incident had taken a serious toll on Reed's relationship with his parents. "It was an awful experience for him, and he was bitter about it. I think Sid knew that, and there wasn't a thing he could do about it. And I don't think Sid actually believed that he was guilty of anything, because he was trying to do the right thing. But Lou never did forgive them for that, and, as far as he was concerned, they owed him something from that point on."

Kronstad left Columbia and began to pursue a career as an actress, and she and Reed took a studio apartment together on the Upper East Side. Reed's drinking continued unabated, and, though Kronstad was unaware of it, his drug use did as well. As often was the case with Reed and the women in his life, his feelings about Kronstad veered between extremes. Part of him idealized her as a beautiful, innocent girl from the country, unsullied by New York cynicism and outrageousness. Another part of him resented her naïveté and wanted to strip that very quality from her — much the way he had nastily shown off the bleach-blonde Shelley Albin to his parents. For Reed, the lure of innocence was always the exquisite possibility of violation. "Lou would tell me how much he loved Bettye and get almost mawkishly sentimental," Reed's friend Ed McCormack said. "He'd go on about how he loved her because she wasn't hip. He'd say, 'Most of the people I know are like the scum of the earth in a way, and I sometimes think that's me, too, that's what I'm like. But I believe in fairy-tale princesses.' Then the next time I'd see him, it would all be about 'that bitch, man. What a bitch she turned out to be. She had some of her square-ass friends over the other night, and she took my gay magazines off the coffee table.' Meanwhile, the last time, she was an angel, a princess."

Like many people, McCormack saw a performative element to Reed's gay desires. "He was unsure about his sexuality, and to some degree he wanted to get even with his parents for the shock treatments they'd given him," McCormack said. "There was a deeply conventional part of him that was very real. I think his parents were very disappointing to him. They didn't turn out right, you know? He longed for them a little bit. He was supposed to be a nice Jewish boy. My feeling was that he had learned from Warhol the art of asexuality. He just didn't seem that interested in it. He seemed more interested in drugs than anything else—drugs and Scotch. Whatever made him feel better. In some ways, he was one of the most miserable people I've ever known. He was not a happy man."

Both Reed and McCormack, to varying degrees, were part of a social scene centered on the Upper West Side apartment of Richard and Lisa Robinson. Record companies, radio stations, and publishing companies were all striving to keep up with the dramatic changes that had reshaped popular music since the midsixties. As often is true in times of change, the people running things were older and, for the most part, out of it. The more discerning ones could see that something important was going on and that they needed people closer to the action to help them address the transformations taking place. For smart, alert, and ambitious young people like the Robinsons, opportunities abounded. Richard wrote about music, hosted a radio show on one of New York's premier rock stations, and worked at a record label. Lisa, who started out doing office work for him, soon followed his path, becoming, in the process, one of the best-known and most in-the-know music writers in the country, a status she retains to this day. The couple married not long after they met, and they surrounded themselves with like-minded friends who were also avid music fans eager to make an impact on the media that surrounded the music.

As something like the poet laureate of the New York underground music scene, Reed was a frequent guest at the Robinsons' soirees. They dubbed their informal group Collective Conscience, and according to Lenny Kaye, "there was some thought about going to corporations and advising them, trying to hip 'em up." Kaye lived with the Robinsons for three months and worked with them on their various projects. Their apartment was on Eighty-Second Street, between Columbus and Central Park West, "in an old Upper West Side building," said Kaye, "and it was one of those apartments that you could actually have more than five people in at a time. It had bedrooms, a small room they used as an office, a dining room. Richard was a mover and shaker—he had his hands in about six different media things. Conflict of interest was rife, but we really liked cheerleading for the groups that we supported. Lou felt like he was not only a part of it, but very much respected by it. I think he felt that the people there cared about him and what he did. When he had gone home to Long Island, I'm not sure he realized how much people did care."

"When Lou would come into the city, Lisa would have us over for that salon she had," Kronstad remembered. "Like everybody else, I would be sitting in an adoring circle around Lou, except I lived with him. Lou would be drinking, and everyone just adored whatever pearls of wisdom came out of his mouth. Lisa adored Lou—anything for him." Unfortunately, the crowd at the Robinsons' gatherings did not hold Kronstad in the same high regard. Generally speaking, they saw themselves as a kind of cultural vanguard, cool insiders with hip tastes and an eye-rolling attitude toward more conventional types. Kronstad did not share either their cultural acumen or their pretensions, but her relationship with Reed granted her a status that would otherwise never have been available to her, had she even wanted it. That she was young and conventionally beautiful can't possibly have helped. Consequently, the Robinson crew's attitude toward her typically ranged from barely polite tolerance to outright condescension. "We made fun of her," said Danny Fields. "We were merciless. We called her 'the cocktail waitress.' It was like, 'How did you get stuck with this person?'" Reed himself would privately reassure her, but at times he shared their contempt.

*   *   *

THE MOST SIGNIFICANT DEVELOPMENT that emerged from the Collective Conscience meetings was that Richard Robinson, who had become a staff producer for RCA, helped arrange for Reed to sign to the label, the genuine launch of his solo career. As dramatic as Reed's departure was from the Velvet Underground, only fifteen months passed between the last gig he played with the band and the announcement of the RCA deal in November of 1971. Reed had a stack of unrecorded songs from his VU days, and he had continued to write new material. Robinson, who would produce the new album, worked closely with Reed in getting the songs in shape for recording. Even though the Velvets had never broken through commercially, they had steadily gathered enough attention to make Reed a cult figure of some renown. Indeed, the Velvets' own cult status was such that Reed and everyone around him thought it best to keep expectations for the album in check. "It's just making a rock-and-roll album," Reed said at the time, continuing his strategy since the Velvets' third album of downplaying his avant-garde ambitions and signaling a turn to the mainstream. Reed and Robinson decided to record the album in London, probably another effort to minimize comparisons to the Velvets and avoid whatever media buildup the scuttlebutt about Lou Reed being back in the studio might have engendered.

The care taken to pry Reed free from his Velvets history makes his sudden decision to do a one-off concert with Nico and John Cale in Paris, just as his solo album was being showcased to the media, seem even more bizarre. Media being as limited as it was at the time, it was unlikely that a concert in Paris would come to the attention of rock fans in New York, or even in London. Still, it inevitably raised the prospect of a Velvets reunion for anyone who heard about it. For an event as momentous as it seems from a contemporary vantage, the show, at the Bataclan theater on January 29, 1972, came together quite casually. Cale was working in London on a project of his own, and Reed simply invited him and Nico to perform with him. At that point, the interactions among the three of them, both in rehearsal and onstage, were, while not cuddly, cordial, even friendly. Clearly, no one wanted to rock the boat. As for the performance, it was riveting, something like a Velvet Underground Unplugged, decades before such a notion would have any currency. Listening to the performance, you can feel the intensity of the sold-out crowd of about a thousand people, and, imperfect though they were, the acoustic performances (Reed on guitar; Cale on viola, piano, and guitar; Nico on harmonium) capture both the delicacy and conceptual force of the Velvets. The three musicians share the spotlight as the set moves through Velvet Underground favorites ("I'm Waiting for the

Man," "I'll Be Your Mirror") and solo work. Reed performed two songs ("Berlin," "Wild Child") that would appear on his forthcoming solo debut. Everyone seemed happy with the performances, and more joint appearances were rumored, though none actually took place. The Bataclan show was Reed's last performance with Nico.

REED'S FIRST SOLO ALBUM, simply titled *Lou Reed,* as if to reintroduce him to a waiting world, was released in May of 1972. Recorded with a crew of top English musicians, including, most peculiarly, guitarist Steve Howe and keyboardist Rick Wakeman of Yes, the album primarily consisted of songs Reed had previously recorded or played live with the Velvet Underground, including "I Can't Stand It," "Ocean," and "Lisa Says." The new versions are not bad, but they seem hesitant and a bit haunted, as if Reed himself couldn't escape the legacy of his former band. The players are fine, but they have no instinctive feel for the material. Their parts are executed, not organic. As a singer, Reed had not yet discovered his post-Velvets voice. Amazingly for him, he sounds indistinctive. That's true of the production and arrangements as well. Moments like the signature guitar part of "Walk and Talk It," which blatantly lifts the indelible riff from the Rolling Stones' "Brown Sugar," are typical—and uncharacteristic of anything else Reed had ever done or would do. Overall, the album sounds strangely anonymous.

Reed went through the motions of trying to sell the album while also trying to manage people's expectations. "This is the closest realization to what I hear in my head that I've ever done," he said. "It's a real rock-and-roll album, and my direction has always been rock and roll. I see it as a life force. I don't think anybody who has been following my stuff is going to be surprised by what I've done with this new album, and I think the general audience will find it more accessible." Meanwhile, in their reporting and reviews, you could feel Reed's coterie of rock critic supporters struggling to make the album what they wished it had been. New York–based rock writer Lillian Roxon heard the album at a London listening party hosted by Richard Robinson, and wrote, "Back in London, the consensus is that the album is beautiful. It's not a Velvets album, of course, but it is Lou Reed. You can dance to it and fall in love to it, and you will certainly buy it for someone you are crazy about. So what Lou Reed has done, if you want to know, is to make being fourteen beautiful again, even for twenty-seven-year-olds. Is that a crime?" In his review for *Phonograph Record,* Greg Shaw said what others were probably thinking: "How successful is an album that keeps you imagining what it would sound like with the rest of the guy's former group? I think that's what it all boils down to."

Defining a pattern he would follow throughout his solo career, Reed soon pivoted from describing the album as the best he'd ever done to effectively disowning it. "There's just too many things wrong with it," he told Mick Rock in *Rolling Stone* before the end of the year. "I was in dandy form, and so was everyone else. I'm just aware of all the things that are missing and all the things that shouldn't have been there." Unfortunately, the "general audience" that Reed had hoped to court agreed. *Lou Reed* barely edged into the *Billboard* Top 200, and then disappeared.

7

TRANSFORMER

WHILE THE *LOU REED* album failed to break Reed commercially in the way he would have desired—or as his fans expected—it nonetheless established him as an active solo artist and brought him back into the public consciousness. Indeed, he had come up from underground and taken his place in the present once again. The challenge now was to transform himself, to come up with the next incarnation of Lou Reed.

The Velvet Underground may have been a commercial failure, but the band's cultural role could not have been more profound. "I've not been particularly good at having my note be what the world's note was at the time," Reed said. "With the Velvets the world's note was 'flower power,' and mine was the opposite."

That oppositional role, however, was essential to the band's appeal and credibility. Not only was the music revolutionary, but supporters could bathe in the coolness that their regard for the band conferred on them.

That was far less true of *Lou Reed,* and not just because of issues with the album's production or Reed's reliance on older material. While he carried a legacy with him, Reed needed to create a new definition of himself that was suited to a new musical era. The straight-ahead rock and roll that for the most part characterized the *Lou Reed* album had gone woefully out of fashion. Harder, noisier rock styles had emerged — Jimi Hendrix, Led Zeppelin, even a band like the Stooges, which would have literally been inconceivable without the Velvet Underground. On a quieter front, singer-songwriters, taking their cues from the softer side of Bob Dylan, had begun exploring more personal, autobiographical subjects. (Jackson Browne, who had been Nico's lover and accompanist for a time, would soon emerge as a defining figure on that scene.) Progressive rock bands were pursuing the sonic and thematic possibilities the Beatles had opened up with *Sgt. Pepper's Lonely Hearts Club Band* and later abandoned.

At first glance, Reed would seem to have little in common with the singer-songwriters, but he himself had started out, as John Cale put it, as something of a folkie. The candor of the singer-songwriters about their

complicated love lives and drug and emotional problems was not far out of keeping with Reed's character-
izations of the denizens of the demimonde as he had
described them in his songs with the Velvet Underground. James Taylor's "Fire and Rain," after all, was
a song about a girl who had been in a mental institution and killed herself. "I been in and out of mental
institutions, strung out on drugs, and living with friends
for the past five years," Taylor told the *New York Times*
in 1971.

But more important, from the perspective of Lou
Reed: it suddenly seemed possible that the oppositional
stance the Velvet Underground had taken might no
longer be necessary. The edge, it turned out, had moved
into the mainstream. The Velvets may have shattered,
but their long-term impact was just beginning to be
felt, particularly in England, where Reed had been
spending so much time, and where the Warhol world
of drag queens, ingenues, ironic superstars, and clever
conceptual art was far more congenial to the British
sensibility than to mainstream Americans. The release
of *The Rise and Fall of Ziggy Stardust and the Spiders
from Mars* a couple of months after the *Lou Reed* album
had made David Bowie a vanguard figure in the rock
world, and of course he viewed the Velvet Underground
as an essential influence, as determinative to him as
Chuck Berry had been to the Rolling Stones.

Beyond Bowie's individual success, his rise indicated

that a critical tonal shift had taken place in rock and roll, a shift that proved aesthetically welcoming to Reed. However much gender-bending had taken place in sixties rock, the music still rested squarely on the assumption of heterosexuality. Even Mick Jagger, who pushed homoerotic posturing as far as it could possibly go with a hugely commercial band, was perceived as a seducer and a womanizer, fronting a band whose swagger and music found its sources in such hypermasculine blues figures as Muddy Waters and Howlin' Wolf. (In contrast, the Velvets "had a rule: no blues licks.... I wasn't trying to be a blues guitar player and play funky licks," Reed once said.) But the sexual revolution that had begun in the sixties took on real momentum as that decade ended and the seventies rolled in. Me Decade indulgence stripped sex of ideology and made it just about doing whatever felt good. Suddenly, it wasn't just hippies, college students, and cultural provocateurs who were overthrowing traditional sexual values, but secretaries, accountants, and schoolteachers as well.

Aspects of sexual life that had previously been marginalized began to rollick into the mainstream. The Stonewall riots of 1969 brought gay sexual life out of the Mafia-run bars and after-hours joints that Reed loved and into the streets. In short order, New York — in particular the West Village, where the Stonewall was located — became a hotbed of flamboyant gay cruising. What had once been closeted was now visible for all to see. Newspaper and television reporters, ever in search of a lurid story, spread the news. Leather bars proliferated near the Hudson River docks, a bustling commercial area during the day that was known, ironically enough, as the meatpacking district. The working-class white men delivering and picking up animal carcasses and cartons of vegetables during the day were replaced at night by a subculture of gay men, often hypermasculinized in their own way, seeking every niche and fetish of sexual pleasure. In the manner of New York nightlife, where the edgiest corners inevitably become emblems of hipness, these hard-core regions would be lined with town cars and limousines on weekend nights and early mornings as celebrities and their hangers-on went in search of vicarious thrills. The sexual carnival would spill out of the clubs and onto the abandoned piers and into the backs of the empty trucks in the area, which, for unknown reasons, were left unlocked at night, as if to more easily accommodate the local gay population.

Hard-core pornography even began to move into the mainstream in 1972, with the cinematic release of *Deep Throat*, a film about a woman (played by Linda Lovelace) whose clitoris is located in her throat. The film, which features extensive oral sex scenes, was widely reviewed and discussed. For a time it became fashionable for couples, particularly in New York, to go see the film together—a far cry from the recent past, when individual men haunted the furtive "adult" film theaters in Times Square—a sign of hip liberation that became known as "porn chic." (Martin Scorsese, who saw *Deep Throat*, would parody this phenomenon in his 1976 film, *Taxi Driver*, when a witless Travis Bickle takes his fantasy girl, Betsy, played by Cybill Shepherd, on a movie date to a porn theater, much to her horror.)

Soon these changes began to influence popular music, particularly in England. Glam rock, emerging in the early seventies, defined a new kind of rock star— one who took the gender play of the sixties to a much greater extreme. In England, Marc Bolan, the driving force behind Tyrannosaurus Rex, later to gain fame as T. Rex, became a star of the hugest proportions on the strength of his lisping vocals, gorgeous head of dark curls, and fey mythologizing. The band started out as mystical folkies, but soon crafted a style of rock and roll that borrowed from greats like Chuck Berry, Eddie Cochran, and Gene Vincent. In a modern touch, the band's sound thinned out the roar of those earlier records, opening up spaces that retained the catchiness of the originals but abandoned the more masculine elements of their force and threat. Bowie would soon follow, and he and his guitarist Mick Ronson would borrow that approach on *The Rise and Fall of Ziggy Stardust*, adding a far more provocative level of homoeroticism with their garb and live performances, which often featured both men in makeup with Bowie kneeling onstage in front of Ronson, who in turn played up the phallic imagery of his guitar to the hilt.

In the States, Alice Cooper cracked the Top 40 with his own American-style brand of gender-bending. As would be true with many metal bands to follow, going so far as taking a woman's name somehow did not cause the band to be perceived in homoerotic terms, at least by its legions of young followers. Gay imagery in the United States was still so outré that it could be hidden in plain sight. The same was true of the Kinks' "Lola," a 1970 song about a man's tryst with a transvestite that restored the band to the American Top 10 for the first time in six years. The only controversy that song generated had nothing to do with the character who "walked like a woman but talked like a man" or his dancing partner who "got down on [his] knees"; it had to do with the song's assertion that the champagne the singer drank tasted "just like Coca-Cola." The BBC rejected that nascent product placement, so songwriter Ray Davies changed the beverage to the more generic "cherry cola" in order to get the single played. The sexual playfulness sailed right through.

Deeper underground, the New York Dolls began their residency at the Mercer Arts Center in early 1972, combining trash, glam, and a zany transvestism with an infectious zeal. It was as if the zonked-out boy-girls of Warhol's Factory scene had become obsessed with Chuck Berry and formed a band. "I seem to inspire transvestite bands. They're very cute," Reed deadpanned at the time. This was no longer the rock and roll of the juvenile delinquent fifties or the high-minded sixties. The rebellion carried over, but this was a new era — and music — of sexual liberation.

WHEN DAVID BOWIE PROPOSED to RCA Records that he produce the next Lou Reed album, Reed knew that was exactly what he needed. "Lou was going through an incredibly bad patch around the time that I first met him," Bowie said about their initial meeting at the Ginger Man restaurant in New York, "and he was being left on the side in terms of what his influence had been. And none of us knew what his influence was going to be — the direction of the Velvet Underground's reputation." When they parted later that night, Bowie told Reed, "I hope we see each other again; this has been such a thrill for me."

Even as Bowie was beginning his rise to superstardom, Reed loomed as a hero to him. "Just the verbal and musical zeitgeist that Lou created," Bowie said, "the nature of his lyric writing that had been hitherto unknown in rock . . . gave us the environment in which to put our more theatrical vision. He supplied us with the street and the landscape, and we peopled it." Reed, for his part, was hardly modest about his impact on the scene that Bowie ruled. "Glam rock, androgyny, polymorphic sex—I was right in the middle of it," he said. "Some say I could have been at the head of the class."

The idea of their working together was not merely charity on Bowie's part nor desperation on Reed's. It was a savvy move by both men. Reed understood that Bowie could make a contemporary figure of him, help him appeal to the new, young audience that had grown up in the wake of the sixties and that Bowie had perfectly described in "All the Young Dudes," the glam anthem he had written earlier that year for Mott the Hoople. Those kids were tired of their older siblings' obsession with the Beatles and Stones and were crazed for T. Rex, all of whom are mentioned in the song. Most important, they never got off on "that revolution stuff," but they were eager for a revolution of their own.

Reed, meanwhile, understood that Bowie represented a new cutting edge—not just in his theatricality, but musically. "I wanted to see how he did things in the studio," Reed later said about his desire to work with Bowie. "What did he do? He seemed really quick and facile. I was very isolated. Why were people talking about him so much? What did he do that I could learn?"

If Bowie could potentially provide Reed with contemporary appeal—as well as the rock stardom and commercial success that he had always yearned for—Reed would provide Bowie with stature, establishing him in a lineage that he very much wanted to be part of. Neither man would admit to such desires—Bowie was too self-conscious a rebel and Reed too determined to style himself as an artist beyond any concern about sales. But those desires were a big part of what brought them together. *Billboard* noted the shifting standing of the two men: "The year started out with David Bowie fast gaining recognition as one of Lou Reed's trendy disciples; the year will end with the tables neatly turned."

"That was a really exciting time," said Bettye Kronstad about the months leading up to the recording of *Transformer* in London during the summer of 1972. "Bowie had a name—he was a big deal. This album would push Lou over the top. And I wanted to marry him *after* he was famous, after he was successful—not beforehand and then get dropped."

Of course, not everyone was enthused about the prospect of Reed and Bowie's union. Richard Robinson, who had produced the *Lou Reed* album, only learned that he had been replaced at the helm of Reed's follow-up the day before he planned to leave New York for London to work on it. Neither he nor his rock critic wife, Lisa, took the news lightly. "While Lou's solo debut had been difficult to make and didn't turn out the way either Lou or Richard envisioned, I was fiercely loyal to Richard and royally pissed off at Lou," she later wrote. "I stopped speaking to, and writing about, both Bowie and Lou for a while."

Angela Bowie, David's wife at the time, arranged for Reed and Kronstad to live in a nicely appointed duplex in Wimbledon, a suburb just outside London, though they ended up spending much of their time in a posh London hotel. Photographer Mick Rock believes that Bowie's manager, Tony Defries, who hoped to manage Reed as well, arranged for Reed to stay in Wimbledon in an effort to keep him clean. On July 8, a month or so before they started recording, Bowie brought Reed onstage with him at a Save the Whale benefit for the Friends of the Earth at Royal Festival Hall in London. Backed by the Spiders from Mars, Reed and Bowie performed "I'm Waiting for the Man," "White Light/White Heat," and "Sweet Jane" before three thousand Bowie devotees. A master promoter, as always, Bowie had already begun the process of introducing Reed to a new audience and creating the sense of an event for their collaboration on Reed's next album.

For his part, the instinctively reticent Reed learned

quickly from Bowie's knack for grabbing attention. Wearing "shades and maroon fingernails," he attended a press event held at the luxurious Dorchester Hotel for junketeering American writers interested in interviewing Bowie about the *Ziggy Stardust* album. While an advance copy of Mott the Hoople's version of "Sweet Jane," which Bowie had produced, played in the background, Reed walked over to where Bowie was being interviewed by a reporter and kissed him. "I was hoping to get a two-way interview," the journalist said. Bowie's reply: "That was a two-way interview." Mick Rock caught the moment in a photograph, though Bowie would be coy about it later. "I remember David in interviews saying, 'Oh, no, we were just about to whisper into each other's ear,' and I would think, 'Well, I saw the kiss, David,'" Rock said. "Lou always just said, 'Of course we kissed.'"

DESPITE HIS STARDOM AND air of supreme self-confidence, Bowie was only twenty-five when work began on *Transformer*. Though Reed himself was just five years older, Bowie was nervous about collaborating with one of his idols. "I was petrified that he said yes to working with me in a producer's capacity," Bowie revealed. "I had so many ideas and I felt so intimidated by my knowledge of the work that he had already done." Still, Bowie's ambitions were not small. "I really wanted it to work for him," he said, "and be a memorable album that people wouldn't forget."

In contrast to his first solo album, Reed came to the sessions for his follow-up with a cache of new songs. Bowie told the press, "I think his new material on the album that we're gonna do will surprise a lot of people as well. It's miles different from anything he's ever done before." Reed had "Walk on the Wild Side," which he had written for a musical based on the Nelson Algren novel *A Walk on the Wild Side* that never came to fruition. Never one to waste a good idea, Reed recast the song as a kind of musical documentary about the Factory scene. For his part, Bowie was fascinated with Warhol (he had written a song about him, "Andy Warhol," for his 1971 album, *Hunky Dory,* and had met him at the Factory). Warhol had already become something of a society figure by this time and the Factory had lost some of its cachet. But the culture at large had caught up with the lifestyle of the Factory characters, so by the time Reed decided to write about them, they seemed very much of the moment.

With its laid-back, soft-jazz arrangement, "Walk on the Wild Side" is often thought to be an anomaly in Reed's catalog, which is more typically characterized by ferocious hard rock or emotionally complicated ballads. But the song, which Bowie called "a classic" and "absolutely brilliant," would become an undeniable milestone, the only U.S. Top 20 hit of Reed's forty-six-year career. In its quiet way, "Walk on the Wild Side" celebrates the sexual transformations of Holly Woodlawn, Jackie Curtis, and Candy Darling, three transgender Factory stalwarts and the stars of Warhol and Paul Morrissey's 1971 satire of the feminist movement, *Women in Revolt.* Two other Factory denizens make an appearance in the song: Joe Dallesandro, who played a hustler in the Warhol trilogy *Flesh, Trash,* and *Heat,* and Sugar Plum Fairy (actor Joe Campbell, a longtime intermittent boyfriend of Harvey Milk, who would be assassinated for his gay activism).

It's not as if Reed knew those characters well, or really at all. "They're just cursory sketches," he admitted, "but the descriptions had to be vivid enough to make an impact in about three minutes." Holly Woodlawn claimed that she had met Reed once at a party, and for years, Dallesandro, who never met Reed and was married and had children when he was starring in the Warhol films, bristled that Reed, intentionally or not, confused the character he played on the screen with his real life. In Reed's mind, he was not creating a literal documentary but drawing on the people he saw around him for material. Of Sugar Plum Fairy, for example, whom Reed also didn't know, he said, "With a name like that it was too good to leave alone."

But the mere presence of those characters, all described with cool, unjudging detachment in Reed's deadpan vocal, captured the empathy and distance so essential to Reed's writing. "They were the ragtag queens of Max's Kansas City, and they got very little in return for all of the groundbreaking things that they did," said Patti Smith, "and to be heralded by someone like Lou was lovingly compassionate without being syrupy." Initially fearful of how the characters named in the song might respond, Reed later said that Candy Darling was so delighted with her treatment that she discussed recording an album of his songs.

But "Walk on the Wild Side" is more than a song. It's a slogan, and an invitation. Its title distills Reed's primary symbolic value: to expose people to worlds they might never have become aware of otherwise. "I have always thought it would be kinda fun to introduce people to characters they maybe hadn't met before, or hadn't wanted to meet, you know," Reed said. "The kind of people you sometimes see at parties but don't dare approach. That's one of the motivations for me writing all those songs in the first place." In the early seventies, millions of people were standing on the brink of taking a walk on the wild side. All they needed was a little push, and Reed provided exactly that. The phrase "soundtrack of an era" is tossed around indiscriminately, but "Walk on the Wild Side" more than lives up to it. It gave a name to a burgeoning reality.

"Writing songs is like making a play," Reed said, "and you give yourself the lead part. And you write yourself the best lines that you could. And you're your own director. . . . And you get to play all different kinds of characters. It's fun. I write through the eyes of somebody else. I'm always checking out people I know I'm going to write songs about. Then I become them. That's why when I'm not doing that I'm kind of empty. I don't have a personality of my own. I just pick up other people's personalities."

Typical radio listeners had no idea who Jackie or Holly or Little Joe or Candy were, but they knew about the changes that were taking place in the society around them, as well as in the sexual (and drug-related: "Jackie is just speeding away . . .") realms of their own lives. For those who were not frightened by those changes (as many were; the battle lines of the culture wars that persist to this day were just being drawn), the dark side of the street, the wild side, began to look not so unfamiliar. In fact, it began to look welcoming.

That the song is so musically accessible, so sinuous and promising, works to its advantage as well. Its indelible bass line, overdubbed by jazz bassist Herbie Flowers on both standup and electric bass so that he could earn an additional twelve pounds according to the rules of the British musicians' union, makes the song immediately identifiable. The searching, lyrical saxophone solo that fades the song out was played by jazz saxophonist Ronnie Ross, who had been Bowie's saxophone instructor when he was younger. That Reed was not screaming, that his guitar was not overloading on feed-back, simply made the call of the wild more seductive. Rather than confront listeners and intimidate them, flaunting his coolness, Reed allowed them to come to him, and to new experiences. What could possibly be so scary about a world that could be described this elegantly and directly, this dryly and wittily, while the "colored girls" serenaded you? Hey, babe, why not just take that next step?

WHILE BOWIE'S PRESENCE WAS critical for reasons that extended beyond music, Mick Ronson, the guitarist in Bowie's band and the coproducer, with Bowie, of *Transformer*, made essential contributions to Reed's second solo effort. It's been argued that Ronson, who also played guitar, piano, and recorder on the album, had a greater role than Bowie—or Reed, for that matter—in shaping and arranging *Transformer*'s songs, and it's ultimately difficult to tell precisely who deserves credit for what. Ronson's influence, Reed said, "was stronger than David's—but together, as a team, they're terrific."

As the years passed after the album's completion, Bowie and Reed's relationship had its ups and downs. Reed, in particular, was determined that it not seem as if he owed the album's success to his superstar bene-

factor, so he tended to diminish Bowie's role in it—
not directly, but by rarely mentioning him. Bowie, for
his part, exhibited a typically English reluctance to
grab the credit—and likely had too much regard for
Reed to want to shove him out of the spotlight. Despite
his considerable talents, Ronson wasn't enough of a
celebrity to be pursued for interviews by the media,
and his death in 1993 ensured that his special role in
many musical ventures (including producing Morrissey's 1992 album *Your Arsenal* and arranging John
Mellencamp's massive hit "Jack and Diane") would go
unheralded.

At the time of the *Transformer* sessions, however, the
three men were getting along famously. "With Ronno
and David there was a real simpatico," Reed said, using
an affectionate English nickname for Ronson, "which
was certainly part of the situation I had with the Velvets, and miles above where I had been with the first
Lou Reed record, where there was nothing simpatico."
On his end, the easygoing Ronson found Reed, whose
cantankerousness in the studio is legendary, a pleasure
to work with. As out of control as he could be, Reed
could take direction when he felt that something important was at stake, as he did with Warhol and Morrissey
for a time. Also, Ronson was not as complex a figure as
Bowie was, not a potential usurper. Consequently, Reed
could relax around him and respond openly to his

suggestions. Ronson recalled meeting Reed at Max's, and then Reed coming to his hotel room in New York a couple of times to play some of the songs he wanted to work on for the album. Ronson would get them down on a little tape recorder so he could think about suitable arrangements and production approaches.

"Lou used to say some funny things to me," Ronson recalled about Reed's method of giving him direction. "Some things like, 'Can you make it a little bit more gray?' That to me was like, what the hell is he talking about? I guess he was just trying to explain things in a more artistic way or something. That was kind of going over my head a bit." Then there was the fact that Ronson hailed from Hull, a town in East Yorkshire in northern England, with a singular local dialect. "The thing with Ronno is that I could very rarely understand a word he said," Reed recalled. "He had a Hull accent; he'd have to repeat things five times. But a really sweet guy. A great guitar player and a really sweet guy." Funnily enough, Reed and Ronson's inability to communicate effectively probably served to smooth the edges of their interactions — and freed Ronson to be as creative as he wanted to be in his approach to the album.

The studio lovefest, as well as the public displays of affection, prompted rumors that Reed and Bowie had fallen in love. True or not, it was a rumor perfectly suited to the times. "I actually wasn't aware of it, if it happened," Kronstad said. "It's the sort of thing that would have happened when I wasn't around."

Neither ever confessed to an affair, and it's possible to make sense of their connection and the rumors surrounding it without assuming a sexual relationship. On the simplest level, studios are hothouse environments, vacuum-sealed from the rest of the world, in which it's possible to bond deeply with the people you're collaborating with so many hours a day. Bowie was a magnetic figure just coming into his own, and, like all producers, he needed to draw the best performances possible out of Reed any way he could. Seduction, whether literal or metaphorical, can be an essential part of that process.

Beyond that, both Reed and Bowie had much at stake, and their mutual sense of self-importance, which would have been high on the most modest day of their lives, escalated due to the urgency of the project. Both men at the time were deeply attracted to outrage, shock, and attention, and neither would have felt any particular need to play down whatever camp element may have been present between them. That the sessions were going well would only encourage their sense that they were invulnerable, subject to no one else's rules of how they should or shouldn't behave. They were free to inspire each other with their mutual admiration both inside and outside the studio, and Ronson was always on hand to make sure the work got done.

*   *   *

IF THE *LOU REED* solo album was haunted by the Velvet Underground, *Transformer* treated that period of Reed's life as a subject, a source of material, rather than a legacy he had to live up to. That writerly distance freed him to create a completely new sound and persona. "Walk on the Wild Side" is the most significant example of this shift, and "Andy's Chest" is another. Originally written in 1968 for the Velvets, the song alludes to the attempted murder of Warhol by Valerie Solanas. "It's what I thought about Andy being shot," Reed said of the song, which strings together a series of gently surrealistic lyrics, including a couple of "bat" references to the Dracula portion of Warhol's nickname, Drella.

Back when Reed was working with the Velvets, Warhol had asked him, "Why don't you write a song called 'Vicious'?" When Reed asked what he meant, Warhol replied, "Vicious, I hit you with a flower." Reed thought it was a great idea, and by the time he got around to completing the song for *Transformer,* it was timely as well. Like the banana cover Warhol had designed for the first Velvets album, his "hit you with a flower" notion was a spoof of hippie idealism. More deeply, it also hinted at the passive-aggressiveness of so much sixties culture—a kind of personal violence concealed in flower power clichés. As the opening line on the opening song on *Transformer,* "Vicious, you hit me with a flower" set the tone for the rest of the album, connecting Reed to his Velvets past while distancing him from the sixties, an era that by 1972 was just beginning to be viewed from a critical distance.

As in his dalliance with Bowie, Reed played with his image in "Vicious," in which the singer refers to himself as "some kind of gay blade" and offhandedly deflects an S and M invitation ("You want me to hit you with a stick / But all I've got's a guitar pick"). "Make Up" and "New York Telephone Conversation" parody the self-involvement of the Factory scene and the back room at Max's, two self-reflecting centers of hipness in the theatrical "city of shows" in which every appearance in public is a performance. "Make Up," however, also nods to the gender-bending kids of the glam movement, for whom makeup and dressing up — and the identity transformations they enact — was at least as important as the music. "Here is this whole glam thing going on, so I just put myself in that head," Reed said about the song. "It's not like I had to go very far to do it. I have about a thousand selves running around. It's easy."

The song's surprisingly direct bridge ("We're coming out / Out of our closets / Out on the streets") drew on the slogans of the gay liberation movement and had an impact well beyond the world of music. Years later, gay activist and writer Don Shewey would describe hearing *Transformer* as a college freshman in 1972 this way: "You can't imagine how profound and delirious it was.... This butch guy talking about drugs and drag queens, sex and self-hatred, without distancing himself, opened up worlds of possibility for me, and for that I will forever be grateful." Reed would never have described himself as a political songwriter, but he wrote a movement anthem.

Reed described "Satellite of Love" as being "about jealousy," a theme that comes through in its gently humorous bridge about the presumably female subject of the song having "been bold" every day of the week with "Harry, Mark, and John," Reed's version of every Tom, Dick, and Harry. The song is sweet and sad, treating emotions that Reed would typically address more corrosively with gentleness and wit. The decade's newly emergent environmental issues also get a nod in the song ("Satellite's gone way up to Mars / Soon it'll be filled with parking cars"), as does the era's fascination with space exploration. Bowie amps up the song's doo-wop aspect with his "bom bom bom" background vocals and the luscious high notes he hits as the song fades. This was neither the first nor the last time that Reed would reach back to his early love of doo-wop, both for its romance and its lyrical rendering of obsession, subjects that always were inextricably linked for him.

The song on *Transformer* that would ultimately rival "Walk on the Wild Side" for preeminence, however, is

"Perfect Day," a haunting ballad raised to stratospheric heights by Ronson's gorgeous string arrangement. Apart from its beauty, the song's enduring appeal stems from its emotional complexity. It describes a couple enjoying all the quotidian pleasures of a weekend date—sangria in Central Park, a visit to the zoo, a movie. The song's melancholic musical setting undercuts the idyllic scene, as do lyrics that fatally jar the mood. "You just keep me hanging on," Reed sings, borrowing a Supremes line to describe an emotional desperation the song has entirely suppressed up to that point. Then, looking on the scene as if from an unbridgeable distance, he sings, "You made me forget myself / I thought I was someone else / Someone good." Those lines, the heart of the song in Reed's view, chillingly distill the part of Reed that longed for a conventional life, even as he courted and reveled in actions, styles, and scenes whose very point was to explode those conventional values. Reed later dismissed the Biblical injunction that concludes the song ("You're going to reap just what you sow") as a cliché, but its complex intent and function in this context make it anything but that. Who is he speaking to? The woman in the song? Or is he addressing that line to himself, frightened and convinced that his own excesses will eventually damn him? The line's religious source in the context of the album's self-conscious, self-styled decadence only strengthens its impact.

According to Kronstad, "Perfect Day" describes one of her dates with Reed. "We had plans to meet in the park," she recalled, "and I went horseback riding beforehand. I'd been stupid and hadn't brought my boots, because I had an appointment before I went riding. So I had sandals on and my ankles were bleeding. We're sitting there having sangria in this very romantic setting. I didn't show Lou. I was so embarrassed." They never discussed what Reed might have meant by the song. "When someone writes you a love song like that and plays it for you, sometimes there's just not a lot to say," she said. Perhaps she also didn't really want to know.

Transformer ends with "Goodnight Ladies," a song that blends an allusion in its title to T. S. Eliot's "The Waste Land" and the weary, fagged-out atmosphere of a music hall evening coming to a close. The song calls attention to the theatricality of the entire album, while echoing the gay theme running through it (it's "ladies," not ladies and gentlemen, archly feminizing everyone who is participating and being addressed). The song's oompah quality, in Reed's description, and woozy, melancholy Dixieland arrangement (done by Herbie Flowers, who played tuba on the track) recall similarly self-conscious evocations of old-fashioned music hall camaraderie by the Rolling Stones, the Beatles, and the Kinks, not to mention Reed's own "After

Hours." For those English bands (and certainly for Bowie and Ronson), such gestures combined wry nostalgia with a sense that the world had forever changed. The reassuring certainties and communal comfort that the music hall represented had utterly vanished.

The title *Transformer* admits multiple meanings, all without diminishing its cool open-endedness. Its definition as a device that controls voltage hints at the album's electrical charge. It also alludes to Reed's role as a change agent, an artist who exposes his audience to characters and situations capable of transforming them. Gender transformations, too, are in there— "and then he was a she," as easy as that. Warhol, who lurks throughout the album, certainly was a transformer, not only in his own life but in creating an environment at the Factory, and eventually in the culture at large, in which characters in search of a new identity could find one. Everyday objects can become works of art as easily as lost boys and girls can become superstars. Finally, the album transformed Lou Reed from a confused underground icon in search of a new direction into the success that, regardless of his ambivalence, he always wanted to be.

As much as its music, *Transformer's* cover generated attention and controversy. The front portrait, shot by Mick Rock before the sessions for the album had even begun, depicts a soulful, vampiric Reed looking out at the viewer, his eyes darkened with makeup, not so much defiant as blithely accepting of his own otherworldliness—another androgynous man who fell to Earth. When Rock showed Reed that shot on a contact sheet, "Lou pounced on it. He immediately said, 'That's the cover, Mick.'...And of course, somehow or other, that came to be the shot that defined him forever."

A *Rolling Stone* writer described Reed at the time as looking like "an effeminate Frankenstein monster in whiteface with baleful blackened eyes." The image became one of the iconic representations of glam rock decadence—"the degenerate side of glam," as Rock put it—and prompted a promotional campaign that dubbed Reed "The Phantom of Rock," a reference to the grisly novel and film *The Phantom of the Opera*. That cadaverous portrait was striking enough, but the back cover features a leggy vamp in high heels and lacy lingerie, a hand artfully placed near her crotch, her eyes closed, the other hand on her hip—evidently a man dressed alluringly as a woman. Opposite that image, and inspired by the gay porn magazines Reed enjoyed, stands a muscular rough trade boy (in fact Ernie Thormahlen, Reed's friend and former road manager) in a white, formfitting crop top T-shirt, black cap, and jeans, with a pronounced bulge in his pants (according to Reed, a banana—yet another Warhol reference?—shoved down his pants). "Haven't you seen the cover?" Reed asked a journalist in 1972. "It's divine. There's this very well-hung stud looking into a mirror and looking back at him is this beautiful girl. There's a lot of sexual ambiguity in the album and two outright gay songs—from me to them, but they're carefully worded so the straights can miss out on the implications and enjoy them without being offended. I suppose, though, the album is going to offend some people." The images defined the twin poles of gay male stereotypes at the time, and it was widely rumored that Reed was the subject of both photos, a view that he thoroughly enjoyed. "I could have had a whole new career," he later joked.

Kronstad took a characteristically pragmatic view of all the homoerotic imagery suffusing the album. "It's just showbiz," she said. "It was marketing. I thought it was clever. We were just selling the album. I was always coming from the point of view of, how do we get his career going?"

RCA was smart enough to take that perspective as well. Rather than attempt somehow to tamp down the controversy the album generated, the company exploited it. "In the midst of all the make-believe madness, the mock depravity, and the pseudosexual anarchists, Lou Reed is the real thing," the label's ad copy ran.

Critical response to the album was mixed, as were

the individual reviews. In *Rolling Stone,* Nick Tosches called *Transformer* a "real cockteaser" and advised Reed to forget "this artsy-fartsy kind of homo stuff." In what eventually amounted to a relatively positive review, Robot A. Hull declared in *Creem,* "This new album is further proof that Lou Reed has turned into something sicker than a homicidal-rapist-mass-murderer-porno editor." As for the album's cover, Hull continued, Reed looked like "he's been giving rim jobs to the Fugs.... Yup, he's a full-fledged social degenerate now, and I really don't see how he could get any lower." In *New Musical Express,* Nick Kent dismissed *Transformer* as "the Lou Reed Chic album.... A total parody of Reed's former genius." Writing in the British publication *Disc and Music Echo,* however, Ray Fox-Cumming wrote of *Transformer,* "It is his best-ever album, beautiful, sad, funny, lyrically impeccable, melodically often very pretty, and it will probably be looked back on as a landmark in years to come."

Amid all the attention, Reed went on the road with the Tots, a hard-charging but virtually unknown bar band from the far-from-trendy New York suburb of Yonkers. Meanwhile, "Walk on the Wild Side" gradually began to draw attention and radio play on its way to becoming a hit, entering the charts more than four months after *Transformer*'s release. In the United States, the verse about Candy Darling was edited out of the single version, but in England, where the term "giving head" was not then current slang, it was kept in, and the song broke into the Top 10. In true Warholian fashion, Lou Reed was now not simply a legend; he was a star.

8

A CITY'S DIVIDED SOUL

A MONTH OR SO before the release of *Transformer,* Lou Reed received a punishing concert review in *Melody Maker* that focused squarely on his new relationship with David Bowie. Following a Friday night performance at the Sundown Theatre in the London suburb of Edmonton, Richard Williams began his review, "The fact is that his association with David Bowie has done Lou Reed no good at all." Further on, Williams wrote that Reed was an original who "shouldn't need the patronage of a second-rate plagiarist, and it's sad that the vagaries of public taste and the music business have put the Long Islander in such an invidious position.... For a start, his stage persona is unconvincing. He seems to feel that he must do the expected: people think he's bizarre, so he must act bizarre (white-powdered face, black lipstick, Monroe wiggles, and silver high heels which forced him to totter on- and offstage like a sad, aging whore)."

Sensing that the critical tide was turning before *Transformer* even came out, Reed began publicly backing away from his connection with Bowie and the glam scene. "I'm not going in the same direction as David," he insisted to an English journalist. "I wanted to try that heavy eye makeup and dance about a bit. . . . Anyway, I've done it all now and stopped it. . . . I don't wear the makeup anymore." When he spoke to journalist Nick Kent in 1973, Reed described the new album he was working on as "a backlash on *Transformer*. Maybe I'll do a song on it called 'Get Back in the Closet You Fuckin' Queers.'"

He continued, "I just think that everyone's into this scene because it's supposedly the thing to do right now. . . . You just can't fake being 'gay.' If they claim they're gay, they're going to have to make love in a gay style, and most of those people aren't capable of making that commitment. These kids can pretend to be as gay as can be, but when it comes down to it they just won't be able to make it. And that line — 'Everyone's bisexual' — that's a very popular thing to say right now. I think it's meaningless."

Despite his ambivalence, Reed knew he was riding a crest; he was more of a public figure than he had ever been before. And with the momentum of *Transformer* behind him, he was set to play his first solo shows in New York in January of 1973 at Lincoln Center's Alice Tully Hall, a dramatic moment in his career. To promote those dates, Reed's record label, RCA, took out subway ads that displayed the black-and-white portrait on the album's front cover (into whose eyes, according to *Rolling Stone,* "some graffiti genius in the IRT Fourteenth Street station had drawn a network of red veins") and challenged viewers with the question, "Will you still be underground when Lou Reed emerges at Alice Tully Hall on January 27?"

Reed played two sets that night at the elegant eleven-hundred-seat theater and told a reporter beforehand, "Did you know that both shows are sold out? That's why I don't give a fuck what the critics say. Fuck the critics." Whether he gave a fuck or not, what the critics thought—and, even more, what the audience thought—mattered. This was Reed's comeback concert, and the stakes were high. By the time of these shows, Reed had already pared back his wardrobe and his stage presentation. "Those who expected the fey Phantom in pancake that they saw on the album cover and in the posters are somewhat taken aback by the Lou Reed who walks out onto the stage at Alice Tully Hall," *Rolling Stone* writer (and Reed buddy) Ed McCormack observed. "More than some campy forebear of glitter rock, he resembles a punk rocker of the early sixties in his skintight stage armor of macho black leather. When he seems to stagger as he fiddles with an amp, one begins to have grim forebodings about the outcome of this concert."

According to McCormack, the first show was disappointing, and before the second one, Andy Warhol went backstage to encourage Reed. "Andy heard the news from the vultures in the lobby as soon as he walked in: the first show had gone badly; Lou's timing was off; he seemed listless through the entire set, perhaps even slightly drunk," McCormack wrote. But in the second set, Reed took the reins. "His presence is cool and benign," McCormack wrote, "his movements spare. He does not camp it up or cavort daintily like David Bowie. He stands behind his guitar and sings; only at intervals does he break formation to remind us of his pansexuality with a subtle wave of the wrist or a less subtle dipping squat that is Chuck Berry–like but decidedly anal in the middle of his song called 'Rock and Roll.'"

"For the most part he just steps up to the mic and sings with a Dylan-like dignity," McCormack continued, "letting the songs create all the auras for him." In the *Village Voice,* Richard Nusser was extravagant in his praise. Reed and his band, Nusser reported, played "the kind of rock and roll that stands up to anything being played in the world today, or, for that matter, anything that has gone before."

Still, the Lincoln Center appearance fell short of

the triumphant homecoming it was meant to be; this was hardly Reed's post-Velvets claim to iconic solo stature. Among other issues, his past continued to haunt him. Regardless of the quality of the performances, the members of the jaded New York crowd that constituted the core of Reed's following were too conscious of their own status to show too much enthusiasm about his return. McCormack described the postshow party at the stately Sherry-Netherland hotel as "funereal." Steve Paul, a hip New York club owner, said, "This is the weirdest party I've ever seen. Everybody seems afraid to make a move, afraid of acting uncool or something." Reed, wrote McCormack, was the "somnambulant heart" of the fete, "slumped in a period chair in his black leather S and M suit, sipping Scotch." At one point, Reed turned to McCormack and, drawing a wry distinction between the reporter covering the event and his friend, said, "Someday in the near future, we'll get together over a couple of Scotches and laugh about this whole scene. . . . Off the record, of course."

ONCE *TRANSFORMER* CAME OUT, Bettye Kronstad was confident that Reed's career was fully established, and in early January of 1973, just three weeks before the Lincoln Center shows, Reed and Kronstad married.

Fred Heller, Reed's manager at the time, arranged for a Catholic officiant to perform the ceremony; "In Fred's mind, that was somewhere between being Presbyterian and Jewish," Kronstad explained. They held their reception in their studio apartment on East Seventy-Eighth Street between First and York Avenues. In the pictures, she said, "he's very happy and I'm really puzzled."

Besides the wedding and the prospect of Reed's commercial success, little had changed about their relationship. Reed's drinking and drug use carried on, and Kronstad continued to have to shift through the roles of supportive wife, nursemaid, confidante, party partner, and collaborator. In addition, she was now a publicity tool. A secretary in the office of Reed's manager assured one writer that "Lou's a changed man. He's really settled down since he married Betty [*sic*]. Like, he's cut down on his drinking drastically and eats watercress sandwiches now. He's got a great sense of humor—he tells Polish jokes, and one time I actually saw him tickling his wife. In public."

In fact, behind that sales pitch, Reed's dependence on Kronstad continued to be frightening. During an interview with Ed McCormack a week or so before the Lincoln Center shows, Reed drank Scotch and suddenly seemed "to sag. His chin drops down on his chest and his lids half close. Presently, he begins to nod out, and Betty [*sic*], his bride of two weeks, leads him inside and puts him to bed." At around that time, an English magazine poll determined Reed to be the second most likely rock star to die prematurely. Keith Richards edged him out.

AMONG HIS OTHER EXTRACURRICULAR activities, Reed was a devoted patient of Dr. Robert Freymann, more casually known as "Dr. Feelgood," a medical doctor on the Upper East Side whose amphetamine-laced vitamin B_{12} shots attracted an extraordinary clientele of celebrities (allegedly including Jackie Kennedy). Freymann was immortalized in the Beatles song "Doctor Robert" ("If you're down he'll pick you up") on their 1966 album *Revolver*.

While Reed concealed much of his drug use, particularly anything that involved needles, from Kronstad, he eagerly turned her on to Freymann, perhaps because the setting of a standard medical practice in the posh environs of Park Avenue and Seventy-Eighth Street somehow made the doctor seem more respectable. Indeed, while Reed was sophisticated and obsessive enough about drugs to know exactly what he was getting from Freymann, he may well have believed that the hormones, vitamins, and other additives that the doctor used in his concoctions somehow made them "healthy." It's common for serious users to study their preferred drugs intently and, ironically, to use their knowledge to rationalize what any objective observer would perceive as obviously destructive behavior. Often a holistic context is created in which other "healthy" behaviors cancel out or even transform the negative effects of the drug use — along the lines of John Lennon using heroin and smoking relentlessly but adhering at times to a strict macrobiotic diet. Baited about shooting speed by Lester Bangs during one of their notoriously combative interviews, Reed, who was roaring drunk, responded, "I still do shoot it . . . My doctor gives it to me . . . Well, no, actually, they're just shots of meth mixed with vitamins . . . Well, no, actually, they're just vitamin C . . . injections."

Regardless, Reed was a convert, and eventually Kronstad was, too.

"It was like going to see God," she recalled, laughing. "You'd go through, like, four waiting rooms and finally you were in God's office. Lou told me it was a vitamin shot, and I believed him. But . . . the doctor, who had a German accent, said to me the first time, 'I vill make you feel like no man has ever made you feel.' And he was right. Holy cow! So we went to get those shots, I think it was every Friday. It would be, like, eight o'clock in the morning and we'd take a cab over and be sitting on his doorstep, waiting for the office to open so that we could get that shot.

"After a while it occurred to me that there must be

something in there other than vitamins. But they served their purpose. The kind of schedule that we were on — I think there were three tours around that time — there's no human way that anybody could perform at that level, and you can't just go to sleep. And there was one time when Lou was really ill; he was so sick he couldn't perform. And those shots fixed it. They brought him back to health."

Ever the enthusiast determined to share his excitement with others, Reed also dragged his writer friend Ed McCormack to Freymann's office for what turned out to be, of all things, a legitimate medical visit. Looking like "death warmed over," according to McCormack, Reed banged on his friend's apartment door early one morning while it was still dark outside. McCormack hadn't been feeling well but wouldn't see a doctor, so Reed took matters into his own hands. "Let's go ... Get dressed," Reed insisted. "I've got a cab waiting downstairs, and I'm taking you to see my doctor." When McCormack protested that it was too early, Reed shut him down: "Don't worry about it. This guy gets in early. And he can cure anything — including cirrhosis — as long as you're honest with him about your habits." Rather than pump McCormack full of speed, however, Freymann took an X-ray, analyzed it, and discussed it with him. His conclusion, according to McCormack: " 'Your liver looks okay, but your bowel is slightly distended,' he informed me in his guttural German accent. 'You better go a little easy on the drinking.'" When McCormack attempted to pay, Freymann informed him that "Lou had already taken care of it."

BECAUSE OF THE SUCCESS of *Transformer,* RCA was eager for a follow-up, and Reed felt the pressure. Speaking about "Walk on the Wild Side," Reed had declared at one point, "That's my masterpiece. That's the one that will make them forget 'Heroin,'" and yet he felt characteristically ambivalent about the prominence the song had brought him. How can you be an underground icon and have hits? How can you define the edge when you've been absorbed by the mainstream? "In the end," Kronstad said, "he kind of resented the song. He resented the very song that made him popular, that pushed him over the edge." Attempting to re-create "Walk on the Wild Side" was the last thing he wanted to do.

Not that it would have been possible. Given the credit that David Bowie was garnering in some quarters for *Transformer*—and the heat that Reed was taking for mimicking him—working with him again was out of the question. Not that Bowie would have been interested. The two men actually had a public brawl at a London club when Bowie said that Reed would have to clean up if Reed wanted to work with him again. It was time for a departure.

Reed and Dennis Katz, who took over managing Reed from Fred Heller, decided that Bob Ezrin was the man for the job. Explaining why Reed was moving on from Bowie, Katz declared, "Lou is out of the glitter thing. He really renounces it. He's not interested in glam rock or glitter rock. Lou Reed is a rock and roller." A twenty-three-year-old from Canada, Ezrin had risen to prominence when, barely in his twenties, he had coproduced Alice Cooper's third album, *Love It to Death,* which included "I'm Eighteen," the song that put Cooper on the commercial map. Ezrin had produced three other Cooper albums: *Killer; School's Out,* which rose to number two on the album charts, with the title track a Top 10 single; and *Billion Dollar Babies,* a number one album in 1973.

While both Reed and Bowie viewed Alice Cooper as a shallow shock monger, a joke version of their own subversive personas, from a record company standpoint his producer was an ideal choice to work with Reed. From the industry perspective, the aesthetic differences among Bowie, Reed, and Cooper were meaningless. Broadly speaking, they were all working the same side of the street—bending gender categories and stunning conventional sensibilities with their cross-dressing, uproarious stage shows, and pushing-the-envelope lyrics. That Ezrin was a talented, ambitious producer was, if anybody even noticed, just icing on the cake. The idea was to transform Reed, like Alice Cooper, into a commercial juggernaut, and no one was better cut out for that task than wunderkind Bob Ezrin.

As far as Reed was concerned, Ezrin's most significant credit might well have been producing the band Detroit, which was fronted by the powerhouse white R & B singer Mitch Ryder; the band's eponymous 1971 album included a muscular version of the Velvet Underground's "Rock and Roll," which had caught Reed's ear in a positive way. In fact, when Ezrin dropped in on Reed's sessions for *Transformer* at Trident Studios, Reed told him "it was his favorite version that had ever been done on one of his songs," Ezrin remembered.

Much as he liked the texture and intelligence that Bowie and Ronson had brought to *Transformer,* Reed believed that the Velvets albums and his solo work lacked punch. Ezrin's albums, in contrast, hit with real sonic power — Detroit's "Rock and Roll" is crushing — and that's what Reed wanted. For his part, Ezrin "fell in love" with Reed when he saw him perform at Massey Hall in Toronto. Not long afterward, Reed was sitting on the floor at Ezrin's house, playing him some new songs on acoustic guitar. "I just found him blazingly smart and challenging and inspiring," Ezrin said. "There was no question in my mind after spending fifteen minutes talking to him that I wanted to work with him."

For the album, Ezrin drafted a crew of stellar musicians, including keyboardist Steve Winwood, bassist Jack Bruce of Cream, drummers Aynsley Dunbar and Procol Harum's B. J. Wilson, and guitarists Steve Hunter (who played in Detroit) and Dick Wagner, both of whom had done sessions for Alice Cooper. Bassists Tony Levin and Eugene Martynec overdubbed parts later in New York. Ezrin played keyboards as well, and Reed played acoustic guitar. The impeccable pedigree of those players was a mark of Ezrin's ambitions for *Berlin*.

But in many ways, Ezrin and Reed met each other while headed in opposite directions — or, perhaps more accurately, they saw opposite sets of possibilities in each other. If Reed viewed Ezrin as the man who could get him the sound he wanted and, as *Rolling Stone* put it, "do justice to his sledgehammer images," Ezrin saw Reed as the vehicle through which he could realize his own literary and artistic ambitions. Ezrin had "always wanted to be a writer," *Rolling Stone* observed, and he viewed Reed primarily through that lens. "Lou is the best living American writer at this point," Ezrin declared. "He's better than Dylan in many, many ways." Perhaps infected by Ezrin's enthusiasm, the author of that *Rolling Stone* piece, Larry "Ratso" Sloman, insisted,

"It's not an overstatement to say that *Berlin* will be the *Sgt. Pepper* of the seventies."

That was not so much an overstatement as an absurdity, but it was typical of the inflated expectations and artificially charged energy that had been generated around *Berlin*. Industry cheerleader *Billboard* joined in on the hype, declaring *Berlin* "a top-notch set from one of the most creative artists on the pop music scene today....A number of potential singles plus the Lou Reed style make this his most comprehensive LP yet."

Though Reed would never credit the notion, this was the time when the concept album was coming into its full glory—that reference to the Beatles' *Sgt. Pepper's Lonely Hearts Club Band,* the inspiration for so many grandiose experiments to follow, was neither irrelevant nor accidental. Heavy metal and progressive rock were both in full flower (Ezrin, not coincidentally, would go on to coproduce Pink Floyd's *The Wall*), and bands in both genres were drawn, in however adolescent a fashion, to grand metaphysical statements. FM radio, with its album-oriented format, was providing an outlet for more extended, exploratory tracks. Singer-songwriters like Bob Dylan, Joni Mitchell, Paul Simon, and Jackson Browne were writing albums of thematically unified songs that emulated short-story collections. Perhaps most important, Reed believed that, having made an actual hit record, he was finally in a position to do something truly ambitious.

With the expansive context of the concept album in mind, Reed and Ezrin began discussing what Reed might do beyond create another record of individual songs. Ezrin was drawn to the quiet drama of the song "Berlin" on Reed's debut solo album.

IT SEEMS STRANGE THAT, of all Reed's songs, he and Ezrin would have identified the dramatic possibilities inherent in "Berlin." On the *Lou Reed* album the song plays like a sketch, filled with suggestive details but never really culminating in any satisfactory way. But perhaps it was the song's unfinished quality that appealed to them, leaving space for them to fill with their fantasies of what it might become.

The two men decided that Reed should write a suite of musically and thematically connected songs based on the disintegrating marriage of the two characters in "Berlin." That Reed's own marriage to Bettye Kronstad was falling apart would only lend the project additional force. It would be something like a film in song form, a "film for the ear," as RCA's movie-style promotional posters for the album described it, or a "movie without pictures," in Ezrin's terms. Those literary and cinematic strategies also served to distance Reed from the visceral power of the material he was drawing on. "*Berlin* was real close to home," he would say later. "People would say, 'Lou, is that autobiographical?'... Jesus. Autobiographical? If only they knew!"

The working notion was for *Berlin* to be a double album, complete with an elaborate booklet filled with lyrics, accompanying text, and photographs illustrating the record's grim story. Setting aside the darkness of *Berlin's* narrative, record companies shiver whenever the notions of double albums and elaborate booklets are mentioned. They are expensive to produce, and therefore the album needs to be priced higher, which tends to diminish sales. Reed had only just established himself as a commercial artist, so this expansive concept for *Berlin* was by no means an easy sell to his label.

Besides that, according to Kronstad, conceiving what the album should be turned out to be much easier than writing it. "Lou had become abusive on our last U.S. tour, when I got him onto the stage as clean as I could.... He gave me a black eye the second time he hit me," Kronstad wrote. "Then I gave him a black eye, too, and that stopped him from using his fists. Everybody knew he was abusive—abusive with his drinking, his drugs, his emotions—with me. He was incredibly self-destructive then." The problem Reed had finishing the songs for the album, she sarcastically explained, "might have had something to do with all the fucking drugs and drinking he was doing. With

Lou, people that he loves become part of him, so I got to be part of that incredible self-destructiveness."

Things had gotten so bad that Kronstad flew to Santo Domingo to get a twenty-four-hour divorce from Reed. The legal standing of such a divorce is complicated, but Kronstad's action is more significant as an indication of how desperate she had become in her marriage. She was frightened and she wanted out. Kronstad remained in their apartment, on which she held the lease, and Reed moved out. "I don't know where," she said. Then, one night, Reed called her from a local restaurant that had been one of their favorites, the Duck Joint, on First Avenue between Seventy-Third and Seventy-Fourth Streets. "He was, like, 'Can you meet me here?'" Kronstad said. "I was in a pretty good mood because I'd basically gotten my name back and I was no longer legally attached to him. So I went. He was there with two other people; I don't remember who they were. They were having a wonderful time, and he was so positive. . . . He said, 'I've stopped. I've quit it. I won't do that stuff. I'll play it straight. We can do this. I need you. Can I just come over and talk about it?'" Kronstad let herself believe him. "I had invested a great deal of my life in him, so I guess there was a part of me that wanted to be convinced."

But even when Reed finally did complete writing the album's ten songs, things didn't get easier. "I remember the morning I woke up and found Lewis in the living room next to a mostly consumed bottle of Johnnie Walker Red," she wrote. "It was eight thirty in the morning and I became upset. His drinking didn't usually begin until at least the afternoon." Reed explained that he had completed writing the album. He handed her his notebook with the lyrics in it, picked up a guitar, and sang the songs he had written.

The songs on *Berlin* trace the disintegration of a couple, Caroline and Jim, through infidelity, violence, and suicide. Caroline is portrayed as unfaithful and promiscuous; Jim swings from yearning for her to icy contempt and malevolence. He beats her and, in the song "The Bed," describes her cutting her wrists and her subsequent death with a truly eerie detachment. The album is tough going for even the most aesthetically objective listener. For Kronstad, listening to it was a devastating experience. Scenes from her marriage and other details of her personal life are woven into the songs. Even when treated as composites or fictionalized in other ways, they were clearly identifiable to her and hit with intense force. It's hard to imagine why Reed would have chosen to play her those songs without any explanation, and even harder to fathom how he expected her to respond.

Kronstad's mother, who had been living in Queens, had recently died. At five years old, Kronstad had been taken from the woman, who had left Kronstad's father when the girl was three. Reed adapted that story and wildly elaborated on it for his *Berlin* song "The Kids." Kronstad had attempted to reconcile with her mother at various points over the years, never completely successfully, so hearing a character based on her mother essentially described as a bisexual whore and drug addict in a song written by her husband was quite a blow.

"The other thing," she added, "is that he was actually writing a lot about what was happening in our relationship. That's what writers do. But who wants their marriage as it's falling apart to be put on an album for the entire world to hear? Or who wants the couple of times that he fucking socked me—who wants that? But there it was."

Kronstad understood, of course, that *Berlin* was not exclusively about her marriage. Talking about the character of Caroline, she noted, "I think Nico is in there. Lou did know her and she was German....Someone once said that the woman in *Berlin* is a combination of all the women in Lou's life, and I think to a certain extent that's true." Despite being hurt, Kronstad remained determined to see her husband through the recording of the album, which was primarily done at Morgan Studios in London.

At the time he wrote the title song and even when he started work on the album, Reed had never been to

Berlin. "I love the idea of a divided city," he later explained, joking that the album could just as easily have been titled *Brooklyn,* tellingly the place of his birth. "It was purely metaphorical." Kronstad's memory of her conversations with Reed support that view. The wall, he told her, represented "what's going on in this relationship between these two people." Berlin, of course, loomed large historically and culturally during the Cold War years of Reed's youth. In the late forties, it was one of the confrontational flash points between the Soviet Union and the West, and in 1963 the city was the site of the dramatic *"Ich bin ein Berliner"* speech by President John F. Kennedy, one of Reed's heroes. The city's divided soul and the absence of a clear identity lent it a morally ambiguous air, a place where black markets, international intrigue, drug trade, and underground activities of all kinds could thrive. The present was tense, the past a horror show, and the future unknowable and potentially frightening. Berlin provided Reed with a different but equally compelling imaginative urban landscape, one with little of the knowing swagger of New York, and one that was more European and weighed down by history. All this made for an album that lacked the note of stoic cheer and upbeat determination that can be heard in even his grimmest New York stories.

Reed's approach to his lyrics and melody writing

on the album was strong and spare. "*Berlin* needed a lyrical approach that was direct," Reed explained. "There could be no mistaking it, no head games. You didn't have to be high to figure out what was happening, or be super hip or anything. It was to the point, whereas some of my other albums and songs had puns or double entendres. In other words, the difference would be, in 'Heroin' I wrote, 'It makes me feel like Jesus's son.' Now, if the Berlin guy had said that, he'd say, 'I take heroin.' That's the difference.... He's consistently saying very short, straight, to-the-point, unmissable things."

Ezrin described Reed's lyrics on *Berlin* as "just magnificent, visceral, elemental writing.... That's Lou. Unadorned but romantic to his core. He found a way to take the reality of the street and make it beautiful." But despite his passion for the material, for Ezrin the album was "a nightmare to make," not least because the self-described "simple Canadian boy" found himself completely out of his element in Reed's decadent scene.

"Keep in mind," said Ezrin, "that with Alice Cooper, I was dealing with a bunch of regular guys who happened to wear makeup when they went onstage. Essentially their lifestyle was very all-American. They were really just hamburger and TV guys, so I understood them.... Lou, on the other hand, was an artist with a capital *A*. His milieu included some of the most cutting-edge and eclectic artists of the time, and their whole approach to everything—from their art to their living—was foreign to me and somewhat scary. That made it tough, and then, when you add to that the fact that many of us were experimenting with drugs...it was disorienting, challenging, and ultimately frightening."

Ezrin was even more direct in another interview. "It drove me literally crazy," he said of making *Berlin*. "I was put away for a little time because I couldn't control myself. I got home and started breaking things, and I've never done something like that before in my life! That album just had me so taut inside."

Berlin was released in July of 1973, just eight months after *Transformer*. A week before the final version of the album was due to be turned in (Reed was on vacation in Portugal at the time), RCA told Ezrin that it would not accept a double album. The album was nearly an hour long, and at the time, artists were encouraged to keep each side of a vinyl LP at eighteen to twenty minutes in order to ensure sound quality. To preserve the conceptual integrity of *Berlin,* Ezrin did not want to remove any of the album's songs. Consequently, he explained, "I dropped fourteen minutes of endings, solos, interstitial material, digressions inside songs." The process nearly killed him. *Rolling Stone* described him as looking "wasted" as he attempted to complete work on the album, the result of "having put in fourteen to twenty hours a day for the last few months." As Ezrin completed a mix of "Men of Good Fortune," he screamed, "Awright, wrap up this turkey before I puke."

Along with the A-list players he had recruited, Ezrin ladled horns and strings onto the album, plus mellotron and a choir, touches that, once again, were unusual for a Lou Reed project and meant to suggest the seriousness of the record's intent. (Interestingly, Ezrin would later use some of those identical parts on seminal Pink Floyd tracks he produced: the strings on "Sad Song" for Floyd's "Comfortably Numb" and a woodwind part from "Caroline Says I" for *The Wall*.) On "The Kids," the song about Caroline's children being taken from her, Ezrin recorded the wails of his own children to scarifying effect. To get his kids to participate, Ezrin told his seven-year-old son, David, that he was doing a play in the studio and he needed some kids' voices to sound scared because their mom was being taken away. The first few attempts didn't sound terrifying enough, but on the third, unprompted, his two-year-old joined in and started screaming. The two children screamed so loud that they distorted the tape. Ezrin further compressed it in the studio. He found that "the more compressed it got, the more anguished it seemed. Most people can't listen to it."

Still, the album was nearly fifty minutes long, but Ezrin was not available to oversee the final mastering of *Berlin*. He was in the hospital. "It was a heroin rebound," he admitted. "I would rather have had a nervous breakdown. I didn't know what heroin was till I went to England on this gig.... We were all seriously ill. It took me a long time to get on my feet. I paid a heavy price. It put me out of commission for quite a while."

Berlin took its toll on Reed as well. "Lou doesn't want to talk about it much," Ezrin said about the album not long after it came out. "He didn't even want to listen to the album. Every time he listens to the album it gets to him. I mean, I can see tears coming into his eyes and everything." Reed himself said, "I think I've gone as deep as I want to go for my own mental health. If I got any deeper I'd wind up disappearing."

For all that, reviews of *Berlin* were mixed at best. In his *Village Voice* column Consumer Guide, Robert Christgau blithely dismissed as "horseshit" the argument that, while depressing and unlikable, *Berlin* was an "artistic accomplishment." Invited to "review" the album in a conversation in *Phonograph Record,* David Johansen, then the lead singer for the New York Dolls, said, "I know why he called it *Berlin*. Because if you called it *Seattle,* or *New York,* or *Cleveland,* you couldn't write a story about it, because everybody would know what you were talking about, and you couldn't convince them you were talking about something when in actuality you weren't talking about anything. But if you give an American kid a flash like 'Berlin,' that's something very exotic to him, and you can say anything to him because he's never been to Berlin, and he won't know you're bullshitting him."

In later years, after the album was acknowledged as a classic, Reed loved to revel in the negative reviews it had received—and, admittedly, some of them were not only harsh but gratuitously personal. Even some of the positive assessments of *Berlin* seemed indistinguishable from attacks. Writing in *New Musical Express,* inveterate Reed watcher Nick Kent declared, "Just when you think your ex-idol has slumped into a pitiful display of gross terminal self-parody, Lou Reed comes back and hits you with something like *Berlin*. It's a creation which leaves you so aesthetically bamboozled you just have to step down and allow him a brand-new artistic credibility for pulling off such a coup in the first place." Perhaps the most scathing negative review appeared in *Rolling Stone,* written by Stephen Davis, who, ironically, would go on to chronicle the salacious on-the-road depredations of Led Zeppelin in his gleefully unauthorized 1985 biography of the band, *Hammer of the Gods*. "Lou Reed's *Berlin*," Davis's review began, "is a disaster, taking the listener into a distorted and degenerate demimonde of paranoia, schizophrenia, degradation, pill-induced violence, and suicide.

There are certain records that are so patently offensive that one wishes to take some kind of physical vengeance on the artists that perpetrate them." He concluded that *Berlin* was Reed's "last shot at a once-promising career. Goodbye, Lou."

A review like that would sour anyone on critics — not that Reed needed any convincing in that regard. "It's one of the worst reviews I've ever seen of anything," Reed said. "I got one paragraph saying I should be physically punished for putting out the album." Characteristically, Reed chose to overlook reviews such as John Rockwell's in the Sunday *New York Times*, which began, "Strikingly and unexpectedly, Lou Reed's *Berlin* is one of the strongest, most original rock records in years." In an informed, authoritative manner, Rockwell covered what would become Reed's own talking points about *Berlin* in subsequent decades. He cited Brecht and Weill, called Reed "a poetic artist who creates unified statements through the medium of the rock record," and described *Berlin* as both "cinematic and operatic." With *Berlin,* Rockwell concluded, Reed "has proven conclusively that he must be counted as one of the most important figures in contemporary rock."

Rockwell wasn't alone. *Circus* called *Berlin* "the most affecting rock effort in recent memory." Even *Rolling Stone,* in a review of Reed's next album four months later, found occasion to counterpoint Stephen Davis's negative review of *Berlin*. Critic Timothy Ferris quoted the lines in Davis's review about Reed chronicling a "degenerate demimonde," and agreed with them. "But I fail to see how that makes it a bad record," he continued. "*Berlin* is bitter, uncompromising, and one of the most fully realized concept albums. Prettiness has nothing to do with art, nor does good taste, good manners, or good morals. Reed is one of the handful of serious artists working in popular music today, and you'd think by now people would stop preaching at him."

Speaking about *Berlin,* Reed would articulate a rationale for his brand of songwriting, and, indeed, for all art that defies accepted pieties. In fact, his argument goes well beyond that. It constitutes a lesson in how to engage art—and how not to. "I don't think anybody is anybody else's moral compass," he said. "Maybe listening to my music is not the best idea if you live a very constricted life. Or maybe it is. I'm writing about real things. Real people. Real characters. You have to believe what I write about is true or you wouldn't pay any attention at all....But a guide to doing things that are wrong and right? I mean, Othello murders Desdemona. Is that a guide to what you can do? The guy in *Berlin* beats up his girlfriend. Is that a guide to what you can do? Is that what you walk away with? I don't think so. Maybe they should sticker my albums and say, 'Stay away if you have no moral compass.'"

It's hard to imagine a more cogent justification not just of *Berlin,* but of Reed's songwriting as a whole. *Rolling Stone* would eventually list *Berlin* among the five hundred greatest albums of all time.

9

ROCK N ROLL ANIMAL

THAT WAS THE BAD move," Lou Reed said jokingly decades later about following *Transformer* with *Berlin*. "That's one of those career-ending moments. They said, 'You want to do *what?*'"

Whether or not it was a "bad move," following a successful album with a dramatic, experimental left turn would be the rhythm that Reed would ride throughout the seventies. He then followed each left turn with an effort to restore the faith of the marketplace and his more mainstream fans with more accessible music. Often, Reed would then pivot again, disowning or disparaging the success such efforts had brought him, as he did with *Transformer* and "Walk on the Wild Side," and ardently defending the more extreme work he had labored so hard to distance himself from.

Part of that pattern could simply be attributed to Reed's contrarianism, his refusal, for complicated and at times contradictory reasons, to be entrapped by what he viewed as the opinions, desires, and expectations of others. Nor is he the only artist among his peers to move in such cycles. Bob Dylan and Neil Young, to cite just two examples, immediately come to mind. Reed's audience had by no means fully solidified in 1973, and even at its height, his following would never reach the sheer numbers of either Dylan's or Young's. In the seventies, his movement in and out of the mainstream seemed driven as much by a fear of success and acceptance as by any aesthetic motivation.

It's tempting—and perhaps accurate—to read that reluctance as, in part, a reaction to his father's wishes for his son's conventional success. For Reed, anything that resembled social acceptance and approval was tainted by that parental association and needed to be cast off. Not that success had lost any of its allure for Reed. His ambivalent feelings did nothing to diminish his desire for stardom and recognition, the result, perhaps, of his mother's bottomless adoration for him. The war between those two competing drives—to reject success and to court it—would rage within him for years, and fuel the addictions that would nearly kill him. He would seesaw precariously between them until he had attained a personalized version of success that allowed him simultaneously to be revered and to be perceived as representing the very epitome of rebellion. That tension within him never fully dissipated, but it would eventually ease enough that he would not need to put his life at risk in order to numb it.

DESPITE REED'S PERCEPTION OF the album as a "career-ending" moment, *Berlin* was no such thing. But it also did not live up to the commercial expectations that *Transformer* had created. Though it was a Top 10 album in the UK, it barely grazed the Top 100 in the United States, peaking at ninety-eight. That was not exactly what RCA had in mind, particularly with hit maker Bob Ezrin handling production. Ezrin, for his part, was philosophical about *Berlin's* fate. "The expectation was that I was going to do something very commercial with him," he said. "Sort of Alice Cooper–ish, real mainstream. In reality, I had become mesmerized by the poetry and by the art of Lou. Maybe I lost sight of my mandate. Honestly, I can look back and say I probably didn't do what I was hired to do."

Finally, *Berlin* "didn't have a radio-friendly single," Ezrin noted, "so it never got the exposure that it should have had.... The truth is, we might have had to sacrifice on the artistic side to get that exposure in a way that maybe we would've regretted later on. It's very hard to go back and say what one would've done, or what one should've done, but I'm entirely satisfied with that album. I think it's one of the best and most complete pieces of work I've ever been involved with." Reed, of course, dismissed the controversy over the album as the result of critical philistinism. The attacks, he said, were "not for good reasons"; they came only because it was a rock-and-roll record. "I've said this over and over again," he emphasized, "but if it was a novel, it wouldn't have been a big deal."

One of the people who most feared that *Berlin* might mark the end of Lou Reed's career was Dennis Katz, his manager. Katz was a lawyer who had worked in the A&R department at RCA before he edged Fred Heller out and took over his role. It was an incestuous affair all around and culminated in a string of costly lawsuits. Heller had been managing Blood, Sweat, and Tears when he took Reed on as a client. Dennis's brother, Steve Katz, was the guitarist and a founding member of the group. Heller had lined up the unlikely touring band Reed had been performing with since he had begun playing gigs in England at around the time he began working on *Transformer:* a rough-and-tumble rock-and-roll quartet from Yonkers, New York, known as the Tots. Heller found them through the band's bass player, Bobby Resigno, who ran errands for the Blood, Sweat, and Tears office in Dobbs Ferry, New York, not far from Yonkers. Resigno, for his part, got that gofer job because his girlfriend babysat for Dave Bargeron, a horn player for Blood, Sweat, and Tears.

When Reed began looking for a band, Heller took him to Yonkers to hear Resigno's group, which also included guitarists Vinnie Laporta and Eddie Reynolds and drummer Scottie Clark. Still in their teens or barely out of them, the band members rehearsed in the basement of Resigno's parents' home in Yonkers. They were hardly devoted Lou Reed fans. "I had heard of Lou because some of my friends were really into dope pretty early and they were into the Velvet Underground," Reynolds said. "So I was familiar with him and knew that he was due respect.... Next thing you know, Bobby's mom answered the door, and she led Lou down to the basement to listen to us."

It might seem ridiculous that Reed would attempt to recruit a barely adult band of suburban unknowns for his first major solo shows after the breakup of the Velvet Underground—and perhaps it was. But a youthful band, free of history and emotional baggage, had its attractions for Reed. In 1972 he had turned thirty, a frightening prospect for anyone playing rock and roll at the time. Proud as he was of the body of work that the Velvet Underground had created, he felt burdened by the band's legend; an anonymous backup group would help wipe the slate clean. Equally important, the band's youthful eagerness and pliability would only reaffirm his standing as the outfit's undisputed leader. After his disagreements with John Cale, Reed had no interest in debating strategy and musical direction with a band of experienced, first-rate players.

Nor, for the most part, was he in any condition to. When he arrived in Yonkers, Reed was hardly in tip-top shape. "As far as I was concerned, he looked like he was stoned on something," Reynolds recalled. For their audition, the band played some original songs that Reynolds had written. The Allman Brothers' live album *At Fillmore East* had come out just the year before, and Laporta and Reynolds modeled much of their playing on the twin-guitar attack of Duane Allman and Dickey Betts. That elaborate style of playing might sound preposterous in a band hoping to back Lou Reed, but while critics and fans might have loved the primitivism of the Velvet Underground, Reed did not. The aspirations of this literal basement band would have made perfect sense to him.

After Reed listened for a while with Heller, Reynolds said, "Lou picked up his guitar and tried a couple of songs with us. We tried to do a lot of that harmony stuff like the Allman Brothers, and that perked Lou's ears. . . . I guess they left with good enough feelings for us to think that maybe it went all right. A month later, we went to England."

The Tots supported Reed on tour in the UK, Europe, and the United States in 1972 and 1973, including the shows at Alice Tully Hall. Reviews of their playing were mixed. These shows were the first appearances by Reed since the breakup of the Velvet Underground, and anyone who showed up anticipating the Velvets' cool, boundary-shattering, avant-garde detachment was going to be sorely disappointed. The Tots were young, sloppy, excited, and energetic; as far as they were concerned, Reed was a rock-and-roll star, and their job was to play his music with as much energy as they could muster. Reviewers who understood that, as Ed McCormack did when he wrote about the second Alice Tully Hall show for *Rolling Stone,* enjoyed and appreciated the band. Others didn't get it.

For his part, Reynolds believed that more showmanship improved the performances — the band's and Reed's. "I had read stuff about Lou being the American Mick Jagger and all that," Reynolds said. "There were a couple of shows where he would really get into it and start dancing, and I could feel the energy."

At other times, the Tots found themselves having to compensate for Reed's lack of energy — and for the condition in which he frequently went onstage. "There would be a bottle of Johnnie Walker Black and a bottle of Johnnie Walker Red," Reynolds recalled, "and if we didn't watch Lou, he would sit there and get bombed before a show." The Tots learned to recognize the "vacant stare he had sometimes," taking it as a cue to help their leader onstage. Reynolds remembered a night when Lou's playing was so off that "one of the roadies had to take his cords out from the bottom of the amp so that he would be deleted from the sound system." After a 1973 show in Detroit, Reed, "looking even more wasted" than usual, chided a group of journalists hanging out at his hotel. "I know why you're all here," he said. "[You] just want to get a headline story—'Lou Reed OD's in Holiday Inn'—don't you?" He walked away laughing.

Some of Reed's other character traits, both negative and positive, were evident to the band as well. Reed could be sweet with his younger bandmates, taking the role of intellectual mentor that he would enjoy playing at various times in his life. But he could also be rude, especially when he'd been drinking, and he had a tendency to lash out unexpectedly. Reynolds remembered the night at the Santa Monica Civic Auditorium in April of 1973 when he broke a D string during the concert's opening number, "Sweet Jane." When the band got backstage after the show, Lou was furious. "He ripped me a new one.... Iggy Pop was standing there watching the whole thing. I felt so bad because it was in front of Iggy."

By the time Reed finished recording *Berlin* and was preparing to tour again, he and Bob Ezrin had a new vision for his music, and the Tots weren't part of it. Reed handled the situation gracefully in Reynolds's opinion, personally sitting down with the band in Dennis Katz's Manhattan office. "I think it did bother him," Reynolds recalled. "He said that we should go on as a band, and that we'd be great. Just by him saying that actually made me feel good about getting fired. He knew how young we were and how much it could possibly hurt us."

WITH THEIR ENTHUSIASM, THE Tots had helped restore Reed's confidence and got him back out on the road. He now believed he could front a band that was older and more experienced and still maintain control. Ezrin was encouraging in that regard. For Reed's touring band, he drafted guitarists Steve Hunter and Dick Wagner, along with keyboardist Ray Colcord and Toronto musicians Prakash John on bass and Pentti Glan on drums. Reed rehearsed the band in the Berkshires at the end of August of 1973. On September 1, Reed and the group played their first gig at the Music Inn in Stockbridge, Massachusetts. Then it was off to Europe for dates that ran into early October.

By the time the North American tour launched at the end of November at Toronto's Massey Hall, Reed was clearly enjoying the muscularity of his new band. Hunter and Wagner, like the Tots but with far more majesty and discipline, employed the sort of twin-guitar attack that had been established by the Allman Brothers and that would become one of the signature sounds of the seventies for bands like the Eagles. For "Sweet Jane," the song that opened the band's sets, the two guitarists had orchestrated — Hunter actually received a writing credit for it — a grand three-minute-plus introduction that was classical in its aspirations. The instrumental section continues for another thirty seconds once the classic "Sweet Jane" riff kicks in, and then Reed enters. Whatever its relationship to the original song, it was a dramatic buildup to Reed's arrival onstage. Reed's charming portrait of a young couple celebrating their love and their kinks with everyday naturalness got transformed into a massive sonic statement.

Reed didn't play guitar onstage; the stylized grandeur of Hunter and Wagner's playing did not at all suit his rawer, less technically proficient style, and he did not feel as if he could play with them. Instead, he poured all his energies into the role of front man and lead singer, which gave him a chance to emphasize his lyrics. "I don't think I'm a singer, with or without a guitar," he said. "I give dramatic readings that are almost my tunes." He changed his look as well. His Jewfro was gone, replaced by a close-cropped near crew cut that mimicked the crisp, cleaned-up look that was becoming fashionable in gay hotbeds like Christopher Street and the West Village docks. (Not long afterward, Reed would dye Iron Crosses into his hair.) He lost weight, looked wiry and spindle thin, and sported a black muscle shirt, black leather pants, a dog collar, and studded black leather cuffs. His movements onstage were jagged and theatrical, and the entire presentation, from its S and M allusions to its guitar pyrotechnics, went over extremely well with audiences. (In a charmingly sentimental move, Reed handpicked the Persuasions, a gospel a cappella group from Brooklyn, to serve as the opening act on most of his UK dates.) By the time the tour got to the Academy of Music on Fourteenth Street in New York, a decision had been made to record the two shows for release as a live album. This would be the antidote to *Berlin*.

Coproduced by Reed and Steve Katz of Blood, Sweat, and Tears and released in February of 1974, the album was titled *Rock n Roll Animal,* and as it was intended to do, it instantly reversed whatever PR damage *Berlin* had done. The cover showed a close-up shot of Reed midperformance, his lips and eyes blackened with makeup and his hands above his head as if he were bound. The promotional campaign for the album featured a black-and-white photo of Reed crouching onstage, with text that read, "After you buy the album, open the jacket and make sure there's a record inside. The 'Rock n Roll Animal' is a bitch to contain." The gender tease caught the tenor of the times in a playful way that even the most mainstream music fan could get a kick out of: Reed, somehow, was both a threatening, butch "rock n roll animal" and a bitch.

The stylized S and M titillation of *Rock n Roll Animal*'s presentation was much easier for fans—and, interestingly enough, most critics—to take than the far more emotionally charged provocations of *Berlin*. Writing in *Zoo World,* critic Wayne Robins opened his review of *Rock n Roll Animal* by arguing, "It's just like Lou Reed to follow the worst album by a major artist in 1973 (*Berlin*) with what might be his best album since the watershed *Loaded*." Robert Christgau awarded the album an A minus and declared, "Reed's live music brings the Velvets into the arena in a clean redefinition of heavy, thrilling without threatening to stupefy.... This is a live album with a reason for living." Writing about the Academy of Music concerts that the album documented, critic Paul Nelson lavished praise on Reed's new backing band, comparing the "mediocre pickup band at Lincoln Center some months earlier" (the Tots) to the new group's "spectacular, even majestic, rock and roll," and calling guitarists Dick Wagner and Steve Hunter "awesome enough so that if Reed were merely competent, the concert would be a success."

The references to the Velvet Underground and specifically to *Loaded* in those reviews were not coincidental. *Rock n Roll Animal* consisted of five songs, four of which were Velvet Underground classics ("Sweet Jane," "Heroin," "White Light/White Heat," "Rock and Roll"), and two of which ("Sweet Jane" and "Rock and Roll") had appeared on *Loaded*. That was a conscious strategy. As the blockbuster age of the music industry was starting to take shape in the seventies, the Velvet Underground, a cult band if there ever was one, was beginning to disappear from view, and Reed did not want that to happen.

Still, reshaping Velvets classics with his new band was a controversial move. Not everyone was as enamored of the new versions as some critics were. The thirteen-minute version of "Heroin" and the ten-minute version of "Rock and Roll," filled with long guitar excursions and elaborate arrangements, overwhelmed the originals and perhaps erased their meaning as well. Eddie Reynolds of the Tots had plenty of reasons to find fault with Reed's new band, but his simple critique is on the money: "I think they got in the way of Lou too much." Reynolds added that his musician friends, who typically had no use for Reed or the Velvet Underground, made an exception for *Rock n Roll Animal* because of the technical prowess of the players. Was that really how Reed wanted those songs to be remembered?

On the other hand, the musical quality, singled out for praise by Paul Nelson and others, meant something important as rock and roll began to be professionalized in the seventies. Despite, or perhaps because of, its length, the elaborate rendition of "Sweet Jane" on *Rock n Roll Animal* became a staple of the then-burgeoning FM radio format. That song and "Rock and Roll" had provided the Velvets with their greatest radio exposure when *Loaded* came out in 1970. Now Reed could enjoy the increased visibility that radio play would provide, and also reach an audience of mainstream rock fans that extended well beyond Velvets stalwarts—something he very much longed for, despite his protests to the contrary. Having tried to distance himself from the Velvet Underground in order to establish his solo career, Reed was now in a position where it was both savvy and necessary to do the opposite. *Berlin* faded from view and, for his audience, *Rock n Roll Animal* became the follow-up to *Transformer* that should have been. It adhered to the classic pop formula for success, sounding at once familiar and fresh. The album made such an impact that six additional tracks from the Academy of Music shows were gathered together and released a year later as *Lou Reed Live,* once again to a positive reception.

Characteristically, Reed disowned *Rock n Roll Animal* as soon as it accomplished what he set out for it to do. "It was the only thing to do at the time," he said, nearly apologizing for the album in an interview with Lenny Kaye. "I wanted to get the Velvets stuff known. That's what I was doing." As for the blustering, extended version of "Heroin," Reed said, "It's just desecrated.

It's so blasphemous that it's horrifying.... I understand why people like 'Heroin' on *Rock n Roll Animal,* but it almost killed me. It was so awful." Of course, thirty years later, he would casually remark of *Rock n Roll Animal,* "A lot of people, myself included, consider it one of the greatest live albums ever. Other than James Brown *Live at the Apollo,* nothing's even close."

Hunter, naturally, had his own views about what he termed "that macabre...ah, majestic" treatment of "Heroin," which he arranged, and about working with Reed in general. "He wanted to do it the old way originally," he said of Reed's feeling about "Heroin," adding, "See, Lou is another one with a problem. He'd start shooting up and just get...uh, illogical, I guess." As for why he and Wagner chose to work with Reed, Hunter just shrugged and said, "It's a living."

REED AND KATZ'S STRATEGY of getting the Velvets' stuff known worked. With Reed reestablished as a commercial force and "Sweet Jane" and "Rock and Roll" on the FM airwaves, the Velvets' legacy came to the cultural foreground once again. Both John Cale and Nico (with Cale producing her albums) had launched solo careers that, while far from commercial triumphs, were distinguished by important, well-received work, and this also helped keep the Velvets' music and reputation alive. Reed understood this and was generous to his former colleagues at around that time. The albums that Cale produced for Nico were, Reed said, "so incredible, the most incredible albums ever made." He noted that "people think that me and Nico and John don't get along, that we fight all the time. Of course we fight. Like cats and dogs. But it's one thing if we fight, and another if somebody said something bad about John or Nico. I'd kill 'em. I'm the only one allowed to say something bad about John or Nico, and vice versa."

Riding the momentum of *Rock n Roll Animal*'s success, in September of 1974 Mercury Records released a double LP titled *1969: The Velvet Underground Live*. It included virtually all the Velvets' best-known songs, culled from performances at a club in Dallas called the End of Cole Avenue on October 19, 1969, and at the Matrix in San Francisco on November 26 and 27 of that same year—a period when the Velvets had been road-hardened and were in top form.

The album was compiled by Paul Nelson, a prominent rock critic, most notably for *Rolling Stone,* who at the time worked in the A&R department at Mercury. As a music writer—and, pointedly, unlike the vast majority of record executives—Nelson understood the Velvets completely and made smart song choices. Not that getting Mercury to put out *1969* was by any means a foregone conclusion. In a piece that was not published until after his 2006 death, Nelson described making the case for a Velvet Underground double album to the Mercury brass this way: "When I made my pitch at an A&R meeting, I got almost nothing back but glazed incomprehension. Suddenly, it dawned on me that practically none of these people knew who the Velvet Underground were. When I mentioned Lou Reed, a slight light went on in a few more pairs of eyes. I talked and talked and talked and finally won the day. We got a double album...for twenty thousand dollars." Nelson's description perfectly captures the state of awareness and appreciation of the Velvet Underground and even Lou Reed in the mainstream music industry at that time. Even after *1969* came out, Mercury's president would routinely confuse the Velvet Underground with Deep Purple.

1969 did not sell well, but it served as a superb document of the group's power onstage for listeners who had never had the opportunity to see them. The album opens with Reed, who is clearly in an affable mood, teasing the Dallas audience before the start of the band's Sunday night set. "Do you people have a curfew or anything like that?" he asked, since many colleges did at the time. Having determined after chatting with the crowd that the band would do one long set rather than two shorter ones, Reed encouraged the audience to "settle back. Pull up your cushions—or whatever else you have with you"—studied pause—"that makes life bearable in Texas." The audience groaned good-naturedly—why would you be at a Velvet Underground show if you didn't expect some attitude?—and Reed laughed. Then, a master showman, Reed combined his unlikely love of football with his stage sense to smooth the edges of his New York condescension. "We saw your Cowboys today and they never let Philadelphia even have the ball for a minute," he said, clearly having watched the Dallas Cowboys crush the Philadelphia Eagles that afternoon by a score of 49–14. "It was ridiculous. You should give other people just a little chance"—another perfectly timed pause—"in football, anyway."

Tracks that the Velvets had never released ("Over You" and "Sweet Bonnie Brown/It's Just Too Much" among them) made *1969* feel like a new album, while Velvets classics, including "Heroin" and "Pale Blue Eyes," solidified the core of the band's legacy. In those days before infinite Internet access, *1969* became a talisman, passed among fans and potential fans one to another, turning on new Velvets devotees one person at a time. By the midseventies, unless you lived in a major city with sophisticated record shops that stocked more than the hits of the day, even the Velvets' four officially released albums (not to mention the curiosity *Live at Max's Kansas City*) were difficult to find.

To that extent, *1969* was a godsend, one whose impact, like that of the Velvet Underground itself, would only truly be felt over time. Even the notoriously difficult to please Reed loved it. When Nelson gave Reed dubs of the record he had put together, Reed "couldn't wait to hear them," Nelson recalled. " 'I've got to hear "Ocean," ' he said. 'I remember the night we played it. I thought it was one of the best things we'd ever done. What side is it on?' I told him, and we listened to 'Ocean' over and over."

Reed also loved the liner notes for *1969*, written by singer-songwriter Elliott Murphy, who greatly admired Reed and the Velvet Underground. "The Velvet Underground must have scared a lot of people," Murphy wrote. "What goes through a mother's mind when she asks her fifteen-year-old daughter 'What's the name of that song you're listening to?' and her daughter replies, 'Heroin.' . . . I hope someday they'll teach rock-and-roll history. I hope that the music on this album is among the more important elements of that class. I hope parents will still get scared when they find their daughter listening to this music."

The notion of his songs being taught in a music history class and still retaining enough subversive power to frighten listeners certainly would have appealed to Reed's literary ambitions. In fact, Reed was so struck by what Murphy had written that he asked Nelson to give him Murphy's telephone number so he could contact him personally. Nelson did, except he did not provide Reed with the current number. Consequently, when Murphy next visited his mother, she told him that "this very nice boy Lewis Reed called."

AS ALL THIS WAS happening, things went awry for the final time in Reed's marriage to Bettye Kronstad. Once *Berlin* was released in July of 1973, Kronstad believed that her wifely duties were done. Through his behavior, Reed helped her along in that decision. He played a show in London with his new band on September 15, 1973, and that marked an end point for Kronstad. "After the show, all these people came over, and there was all this drinking, and I have no idea what was going on with the drugging thing," she said. "Lou was belligerent. Physically belligerent. So he hadn't changed. . . . I didn't like the way he was treating me. I was hurt. So I said to myself, I'm out. I did try. But it's not working. That's what I said to him: we tried. It's not working. I'm out."

Two days later, on September 17, 1973, Reed head-lined the Olympia theater in Paris, and Kronstad made her escape. Just before she and Reed were set to leave their hotel for the theater, she took off after leaving a message for Dennis Katz that she needed a plane ticket back to New York. "While everyone else was at the show, I wandered around the city in the rain, crying, until a Parisian policeman stopped me under the Arc de Triomphe and told me I should go back to my hotel and get some sleep," she wrote. "I was twenty-four years old." Her departure, predictably, had a damaging impact on Reed. He would collapse onstage five days later, forcing a show in Brussels to be canceled. Another show, in Manchester, would be cut short three days later.

When Kronstad returned to New York, she got a new apartment, in the East Sixties, and resumed her acting career. She worked with William Esper, a now legendary acting teacher who had trained with Sanford Meisner at the Neighborhood Playhouse School of the Theater on East Fifty-Fourth Street, where Kronstad had studied for a year after leaving Columbia. The community of actors provided a social life for her until the spring term ended. "Then things calmed down," she said. "It was summer, and everybody either went back home or on vacation. I was pretty much on my own, because the people who had been friends of Lou's didn't continue to stay friends with me. I wasn't the star. He was the star, so that was the most logical and interesting place for them to go. I couldn't go anywhere I used to go because he would be there with his friends."

One significant member of Reed's circle did get in touch with Kronstad. "I got a message from Dr. Feelgood," she said, referring, of course, to Dr. Robert Freymann. "He actually called me, God himself called me, and said, 'Look, I'm calling on Lou's behalf. Lou needs you. He wants you back.' I don't know exactly how I answered him, but to myself I said, 'No. I can't.'"

Her class with William Esper had managed to stave the emotional devastation of her divorce, but once that was done, it hit her full force. In order to try to restore herself, Kronstad traveled to Richmond, Virginia, to spend time near her Uncle Babe, her father's youngest brother. Babe, who had served in Korea, had been a Marine training sergeant specializing in underwater demolition. Rendered quadriplegic in a tragic accident, he now resided in a veterans' hospital. Kronstad had phoned him and explained that she was depressed and had no clear sense of what next steps to take. He had always tried to look after her at important transitional moments in her life, and this time was no different. "He said, 'Kid, put your stuff in storage and come down here and let me talk to you,'" Kronstad recalled. "So that's what I did, and he put me back together."

During their meetings, she chronicled, among many other things, the dissolution of her marriage to Reed. It's difficult to imagine what a quadriplegic former Marine from a small town in western Pennsylvania could possibly have thought about his niece's experiences with the bisexual, drug-addled, Jewish inventor of avant-garde rock, but Babe listened patiently and seemed less interested in judging her life than in trying to understand and helping her to move forward with it.

As part of that effort, he wanted to hear *Berlin*. Kronstad's copy was in storage, and in any event, she told her uncle, "Babe, you don't want to hear that album." He simply responded, "Yes, I do. I want to know what you went through." She visited a local record store, found the album, brought it to the counter, and began to write out a check to pay for it. "I swear I'm not making this up," Kronstad said. "As I was writing the check, the guy behind the counter said to me, 'Are you sure you want this album? This is the most depressing album in the world. People are returning it.' And here he was talking to *me!* I didn't say anything. I just kept writing the check."

She then played it for her uncle. "He was very quiet. And when he's very quiet, he's very angry. Very upset. He just said, 'You know, kid, this is what happens when you don't take care of yourself, because no one is going to take care of you in life but you. So learn from it. Learn from it.' And he's right, isn't he?"

Kronstad never made an effort to reestablish contact with Reed after their divorce, nor did she follow his subsequent career with much beyond a cursory interest. Of the time she spent on the road with Reed, playing nursemaid and helpmate, she said, "Bob Dylan's girlfriend Suze Rotolo had the best line about that sort of life. She said that the girlfriend of a rock star isn't really there. It was awful how people treated you, just awful."

After Kronstad remarried, her testimony was subpoenaed in a lawsuit that Reed had filed against a former manager. "I had to testify that Lou was of sound mind during the time he was with me, and so I did," she said. "I said he wasn't more drunk or disorderly than anybody else during that time.... Then, of course, the manager's lawyer said to me, 'Well, in fact, wasn't there a time when you were so drunk and drugged out yourself that you fell off an escalator and someone had to pick you up?' Anything they could find to discredit me and my testimony. I said, 'Yeah, but that had to do with the seven-inch, fuck-me platform heels I was wearing, and my heel got caught in one of the treads of the escalator.' That's actually what happened. But again, I was being attacked. Whatever joy Lou brought me, there was an equal amount of pain."

Until his death, Kronstad rarely spoke about her marriage to Reed, even privately. After that, she felt that it was important to get her side of the story out, to help shape the narrative rather than simply be a character in other people's versions of it. Part of her initial silence was an innate desire for privacy. Part was an urge to move her life forward and not get caught up in the impossible-to-replicate glamour or luridness of those years. And part was an understandable wari-ness about how the more conventional people she lived among would react to knowledge of her past. "It was Lou Reed," she said simply. "Lou Reed was the devil incarnate to many people."

10

ONE MACHINE TALKING TO ANOTHER

ONE OF THE KEY moves Lou Reed made as he planned his follow-up album to *Rock n Roll Animal* was to draft keyboardist Michael Fonfara as one of the players. Reed had wanted Fonfara, who, along with bassist Prakash John and drummer Pentti Glan, was a member of the Black Stone Rangers, to go on the road with him after *Berlin,* but Fonfara had chosen to stay with his band, which was on the verge of signing a label deal. Ironically, John and Glan chose to leave the band in order to work with Reed, and Fonfara moved to Los Angeles with the Black Stone Rangers' guitarist, Danny Weis. (Weis and Fonfara had both been members of the sixties band Rhinoceros, and Weis was also an original member of Iron Butterfly.) Fonfara did not turn down the second offer when Reed proffered it, and Weis was also asked to play on the sessions. Soon both Steve Hunter, who went off to play with Alice Cooper, and Dick Wagner left Reed's band. "Steve left because he thought, 'Well, three guitars is too much for what we're doing,' and eventually Dick left because he said, 'Well, two guitars is too much for what we're doing,'" Fonfara said. "The fact is, when Weis is on, nobody else needs to be there." At that point, the Black Stone Rangers essentially became Reed's backing band.

At the time, Fonfara didn't know much about Reed, beyond Velvets lore and "Walk on the Wild Side." He believed that he was brought into the sessions because "they wanted somebody funkier than what they had." (Reed had been dissatisfied with Ray Colcord's playing on the tour that yielded *Rock n Roll Animal*.) Initially, "Lou was in the mood to make an R & B record," Fonfara said. "He wanted to be a Lou Reed version of James Brown."

Reed decided to record at Electric Lady Studios, which had been built by Jimi Hendrix, whom Reed much admired, on West Eighth Street, in the heart of Greenwich Village. This would be the first of Reed's solo albums to be recorded in New York. Steve Katz was chosen to produce the new album, an obvious pick given the success of *Rock n Roll Animal,* which he had produced, and the fact that his brother, Dennis, was Reed's manager. But successfully recording a crack band onstage proved to be a very different experience from working with Lou Reed in the studio. "Steve had an ear for production and he had production chops, but Lou was just way too much for him to handle," Fonfara said.

Among other things, what Steve Katz couldn't handle was Reed's propensity to switch conceptual gears midproject while refusing to communicate his ideas to the people around him. Reed eventually backed off on his original R & B vision of the album, but he didn't know exactly where he wanted to go after that, and no one else—including Katz—was in a position to take the reins. "Steve didn't understand what Lou's concept was going to be," said Fonfara, "and he ended up pulling a sort of R & B album out of it, more so than what Lou wanted....Lou was having fun when we did it, but...I think he wanted something a little more sensitive, more of an esoteric feeling to the album."

It was not unlike Reed to start out wanting to make a "fun" R & B record, and then decide that such a project might be too frivolous and back away from it. Reed had loved R & B since childhood, and the genre was experiencing a heyday in the midseventies. James Brown's funk, Philadelphia soul, and George Clinton's extraterrestrial excursions with Parliament-Funkadelic were all in full flight. The late-night—or, really, all-night—gay clubs that Reed liked to frequent were already pulsing with the highly rhythmic, Latin-tinged R & B that would eventually erupt in the mainstream culture as disco. Equally androgynous and more commercially savvy white artists like Elton John, David Bowie, the Rolling Stones, and Rod Stewart were starting to take R & B styles straight to the bank at around this time. But Reed lacked their self-assurance and, consequently, pulled back.

As the sessions got under way for the album that would become *Sally Can't Dance*—the title itself perfectly captures Reed's ambivalence about making an R & B album—Reed turned to Michael Fonfara as his musical director, a role that he would play for the next six years. Fonfara's first impression of Reed was that he was "brilliant with lyrics and could write songs, but he didn't know how to do rhythm and blues at all. It was up to us to more or less take these lyrics and put them with songs that were more like R & B than the rock-and-roll style he had been doing." A horn section and soulful background singers joined the sessions, Fonfara recalled, "and Lou was pretty gung ho about it. We were doing the job that he wanted us to do."

The success of *Rock n Roll Animal* meant that Reed had a sizable audience awaiting the release of his next album, and *Sally Can't Dance,* which came out in August of 1974, became the highest charting album of Reed's career when it rose to number ten. It was his first (and only) Top 10 release. No doubt partly because of the album's success—and partly because he believed that he had lost control of the album in the studio—Reed would disparage *Sally Can't Dance* more strongly and consistently than any other album he put out. "This is fantastic: the worse I am, the more it sells," he told Danny Fields in *Gig* magazine. "If I wasn't on the record at all next time around, it would probably go to number one." That was a hypothesis he would soon test.

Though it didn't sell well as a single, the title track on *Sally Can't Dance* proved an effective advertisement for the album. Since most of Reed's new fans were unaware of *Berlin,* they probably didn't need reassurance, but for anyone who did, "Sally Can't Dance," with its pumping horns and catchy riff, suggested an album that was upbeat, of the moment, and even light-hearted. RCA supported the album's release with a thirty-second television ad featuring a disaffected Reed glumly staring at the camera while the chorus and part of a verse of "Sally Can't Dance" play and famed voice-over genius Don Pardo encourages viewers to "sing along with Lou!" as a bouncing ball highlights the lyrics. According to one of the spot's producers, a more elaborate shoot and ad were planned, but Reed was so high and incoherent when he arrived at the studio that a more bare-bones concept was rushed into effect. Nonetheless, the ad won the 1974 award for best commercial from *Art Direction* magazine.

"Sally Can't Dance" notably offered a checklist of expected post–"Wild Side" references for a Lou Reed single—mentions of hip New York hot spots like St. Marks Place and the gay nightclub Le Jardin, allusions to drugs (meth, in this case), and a whiff of the trash-glam underground—all without posing the slightest threat. Even the album's cover—a pouty portrait of a bottle-blond Reed, his hair close-cropped, wearing dark sunglasses, his head seductively tilted to one side—was designed to titillate rather than menace, an expression of the easy, off-the-shelf decadence that had, rightly or wrongly, troubled so many critics about the artist's solo work. (Evidently the look was inspired by a photograph Reed had taken of a transvestite street hustler he had picked up.) The album's title, too, was reassuring. For one thing, it suggested heterosexual desire from that bitch of a rock-and-roll animal. In addition, starting with Little Richard and Wilson Pickett, Sally had been enshrined as a delectable rock-and-roll name. The entire culture was awakening to dance music, and if Sally couldn't dance, there had to be a funny story behind that incapacity.

Other songs on the album explored darker themes,

most notably "Kill Your Sons," which, though a relatively inert track on the album, would go on to become a roaring staple of Reed's live shows. The song had its origins in 1970, when Reed recorded it on acoustic guitar as "Kill Our Sons." In that incarnation, it was a folkie antiwar song—a generational battle cry and somewhat of a cliché—about old men sending young men off to war to die while living lives of ease themselves. For the version on *Sally Can't Dance,* Reed transformed that sociopolitical context into a psychological one, and the song became a vicious denunciation of his parents for subjecting him to electroshock therapy. It's Reed at his best: simultaneously biting, sardonic, rageful, and poignant. He sneers at "two-bit psychiatrists," savages the straight lives of his parents and sister, wryly compares the treatment he received in two different mental wards, laments being ignored by his family after a drug freak-out, and reports that his brain was so rattled by the convulsive shocks he received that he "couldn't even read" afterward. The song is funny, frightening, and, ultimately, devastating—and its power was totally lost amid the laid-back lounge R & B on *Sally Can't Dance.*

The album was not well received by critics, but perhaps Reed himself delivered the most damning review. "Oh, I slept through *Sally Can't Dance*—that's no big secret," he told Caroline Coon in *Melody Maker.* "They'd make a suggestion and I'd say, 'Oh, all right.'

I'd do the vocals in one take, in twenty minutes, and then it was goodbye." He was more virulently dismissive when he discussed the album with Lenny Kaye. "What a horror. It went Top 10 and it sucks. People who want more *Rock n Roll Animal,* sorry. I mimic me probably better than anybody, so if everybody else is making money ripping me off, I figured maybe I better get in on it. Why not? I created Lou Reed. I have nothing even faintly in common with that guy, but I can play him well. Really well."

By now Reed's drinking and drug use were affecting every aspect of his life, but what seemed to concern him most was that he had had two successful albums in a row. This became a recurring theme in Reed's interviews: "The worse the albums were, the more they apparently sold." The merits of *Rock n Roll Animal* and *Sally Can't Dance* can be debated, of course. But are they really as out of character as Reed insisted? Or did Reed choose to stop the momentum of his career as part of an effort to maintain control over it, to feel the impact of his own agency, even if the results were negative?

Given the success of Reed's last two albums, which came out within six months of each other, RCA was eager for him to deliver something new. He went back to Electric Lady in early January of 1975 to begin work on a new album. Steve Katz was supposed to produce again, but he and Reed had completely fallen out by that time, and Katz did not even attend the sessions. Reed stopped recording after less than a week, and fired his manager, Dennis Katz, after a dispute about the direction the album was taking. The inevitable legal battles ensued and would persist for years.

In March of 1975, the label put out *Lou Reed Live* from the same concerts that had yielded *Rock n Roll Animal,* but that was not enough. Reed would honor RCA's request for another album, and the label would come to regret it. After *Sally Can't Dance* and amid all the chaos surrounding him, Reed felt the need to get behind the wheel of his career—and drive it into a wall. And he did exactly that.

"I kept thinking that somehow it would stop," he said, referring to what he regarded as the meretricious success of *Rock n Roll Animal* and *Sally Can't Dance.* "But it didn't. So I decided to put a stop to it. For those who wanted to hear the real thing, and wanted to hear a guitar solo, they got *Metal Machine Music.* And that put *a stop* to it! There wasn't going to be any more records after that."

Even allowing for his characteristic exaggeration, you could see why Reed might believe *Metal Machine Music* would be the last anyone heard from him. A double album released in July of 1975, less than a year after *Sally Can't Dance,* the album was exactly what its title described: four vinyl sides of nonstop, reverberating, distortion-laden, clamorous guitar feedback. Each of the sides was listed as running exactly sixteen minutes and one second (with side four designed to keep repeating until the listener physically removed the needle from the groove), but in fact the pieces vary in length by twenty seconds or so.

Reed has variously described how the album, which was partly subtitled *An Electronic Instrumental Composition,* was made, but it's now generally accepted that he recorded it alone in his loft in the garment district of Manhattan, with three guitars, two amplifiers, and a four-track analog tape machine. Guitars wildly feeding back, essentially playing themselves, for a bit over an hour in full metallic glory constitutes the record's "music." "My goal at the time," Reed later wrote, "was to have a keyless album of ever-changing rhythm with no lyric or vocal—pure guitar-driven sound in which to surround and intoxicate yourself. I made it out of love for guitar-driven feedback and the squall of the metal machine." It's as if Reed made good on his joking comment to Danny Fields that he might not be "on the record at all next time around."

But contrary to his prediction to Fields, *Metal Machine Music* did not go to number one. From the standpoint of Reed's record company and his fans, the album was most notable for the absence of his voice, lyrics, and anything that might remotely be called a song. As the *New York Times* put it, "Warhol once said that his ambition was to become a machine; Lou Reed has gotten there before him." Reed agreed. Asked about the back cover shot depicting him onstage with a microphone in front of him (an odd choice for an album with no vocals), Reed replied, "It's just one machine talking to another."

Predictably, *Metal Machine Music* immediately incited controversy. No rock artist on a major label had ever released anything like it. When stunned RCA executives heard the album, they considered releasing it on their Red Seal classical label, a suggestion that actually made sense but would immediately have identified it as a niche recording, which, of course, it was. Reed opposed that strategy, regarding it as "pretentious." Instead, the album was released on RCA, giving it the same commercial positioning as his previous albums.

Reed had said that he wanted the album's cover to include a disclaimer that read, "Has no songs, no vocals," a clearly unrealistic expectation. How much Reed approved—or was in any condition to approve—the artwork and visual presentation of *Metal Machine Music* is open to question. Part of him loved the sounds he had created for the album, but he was also motivated by revenge on a company that seemed to be trying to squeeze as much profit out of him as it possibly could. *Metal Machine Music* would be his seventh album release on RCA in three years, and Reed had decided that enough was enough.

Reed had a sizable audience by this time. Particularly for younger fans who had come to him since *Rock n Roll Animal,* a new album from him was a very big deal—and these were not the sort of fans to be dissuaded by the *Electronic Instrumental Composition* subtitle, which, in any event, was not printed in especially large type. Far more compelling to them would have been the striking image of a meth-thin Lou on the cover in his full black-leather-and-studs *Rock n Roll Animal* regalia. For the heavy metal fans of *Rock n Roll Animal* and *Lou Reed Live,* that cover and a title like *Metal Machine Music* suggested a muscular return to form after the relatively somnolent *Sally Can't Dance.*

Like the product-hungry suits of RCA, those fans seemed to be a target of Reed's nihilistic gesture. When Reed said that those who "wanted to hear a guitar solo...got *Metal Machine Music,*" that's whom he was talking about: the heavy metal kids who loved the twin-guitar pyrotechnics of Dick Wagner and Steve Hunter even as Reed believed those arrangements betrayed some of his own best songs. He was talking about the fans who called out for Wagner and Hunter when Reed hit the road with his new, more R & B–inflected band after *Sally Can't Dance* came out.

Compared to *Metal Machine Music, Berlin* was, as *Rolling Stone* had insanely predicted, the *Sgt. Pepper* of the seventies. Fans returned the album in such numbers that RCA felt compelled to issue an apology to retailers. That appalled Reed, but the label had little choice. It's said that the album sold a hundred thousand copies, which seems inflated, even at this juncture, given the extremeness of the music. But if one considers the young, enthusiastic audience waiting for a new Lou Reed album and the fact that none of them would have heard the music before seeing that enticing cover, that number is not inconceivable. The real question is how many of those copies came back to the stores. RCA ended up pulling the album after three months.

In strictly artistic terms, what can be made of *Metal Machine Music*? Most obviously, it's a punk gesture on a scale that remains unrivaled, a screeching fuck you not only to Reed's record company but to his fans. Musically, it can be heard as the furthest extension of sounds that had been part of Reed's creative life for many years, from the squalling free jazz he had loved as a college student to the barrier-shattering drones of La Monte Young that John Cale had introduced him to. Bob Ludwig, who engineered the album, insisted that nothing about it shocked him. As a graduate of the prestigious Eastman School of Music, Ludwig was familiar with the avant-garde compositions of Karlheinz Stockhausen,

Iannis Xenakis, and Elliott Carter, and he heard what Reed was doing in that aesthetic context.

Reed claimed a more prosaic lineage. "I did tons of shows with the Velvet Underground where we would leave our guitars against the amps and walk away," he explained. "The guitars would feed back forever, like they were alive. *Metal Machine Music* was just me doing that—lots of it." As relentless and monochromatic as the album can sound to—and this hardly seems the correct term—a casual listener, critic David Fricke pointed out that as you engage it, "you start to hear a certain oblique cohesion, patterns and effects that surge in and out of the chaos: shrill pipe organ–like chords, trebly shivers of demented surf guitar. And there are moments when the stereo halves of the mix suddenly erupt into a combined burst of feedback sunshine. It is a clarity that hurts; it leaves you blinded and shaken."

For all that, *Metal Machine Music* is—in its conception, motivations, execution, and consequences—a hymn to speed. (Reed even included the chemical symbol of the Benzedrine drug group as part of the album art, and one wag referred to the album as *Methedrine Machine Music*.) Reed's extensive liner notes, including a completely made-up list of sonic and equipment "specifications" ("All the specs were a lie," he later declared), are little more than a deranged amphetamine rant. "This record is not for parties/dancing/

background/romance," Reed wrote, stating the obvious. "This is what I meant by 'real' rock, about 'real' things. No one I know has listened to it all the way through, including myself. It is not meant to be." Those quotation marks around "real" say just about all that needs to be said about Reed's frame of mind. He chides his fans: "Most of you won't like this, and I don't blame you at all. It's not meant for you. . . . This is not meant for the market." He concludes with a strangely adolescent insult — "My week beats your year" — which he described as "a try at a Warholian soundbyte."

Typically, Reed exulted in the negative reactions the album garnered, often referring specifically to a *Billboard* review that concluded, "Recommended cuts: None." And yet, as so often was the case with Reed's output, critics tended to accord the album far greater consideration than he acknowledged, even when the reviews were negative. It's as if Reed believed that his fuck you gesture to the music industry could be meaningful only if it had no support at all. While there was a certain amount of the adolescent sneering so common in rock criticism, for the most part, major journalists wrote at length about the album in prominent venues and struggled to come to grips with it. In the *New York Times,* John Rockwell, who had praised *Berlin,* wrote with genuine appreciation, as well as concern for the impact the album might have on Reed's career. Citing what he described as Reed's "onstage image of off-the-wall instability" and pointing out that the album's grinding roar was "hardly unprecedented in the world of the classical avant-garde," he speculated that *Metal Machine Music* might "convince many of his admirers that he has finally tripped over the line between outrageousness and sheer self-destructive indulgence." Rockwell did not shy away from the complex issue of Reed's anger, noting that Reed was "clearly full of hostility about the whole problem of balancing his rock star career with his need to experiment." Rockwell concluded, "One would like to see rock stars take the risk to stretch their art in ways that might jeopardize the affection of their fans. But one can't help fearing that, in this instance, Mr. Reed may have gone further than his audience will willingly follow."

Writing in *Rolling Stone,* James Wolcott, too, expressed concern about the self-destructiveness evident in *Metal Machine Music.* "What's most distressing is the possibility that *Metal Machine Music* isn't so much a knife slash at his detractors as perhaps a blade turned inward," Wolcott wrote. "At its very worst, this album suggests masochism. He may be, to shift weaponry images, moving to the center of fire so that we critics-as-assassins can make a clean kill. Fine, Lou, go ahead. Just stand there. Don't move. But damned if I'll squeeze the trigger."

As shaky as Reed's emotional state was at the time,

and as much as *Metal Machine Music* was both a symptom and an expression of that precarious state of mind, Reed seemed somehow to understand both the musical and the symbolic importance that would eventually accrue to the album. "In time," he said, "it will prove itself." Years later, he would say, "I run into different musicians in my travels, and it's odd how many of them tell me that *Metal Machine Music* is a seminal thing.... [O]nce you hear *Metal Machine Music,* it frees you up. It's been done—now you can do anything."

And the album did go on to "prove itself." It would become a foundational document for the genre of industrial music, and, incredibly, it would be transcribed and performed live. About a year after the album's release, Lenny Kaye asked Reed if he thought that *Metal Machine Music* had established him "as an underground artist again." That was a smart question, and as a member of the Patti Smith Group, Kaye was the perfect person to ask it. As the punk movement was gearing up in New York and London, Reed had to be aware that for the first time in his career, it was possible that he could be outflanked on his left. The burgeoning movement owed Reed and the Velvet Underground an essential debt, needless to say. He would soon be dubbed the "Godfather of Punk." But Reed had no interest in becoming a father figure of any kind. This was still an era in which anyone over thirty who was still playing rock and roll was suspect. The media had already felt the need, for example, to anoint a dozen-odd so-called new Dylans despite the fact that the old Dylan had not yet reached thirty-five. So, after two commercially successful albums that carried him into the mainstream, did Lou Reed need to be established "as an underground artist again"? Absolutely. And with *Metal Machine Music,* he outgunned the punks before their movement had even managed to get off the ground.

11

A SPEED-ADDLED, LEATHER-CLAD VIRGIL

THE SEVENTIES WAS A decade defined by sexual excess, and Reed distinguished himself in that regard as well. He became a regular at the gay bars that lined the docks along the Hudson, the west-of-everything boundary of Greenwich Village where the sex shows—and the sexual encounters available to patrons—established the outer limits of deviance, perversion, and fetishism. Whatever else he did, Reed took a voyeuristic delight in those environments, often photographing and interviewing the hustlers, transvestite hookers, and other erotic adventurers he met there. (That urge to document the extreme from a cool distance was another attribute he shared with his mentor, Andy Warhol.)

Reed liked to test people—sometimes gently, sometimes not so much—and one of his ways of doing that was to escort carefully chosen friends through the wilds of the sex bars, like a speed-addled, leather-clad Virgil guiding a series of aspiring Dantes through the underworld. To be asked to accompany Reed on one of these jaunts was, in a sense, to be accepted by him. He would invite only people he already trusted. But it was an intriguing impulse nonetheless. For Reed it was a gesture of friendship, an invitation to get to know him better. Welcome to my world.

Music mogul Clive Davis was one of the friends Reed took on a night journey through his favorite clubs. Reed and Davis, who had run Columbia Records and then founded his own label, Arista, in 1974, seemed an unlikely pair. A graduate of Harvard Law School, married, and a father, Davis was ten years older than Reed and maintained a formal bearing; a suit and a matching tie and pocket handkerchief were his standard uniform. And, of course, he was the epitome of a record executive, a music industry powerhouse, and, to that extent, the sort of figure Reed would typically hold in contempt. But they shared a number of key attributes. Both were Jewish and had been born in Brooklyn and attended public schools. New Yorkers to the bone, they still shared an outer-borough, rough-

Lou Reed (with guitar) at his high school talent show, March 1959, along with (from left) Richard Sigal, Judy Titus, and Johnny DeKam. (Courtesy of Richard Sigal)

Reed's senior year high school yearbook photo, inscribed to his friend Richard Sigal. Reed "naturally" likes girls, and intends to "take life as it comes." (Courtesy of Richard Sigal)

LEWIS REED

Tall, dark-haired Lou likes basketball, music, and naturally, girls. He was a valuable participant on the track team. He is one of Freeport's great contributors to the recording world. As for the immediate future, Lou has no plans, but will take life as it comes.

Reed performs with his band on the front porch of the Sigma Alpha Mu fraternity at Syracuse University during the 1961–62 academic year. (Syracuse University Archives)

Reed's college girlfriend, Shelley Albin, in 1963, with her brown hair bleached blonde out of depression over breaking up with Lou. Her mother commented about her "trashy" look: "Why not carry a mattress on your back, too?" Reed loved it. (Photograph by Marsha Bromson)

Reed (center) and the Velvet Underground perform for *Venus in Furs,* a film by the band's friend Piero Heliczer, November 1965. (Adam Ritchie / Redferns / Getty Images)

Reed and Warhol hold one of the helium-filled balloons from Warhol's *Silver Clouds* exhibition at the Leo Castelli Gallery in New York, 1966. (Estate of David Gahr / Getty Images)

The Velvet Underground at the Trip in Los Angeles in 1966. Said Cher, an attendee: the Velvets "will replace nothing, except maybe suicide." (© Lisa Law)

Only boys wear shades: (from left) Nico, Andy Warhol, Maureen Tucker, Reed, Sterling Morrison, and John Cale in Los Angeles, 1966. (Steve Schapiro / Corbis via Getty Images)

Nico and Reed rehearse outdoors in Los Angeles, 1966. (© Lisa Law)

Hey, hey, we're the Velvets: (from left) Morrison, Reed, Tucker, and newcomer Doug Yule, 1969. (Michael Ochs Archives / Getty Images)

Did we miss the Summer of Love?: (from left) Tucker, Morrison, Yule, and Reed in unlikely psychedelic garb, 1970. (Consolidated Image Foundation / Cache Agency)

Reed comes up from underground, backed by the Tots at Lincoln Center's Alice Tully Hall, January 1973. (Steven Rossini / Frank White Photo Agency)

Bettye Kronstad and Reed at the party following Reed's Alice Tully Hall performances, January 1973. (Photo by Anton Perich)

Reed and David Bowie reach across Mick Jagger for an intimate moment at the Café Royal in London, July 1973. (Photo © Mick Rock 2017)

The "Phantom of Rock" onstage in Amsterdam, Holland, September 1973. (Laurens Van Houten / Frank White Photo Agency)

Reed, blond and not having more fun. (Photo © Mick Rock 2017)

Reed mimics shooting up onstage, November 1974. (Michael Zagaris)

Reed enacts his fondness for the press, San Francisco, November 1974. (Michael Zagaris)

Reed, whip-thin at the cover shoot for *Coney Island Baby,* 1975. (Photo © Mick Rock 2017)

Reed takes aim. (Photo © Mick Rock 2017)

"I'll be your mirror": Reed at home. (Photo © Mick Rock 2017)

(From left) John Cale, Reed, and Andy Warhol at the Ocean Club, New York, July 1976. (© Bob Gruen)

Patti Smith and Reed at the Ocean Club, July 1976. (© Bob Gruen)

Pietà: Rachel comforts Reed at a London party celebrating their third anniversary, April 1977. (Photo by Jill Furmanovsky 1977)

Rachel and Reed, April 1977. (Photo by Jill Furmanovsky 1977)

Reed, from the cover shoot for *Street Hassle,* 1978. (Michael Ochs Archives / Getty Images)

"Standing on the corner": Reed, New York City, May 1980. (Estate of David Gahr / Getty Images)

"A chocolate egg cream was not to be missed": Reed enjoys an egg cream at Cafe Figaro on the corner of Bleecker and MacDougal, 1982. (Waring Abbott / Getty Images)

"I took my GPZ out for a ride": Reed in New Jersey, 1982. (Waring Abbott / Getty Images)

Reed and Robert Quine lock in and roar at the Beacon Theatre, New York City, October 18, 1984. (© Ebet Roberts)

Reed and his wife Sylvia arriving at a party hosted by Ahmet Ertegun at Mortimer's, New York City, January 1989. (Ron Galella, Ltd. / Getty Images)

John Cale and Reed, 1989, for *Songs for Drella*. (Waring Abbott / Getty Images)

The Velvet Underground reunited and on tour at the Forum, London, June 5, 1993: (from left) John Cale, Lou Reed, Maureen Tucker, and Sterling Morrison. (Leon Morris / Redferns / Getty Images)

Laurie Anderson and Reed at Josie's, New York City, March 1996. (© Ebet Roberts)

Bono (left), Anderson, and David Bowie (right) join Reed, who is being honored as a distinguished alumnus by Syracuse University, April 2007. (Eric Weiss Photo)

Reed, backed by a choir, performs *Berlin* in Hamburg, Germany, July 2008. (Krafft Angerer / Stringer / Getty Images)

Reed backstage at an event celebrating the Velvet Underground at the New York Public Library, December 2009. (Steve Pyke / Contour by Getty Images)

James Hetfield (left) and Lars Ulrich of Metallica flank Reed at a listening party for their album *Lulu* at the Steven Kasher Gallery in New York, October 2011. (Kevin Mazur / Getty Images)

Reed, in one of his last public appearances, joins his friend and collaborator Mick Rock at an event celebrating the publication of *Transformer,* October 3, 2013. (Theo Wargo / Getty Images)

Lou Reed, 2009. (Steve Pyke / Contour by Getty Images)

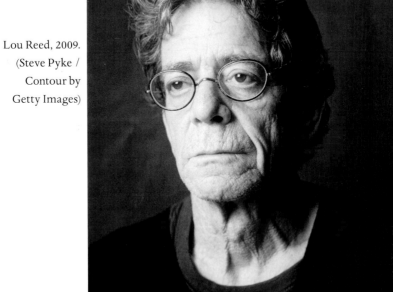

around-the-edges defensiveness. For all his high style, Davis prized his Brooklyn roots as well as his ability to get along with anyone, regardless of station. Now in his eighties, he is an innately curious person and values his ability to move in any world with poise and confidence.

Reed, for all his rebellious attitudes, could not help but be impressed by highly educated people. That Davis, unlike the vast majority of record company executives, had graduated from Harvard Law and was highly articulate was not lost on Reed. Davis often noted how smart and funny Reed was, how entertaining as a conversationalist. As a perennial music business outsider, Reed would have enjoyed the irony of his highly visible friendship with Davis, the quintessential insider. And for Davis, befriending the notorious Lou Reed provided the ultimate street cred. Years later, Davis would identify himself as bisexual, and his primary relationships would eventually be with men. Those impulses, however latent at the time, may well have also played a role in the closeness between the two men.

Davis was a regular at Studio 54 in those heady days (as was Warhol), and Reed, who shunned venues as mainstream and self-consciously exclusive as that club, would ask him about it. According to Davis, Reed wanted to know "what made it special? Was I attracted to explore the nightlife?" The answer was yes; both men relished New York after hours, and Davis was game for a tour of Reed's favorite late-night haunts. "There was never any lecturing or acting like a guide," Davis noted. "It was just visual. His demeanor was very straightforward and matter-of-fact—not fun or conversational or looking to see my reaction. I was his friend Clive joining him for a walk through his night-life. None of it was designed to shock or impress—it seemed more intended to expose: 'This is my everyday life.' And I got it, that he was this fascinating, complex mixture, drawn to the wild side. Maybe he was curious to see how I would handle myself, if I would act and dress the same way I always did—which I did. I think it was to show me more than he could articulate or verbally express, that I would learn more and be more in sync with who he really was."

At other times, Davis took the lead. In August of 1975, Davis brought Reed to the Bottom Line on Mercer Street to witness one of the now legendary break-out performances by Bruce Springsteen and the E Street Band. By this point the founder and president of Arista Records, Davis had signed Springsteen to Columbia Records when he was the president of that label. Springsteen fever was running high. *Born to Run* was just about to be released, Springsteen would soon be on the cover of both *Time* and *Newsweek,* and his ten-night stand at the Bottom Line was a seminal event.

Characteristically, Springsteen more than lived up to the hype surrounding him, delivering galvanizing performances night after night. Critics were exultant, and fans were rapturous. Springsteen blew everyone away — except, seemingly, Lou Reed.

"I don't think he loved it," Davis said. "I was so enthusiastic at the transformation of Bruce that I was flying, but artists have a way of being innately competitive with each other. All I can say is that Lou didn't look upon that moment as the emergence of a new poet laureate or a new pioneering rock spirit. He was much more measured and not overly impressed. He didn't know why I was so ecstatic."

Having just a month earlier released *Metal Machine Music,* the polar opposite of a rousing, crowd-pleasing album like *Born to Run,* Reed might be forgiven for not being able to recognize a "new pioneering rock spirit" at that particular moment. Nonetheless, as was often the case, Reed may also have taken in more at that Springsteen show than he was willing to let on. Springsteen would soon become a friend, and the Bottom Line would for years be one of Reed's favorite places to play.

English photographer Mick Rock, who took the iconic shot of Reed that became the cover of *Transformer,* became another student of New York nightlife, though Rock stood in a much different relationship

to Reed than Davis did. Rock was seven years younger
than Reed and, in many ways, emerged out of the subversive cultural world that Reed and the Velvet Underground had shaped for the musicians and artists that
followed them. His own career progressed in parallel
with Reed's and David Bowie's, and both men perceived him not as an outsider, but as an organic part
of their world. Rock viewed his role as helping those
artists convey the compelling images they wanted to
present to the world. "I saw them the way they wanted
to see themselves," he said. He looked like them, acted
like them, and was one of them. He used the same
substances and indulged the same vices they did. And,
like Bowie, he'd regarded Reed as a hero since his days
with the Velvet Underground. "He was my rock-and-
roll Baudelaire," Rock said. "He was so big in my mind
since I was a teenager. I could see the Rimbaud in
him, too—no food, no sleep, into all kinds of mis-
chief, coming up with great art. I related him more
than anybody else back to that."

Rock, who had studied literature at Cambridge University and started out as a writer, could talk poetry
with Reed. "Look at all the poetry he wrote that he
never set to music. He'd carry around these typewrit-
ten pages, and he'd show that stuff to me." Rock worked
often with Reed throughout the seventies, eventually
spending half his time in New York. "In the end, I

know that my pictures defined him more than anybody else's," Rock said. "I think I also took the sexiest
pictures of him.... He was playful, and there was a
thing between us. It was the seventies and we were
young. We were close. It was like his door was always
open to me back then. I know he in some way found
me attractive, and he was certainly very affectionate
with me." Beyond that, as with Davis and his Harvard pedigree, it was not lost on Reed that Rock had
attended Cambridge. "Rock's educated, but I am, too,"
Reed said. "It's just that no one knows this about either
one of us. So you're out there doing the whole punk
thing and people make a deadly mistake: they think
you're only that. The fact that I have a degree with
honors and Mick has his from Cambridge—they miss
that. So there's a lot of smart stuff going on, but no
one gets that it's there. They go, 'Oh, it's androgyny!' "

On Rock's trips to New York, Reed would occasionally take him on a tour of his underground haunts.
"I had been around interesting clubs in London where,
shall we say, there was a mixed sexual vibe," Rock
recalled. "But Lou took me to places that were certainly darker and deeper. Sweetly, he was actually very
protective of me, because if you came from London,
you were going to be a bit naive when you got taken
into the cultural depths of New York. I had played
around in London, but that was strictly amateur time,

strictly a warm-up. Like those gay clubs that started showing up in New York as the seventies rolled on — there was never a place in London like the Anvil."

The Anvil was a notorious leather bar on the corner of Fourteenth Street and Tenth Avenue that featured live sex shows, most notably including fist fucking, drag queens, and a downstairs room packed with male patrons openly having sex of every variety. The Anvil gained sufficient notoriety that celebrities frequented it for the sex shows, and sightings of famous visitors were common. "Freddie Mercury got his look from a guy who used to dance on the bar at the Anvil who had a mustache and wore gold shorts with suspenders and a cap," Rock said. "Of course, Freddie had been down to the Anvil and seen him and grabbed the image."

Rock found his Anvil visit memorable. "There was some stuff going on that even shocked me, and I thought I was hip and unshockable. Lou did live that kind of life. Talk about sex and drugs. And finally, of course, we're also talking about a lot of dead people. I mean, Lou collected people, and I met all kinds of bizarre characters. . . . I took photos in his apartment during that Desoxyn period, let's call it. He had immersed himself deep in the underbelly of New York—no doubt. He liked to dip into the belly of the beast."

Like Davis, Rock saw Reed's invitation to explore his night world as a gesture of friendship, combined with a writerly interest in anything that might stir his imagination. And, according to Rock, Reed's fondness for strange characters extended beyond the sexual demimonde. "He introduced me to a friend of his who was apparently from a very wealthy family, and Lou said, 'This man is the greatest B and E man in New York'—which is 'breaking and entering,'" Rock said. Reed would soon refer to this character in one of his songs. "Apparently, the guy was a master," Rock said, "and he didn't do it for the money, because he didn't need it. It just was his thrill in life."

Reed also explored the sexual underground with Erin Clermont, the Syracuse friend he stayed in touch with intermittently throughout his life. He would often phone her in the middle of the night and come by her apartment in the Village for a visit. Other times they would head out—to Plato's Retreat, a well-known and relatively mainstream sex club, or to the notorious gay club Hell Fire, among other places. They attended meetings of the Eulenspiegel Society, an organization designed to educate and provide social interactions for people interested in BDSM—bondage, discipline, and sadomasochism. "It's very buttoned-up," Clermont said of the Eulenspiegel Society. "Nothing happens at the meetings; they're like mixers. It's no Hell Fire— everyone wears clothes. You have conversations with people. There was a guy there who was begging to come clean my apartment on his hands and knees. I laughed, but if you laugh, they like it, so I was perfect. I took his card; I think it said 'sex slave' on it."

"Lou and I did watch a bit of porn together," she continued. "I'm one of the small group of females who like gay porn. There was this one gay filmmaker, Fred Halsted, who made *L.A. Plays Itself,* which is considered a fine film aside from its incredible topic, which is fisting. And we'd go up to Forty-Second Street and look at the peep shows, which wasn't gay. I know the big question is, 'Do you think Lou was gay?' I do not. I think he was inter. He was bisexual, I guess, to a certain degree. But primarily his focus was women. He liked women, and not just for sex. That was part of his neediness. I think he got the emotional succor from women that he could not get from a man. But I saw our adventures as a walk on the wild side. Experiencing those parts of New York and doing things. It was the seventies."

WITHOUT QUESTION, THE MOST significant character Reed met on his late-night rambles through the city was the mysterious Rachel, the transsexual male who would become his live-in lover for three or four years in the seventies. "It was in a late-night club in Greenwich Village," Reed said, describing the first time he met Rachel. Reed had been in a romantic, methamphetamine haze. "I'd been up for days, as usual, and everything was at that superreal, glowing stage. I walked in there, and there was this amazing person, the incredible head, kind of vibrating out of it all. Rachel was wearing this amazing makeup and dress and I was obviously in a different world to anyone else in the place. Eventually I spoke and she came home with me."

It was not exactly a Hollywood-style meet-cute, but it did turn into something like a Lou Reed dream date: "I rapped for hours and hours, while Rachel just sat there looking at me, saying nothing. . . . Rachel was completely disinterested in who I was and what I did. Nothing could impress her. He'd hardly heard my music and didn't like it all that much when he did." Very quickly, the couple became inseparable. "At the time I was living with a girl, a crazy blonde lady, and I kind of wanted us all three to live together, but somehow it was too heavy for her. Rachel just stayed on and the girl moved out. . . . Rachel knows how to do it for me. No one else ever did before. Rachel's something else."

However much more accepting society has become of sexual expression of all kinds over the past four decades, it's impossible to conceive of another highly visible star of Reed's stature openly presenting a trans-sexual as his significant other at that time. While Rachel identified as a woman, she had not had her male genitalia removed, and it is not entirely clear whether she had undergone hormone treatments to grow breasts, though some people think she had. Reed and just about everyone else who knew her alternated between male and female pronouns in referring to her, less for ideological reasons than simply out of confusion over what would be the most appropriate term in any given situation.

Even the physical descriptions of Rachel varied from observer to observer and situation to situation. The most notorious of those was Lester Bangs's vicious and homophobic takedown of Rachel, whom he met in a Detroit hotel room while interviewing Reed on his tour promoting *Sally Can't Dance*. Rachel, Bangs wrote, was "a strange, somewhat female thing." It got worse from there. "You simultaneously wanted to look away and sort of surreptitiously gawk," Bangs continued. "At first glance, I'd thought it was some big dark swarthy European woman, with long rank thick hair falling about her shoulders. Then I noticed that it had a beard, and I figured, well, cool, the bearded lady, with Lou Reed, that fits. But now I was up closer and it was almost unmistakably a guy. Except that behind its see-through blouse, it seemed to have tits. Or something. . . . It was grotesque, it was abject, like something that might have grovelingly scampered in when Lou opened the door to get the milk and papers in the morning, and just stayed around. . . . If the album *Berlin* was melted down in a vat and reshaped into human form, it would be this creature."

One of the first generation of prominent rock critics, Bangs had been a significant supporter of the Velvet Underground, but, as so often happened with him, his hero worship degenerated into obsession and, finally, a desperate need to tear down his idol. His goofy—and sneering—description of Rachel expressed the adolescent sensibility that characterized all his writing. Still, being the focus of Bangs's attention somehow appealed to Reed in a way that was at least in part masochistic. In a series of articles and interviews, the two men sparred and debated, insulted and battled, baited and chided each other in ways that, for all their self-indulgent bluster, assumed their mutual importance—and self-importance. Reed's bearing, reputation, and cultural stature demanded that people tiptoe around him—a suggestion that Bangs, in his bull-in-a-china-shop way, gleefully took as a provocation. Reed enjoyed that bravado. Typically, beyond whatever other substances Reed may have ingested before their confrontations, he and Bangs were drunk to the point of incoherence. Still, Reed remarked to Bangs at one point, "You know, I basically like you in spite of myself." Later, though, after Bangs died of a drug overdose in 1982, Reed explained to guitarist Robert Quine, who was a close friend of Bangs, that

Bangs's comments about Rachel were part of the reason he had come to detest him. "Do you understand, Quine? This is a person I was close to," Reed said. "And he is calling her a creature and 'thing.'"

It's telling, however, that as different a figure as Rachel was from Bettye Kronstad, Shelley Albin, and Reed's other female paramours, she was called upon to play a very similar role and was expected to comport herself in a similar way. While Rachel accompanied Reed virtually everywhere, she was invariably described as quiet, attentive to Reed, and reluctant to say much of anything in his presence. Bangs reported that Rachel had been introduced — or, more likely, described — to the production staff at the Detroit venue as "Lou's babysitter." For all his adolescent condescension about Rachel, Bangs allowed that there was "a sense of permanency, even protectiveness, about the relationship." Reed's substance abuse problems determined that he needed a minder, and whether that person was female by birth or predilection was insignificant. As Erin Clermont put it, "She took care of things for him. She was an assistant, but also probably gave him blow jobs, I would guess." Meanwhile, when Clermont asked Reed about Rachel, he replied, "Listen, she's more beautiful than any fucking woman."

Perhaps it's most indicative of the complicated messages, visual and otherwise, that a transsexual embodies—and certainly embodied in the seventies—that Rachel conveyed wildly contradictory meanings. She was beautiful, womanly, and feminine; she was clearly a man and often described as showing stubble. She was not only quiet but virtually never spoke; she was vivacious and friendly. Reed believed that Rachel had no idea who he was when they met, and he was charmed by that. Others on the scene claim that Rachel was triumphant about landing in a relationship with a rock star like Reed. Of course, none of those descriptions precludes the others. It's perfectly possible that Rachel, like anyone else, was outgoing with certain people or at particular times, and withdrawn and silent at others. For all its pretenses to rebellion and openness, the underground rock scene—and certainly the mainstream music business—was hardly free of homophobia and misogyny. Far from it. And however wild and determined a character Rachel might have been, moving through that world, even as Lou Reed's girlfriend, would have called for some deft manipulations. She could not possibly know whom to trust and of whom to be wary. A silent watchfulness must often have seemed to her the most effective strategy. If Rachel did take hormones, it's likely that she could have looked or seemed feminine at some times, more masculine at others. What's interesting is that very few of the descriptions of her seemed to allow for that range of possibilities.

Each person, including Reed, seemed to believe that his or her version of Rachel was who she was in some essential way.

Even if Rachel wasn't aware of who Reed was when they met, it's inconceivable that she would not have quickly figured it out and become excited about what being involved with him could potentially mean. Reed's demeanor at around that time would have ensured that. "When Lou walked into a room, if everyone didn't stop talking and look at him, he'd make sure they did," Michael Fonfara said. "He dominated a room. That is just the way he was. He demanded that kind of thing."

Clive Davis lived with his wife and children in an apartment on Central Park West, and he regularly invited Reed to the Thanksgiving brunch he would host so that his guests could watch the Macy's parade floats make their way downtown. Reed would invariably attend, accompanied by Rachel. "It was an amazing picture," Davis said. "Maybe fifty or sixty people. Eggnog and bagels. Most of them families with younger kids. The parade is going by. And there were Lou and Rachel. But Lou was very approachable, very down-to-earth, very good company."

Reed dedicated his next album, *Coney Island Baby*, to Rachel. Though he had been convinced that *Metal Machine Music* would put an end to his career, that obviously did not prove to be the case. To his credit,

Ken Glancy, the president of RCA Records at the time and a believer in Reed, recognized that, as had happened with *Berlin,* the career damage that *Metal Machine Music* had caused could easily be reversed as long as Reed released another, more mainstream album soon afterward. Glancy exacted a promise from Reed that his next album would be nothing like *Metal Machine Music,* and everybody decided to move on.

Released in January of 1976, *Coney Island Baby* is perhaps the most romantic album of Reed's career, reflecting a desire to distinguish it as starkly as possible from *Metal Machine Music.* If that album gave expression to the grinding, inhuman, metallic assault of the modern age, this one tapped into the deepest recesses of the human heart, the wish, the belief, the conviction that "the glory of love / Might see you through."

The album's cover, a soft-focus, black-and-white portrait of Reed taken by Mick Rock, is the polar opposite of the hard-edged, leather-clad figure that Reed had presented in recent years. His hair is neither close-cropped nor blond, but gracefully styled and its natural dark brown color. He is not wearing sunglasses but is covering one eye with a bowler hat and peering at the camera — and the viewer — as if he were trying to determine how much of himself to reveal. He is not smiling, but neither is he flashing the intimidating scowl that had become his signature expression. His pale white skin blends seamlessly into the photo's white backdrop, creating a sense of vulnerability, as if the hard outlines of his body had dissolved, his impregnable studs-and-leather physical fortress now a thing of the past. He is wearing a black-and-white tuxedo-style shirt and bow tie, a parody of formality that had become fashionable in the seventies. The outfit reveals his collarbone and some of his chest and shoulders, a feminine look that further adds to his vulnerability. He looks something like a mime, a particularly introspective vaudeville hoofer, or Charlie Chaplin's Little Tramp—all highly aestheticized images, once again in stark contrast to the gritty street realism that had more recently been his mode. Across the light-colored block capitals of the album's title is Lou Reed's signature in stylized script, another self-consciously personal touch, as if, in opposition to the contempt of *Metal Machine Music*, each fan was getting a personally autographed copy of this much more friendly work.

The title track, which closes the album, borrows the name of a 1962 regional hit by the Excellents. By 1962, doo-wop had lost most of its cultural relevance, and even the artists who emerged from its influence, like Dion DiMucci and the Four Seasons, had been touched at least as meaningfully by rock and roll. The Excellents' "Coney Island Baby," however, was among the last classic expressions of the form—all wistfulness, earnestness, and youthfulness. A true aficionado like

Reed would have appreciated that. The song's reference to an amusement park in an urban setting—Brooklyn, Reed's birthplace—only enhanced its evocation of an innocent teen romance that would soon be as much an anachronism as the song's perfectly constructed harmonies. Reed wanted to tap that purity, that sense of perfect love as it can only be experienced in adolescence, for his hymn to Rachel.

Over a spare, meditative guitar-bass-drums arrangement, soulful backing vocals, and an impossibly slow tempo, Reed's vocal delivery in the song's verses is essentially a recitation, which lends it an extremely intimate feel, as if he were struggling to find the words for the memories he's recalling, giving voice to them in real time as they emerge in his mind. He thinks back to high school and talks about wanting to "stand up straight" and play football for the coach, the "straightest dude" he ever knew. He conjures a John Wayne world of stoic masculine virtue: strong, silent, undeniable. Performing the song onstage, Reed would sometimes evoke Green Bay Packers coach (and fellow Brooklyn native) Vince Lombardi by name, as well as the declaration "Winning isn't everything; it's the only thing," which is frequently—and incorrectly—attributed to him. As his spoken introduction to "I'm Waiting for the Man" on *1969: The Velvet Underground Live* demonstrates, Reed was not above drawing life lessons from football, and the stark, black-and-white thinking of that quotation is not much different from the unforgiving street code by which many of Reed's characters live and die. To play football for the coach is to be willing to live according to your beliefs — and to be willing to be judged on how uncompromisingly you've done that.

In Reed's case, the song seems to be simultaneously about a desire to please and outrage his father, impulses that warred within him his entire life. Against the desire to live up to the standards defined by the coach, Reed presents a haunted vision of a nighttime self alone and lonely in the "midnight hour," a morally degraded figure who, far from striving to live up to clearly defined principles, has put his soul "up for sale." That character's sleepless memories drift back not to afternoons on the high school football field but to "all the things that you done," to having made "every different scene," to never being able "to be no human being" — all those references more lurid and harrowing for remaining entirely unspecified, the listener's imagination all too readily filling in the gaps. As if channeling Travis Bickle in *Taxi Driver*, the singer declares that New York is "something like a circus or a sewer," a moral cesspool in which it's all too understandable that some people have "peculiar tastes."

To resolve the tension in the song, Reed once again turned to doo-wop, proclaiming, "The glory of love / Might see you through." "The Glory of Love" is an R

& B standard recorded by the Five Keys, the Platters, and the (happily named) Velvetones, and its title alone is something of a doo-wop statement of purpose. In Reed's "Coney Island Baby," the glory of love is embodied in the devotion of a "princess... / Who loved you even though she knew you was wrong." Beyond the trope of the good girl who falls for the bad boy, "wrong" in this case suggests "gay," "perverse," or "addicted," as well as alluding to Reed's penchant for falling for women—in marked contrast to Rachel—whose tastes in virtually all regards tended to be far more conventional than his own. The song is an experiment, according to Reed, in "using those kinds of pop doo-wop phrases and trying to actually breathe meaning into them beyond the cliché."

Reed ends the song dramatically, with the sort of radio dedication he heard so often growing up. "I'd like to send this one out to Lou and Rachel, and all the kids, and P.S. 192," he intones, reaching back even to the local Brooklyn public school he loathed. "Man, I swear I'd give the whole thing up for you." It's unclear what the singer would be willing to give up for his love—or for the presumed groundedness, the realness, the normalcy, of the kids at P.S. 192. His ambitions? His fame? His art? His success? All of it?

That Reed would bring the deepest and most sentimental of his musical tastes to bear on his relationship with Rachel, going so far as to mention her by name in the title track of his album, suggests the seriousness of his feelings for her. Rachel, "a tall, exotic person with cascading hair, arching eyebrows, and hands whose fragile elegance is enhanced by two glinting diamond rings," one critic wrote, "has put the heart back into Lou's rock and roll."

It would take decades before American culture would begin to grapple with the notion that gays, let alone transsexuals, experience love in anything like the romanticized terms then reserved for heterosexuals. Yet there was Reed doing just that on an album released in America's bicentennial year, and managing simultaneously to express all his conflicted feelings about his own sexual identity and desires. It is one of his greatest achievements as a songwriter. As vulnerable as he seems in the song, however, Reed heard it as a statement of defiance. "Saying 'I'm a Coney Island baby' at the end of that song is like saying I haven't backed off an inch," he said, "and don't you forget it."

JUST AS ROCK N *Roll Animal* erased the career damage done by *Berlin, Coney Island Baby* succeeded in making *Metal Machine Music* seem like some kind of bad dream from which Reed had miraculously awakened. Reed himself may have felt that *Metal Machine Music* "made it that much harder for *Coney Island Baby* to prove itself," but, in fact, it made it much easier. As with *Berlin,* fans wanted to forget about *Metal Machine Music,* and Reed called his new album "a continuation of what I was doing with the Velvet Underground"—in other words, exactly what his fans were hoping he would do. And the critics, ever eager to proclaim that "Lou Reed is back!" loved *Coney Island Baby.* John Rockwell called it his "best album in years"; Lenny Kaye described it as a "self-renaissance." In a rapturous lead review in *Rolling Stone,* Paul Nelson concluded that when Reed sang about wanting to play football for the coach, "he is expressing the profound dream of the damned—and his loss is given greater intensity because both he and we know that such wishes were impossible from the very beginning. So we reaccept it. And it hurts all over again."

Nelson's final comment? "You can play on my team any day, Lou."

12

THIS GENDER BUSINESS

AS INSIGHTFUL A CRITIC and as visionary a record executive as he was, Paul Nelson didn't understand that Lou Reed had no desire to play on his team. Reed took the team of sophisticated critics and sympathetic executives who supported him entirely for granted, as well he might have. To him, the imagined world of the high school football coach represented something else entirely—a realm of male-defined normalcy, epitomized by his father, that would forever elude him. Reed would alternately seek to gain entry to this world and to outrage it. In the case of "Coney Island Baby," he did both, and brilliantly.

While the album succeeded in changing the perception of Lou Reed by the public and within the music industry, it was hardly a blockbuster. It rose to number forty-one on the *Billboard* album chart—a respect-able showing, particularly for him—but nothing dramatic. Reed worked hard by his own standard to sell the album, doing as many interviews as he could bear. But as was so often the case during this period, his emotional and physical condition did not make him the most effective messenger for his own work. Understandably, he was under a great deal of stress. He was massively in debt to RCA, drowning in law-suits with his former manager Dennis Katz, still drink-ing prodigiously and shooting speed, and involved in a highly public relationship with a transsexual. That's enough to make anyone's behavior erratic, and for some-one as prone to walking along the ledge as Reed was, it was enough to tip him into the pit.

For a *New York Times* interview with John Rock-well, Reed showed up late, "complained vituperatively" about the executive office his record company had selected as the site for the interview, and insisted on relocating the chat to the bar at the Algonquin Hotel, where, Rockwell wryly noted, "a couple of drinks improved his mood marginally." Rockwell concluded that Reed, for all his scary posturing, is "the Don Rick-les of rock, but the humor gets lost in translation."

For a *Rolling Stone* interview, Reed was in even finer form, as revealing of his private life as he would ever be in such a situation. At dinner with the reporter Timothy Ferris, he rattled off "a chain of racist and anti-Semitic remarks calculated to 'clear the air.'" (Such provocations were characteristic of Reed at the time. He told one friend that he needed to get a "nigger comb" to tame his unruly hair, and explained to a reporter from *Creem* that "nigger music—pardon me—soul brothers and their turbulent rhythm" takes over the music scene when there's "nothing happening.") Then, in an extremely unusual gesture, Reed brought Ferris back to the Upper East Side apartment he shared with Rachel, whom the reporter described as Reed's "live-in boyfriend." Reed poured Ferris a "water glass of bourbon" and showed him a tape of interviews he had done with transvestite street hustlers. "He picks them up—on Tenth Avenue, the lowest rank in the hierarchy of New York whoredom, where they hustle motorists headed for New Jersey who mistake them for women—brings them home, [and] makes recordings and Polaroids (one of which was the basis for the *Sally Can't Dance* cover)," Ferris wrote.

While this assessment was essentially accurate, Ferris overlooked the fact that, New Jersey suburbanites or not, at least some of those horny motorists were there precisely because those street hookers were not women. That was the attraction. Nonetheless, Reed's habit of photographing, filming, and interviewing these men was long-standing and, among other things, demonstrates that, to one degree or another, Reed's relationship with Rachel occurred within the context of a larger fascination. Speaking of Rachel, photographer Mick Rock said that he had pictures of Reed "with similar characters, and those do not get published. They're buried, and I show them to nobody. But yes, I have all these other pictures, too."

The tape Reed showed Ferris featured a drag queen discussing a character named Arman, whom she described as a "glass-coffee-table queen." Asked about that term, she explained that Arman "lies under the glass coffee table on little velvet pillows, and you gap yourself over the coffee table and shit onto the glass while his face is pressed up against it. And then afterward you can make him eat the shit off." Clearly amused and titillated, Reed pressed for more details about the encounter, which his guest matter-of-factly provided.

To assume that Reed was entirely out of control at the time is perhaps the only way to understand why he would show a tape like that to a reporter for a major national magazine—an interaction that inevitably resulted in a huge, all-caps headline that read, "WHAT HAPPENS WHEN YOUR AVERAGE INTRO-VERT MEETS THE GLASS-COFFEE-TABLE QUEEN." It certainly explains why, in the future, Reed would typically flat-out refuse not only to discuss his personal life but to comment on things he had previously said in interviews. On a few occasions, Reed would almost sheepishly admit to having done too many interviews while drunk or stoned. The anger he would often express to reporters was, in part, a projection of the anger he felt toward himself for having allowed himself to lose control. He was embarrassed and humiliated and, consequently, lashed out. He once warned Jeffrey Ross, who was in his early twenties and playing guitar in his band, "You're going to get interviewed, and you'd better figure out who you are right now, because that's who you're going to be forever." That was a fate Reed viewed as a kind of hell, all the worse because he had condemned himself to it with his excesses.

To his credit, Ferris rendered the scene in a completely understated way, allowing Reed's jaw-dropping anecdotes to speak for themselves. And Reed suggested a more sensible reason for why he might have been so open with Ferris. "The critics think I'm that tape," Reed explained. "That's why I get such bad publicity. They assume I am what's on a tape like that, which they find offensive. It's not me, though I don't find anything wrong with it at all. If only they knew that not only am I such a worthless churl as to write songs about these things, but on top of that, I stole it all. Stole it from the people."

It's possible to believe that for Reed, such encounters, at least in part, constituted a kind of research, his questioning of the hustler and fascination with the answers an aural version of his voyeurism. But the scatological nature of his interests — he eagerly grilled his visitor with questions about Arman's habits — attests to his extreme state of mind. A young artist and enthusiastic Lou Reed fan named Duncan Hannah, who hung out in the back room at Max's and was introduced to Reed by Danny Fields, reported that Reed's approach to him consisted of this invitation: "Well, look, why don't you come back to my hotel with me? . . . And you can shit in my mouth." When the young man demurred, Reed asked, "Does that, does that repulse you?" Assured that it did repulse him, Reed offered a compromise: "Well, I'll put a — I'll put a plate over my face, then you can shit on the plate. How'd you like that?" That didn't work either. Hannah was gobsmacked. "I was really depressed because I'd imagined something really different," he said. "It wasn't like it was in the books: 'God, I met my hero and we were talking about Raymond Chandler!' Instead, it was, 'Can I shit in your mouth?'"

Reed's question — "Does that repulse you?" — suggests that the shock factor of his seduction was as much the point as getting Hannah to agree to his request. That certainly is the impression one would get from Jonny Podell, the high-flying New York booking agent who managed Reed for a year when his relationship with Rachel was in high gear. Asked about Reed's relationship with Rachel, Podell replied, "You want me to tell you my real feelings? I almost feel bad saying this, but I mean it with real love. I think Lou was a total act.... Look, we all present a certain way, and for me, he was Lou from Long Island seeing how far he could rebel against Daddy the accountant. I thought he became a drug addict because it was cool and rebellious. I thought he wanted to be with a guy— or a guy-girl—because it was shock and awe. Lou's feelings about music were real, but the rest was shock and awe." Even Reed's friend the *Rolling Stone* writer Ed McCormack, referring to the shock treatments to which Reed's parents had subjected him, speculated that "one had to wonder if his very public relationship with Rachel was yet another way of letting Mom and Dad know that they had not 'cured' a fucking thing." Reed himself would later observe that "I always thought one way kids had of getting back at their parents was to do this gender business. It was only kids trying to be outrageous."

Mick Rock, who spent a lot of time with Reed and Rachel and took the best-known—and best— photographs of them together, had a different take. "I never regard other people's relationships as being my business.... But to be quite honest with you, Lou was so high a lot of the time, I don't even know what he would have been capable of." To Michael Fonfara, Reed suggested otherwise. "We used to have this joke going," Fonfara recalled. "Lou would say, 'Michael, you don't know what it's like until you've been with a guy.' And I'd say, 'No, Lou, you've got it backwards. You don't know what it's like until you've been with a proper woman.' We had this argument going for a couple of years. I never put Rachel down. Rachel and I were good friends. But Rachel had an extra life in addition to the one she lived with Lou. And that was the drag-queen-on-the-street life."

Fonfara also touched on the persistent rumor of street violence that surrounded Rachel. Reed, he said, "knew how tough she was. He knew how good she was with a knife. She was pretty swift." Clearly, Rachel, along with the B and E expert to whom Reed introduced Mick Rock, was part of the world of criminality that fascinated Reed. It was even rumored that Rachel had killed a man in prison. Writer and artist Richard Sassin recalled a jealous and "very stoned" Rachel drawing a switchblade on a female friend of his backstage at the Bottom Line, warning her, "Don't ever look at Lou like that again!" The friend lived in the same Upper East Side building as Lou and Rachel, and Sassin described often seeing Rachel sleeping in the lobby all night, "beat up and locked out of their apartment. I never saw Lou hit Rachel. She would be curled up as much as she could on the small lobby couch with black eyes or a swollen face. I asked if she was okay once, and she told me to fuck off, so we just ignored her after that."

An entry in Andy Warhol's diary for Sunday, December 19, 1976, provides another glimpse into the rougher life that Rachel may have been leading. "Lou Reed called and that was the drama of the day," Warhol wrote. "He'd come back from a successful tour, he was a big hit in L.A., but he said Rachel had gotten kicked in the balls and was bleeding from the mouth and he wanted the name of a doctor. Lou's doctor had looked at Rachel and said that it was nothing, that it would stop, but Lou wanted another doctor to check. I said I'd get Bianca [Jagger]'s. But then Lou called back and said he got Keith Richards's doctor to come over. I told him he should take her to the hospital. I was calling Rachel 'she' because she's always in drag but then Lou calls him 'he.'"

For all that turmoil, in some ways, Reed and Rachel's life together followed a conventional domestic script. The couple had a pair of miniature dachshunds, the Count and the Duke. Reed doted on the dogs, and Fonfara, a neighbor when Reed and Rachel moved to Greenwich Village, would occasionally walk them when Reed was busy. Mick Rock accompanied Reed when he went to purchase one of the dogs and photographed him. "I have these pictures of Lou holding this puppy, and he's so gentle with him," Rock recalled. "I often used to threaten him: 'I'm going to publish those pictures and ruin your image!'" On the home front, Rachel, Fonfara remarked, "couldn't cook. She tried desperately, but she'd make a mess and burn everything. But Lou insisted on letting her try to be the hostess. And when she dressed up, she looked like Sophia Loren."

Indeed, Rachel's charm and elegance were much noticed. Susan Blond, a prominent New York publicist and Warhol acolyte, recalled meeting Reed and Rachel while on vacation in the Caribbean. "I was walking along the shore with my husband at the time," she said, "and I saw a figure in the distance and thought, 'That's just the most elegant person on this whole beach.' When I looked closer, I realized this elegant woman was Rachel. Lou was with her — the two of them were there, just like we were, having a romantic trip on an island. She was wearing, like, a short, see-through cover-up, like something you'd see on a Greek statue. Maybe off one shoulder, and short enough that you could see her legs. She just looked great."

For the one tempestuous year that he and Reed worked together, Jonny Podell adored Rachel, whom, he said, Reed would occasionally refer to as Richard. (Richard Humphries was Rachel's birth name.) Podell's managerial relationship with Reed was far more complicated, in part because he was as enthusiastic a drug user as Reed was; singer-songwriter Elliott Murphy described their relationship as "a marriage made in the emergency room." For Podell, Rachel was much easier to handle. "I totally dug Rachel," Podell said. "She was charming and lovable—not like Lou, who was very subject to mood swings. She would come bounding into my office and say, 'Hi, Jonny, I want to show you my new pumps!' I'd always raise my arms and say, 'Stop right there. Before you even come in, just let me know: are you Rachel or Richard today? I just want to get my dialogue straight.' And she'd laugh."

Podell's wife, Monica, was a prominent model at the time, and the couple was much in demand on the hip New York social scene as a result of her beauty, Podell's flamboyance, and his client list, which included, along with Reed, George Harrison, Alice Cooper, the Allman Brothers, and Crosby, Stills, and Nash. "We were the hot couple in town, but Lou hated Monica," Podell said. "Lou hated women. And Monica didn't love Lou. I took coke. Lou took speed. I don't know what the fuck Rachel took. One night we were going on a double date to a bar called Willy's on Third Avenue and Eighty-Third Street. So I say to Lou, 'Monica's coming tonight. I don't care how you feel about her. She's the most popular girl in New York, and I would love it if you loved her, but whatever. You're my client; she's my wife. Monica gets respect. This should be fun, not a fucking world war.'"

"Then I go to Monica," he continued, "'Listen, this

guy is my client. I know he's rude. I know he hates women. I know he's a speed freak. They can't all love you like Alice Cooper loves you or Graham Nash loves you. He don't like you.' So we're at Willy's, and within minutes Lou says something about Monica having no tits. So Monica goes right into, 'I have little tits? At least my nipples are bigger than the pimple on your nose that you get from shooting speed, you junkie!' And she runs out of the restaurant. I go to Lou, 'You run after her, or I'll kill you!' Now it's like a scene out of the Beatles' *Help!* There's Monica running. There's Lou running. Behind Lou was Rachel, and behind them all was me. Hysterical. I mean, can you imagine? The drugs ruled everything."

Podell recalled another chaotic moment with Reed. "I was hosting a party at my apartment one night, and Dickey Betts was coming," Podell said, referring to the guitarist best known for his work with the Allman Brothers. "Dickey was a redneck—powerfully built, strong, an angry alcoholic. He hates everything about the likes of Andy Warhol and Lou Reed—'a bunch of fags,' you know what I mean? He's a macho motherfucker. And Lou's coming to the party, too. So, again, I tell everybody, 'Dickey, listen, Lou Reed's going to be here. You don't have to like him, but you do have to respect my home.' And then, 'Lou, Dickey Betts will be here. His money is funding our operation. Just be

polite. You don't have to like him, but when I introduce you to him, be on your best behavior.' I don't
remember the details, but in the first five minutes they
got into a fistfight. I think Dickey punched him in the
face and then left. But that was Lou. I mean, 'Just say
hello to Dickey Betts and go in the other room.' But it
was like, when your parents tell you no, what do you
do? Yes."

Others' memories of Rachel do not depict her as
vivacious and outgoing as Podell's do, but as a quiet,
almost passive presence in Reed's life. Writer Ed McCormack recalled waking up on a black leather couch in
Reed's East Side apartment after blacking out the night
before. When he awoke, Rachel was watching over
him in a living room distinguished by "an elegant glass
coffee table, on top of which was a very strange still
life: a bottle of prescription pills, a circular silver dish
with twelve disposable hypodermic needles neatly
arranged along its edges in a sort of speed-freakishly
compulsive sunbeam pattern, and a row of test tubes
filled with water, little white pills dissolving in milky
bubbles within each one." Rachel, wearing a blue silk
kimono, was on the phone, speaking in a male voice
and leaving a message for her sister. McCormack
described her as reminding him "of Cher, only pret-
tier...with large dark eyes, curtained between sheets
of shiny black hair." Rachel asked how he was feeling,
and then explained that she and Reed had brought

him back to the apartment "to sleep it off" because "You were really out of it. Lou was worried that you were so out of it you might not know what you were doing. . . . He doesn't like to see his friends getting into trouble." When Rachel turned around to walk McCormack to the door, he swiped a prescription bottle of Desoxyn off the coffee table.

Charlie Messing, a guitarist with Peter Stampfel's Unholy Modal Rounders, got a brief glimpse into Reed's domestic life one night after he and Stampfel ran into Reed at a reading by a poet and painter named Camille O'Grady, a mutual friend who had an "S and M following." (O'Grady would later open for Reed at the Bottom Line.) After the reading, Reed hung around, sitting on the floor of the loft with a crowd of about a dozen people, including a "chubby black leather/black guy" who "was offering his ass to Lou, extolling its virtues. Lou was not taking him seriously." Stampfel approached Reed, who explained that he was conducting a study on the "long-range effects of speed" and wanted to solicit Stampfel's views on the subject. So he invited Messing and Stampfel to his apartment on East Fifty-Second Street.

When they arrived, Reed wasn't there, but Rachel invited them in to wait for him. "I honestly could not tell if Rachel was a man or a woman," Messing said. "Low voice, long hair, long fingernails, certain way of walking and sitting. . . . Rachel was a lot like a woman.

And yet... Anyway, he/she was gracious but carefully noncommittal, and so we sat and waited together."

The sparsely furnished apartment had a "spotless polished maple floor," and the two men removed their shoes upon entering. It was the holiday season, and Reed and Rachel had set up a tall Christmas tree. Otherwise, the apartment was filled with up-to-the-minute electronics equipment (including then-new digital clocks, a video camera, and a VCR) provided to Reed by his label at the time, RCA Records. Messing noticed that there were two rows of hardcover books along the windowsill, "all related to Warhol or the Beats." Also resting on the windowsill was a "huge *Physicians' Desk Reference*... the bible for pillheads. It had a photo of, and told the effects of, every pill in existence." Near the stereo was a row of vinyl records; the front one was Aerosmith's 1975 album *Toys in the Attic,* which had come out earlier that year. Messing asked Rachel for something to drink, and she invited him to look in the refrigerator to see what was there. "So I shuffled into their totally clean kitchen and opened the fridge," Messing said. "Sparkling clean inside, too. And the only contents were a package of bacon, a quart of milk, and an almost empty quart of Tropicana." On his trip back from the kitchen, Messing peeked into the apartment's master bedroom: "Absolutely bare except for yet another digital clock."

When Reed arrived home with grocery bags, he pulled out a rawhide toy for one of the small dogs he and Rachel kept in the apartment. He baby-talked with the dog, who went wild greeting him and then chased his new toy around the floor. Reed had also purchased a new pair of aviator sunglasses, which he took out and tried on. He then tossed the pair he had been wearing into a wastebasket.

Ever the gracious host, Reed first chided Stampfel and Messing for not phoning ahead; he didn't have time now for the discussion of speed and its effects. Then he relaxed and sat with the two men on a large futon in the living room. He played them test pressings of *Coney Island Baby,* which would come out a month later, in January of 1976. After Stampfel left, Messing hung around until some of Reed's other friends arrived, and everyone decided to go to dinner at the Carnegie Deli. Messing didn't have enough money to cover his meal. On his way out, like Ed McCormack with Reed's bottle of Desoxyn, he swiped the pair of sunglasses that Reed had thrown in the trash. Decades later, he would sell them on eBay, after "a fierce bidding war," for $250.

The complex nature of Reed and Rachel's relationship—who is taking care of whom?—played out in public as well. On Thanksgiving Day in 1976, Reed had lunch with Rachel and a British journalist at the Beverly Wilshire Hotel after a show the night before at the Santa Monica Civic Center. Rachel was sick with an "infected lung," and Reed asked the journalist to feel Rachel's head to see if she was running a fever. "How is it that *I'm* the voice of reason?" Reed asked Rachel. "I'm running after you. It really seems that way. It's me who tells you to put your coat on, and it's you who should be looking after *me*. We'll end up this tour hating each other!" Rachel replied, "No we won't." The journalist noticed that despite Rachel's illness, she "left the table several times to check that all [was] well at the theater, organized the car to take Lou to the gig, worried whether Lou's two traveling companions — his miniature dachshunds, the Count and the Duke — [were] behaving themselves in the hotel bedroom...and made several calls to New York — acted, in fact, the perfect aide-de-camp."

Jeffrey Ross, who played guitar in Reed's band when he was in his early twenties, described himself as having been "adopted" by Reed and Rachel. "As soon as you met Rachel/Richard — whatever — you were struck by a couple of things," he said. "One was vulnerability. Another was this almost maternal concern for Lou. I know a lot of rock stars and girls, a lot of people who were famous, and you watch the way their partners behaved, as if somehow this is their fame, this is their success. Rachel wasn't like that. Rachel was Lou's partner. Rachel really cared for Lou. By 'vulnerability,' it was a sense I had that she could be hurt easily, that she was eager and excited about everything that went on around Lou in a let's-make-this-better kind of way. Not like, 'I can be famous through this,' but a pride in Lou and concern for him. She was like nonstop energy and enthusiasm, coupled with making sure that Lou's comfort zone was never disturbed."

In all these stories, Rachel conducted herself in the traditional way that Reed liked his partners to comport themselves in public. She was quiet and deferential, "gracious and carefully noncommittal"—very stereotypically wifely, in fact. She did not draw attention away from him, but did whatever she could to make his life easier. She essentially disappeared when he came on the scene, and worked to his benefit in the background. But however well Rachel presented in these situations, Reed had evidently found in her someone whose secret life rivaled or perhaps even exceeded his own—which likely only drove his level of interest in her higher. Reed may have, in part, been joking about having to look after Rachel, but to the degree that he did have to, it was likely both a source of attraction and a problem—the bottom line was, "It's you who should be looking after *me*." If Reed and Jonny Podell had a marriage made in the emergency room, Reed and Rachel had one that drew its power from the vivid inner realms of their psychological lives—and, regardless of everything else, their profound affection for each other.

AFTER *CONEY ISLAND BABY* was released and failed to alter Reed's commercial fortunes in any appreciable way, he pondered his options. He was shopping a manuscript of poems and making noises about possibly working with John Cale again. But despite his debt to RCA, the managerial lawsuits plaguing him, and his perennial substance abuse, Reed's cultural standing was as high as it had ever been, thanks in part to the punk movement burgeoning around the Lower East Side of Manhattan, most notably centered on the club CBGB, on the Bowery where it intersects with Bleecker Street. Aware that he was the movement's spiritual godfather, Reed kept a close eye on it, often going to hear new bands and following their development, both artistically and commercially. These bands may have been his artistic inheritors, but he nonetheless felt competitive with them. It was fine to be seen as an important influence, but he did not want to be shoved to the sidelines by a new generation of rebels. By his own reckoning, he had not yet achieved what he deserved commercially—far from it. In fact, he was at a financial low point, finally living at the Gramercy Park Hotel with Rachel, with RCA picking up the tab.

At around this time, Clive Davis invited Reed to join him and Arista A&R man Bob Feiden at Feiden's modest beach house on Long Island. "We'll listen to music, we'll relax," Davis told him. "It's totally isolated. It will really be fun."

"Clive," Reed responded, "you don't understand. If I ever get a tan, my career would be over."

It's unclear who approached whom about Reed moving from RCA to Arista. Reed always claimed — and took palpable pride in asserting — that Davis contacted him. "There was just me and Rachel . . . living at the fucking Gramercy Park Hotel on fifteen dollars a day, while the lawyers were trying to figure out what to do with me," he said. "Then I got a call from Clive Davis . . . and he said, 'Hey, how ya doing? Haven't seen you for a while.' He *knew* how I was doing. He said, 'Why don't we have lunch?' I felt like saying, 'You mean you want to be seen with me in public?' If Clive could be seen with me, I had turned the corner. I grabbed Rachel and said, 'Do you know who just called?' I knew then that I'd won."

Davis claimed that Reed got in touch with him, complaining about his financial situation at RCA and wanting to see if there might be a place for him at Arista. Davis, then in his midforties, had already become a music industry legend. He had founded Arista Records, and the label instantly became a success story.

Notably, as the punk rock scene began to attract attention, Davis signed Patti Smith, whose incendiary debut album, *Horses,* came out in December of 1975 and became a sensation. That John Cale produced the album, that Smith was hailed as a poet as well as a rock star, and that the Patti Smith Group frequently performed Velvet Underground songs did not escape Reed's attention. With his keen industry perception, Davis certainly understood the value of having both the hottest star on the punk scene and its most seminal influence on his label. That Davis and Reed were friends made the business relationship all the easier.

In a sense, both Reed and Davis wanted the same thing. Their difficulties arose in determining how to get there. Davis was adventurous in his signings, but he never took on artists he did not believe could be commercially successful. He viewed the music industry as a business, and while he strongly supported the need for important songwriters to take left turns, he also believed that having hits was a significant part of what made those left turns credible, or even possible. "Lou doesn't sell albums, but Clive believes in him," an Arista publicist said, and that was true. Overlooked in that statement is that what Davis believed in about Reed, rightly or wrongly, was his *eventual* ability to sell records. Certainly, he took Reed seriously as an artist and would never have attempted to force Reed to do something he didn't want to do. Nor would he have been able to, according to Reed. "I didn't make a record because I couldn't have it my way," Reed said, alluding to his days before the Arista deal. "But I got lucky and met Clive. And now I've got my way — top to bottom control all the way."

Jonny Podell, who became Reed's manager at around this time, summed it up this way: "Lou had relevance. He wanted mass popularity." Then he added a key phrase: "On his own terms." Like so many artists who are not hit makers, Reed viewed his second-tier commercial status as the result of record companies that didn't understand him and, for that reason, couldn't promote and market him properly. Despite occasional moments of accepting his status as a cult artist, he would feel this way until his death.

Reed's and Davis's expectations collided when Reed completed *Rock and Roll Heart,* his first Arista album. Knowing that Reed was hoping for greater commercial success, Davis suggested that the title track had radio potential and could do well if Reed was willing to do some additional work on it. "I felt it was a little sparse for radio," Davis said. "So I said, 'Can you sweeten it up a little? I really feel this could be a radio record with just a little tweaking.'"

Reed allowed that Davis had "good ears," but he was having none of it. "I'm a control person," Reed said. "I fought so hard to get things to the point of having that control that I wouldn't relinquish it...."

I'm like a brick wall sometimes." Davis established a solid rapport with Michael Fonfara, and over the years he would occasionally solicit Fonfara's help in dealing with Reed. "Clive is a genius," Fonfara said. "He would call me into his office once in a while and basically say, 'Lou's not listening to me. You're his bandleader. Won't he listen to you?'" No, he would not. "Every once in a while," Fonfara recalled, "Lou would say, 'Yes, I know you're giving me the perfect commercial way to present my stuff. I don't want it perfect. I want you to mess it up for me. If you can't, I'll mess it up myself.' He used to demand wrong bass notes, ones that just don't belong. He'd say, 'I don't care if it's wrong. It's there.'"

For his part, Davis understood Reed's reluctance. "If I were a painter and I unveiled my painting to a gallery owner and he said, 'If you put more blue in it, I could do better with it....' I mean, I've just created my work. It is what it is. I have a feeling that's what Lou felt. But there is that borderline case where you don't feel you're compromising somebody's art by asking them to do what they need to do to attain the commercial success they keep telling you they want. So it was frustrating. I have the greatest respect for Lou. But the simple fact is that we needed more ammunition, a song that could go to radio, if he was going to break through."

Despite all his resistance, the accessibility of the songs on *Rock and Roll Heart,* which led one wag to dub the album "Lou Reed lite," suggests that he actually was willing to nuzzle a bit closer to the mainstream. While explaining to a pair of journalists "the merits of amphetamines over liquor"—though Reed was consuming plenty of both—he described *Rock and Roll Heart* as "very danceable, the kind of thing that, if you were sitting in a bar and either wanted to punch somebody or fuck, you'd probably play it on the jukebox."

The album's edgiest moment comes on its closing track, "Temporary Thing," a grippingly dramatic confrontation between lovers that Reed acts out as if it were a play. The singer's bitter condescension and angry insistence that the relationship is "just a temporary thing" suggest, conversely, that he's much more deeply invested than he is letting on, or maybe more than he even understands. The effect is powerful and unsettling. The track suggests, as John Rockwell noted in the *New York Times,* that by this point in the album, "Mr. Reed had paid his debts to Mr. Davis or his own commercial demons and felt that he could finally do his thing." Reed, Rockwell correctly noted, "has always been torn between a desire for artsiness and outrage on the one hand and commercial success on the other, but his records have tended to fall into just one of those categories."

Rock and Roll Heart appeared in the fall of 1976 and made a respectable showing, but as usual, and despite Reed's move to Arista, it did not prove to be the commercial breakthrough that part of Reed—and all of Clive Davis—had hoped for.

13

FUCKING FAGGOT JUNKIE

REED'S RECORD SALES MAY have plateaued in the midseventies, but because of the success of the live *Rock n Roll Animal* album and the reputation he had earned for outrageousness, he became a significant attraction on the road. He did well in the United States, typically playing in theater-size halls, but in Europe he could fill much larger venues, often playing outdoor shows to tens of thousands of fans. Tours on that scale need to be run with military precision, but Reed's drug use and general irritability typically made those tours as chaotic as the rest of his life. Admittedly, the infrastructure was not yet in place to smooth the bumps of life on the road, and for someone with Reed's temperament, suspicion of journalists, and increasing need for sonic perfection, it was a hard go—for him and, consequently, everyone around him. "There weren't sound systems," Reed said of that period. "It was like the Wild West out there. The idea of being able to hear the lead singer was a whole new idea. It was like the Wright brothers and the airplane."

"Lou always had lots of issues on the road because he'd be surrounded by people," Fonfara said. "When you'd look out the hotel room window, down in the parking lot there would be thirty or forty people, kids, mostly, all dressed exactly like Lou, staring up at the windows, waiting for a glimpse of him." Reed could be rude even to the most expert, sophisticated, and supportive journalists, so when he would meet the gaggle of reporters randomly assigned to cover one of his press conferences, the results were not likely to be good. Reed became the master of the Dylan-style put-on and put-down. Like Dylan, he had decided that it was pointless to expend energy determining if a question was smart, witless, well intended, or hostile. Everyone received the same dismissive treatment, often to hilarious effect, as in the exchanges that took place at an airport press conference Reed submitted to in Sydney, Australia, in August of 1974. His hair blond and close-cropped, Reed was wearing sunglasses and sipping a pastel-colored drink as a roomful of reporters peppered him with questions:

You said a little while ago that you sing mainly about drugs. Is that right?
Sometimes.

Why do you do this?
Because I think the government is plotting against me.

Were you searched by our customs men for drugs?
Oh, no, because I don't take any.

No drugs at all?
Uh-uh. I'm high on life.

And yet you sing about them. Do you want people to take drugs themselves?
Oh, yeah. I want them to take drugs.

Why is this?
Because it's better than Monopoly.

Why is your music so popular, Lou?
I didn't know it was popular.

Do you think it's a decadent society we're living in?
No.

Would you describe yourself as a decadent person?
No.

How would you describe yourself?
Average.

You're a man of few words. Why is this?
I don't have anything to say.

Do you like press interviews in general?
No.

You shun publicity?
No.

What message is it that you're trying to get across?
I don't have one.

Would it be right to call your music gutter rock?
Gutter rock?

Gutter rock.
Oh, yeah.

Where do you spend your money?
On drugs.

For other people.
Right.

Who writes these things about you if they're not true?
Journalists.

[Laughter] Is that perhaps why you don't like journalists?
Oh, I love journalists.

Reed delivered his responses in the affectless style perfected by Andy Warhol in his own interviews. Reed had learned well from the master: his music, attitude, and look encouraged questions about decadence, shock, and outrage—"gutter rock," indeed—but rather than credit those questions by addressing them, Reed employed the Warholian strategy of admitting to being exactly whatever his interrogators believed him to be ("Oh, yeah. I want [people] to take drugs"), all in a tone that suggested it was the most natural thing in the world. At the same time, Reed rejected the charge of being decadent and, once again borrowing from the Warhol playbook, described himself as "average." The reporters at the press conference grew increasingly irritated and attempted to bait him, accusing him of, among other things, hypocrisy. One asked if his "anti-social behavior"—that is, his refusal to cooperate with them—was just part of a "show business gimmick," just an expression of his being in the "entertainment game," a phrase Reed repeated with some amusement. But he never bit back. As with the questions about "gutter rock" and whether or not he wanted people to take drugs, Reed seemed on the verge of laughter, but never broke the numbed serenity of his character.

On the tour in support of *Sally Can't Dance,* Reed began the onstage ritual of pretending to shoot drugs. It became a staple of his shows—another example of the self-conscious, shock-the-bourgeoisie, titillate-the-suburban-masses ethos that his critics despised in him. "In the middle of that tour, Lou decided that he didn't want to be James Brown anymore—he was going to go back to being Lou Reed," Fonfara said. "So he'd tie himself off with the microphone cord and then pretend to shoot speed onstage. Because of his song 'Heroin,' he knew he was fooling the audience. Most people who didn't know any better—and that's ninety percent of them—thought he was a heroin addict. But anyone who did know knew he was a speed freak."

Reed, of course, was playing a character in these performances, regardless of his actual preference in drugs to inject. The Velvets' "White Light/White Heat" made his fondness for speed palpable, but he would enact his shooting-up ritual during "Heroin," a far more dramatic setting for his mock needle play. For addicts, organizing their drug gear—their "works," as the slang term has it—as they prepare to shoot up has a ritualistic, even sacred, element. Reed fully understood the power of taking that private, intensely intimate act public in a concert setting. The vast majority of his audience, needless to say, was entirely unaware of anything remotely that high-minded in his actions. Fonfara was correct in stating that Reed was becoming "Lou Reed" again, or at least the version of Lou Reed that the audience expected to see. To that extent, he was playing to the cheap seats, going for the obvious effect.

Not to say that such gestures couldn't have a significant impact. Suzanne Vega first saw Reed, whom she had barely paid attention to previously, perform at Columbia University in 1979, when she was taken to the show on a date. "Lou was smashing things, lighting cigarettes, and throwing them at the audience and pretending to shoot up, tying up his arm and all that," she recalled. "He played 'Caroline Says II,' and that verse is so clear, it's like a play: 'Caroline says / As she gets up from the floor / You can hit me all you want to / But I don't love you anymore.' That's so brilliant. That's the whole story right there. I was like, I didn't even know you were allowed to say things like that on a stage. It just had never occurred to me. I came away from that night thinking, wow, he really tells the truth about things. After that, whenever he played in New York, I would go see him." Vega's epiphany is especially significant when one considers that "Luka," her best-known song, would be about a victim of abuse.

REED'S DRINKING AND DRUG use, of course, played a role in how well life on the road went for him and the band. "If he didn't do too much, he'd be right on the money. He'd be great," Fonfara said about Reed's use of speed. "But if he did a little too much, he'd get nervous, he'd be cranky before we went on. Then once we got onstage, he'd be fine."

Of course, getting onstage presented its own set of challenges. "We'd be staying in a hotel, and Lou would call me in the morning and say, 'Meet me down in the courtyard,'" Fonfara said. "So I'd go down, and there would be these white-jacketed waiters with big jeroboams of Dom Perignon and a guy squeezing fresh orange juice, and we'd drink mimosas until we could hardly walk. Then he'd say, 'Well, now we've got to go to the gig.' I'd look at him walking across the floor, and I'd think, 'I can't even get up. How can he do it?' But he could handle a lot of booze. Eventually, that's what put his liver over, I think."

Reed's taste in alcohol was not always so refined. Primarily, he was a Scotch drinker, and he preferred Johnnie Walker Red to anything more top-shelf. "Of course, when people found out he liked Scotch, they would present him with the high-end, single malt stuff," Fonfara recalled. "He would look at me and say, 'Here, you take this,' and he'd hand me a beautiful bottle of Glenmorangie or some other brand worth twenty times what he was drinking. He'd say, 'Fonf, you can have this wimpy stuff for people who don't know about Scotch. Give me the good industrial stuff!'" And occasionally Reed wouldn't make it to the stage. On August 5, 1975, he was scheduled to perform at the Wellington Town Hall in New Zealand, but the promoter, Ron Blackmore, abruptly canceled the show. Blackmore told the *Evening Post* that Reed had "a very, very personal problem that should never have damned well happened. It's so personal and serious that I can't even tell you about it off the record." Reed made up the show the following night, but many of the more than two thousand fans who had bought tickets for the previous night failed to show up.

The audiences, too, used the occasion of a Lou Reed show to act out their own excesses. Reed told his friend Eric Andersen that audiences "at Tom Jones's shows would throw roses, panties, and hotel room keys. On my European tours, they'd throw loaded syringes onstage."

"For the most part, the audiences were terrific," Fonfara said, and hearing tens of thousands of people screaming *"Loooouuu"* night after night was exhilarating. But if the band was extremely late or didn't even show it was quite another story. And if Reed sensed a problem of any kind, he wouldn't hesitate to cut the show short. That created its own problems. "That was one thing Lou was never afraid to do," Fonfara said. "If he thought things weren't going right, he'd snap his fingers and tell the roadies to get the band off the stage. So we had a number of riots, and it would take an awful lot of police to calm the people down." It seemed as if every country eventually got its own Lou Reed story. "We did some gigs in Japan where all these black belts would be holding arms in front of the stage," Fonfara said. "I had my elbow shattered once by a group of kids who leaped on me. In Europe, they would throw bottles and shoot fireworks like Roman candles at the stage. We were playing in Glasgow once and I got knocked out cold by a quart bottle of wine."

Perhaps the most extreme event occurred in Portugal. According to Fonfara, the band was "supposed to play in this huge Christians-and-lions-type stadium. As we were getting close in our limos, Lou could see people were scaling the walls and climbing on each other's shoulders to get in for free. He flipped and decided that the band wasn't going to go on, so we drove away. They rioted so bad we couldn't get out of town. The streets were filled with gangs of thugs looking for Lou and the band.

"So the audiences loved Lou as long as he'd go on. But it was like Sly and the Family Stone back in their day. They had all these great fans, but when they didn't actually turn up for the show, the crowd would turn ugly."

Things could turn ugly on the streets as well, given Reed's look and propensities. Fonfara believed that Reed's interest in martial arts had its origins in one edgy night in Sweden. "We were walking down the street in Stockholm, and Lou was dressed especially poufy—earrings, face painted, everything. A couple of Russian sailors started to push him around. So I took them out. After that, Lou followed me like a puppy, begging me to teach him how to do that. I'd been in martial arts maybe ten, twelve years—I did three kinds of karate, two kinds of kung fu, and I was a kickboxer. Lou was quite impressed. I didn't even have a scrape on my knuckles. I used my feet. Anyway, they were down, and I took Lou back to the hotel. He was just, 'You've got to show me how to do that.' So when we got back to New York, I got him into a martial arts club, and we started working out. He became fanatic— Lou was fanatical about everything. We'd work out for a couple of hours, and I'd be ready to leave, and he'd say, 'I want to go another two hours.' He got pretty good at it and started getting himself into shape, but he'd have constant relapses into speed and booze."

Reed continued to experiment onstage, most notably with his tour in 1976 in support of *Rock and Roll Heart*. For those shows, he performed in front of a phalanx of television monitors, many of which he had found on the street with the help of Mick Rock and guitarist Jeffrey Ross. Obviously, it was an idea well ahead of its time—an introduction of randomness into his stage presentation—as well as a smart nod back to Warhol and his fascination with media. As Warhol and Paul Morrissey had during the Exploding Plastic Inevitable events, Reed had Mick Rock feed imagery from backstage into the monitors, providing a meta aspect to his shows. Bathing himself in a flood of images somehow rendered his music that much more unsettling.

Reviewing one of the New York shows at the Palladium, John Rockwell wrote in the *New York Times* that "the mood was only enhanced by forty-eight black-and-white television monitors that half surrounded him on the rear in three squat banks of sixteen each. In quaint moments, most of the sets glowed blankly, and a few picked up real programs; during the music, they all pulsed together in abstract patterns." Rockwell also described the emotional impact of Reed's singing, which is easy to frame as minimalist without understanding the power that his small gestures unleashed. "Mr. Reed's singing remains about the most dramatic instance of a voice that fails by most ordinary standards of musicianship and yet functions superbly as a communicative instrument," he wrote. "His ability to skirt the notes consistently is an act of near genius, and tone quality is almost an irrelevant category. Yet the very instability of pitch lends an ominous undercurrent to the sound, and the phrasing, with its quick bursts of anger seemingly unrelated to the text, is as chilling as ever."

Still, Rockwell concluded that the show was a disappointment. Backed by a band that consisted of saxophone, keyboards, bass, and drums, Reed apparently did not play guitar until the very end of the show.

While Rockwell complimented the band's technical skills ("as fluent an ensemble as Mr. Reed has had"), he took issue with the music as a "rather faceless, jazz-ish idiom" that lacked "a true rock aura." It's telling that as punk was beginning to strip rock down to its absolute basics, Reed began to reexplore his youthful fascination with jazz and toured with the most elaborate staging of his career—yet another example of his refusal to allow external forces of any sort to dictate his direction. But if you're insistent on not following trends, are you really immune to them? Are your choices then as much a function of trends as if you'd blindly followed them? Reed's musical progression would raise those questions time and time again. Nonetheless, jazz continued to move in and out of his music through the end of the seventies—an era in which "jazz-rock" entered the musical lexicon as fully as punk did.

The Palladium set may have been "faceless," but the 1976 tour soon heated up thanks to a chance encounter at an airport. Reed and the band ran into the trumpet player Don Cherry when they arrived at LAX in Los Angeles; Cherry was about to fly out after a visit. Fonfara recalled Reed recognizing Cherry from an Ornette Coleman album cover and walking up to introduce himself. Bassist Bruce Yaw, who was playing with Reed at the time, recalled that the band's saxophonist, Marty Fogel, knew Cherry from New

York and provided the introduction. Regardless, the two men hit it off immediately. According to Fonfara, Reed said, " 'We're playing the Anaheim Convention Center tonight. Will you please hang out for an extra day and come and sit in with us? I'd give anything to have you onstage with us.' Don said 'Fine,' canceled his flight, and came down to the hotel. Lou got him a room and we went and did the Convention Center that night."

Playing with Cherry was a thrill Reed would refer back to for the rest of his life. One of his many, oft-repeated critiques of punk was its musical primitivism, its lack, in his view, of subtlety or nuance. In the shows the two men played together, Cherry pushed the jazz element in Reed's sound to the edge, dramatizing Reed's fondness for the out jazz Cherry had pioneered with Ornette Coleman—the sort of music Reed used to love to play on his radio show in college. The band, too, lifted off with Cherry on board. "Don Cherry is positively spiritual onstage," Fonfara recalled. "He was like some ghost that was floating above the ground. He'd suddenly come creeping in from between the amplifiers, and all of a sudden he's here like an apparition, and then he'd hit two or three notes that are outside, take a Sunday stroll, and then [come] back in. But [those notes added] a lot of meaning to what Lou was saying. Lou loved him, and he loved Lou."

*   *   *

AMID THE CHAOS THAT was his life in the late seventies, Reed met Sylvia Morales, the woman who would become his second wife. The story of how they met varies with the teller. Michael Fonfara claimed that he introduced Morales to Reed after spotting her in the audience one night. "I looked at this group of girls in front of me, and one of them was waving," he recalled. "So I pointed to her and told my keyboard roadie, 'I'd like to have that one backstage.' So he brought her back, and she ended up coming back to the hotel with me. We were going up in the elevator, and she said, 'Michael, I've got to tell you the truth. I'm really doing this so that I can meet Lou.' So when we got to my room, I said, 'Okay, just wait here a minute.'

"I went to Lou's room and said, 'Just give this girl five minutes. She's a nice girl.' He said, 'As long as you come back—and she only gets five minutes.' They started to talk and I could see their foreheads coming closer together. Then Lou looked up at me, jerked his thumb at the door, and said, 'Get out.' The next morning we met for breakfast and he was already talking about Sylvia."

However, Reed's friend Erin Clermont said that Reed first encountered Sylvia at a meeting of the Eulenspiegel Society, the BDSM support group based in Manhattan. For her part, Morales said she was introduced to Reed by Anya Phillips, a downtown New York scenester, cofounder of the New Wave dance emporium the Mudd Club, and, eventually, manager of the No Wave band James Chance and the Contortions. Phillips also worked as a dominatrix and had been friends with Morales since their high school days in Taiwan, where Morales's father, who was in the military, had been stationed. According to Morales, she and Phillips spotted Reed in a bar on Eighth Avenue in Manhattan, Phillips walked over and introduced herself to him, and the three of them got into a conversation. At the time, Morales was in her early twenties and a student at Sarah Lawrence College in Bronxville, just north of New York City. She was intimidated by Reed but determined to hold her own in his presence. "Lou's very, very smart, and I fancied myself to be very, very smart, and Lou made some remark that I was not as bright as he was," she said. "But I was not gonna let this guy think that he was some rich famous rock star that was impressing me."

But of course she was impressed. Like so many of the people Reed was drawn to, Morales was poised, well-read, and articulate. She talked with him about writers and books, his favorite subjects. He also would have noted her Sarah Lawrence pedigree. That Reed even bothered to make a joke about being smarter than Morales indicates that he was taken with her. Typically, he would assume his intellectual superiority, or, if he truly didn't care, he would ignore the other person or insult her. His teasing was a mark of his attraction. Even so, when they parted, Morales and Reed did not exchange numbers, so Morales hatched a plan to find out Reed's address in order to write him a letter—a gesture far more intimate than a phone call. The strategy worked. After he received her letter, Reed contacted Morales, and the two began to see each other.

Fonfara instantly noted that Morales understood how to behave around Reed, and she honed that understanding as their relationship developed. "She was very smart, and she knew when not to talk," Fonfara said. "She knew when to give Lou the floor. She'd just sit there and nod. And whenever she disagreed with him, she would make her views known, but not publicly. She'd talk to him on the side." Before long, Morales moved into the apartment Reed had been sharing with Rachel on Christopher Street, near Sheridan Square. Fonfara, who lived nearby with his wife, said, "Soon Rachel was gone, Sylvia was there, and they kept the dachshunds."

As for Rachel's disappearance, Reed was determined to keep that as mysterious as possible. "I never found out what happened," Fonfara said. "All I knew was that Rachel dropped off the scene, and I never saw her again. Never. I asked Lou about Rachel a couple of times, and he just said, 'Never mind. You don't want to know.'"

There was talk that Rachel had been taking hormones

and was interested in a sex change operation, and that Reed began pulling away from her; whether this was because of a discomfort with that transition or for other reasons is unknown. One of the last people known to have seen her was guitarist Jeffrey Ross, who ran into her near the intersection of Eighth Street and Sixth Avenue in the Village, in either the late eighties or early nineties. "I was walking across the street, and on that little triangle in the middle of the street comes Rachel," he recalled. "'Oh, my God, Jeffrey, how are you? I can't believe it!' I recognized him right away. There had been no further treatments, I guess, or whatever was going on when she was with Lou. She had been on hormones, trying to grow tits, basically. She was very proud of them, too, these little nine-year-old breasts under a T-shirt. I guess all that stopped when she wasn't with Lou anymore. This is much later—you've got to figure this is ten, twelve years of living over in the West Village, doing whatever you do there to earn money when you're a transsexual—with what I self-diagnosed as an obvious crack problem. She was absolutely rail thin, very unhealthy. AIDS had basically taken over New York and the crack surge had started." Reed would almost never again speak of Rachel, publicly or privately.

WHATEVER RACHEL'S FATE, HER breakup with Reed became one of the subthemes of Reed's next album,

Street Hassle, which came out in February of 1978; *Rolling Stone* referred to Rachel as the album's "raison d'être." *Street Hassle,* which combined live performances of shows in Germany with studio overdubs, marks something like the beginning of Reed's obsession with technology, although *Metal Machine Music* might contend for that honor as well. *Street Hassle* was the first album released using the binaural process created by sound architect and engineer Manfred Schunke; it involved computer-designed models of the average human head. "The detail was as precise as possible down to the size, shape, and bone structure of the ear and ear canal," wrote music historian Rob Bowman. "Microphones were then designed to fit each ear so, theoretically, what they recorded would be exactly what a human being sitting in the position the head was placed in would actually hear." Schunke engineered *Street Hassle,* as well as Reed's next two albums.

Using the binaural technique, which pretty much assumed that fans would be listening to the album through headphones, was a characteristically confounding gesture on Reed's part. By 1978, punk had fully enshrined itself as a national movement in the United States. Patti Smith's *Horses* was already regarded as a classic, and the Ramones, Talking Heads, and Television had emerged as important groups. While all the bands gathered under the punk rubric were different, the very idea of punk rested on rawness and irreverence.

The preciousness of recording an album meant to be heard through headphones seemed entirely antithetical to everything punk represented. Reed, of course, completely understood the appeal of punk. When Danny Fields first played him a demo tape of the Ramones, Reed couldn't have been more excited. "They're crazy!" he exclaimed. "I mean, it makes everybody else look so fucking wimpy, Patti Smith and me included, man.... They got them an amp, they got them a guitar, and now look—there they are.... It doesn't take any talent. All they're doing is banging it, and look at this. That is the greatest thing I've ever heard."

But Reed clearly believed that what was good for the Ramones, or for the punk aesthetic generally, did not really apply to him. The notion that it "doesn't take any talent" to play rock and roll was fine for a laugh about a new band with an old friend. But Reed had premised his entire career on the idea that rock music could bear the weight of great literature. Writing lyrics—or, for that matter, making music—as cartoonish as the Ramones' was the last thing he wanted to do. He described his song "Banging on My Drum" on *Rock and Roll Heart* as "what the Ramones *should* do. Three chords is three chords, but there is a finesse to it." As for the Sex Pistols, Reed said, "Shakespeare had a phrase for that....'Sound and fury signifying nothing.' I'm so tired of the theory of the noble savage. I'd like to hear punks who weren't at the mercy of their own rage and who could put together a coherent sentence." The poet and performance artist Camille O'Grady aptly summed up Reed's complicated attitude toward punk: "The kid adopted me, so I might as well make the best of it." But his contrarian nature and fierce artistic independence finally would not allow him to fully exploit the possibilities that the punk revolution offered him. Instead, *Street Hassle* reflected the most sophisticated recording technology that Reed could find.

Thematically, however, *Street Hassle* pushed up against and overwhelmed the aesthetic challenges that punk represented and demonstrated why Reed was a founding father. In a brilliant nod to his multiple personalities and image shifts, Reed opens the album in jagged conversation with himself. He references some career high points as the rugged riff from "Gimmie Some Good Times," the album's first song, plays in the background. "Hey, if it ain't the rock-and-roll animal himself," he says in an excited voice, as if mimicking a fan running into him on the street. "What are ya doin', bro?" He answers in his characteristic speech-singing with the opening line of "Sweet Jane": "Standing on the corner / Suitcase in my hand." As if enthused by hearing the opening line of a Velvet Underground classic, Reed the fan exclaims, "No shit! What it is!"

Reed the artist continues to sing, "Jack is in his corset, Jane is in her vest." In a withering tone, Reed the fan responds, "Fucking faggot junkie."

At around the time of the release of *Coney Island Baby*, Reed had told Lenny Kaye, in language predictive of the opening exchange on *Street Hassle*, that he was done with the stereotypical "Lou Reed" image — "No more bullshit, dyed hair, faggot junkie trip," he said. It's hard not to hear those words repeated on *Street Hassle* as a repudiation of the life he had been living with Rachel. The three-part title track, one of the masterpieces of Reed's solo career, stands as something of a requiem for Reed and Rachel's relationship, as well as for the tawdry, dangerous street life out of which Rachel had emerged. Indeed, Reed once described the nearly eleven-minute "Street Hassle" as his answer to the question, "What would happen if Raymond Chandler wrote a rock-and-roll song?"

The first section of "Street Hassle," "Waltzing Matilda," is set to an elegant cello riff and describes in unapologetically romantic terms a woman or transvestite picking up a young male hustler for sex. Rather than quick, furtive, and anonymous, the act is described in lovingly erotic terms: "He made love to her gently / It was like she'd never ever come." The "sha-la-la-la" interjections in the lyrics recall both innocent children's rhymes and doo-wop rhapsodies, both helping to sweeten the sexual encounter. In a sense, Reed is revisiting the meet-cute he described in *Coney Island Baby*'s "Crazy Feeling," in which a chiming guitar and a lilting melody lend a shimmering quality to an after-hours gay bar pickup. The two songs, then, frame Reed and Rachel's relationship, the first describing the headiness of falling in love, the second fixing that emotion in an equally romantic but ultimately finite context. "Neither one regretted a thing," Reed concludes "Waltzing Matilda." The line lends dignity to the two characters in the song but also makes it clear, with an undercurrent of sadness, that whatever passed between them is now over.

The second section of "Street Hassle," itself titled "Street Hassle," takes its inspiration from the 1975 death of Eric Emerson, a musician, dancer, actor, and Factory regular, as well as the man who caused the Verve recall of *The Velvet Underground and Nico* when he threatened to sue the label because a photograph of him appeared on the album's back cover without his permission. Emerson's body was found near the docks by the West Side Highway, and his death was attributed to a hit-and-run accident. It was widely rumored, however, that he had died in another location from a heroin overdose and that his body had been left in the street to create the impression of an accident in order to avoid a police investigation. Reed used that incident and the speculation surrounding it as the basis for "Street Hassle," a riveting, streetwise, morally compromised dramatic monologue delivered by a man in whose apartment a young woman dies of an overdose. In a delivery bristling with nervous, suppressed urgency, the singer tells the man who brought the girl with him that he has to get her body out of the apartment, and "by morning she's just another hit-and-run." In one of the record's most chilling moments, the singer takes the "slip away" line that is the heart of the song's romance—"Why don't we slip away?" the hustler is asked in "Waltzing Matilda," and that notion becomes the title and main theme of the song's heartbreaking third movement—and transforms it into a suggestion to get rid of the girl's body. "Sha-la-la-la, man," the singer recites with a kind of weary contempt. "Why don't you just slip her away?" Reed said he wasn't sure why he changed the gender of the drug overdose victim in the song from male, as in the case of Eric Emerson, to female, but doing so adds to the sexual blurring that characterized Reed's relationship with Rachel, as well as his decision to move on from Rachel to Sylvia Morales.

Dramatically, "Slipaway," the third and final section of "Street Hassle," begins with a recitation by Bruce Springsteen. By this point, Reed recognized that, like himself, Springsteen was writing about a community of outsiders who rarely received recognition in works of art. To end the "Street Hassle" section of the song, Reed had observed of the lost souls he was singing about that "some people got no choice / And they can never find a voice / To talk with that they can even call their own / So the first thing that they see that allows them the right to be / Why, they follow it / You know, it's called bad luck." Those lyrics could easily find a place in any number of Springsteen songs, and as it happened, Springsteen was working on *Darkness on the Edge of Town,* his bleakest and most unsparing album, at the time. Springsteen's voice then, a mumbled drawl that sounds world-weary and defeated, seems entirely at home in Reed's portrayal of a Dantean urban inferno. Reed said that if he had recited those lines, they would have "come out funny. And when he did it, it sounded real." Springsteen's spoken part ends with a sly reference to perhaps the most famous line that he has ever written: "You know, tramps like us, we were born to pay."

Springsteen's speech introduces what may well be the most poignant passage in any of Reed's songs. A bass guitar continues the musical theme the cello established, and a mournful, droning organ contributes to an atmosphere of irretrievable loss. "Love has gone away," Reed sings, "And there's no one here now / And there's nothing left to say / But, oh, how I miss him, baby." Such speculation is always problematic, but, in the simplicity and sheer heartache of those lyrics, it very much sounds as if Reed is singing in his own voice, not that of a character. In any event, the breakup of Reed and Rachel's relationship lurks in the

background. While Reed had explored gay relationships in songs before, it had always been with an element of theatricality and self-conscious provocation.
But that "oh, how I miss him, baby," delivered in a
quavering voice on the verge of breaking down, hits
with extraordinary power. "Slipaway" tells the story of
two human beings whose bond has disintegrated, leaving emotional devastation in its wake. Writing with
that kind of vulnerability about a love affair between
two men in a rock song was revolutionary at the time
and has lost little of its impact.

In an interview following the release of *Street Hassle*, Reed backed off his frequent claim that he had
nothing remotely in common with the "Lou Reed"
character. Speaking about that album and *Coney Island
Baby*, he said, "There are some severe little tangent
things in my songs that remove them from me, but,
ah, yes, they're very personal. I guess the Lou Reed
character is pretty close to the real Lou Reed, to the
point, maybe, where there's really no heavy difference
between the two, except maybe a piece of vinyl. I keep
hedging my bet, instead of saying that's really me, but
that is me, as much as you can get on record." In the
same interview, Reed, who typically resisted interpreting his own songs, offered a deep reading of the "Street
Hassle" and "Slipaway" sections of "Street Hassle" that
beautifully ties them together.

The character in "Street Hassle" who suggests dragging the young girl's body out of his apartment, Reed suggests, "may come off as a little cruel, but let's say he's also the guy who's singing the last part about losing love. He's already lost the one for him. He's not unaware of those feelings; he's just handling the situation, that's all.... That's what my songs are all about: they're one-to-ones. I just let people eavesdrop on them. Like that line at the end of 'Street Hassle': 'Love has gone away / Took the rings right off my fingers / There's nothing left to say / But oh, how I miss him, baby.' That person really exists. He *did* take the rings right off my fingers, and I do miss him."

That image of removing rings resonates as a primal symbol of a relationship that has come apart but also as an allusion to the criminality and thievery that were so much a part of the hustling world Rachel lived in. To make that point explicit, in the interview, Reed emphasized the word "him" in the lyrics he quoted, and then explained why it's there. "They're not heterosexual concerns running through that song," Reed said. "I don't make a big deal of it, but when I mention a pronoun, its gender is all-important. It's just that my gay people don't lisp. They're not any more affected than the straight world. They just *are*. That's important to me. I'm one of them and I'm right there, just like anybody else. It's not made anything other than what it is. But if you take me, you've got to take the whole thing."

That interview marked one of the last times Reed would publicly describe himself as gay. As Rachel receded and Morales became more of a force in his life, Reed increasingly identified as heterosexual. To that extent, the song "Street Hassle" was a farewell to both a person and an identity. Beyond its extraordinary title track, however, the *Street Hassle* album was something of a hodgepodge. Among its stranger aspects is the notorious "I Wanna Be Black," which channels into a song the racial provocations Reed had indulged in interviews and elsewhere. A swipe at white artists who mimic black styles—odd coming from a man who, as Michael Fonfara said, had decided he wanted to be James Brown just a few years before—the song expresses the wish to no longer be a "fucked-up, middle-class college student" and instead to have "a stable of foxy whores," "shoot twenty feet of jism," "have a big prick," and "fuck up the Jews." Beyond those coarse stereotypes, both Martin Luther King Jr. and Malcolm X come in for equally dim-witted treatment. Reed played the song live many times but eventually grew uncomfortable with it, though it continued to turn up on various anthologies over the years.

Such songs doomed *Street Hassle* commercially. According to Reed, Clive Davis lost patience with him when he heard the stunning opening line of the "Street Hassle" section of the title track: "Hey, that cunt's not breathing." Davis did not recall it that way, and said he encouraged Reed to expand "Street Hassle" into the extended tour de force that it became. Regardless, the album did not perform "meaningfully," in Davis's terms, i.e., commercially. Critically, however, it was a major success. To John Rockwell, it sounded "as if Mr. Reed were finally beginning to make some sort of productive synthesis of the warring tensions within himself." In a lead review, *Rolling Stone* called *Street Hassle* "a stunning incandescent triumph—the best solo album Lou Reed has ever done." The review concludes, "After all this time, he still cares. How strangely moving that is."

REED HAD BEGUN TO make the Bottom Line something like his New York headquarters, as he had seen Bruce Springsteen do. Ever since the four-hundred-seat club had opened in 1974, the small, comfortable venue on the corner of Mercer and West Fourth Streets in Greenwich Village had become an essential part of the music industry and media scene. Record companies would showcase new performers there in order to generate coverage and buzz. More-established acts like Reed, who could easily fill much larger venues, played there to rally the faithful and create a sense of occasion. Reed concluded his tour in support of *Street Hassle* with a five-night stand at the club, from May 17 to 21, 1978, for a total of ten shows—two per night for an admission charge of seven dollars. As always when Reed played his hometown, expectations ran high. He was particularly excited by his band at the time: a ferocious combo that consisted of Michael Fonfara on keyboards, Stuart Heinrich on guitar, Ellard "Moose" Boles on bass, Marty Fogel on saxophone, Michael Suchorsky on drums, and Angela Howell and Chrissy Faith on backing vocals. "I thought I had a killer group," Reed said. "I couldn't play guitar with a lot of those earlier bands. I loved playing guitar with this one." Reed decided to record the Bottom Line shows for a live album.

Take No Prisoners was released in November of 1978, just in time for the lucrative holiday record-buying season. No doubt it was intended to be something like a live greatest hits set that would appeal to both initiates and the curious. Instead, it turned out to be one of the most notorious albums of Reed's career. It was a double album with a gatefold sleeve running more than ninety minutes and featuring a mere ten songs. Reed was right about the band. When it was allowed to play, it was funky, jazzy, and rocking, injecting contemporary life into Velvet Underground classics like "Sweet Jane" and "I'm Waiting for the Man," while delivering all the emotional drama of "Street Hassle" and "Coney Island Baby." Repeatedly, however, Reed halts the proceedings to bait and insult the audience, complain about his career, and ramble on about his personal history, the characters in his songs, the denizens of Andy Warhol's Factory, and life in New York City. He rails against critics, mentioning John Rockwell and Robert Christgau by name even though both had been supporters of the Velvet Underground and his solo career. Perhaps that very support was part of the problem. "Fuck you! I don't need you to tell me I'm good," Reed spits. (Christgau's response in his *Village Voice* Consumer Guide column: "I thank Lou for pronouncing my name right. C+.") The album is cringeworthy at times and funny at others, as if Lenny Bruce had morphed into Henny Youngman in a comedy club version of Max's Kansas City. It's unlike any album, recorded live or in the studio, before or since.

Reed put Michael Fonfara in charge of assembling the live album. As far as Reed's rants from the stage went, Fonfara simply said, "I thought he was too drunk. But his audience worldwide expected him to be drunk. If they saw him walking up onstage totally straight, they'd say, 'This isn't the Lou Reed we came to see.' I know he felt that he had to live up to his image." That insistence from his fans that Reed push to extremes is part of what led Reed to title the album *Take No Prisoners*. "When we were in Montreal before we went on, somebody out in the audience was yelling, 'Take no prisoners, Lou, take no prisoners!'" Reed said. "Then the guy would just bash his head against the table. 'Lou Reed, take no prisoners!' — *smack!* I thought the phrase was great. It couldn't have been more appropriate. 'Don't take prisoners; beat us to death. Shoot us. Maim us. Kill us. But don't settle for less. Go all the way!' That's what I took it to mean."

Reed compared the album to *Metal Machine Music* in both its impact and its intent. After describing the album as "manly," he said, "I wanted to make a record that wouldn't give an inch. If anything, it would push the world *back* just an inch or two. If *Metal Machine Music* was just a hello note, *Take No Prisoners* is the letter that should have gone with it. You may find this funny, but I think of it as a contemporary urban blues album. After all, that's what I write — tales of the city. And if I dropped dead tomorrow, this is the record I'd choose for posterity. It's not only the smartest thing I've ever done, it's also as close to Lou Reed as you're probably going to get, for better or worse."

Reed wanted an album documenting the highly idiosyncratic Bottom Line shows, and that's exactly what he got. Whereas his introduction to "I'm Waiting for the Man" on the Velvet Underground's live album *1969* is a perfect example of his ability to turn on the charm from the stage while maintaining his tough-as-nails persona, on *Take No Prisoners* he succumbs to a fatal case of logorrhea. "Everybody said, 'You don't talk enough onstage. Can't you just introduce songs?'" Reed joked about the album years later. "Well, there it is: Lou Reed talks — and talks and talks and talks." In his *Rolling Stone* review, critic Ken Tucker accurately described *Take No Prisoners* as "a barrage of invective, self-laceration, barbarity, and the all-out savaging of just about everybody who happened to pop into Reed's head."

A *Rolling Stone* review of Reed at the Bottom Line in 1979 noted that his shows at the club were more like family reunions than concerts, and indeed, the performances captured on *Take No Prisoners* do have the feel of a rambunctious Thanksgiving dinner with relatives. Even at their most abrasive, Reed's screeds and his exchanges with the audience imply an intimacy that could have been achieved only in front of a New York crowd, and in as tight a space as the Bottom Line. "I always think of the audiences in New York as friends," Reed said. "Or else they'd shoot me." In its credits, *Take No Prisoners* is dedicated to "Cecil and Beanie" (correctly spelled "Beany"), two puppets and, later, cartoon characters whose smart, satirical antics date back to the 1940s. Asked about the dedication, Reed responded, "Why did I do it? Who knows? It was just there to show you, hey, we're not always so serious. But I guess you could already tell that from the recording, right?"

If, as he did throughout the seventies, Reed followed up a triumph—such as *Street Hassle*—with outrage—such as *Take No Prisoners*—he once again tried to get back on track, this time with *The Bells,* which came out in April of 1979. Not that *The Bells* is

immediately accessible. Some songs on it seem con-
foundingly simple, even one-dimensional; the rest, in
contrast, are thick with sound and emotion. Trum-
peter Don Cherry joined the group in the studio for
these sessions, and Reed made much of the jazz elements in the band's sound on the album. But it's not
jazz that anyone who typically listened to jazz would
be likely to enjoy or even want to hear. As Reed himself joked, "If you can't play rock and you can't play
jazz, you put the two together and you've really got
something." The album's jazz components, its descent
into atmospheric noises and effects, particularly on the
title track, are part of its intense experimental impulses.
Like so much of Reed's work, *The Bells* moves back
and forth across a line separating commercial gestures,
attempting to grapple with the recognizable sounds of
the contemporary moment while compulsively pushing the music well beyond the boundaries of mainstream acceptability. Reed delivered his vocals in the
same staccato, strangulated style he had defined on
Street Hassle, and in a bid for spontaneity, he wrote
most of his lyrics in the studio. The album's title nicely
gets at the extremes Reed was always attempting to
bridge. "The Bells" was a highly dramatic early fifties
R & B single by Billy Ward and the Dominoes (with
the great Clyde McPhatter on lead vocals) and was
later covered by James Brown. Reed doubtless knew
both versions. On the opposite end of the spectrum,

"The Bells" is also the title of one of Edgar Allan Poe's most wildly obsessional poems.

The Bells was the fourth album of Reed's five-album deal with Arista, and it's the one that drove a stake through the heart of his relationship with the company. There was nothing remotely like a single on it, and whatever hopes Reed and Clive Davis had once entertained about Reed's reaching a wider audience had been buried. Reed claimed that Davis wrote him a long letter explaining that he thought the album was not really finished and needed more work. (Davis did not recall doing that but admitted that he might have.) Reed, of course, dismissed Davis's suggestions. Characteristically, Reed believed that, because of his refusal to address Davis's concerns, Arista refused to support the album. "It was released and dropped into a dark well," Reed said. No question, if Davis believed that *The Bells* did not have sales potential — and it didn't — Arista would not have promoted it extensively.

Reed chose to confront Davis from the stage of the Bottom Line, giving him the finger and demanding, as Davis sat in front of him, "Where's the money, Clive? How come I don't hear my album on the radio?" Davis had never been accused of cheating artists, and as for the possibility of Reed hearing his music on the radio, Davis took his best shot at that with *Rock and Roll Heart*. Reed issued an apology: "I've always loved Clive and he happens to be one of my best friends. I just felt like having a business discussion from the stage. Sometimes out of frustration you yell at those you love the most."

In addition to cowriting two songs on *The Bells,* Michael Fonfara served as the album's executive producer. Other band members were also listed as cowriters on songs, making *The Bells* the first occasion on which Reed acknowledged cowriters since his days with the Velvet Underground. (Reed also cowrote three songs on the album with guitarist Nils Lofgren, who does not play on the record. According to Reed, their collaboration took place as a "first-class mail correspondence.") The rocker "Looking for Love" is the only song on the album credited to Reed alone.

Reed closed the album with four songs that seemed to have a strongly personal perspective, an approach presaged by the album's cover. In marked contrast to the cartoonish cover of *Take No Prisoners,* the photo on the front of *The Bells* depicts a straightforward, conventional-looking Reed gazing directly at the viewer. It's a cleaned-up, nontheatrical visual. His face is intent and focused but expressionless, and with his right hand he's holding up a mirror to his face. It's as if he had momentarily turned away from examining himself to stare at the viewer, implicating his audience in the reflections the album contains.

"City Lights," the first of the four songs that close the album, borrows its title from Charlie Chaplin's

classic 1931 silent film. The song is a touching meditation on Chaplin's banishment from the United States,
the result in large part of moralistic media attacks on
him orchestrated by the FBI and its Red-baiting director,
J. Edgar Hoover. Reed clearly saw something familiar
in the notion of one of America's greatest artists being
hounded into exile for issues in his personal and political life. Interestingly, the song is not a screed. The
music, defined primarily by a lilting piano part, is almost
whimsical—a sonic representation, it would seem, of
the Little Tramp's genial appeal. Reed delivers the lyrics in a thoughtful recitative, and the tone carries regret
that the United States, a nation founded on the con-
cepts of freedom and liberty, had become so oppressive that one of its most distinctive talents would be
driven to foreign shores.

The next track, "All Through the Night," is set in a
party atmosphere, with Reed's vocal competing with
cocktail conversations ("The drinks are on the house—
they're on me," Reed announces right before his vocal
kicks in). The song offers an affecting portrait of the
city's night crawlers struggling to maintain an emotional grip on their lives. Over a repeated, almost childlike trumpet figure played by Don Cherry, Reed tells
a tale of junk sickness and hospitalization, of "a daytime of sin" that descends into "a nighttime of hell,"
and the struggle to make it all through the night to
the following day. He sings with empathy about the

fear and loneliness that plague so many lives, not just those on the fringes. No one is excluded from the song's compassionate embrace, which is both sustaining and unsentimental. The quaver in Reed's voice, which could sound affected, perfectly suits the song's emotional tenor. The singer's handle on his feelings is precarious, and his unreliable relationship to pitch underscores that tenuousness.

"Families" is one of the most personal songs Reed ever wrote, and one of the fairest. In it he takes on the life he grew up living with his family on Long Island, but he doesn't treat it in the extreme ways he sometimes did. Musically, the horns establish a groove that is both insistent and mournful, and apart from some inevitable sarcasm, Reed treats the breakdown of his relationship with his mother, father, and sister with some ruefulness. The familiar charges are leveled once again. His parents are disappointed because he's not living a more conventional life. He isn't married, hasn't given them grandchildren, doesn't want to take over his father's business, isn't as recognizably pleasing to them as his younger sister is. Even his dog is underappreciated. But the line "And families that live out in the suburbs / Often make each other cry" and the plural noun of the title indicate Reed's understanding that, serious as they were, the problems in his home were by no means exclusive to the Reeds. "There's nothing here we have in common except our name," he concludes.

"And I don't think that I'll come home much anymore."

The title track ends the album on a bold note, recycling an experimental technique Reed had used previously in which the lyrics and vocal are buried within the sound of the song, meant not so much to be heard as suggestively wondered about. More than halfway through the nine-minute track, Reed's voice emerges from the instrumental sludge and he offers a meditation on the emotional fragility of performance — and, by extension, the vulnerability and dangers of the artistic life. In its portrayal of artists as isolated, misunderstood, and suffering figures, the song pulls together and deepens themes articulated in "City Lights," "All Through the Night," and "Families." The music grows more portentous as Reed repeats the line "Here come the bells" — with all the associations of alarms, funerals, and other endings that the tolling of bells connotes — and the track comes to a dramatic conclusion. "I had rented a fifteen-foot gong for the occasion and it is still thrilling to hear it end the work."

"The Bells" remained a favorite of Reed's. He claimed that he improvised the lyrics in the studio. "It was a spontaneous piece," Reed said. "The vocal came to me as I sang, and each year since, I wonder at its meaning." Clearly, the song's lyrics touch on ideas that had been running through his mind and evocative as they are, they serve as an eloquent, poetic summary of the album's themes. "Love and the desire for transcendence run through these songs," Reed said. "The characters in these songs are always moving toward something.... They understand the desire to see 'The Bells,' to hear the announcement of transcendence and freedom. And that's what all the lyrics are about."

Unsurprisingly, *The Bells* did not do well commercially; it rose only to number 130 on *Billboard*'s Top 200 albums chart. Critics, however, responded strongly to both the album's musical boldness and the apparent sincerity of its lyrics. In that regard, *The Bells* pushed aside *Take No Prisoners* and became the true thematic descendant of *Street Hassle*. In the *New York Times,* John Rockwell rightly placed *The Bells* among Reed's most "personal, intense" efforts, adding, "If he didn't seem so genuinely confused a person, one might almost suspect that he had created [his] hostile image to make a more striking contrast to the tenderness." In *Melody Maker,* Jon Savage called *The Bells* "the likely keynote for the final year of the seventies." Reed's old sparring partner Lester Bangs reviewed the album for *Rolling Stone;* it was the last piece he wrote for the magazine before his death in 1982. "*The Bells* isn't merely Lou Reed's best solo LP," Bangs declared. "It's great art." He added that "with *The Bells,* more than in *Street Hassle,* perhaps even more than in his work with the Velvet Underground, Lou Reed achieves his oft-stated ambition: to become a great writer in the literary sense."

14

GROWING UP IN PUBLIC

A S THE SEVENTIES DRAINED into the eighties, a sense of cultural exhaustion permeated American society. President Jimmy Carter, an unpretentious man from rural Georgia who had risen to the presidency on the strength of a post-Watergate desire for decency in government, described that mood as a "crisis of confidence" in a speech he delivered in July of 1979. Though Carter never used the word, that speech became known as his "malaise" speech, and it proved to be one of a number of significant factors that led to his crushing defeat at the hands of Ronald Reagan in the presidential election the following year. The revolution in Iran that overthrew the shah and installed an Islamic government disrupted the country's oil production, which affected supplies throughout the world. For Americans, who regarded cars and cheap gas as essential elements of their national identity, the long lines at filling stations represented an emotional as much as an economic blow. In November of 1979, Iranian students seized the U.S. embassy in Tehran and took fifty-two American citizens hostage—another shock to American pride. A planned helicopter raid in April of 1980 to free the hostages failed utterly, compounding what was seen internationally as a humiliation for the United States.

Many Americans viewed these setbacks as part of the inheritance of the sixties counterculture, a post-Vietnam unwillingness to exercise America's strength around the world. America was losing its global stature, and at home the sex-and-drugs indulgences sanctioned by the counterculture were coming under suspicion. Concern about sexually transmitted diseases was on the rise, and in 1980, the first cases of what would eventually be known as AIDS were reported. Rehab programs sprung up as the toll of drug and alcohol dependence became increasingly clear. Former hippies magically transformed into yuppies, young urban professionals in search of the materialistic good life rather than social change. Riding the wave of these developments, Ronald Reagan vowed to combat the excesses of the sixties and reinstate traditional patriotic values, intensifying a culture war that persists to this day.

It was within that cultural context—and strangely congruent with it—that Lou Reed and Sylvia Morales got married on Valentine's Day in 1980. Reed had announced their forthcoming nuptials from the stage of the Bottom Line during a run of Christmas shows in 1979. The choice of Valentine's Day reflects Reed's deep romanticism, which could border on Hallmark card clichés. Of course, in the life of Lou Reed, even such heartwarming gestures had a serrated edge. Reed and Morales were married in Reed's apartment on Christopher Street near Sheridan Square in Greenwich Village, the same space he had shared with Rachel. Now Rachel was gone and Sylvia was fully installed there, with all the institutional and legal legitimacy that marriage provides. Reed, looking like a promising young banker, wore a dark suit and a white shirt and tie, and Morales wore a white wedding dress. His hair was cut short—not the butch short style he had favored at around the time of *Rock n Roll Animal,* but respectably cleaned up. A telling photograph from the event shows the smiling couple, looking cutely self-conscious, cutting the wedding cake together, both of Reed's hands carefully enfolding Sylvia's right hand as she holds the knife. It's the sort of photograph that graces the wedding albums in every one of those suburban homes that Reed indicted in "Families." Reed's old friend the singer-songwriter Garland Jeffreys, himself wearing a suit and tie, looks on appreciatively, if a bit confusedly. After the wedding, the guests repaired to Playland, a pinball arcade in Times Square. Reed was an obsessive player, and Sylvia joined him in his enthusiasm.

With encouragement from Sylvia and his doctors, Reed would soon be on the road to cleaning himself up, in keeping with the tenor of the times. But the sessions for his next album, *Growing Up in Public,* were something like one final lost weekend. To make the album, Reed and his band journeyed to the island of Montserrat in order to record at the AIR studio that Beatles producer George Martin had established there in 1979. For Reed, who loved beaches and the water, it was an ideal environment. He and Michael Fonfara lived and worked together throughout the project. "I was pleased with that album, because Lou allowed me to write all the music for it and to produce it," Fonfara recalled. "We split the writing. George Martin provided housing for everybody, and Lou and I shared a house overlooking a cliff. It was a big estate on the water. Lou and I would get together every night. He'd bring his guitar, and we'd write the songs at night and teach them to the band in the morning. In the studio, the recording console sat next to a floor-to-ceiling window and an Olympic-size swimming pool right outside the door. All you had to do was get up out of the producer's chair, take three steps, and fall into the water. It was a beautiful thing."

As he did about so many things, Reed made contradictory remarks about the Beatles over the years, so it's fascinating to think about his interactions with George Martin, the fifth Beatle if anyone was. Speaking about the Velvet Underground's approach not long before the sessions for *Growing Up in Public* began, Reed said, "I got off on the Beatles and all that stuff, but why not have a little something on the side for the kids in the back row?" Later his remarks about the band were much harsher. "I never liked the Beatles," he said bluntly. "I thought they were garbage." Still, Reed's obsession with technology and sound made the prospect of meeting and working, at least informally, with one of the century's most distinctive producers extremely attractive. "Lou and George got along perfectly," Fonfara said. "Absolutely perfectly. They had a huge respect for each other. It was a great advantage to have George come around and tell us which he thought were the better songs and the better takes. Lou and I sat with him and his wife every night."

For better or worse, Montserrat offered other pleasures as well. Reed had begun to cut back on his use of speed but had not yet stopped drinking. "*Growing Up in Public* is one of the great drinking records of all time," Reed said. "We were in Montserrat, where they come up to you: 'Sir, would you like another mai tai?' Me and Fonfara were ridiculous. We both almost drowned in the pools they've got there. It's not a good way to make a record. We were animals." Fonfara had similar recollections. "This was a studio where they had waiters come by constantly with trays of beautiful tropical drinks," he said. "I mean, we wrote a song called 'The Power of Positive Drinking.'"

That song, its title a clever riff on *The Power of Positive Thinking*, Norman Vincent Peale's classic tome of optimistic self-improvement, provides one of the lighter moments on *Growing Up in Public*, which came out in April of 1980. The song declares Reed's love for Scotch, skewers drinkers who become morose or overly familiar after having a few, and promises, "When I exit, I'll go out gracefully, shot in my hand." The rest of the album, however, takes on far more serious themes. Despite the lavish circumstances under which it was recorded, *Growing Up in Public* continues, as that title would suggest, the personal exploration and reevaluation that Reed had begun on *Street Hassle* and *The Bells*. He was now approaching forty. His journey into the sexual underworld with Rachel was in the past, and marriage to Sylvia Morales was looming. The album marked the end of his relationship with Arista. The seventies were coming to a close. And even if Reed was still swimming in alcohol, his doctors had told him he had to clean up, and he was beginning to. He told Fonfara, "When we get through with this album, I'm going to go on the wagon." And he stuck to his word.

Reed's journey to some semblance of health was gradual but determined, and Sylvia played a crucial role in it. "When I met Lou, he was living with Rachel and he was taking a lot of drugs, just a lot," Sylvia recalled. "Episodes of being up for two days, three days." But, she added, "there was enough of his self-preservation instinct still functioning that he'd come out of those episodes and there would be this drive to move things forward. The end result was going to be that he moves toward getting clean, moves toward health, and moves toward pulling his business situation together. Somewhere in there he had a very clear focus that change needed to happen and that I was the vehicle for it."

The cover of *Growing Up in Public* dramatically reflects that sense of transition. "Look at that cover," Mick Rock said. "He antis his entire image. And he gets me to shoot it." The cover shot is a stark portrait of Reed, wearing a green V-neck sweater with no shirt underneath. He is looking directly into the camera, but not with his usual sneering defiance. His eyes and his facial features are soft, and his shoulders are relaxed, even a bit slumped. His look is questioning and open, not the look of the Lou Reed determined to convince you—and perhaps himself—that not only does he have all the answers, but that you don't dare question him. His face looks weathered; he's grown up in public and then some. He's taken some hits—and given some, too. Maybe he's learned something as well.

The notion of growing up in public is one that Reed would return to in interviews. Though he would never admit it, part of him came to feel embarrassed about things he had done and said during his years of greatest excess in the seventies. It was one of the reasons he refused to discuss his personal life in interviews after 1980. "You do interviews and what they want to know is, 'Did you and David Bowie fuck a goat in Central Park in 1974?'" he said. "'Did you live with a drag queen?' 'What were the drugs like?' What bullshit is this?" Having done interviews while under the influence of drugs and alcohol, Reed came to hate being asked to respond to statements he had made in the past. That resentment—and underlying sense of humiliation—typically expressed itself as anger. "Most of [my] major mistakes were in public," he said, "and I put them on record to boot." He found that idea excruciating but eventually came to accept it. *Growing Up in Public* was a key moment in that process.

The album begins where "growing up" begins: in the family. The first song is "How Do You Speak to an Angel," which, on the basis of its title and lilting piano riff, one might think would be a syrupy ode to his new heteronormative love. Instead, the song's first verse is as raw as anything Reed had ever written. "A son who is cursed with a harridan mother / Or a weak simpering father at best / Is raised to play out the timeless classical motives / Of filial love and incest," Reed sings in the pinched, quavering vocal style he had begun to define on *Street Hassle*. Casting his struggle in explicitly Oedipal terms, Reed portrays his father as "weak" and "simpering," not the overbearing bully he would sometimes conjure, suggesting that the boy's taboo passion ("filial love and incest") provokes both feelings of manic omnipotence against which the "weak" father is defenseless and feelings of guilt—frightening feelings that evoke the specter of inevitable paternal revenge.

Those feelings are all summoned by anxiety over the question of "how do you speak to the prettiest girl?," a reference to Sylvia, whose beauty was one of the first things anyone who met her mentioned about her. The question has a strangely adolescent quality, the nervousness of a teenage boy approaching one of the best-looking girls in his school. "What does he say if he's shy?" Reed wonders, an astonishing question coming from an artist known for his boldness and aggression. Those elements of the song, along with its title, recall the high romance of doo-wop, even as musically the song bears no resemblance to that genre. Reed refers to his obsessiveness, how his thoughts "dance on the head of a pin," as well as his sense of alienation, how he always feels as if he is "on the outside looking in," a reference to the gorgeously agonized 1964 Top 20 hit by Little Anthony and the Imperials. By the end of the song, Reed is screaming in his most guttural voice. "How Do You Speak to an Angel," in short, introduces the album on an unnerving note of sexual panic.

Next comes "My Old Man," a song that directly addresses Reed's feelings about his father. Once again, the song begins with an immersion in the emotions of childhood, with Reed attending public school in Brooklyn and longing to "grow up to be like my old man." But as he gets older, he grows "sick" of his father's "bullying." The Oedipal combat continues, particularly when he describes his father beating his mother— "It made me so mad I could choke." The man who in the previous song was weak and simpering is now a physically abusive tyrant, so threatening that the singer vows to return to his home only when he is "much richer, in every way so much bigger / That the old man will never hit anyone again." The phallic connotations of "in every way so much bigger" emphasizes the sexual competitiveness of the father-son relationship, part of the entangled nexus of desire, fear, and rebellion that Freud brilliantly termed "the family romance." Reed ends the song singing in a staccato fury, this time triggered by the outrage he felt when his father confronted him. "And can you believe what he said to me?" Reed sings, rage bristling in his vocal. "He said, 'Lou, act like a man' " — and here's another reference to a period hit: the Four Seasons' 1963 number one single, "Walk Like a Man." In the previous song, he impugned his father's manhood; now his father undermines his.

It's important to note that no evidence whatsoever exists for Reed's assertion in "My Old Man" that his father beat his mother. Reed himself admitted as much. Speaking about *Growing Up in Public* and the notion that he was "baring his soul" on the album, Reed explained, "Well, actually, my mother's not dead, my father never beat my mother—you've gotta take it, like, I'm a writer, you know what I'm saying? I take a thing and...I'm not restricted to me....Whether my mother's dead or not really doesn't matter; it's the attitude I'm interested in. I wanted to express a view, so I manipulated the events to justify the view."

Reed's family, all of whom were still very much alive, predictably, did not see it that way. His sister, Merrill, felt strongly enough about Reed's allegation that she published an article after his death explicitly countering his claim. Of course, Reed had the right to assert whatever he wanted within the context of a song. But he must have known that his lyrics would be heard as autobiographical. Having the father in the song address his son as "Lou" only reinforces its seeming realness. It's a reflection of the continuing hostility Reed felt for his family, and particularly his father, that he would feel compelled to go to such lengths.

On "Standing on Ceremony," Reed sings in the voice of a father commanding his son to observe the basic requirements of etiquette ("Remember your manners / Will you please take your hat off?") because his mother is dying. It's another revenge fantasy, and it ends with Reed, as he often did in real life, ordering his family that if anyone asks about him, "Tell them that you haven't seen me." On "Smiles," Reed blames his mother for his notorious flat expression, saying he was "taught never to smile" and that his mother warned him to never "let anyone see that you're happy," unless he was "in front of a camera"—a slap at what he perceived as his parents' concern with appearances. The song ends with Reed singing "Doo doo doo," evoking the chorus of "Walk on the Wild Side," and suggesting that the ironic result of his family's suppression of his emotions is his journey into the sexual underworld.

The last two songs on *Growing Up in Public* are the most affecting and the most nakedly vulnerable. The ballad "Think It Over" is a marriage proposal in song, presented in terms that are both ultraromantic and tentative. In a clear rendering of Reed's relationship with Morales ("I wrote that song specifically for Sylvia," he said later), he offers her "his heart / Once and for all, forever to keep," but exerts no pressure, asking her simply to "think it over." She responds, "When you ask for someone's heart / You must know that you're smart / Smart enough to care for it." Hidden within the gentleness of those lines, one hears a warning from Reed to himself, an awareness of his anger and its self-sabotaging ability to destroy the things and people he loves the most. That the quality that will preserve their love is intelligence is worth remarking. It's Reed's reassurance that the trait he felt most certain of and valued the most in himself would see the marriage through. The female character's "lah-dee-dah-dee-dah" refers to Diane Keaton's verbal tic in *Annie Hall,* Woody Allen's most romantic film.

Growing Up in Public closes with "Teach the Gifted Children," a song that offers, of all things, Reed's own highly idiosyncratic version of Crosby, Stills, Nash, and Young's "Teach Your Children." Along with the pieties you would expect in such a song ("Teach them about flowers"), Reed offers a darker vision of what children must learn to survive in the world. "Teach them about anger," he sings, "or the wages of their sins." He views childhood not as a paradise of innocence but as a state corrupted by original sin and requiring the cleansing of baptism, which he evokes by quoting Al Green's "Take Me to the River." Emotionally, "Teach the Gifted Children" looks backward and forward. It creates a portrait of the nurturing childhood Reed wished he had, and it also suggests the possibility of having children with Morales and assuming the adult role of a parent himself.

In Reed's view, *Growing Up in Public* is a redemption

story, with salvation coming in the person of his female lover and the possibility of marriage. Speaking of the character at the center of the album, he said, "I think of the whole thing as being on a very up note. Like he's going ahead, like he's found the perfect lady with the incredible grace." Reed felt strongly enough about what he had to say that he included a lyric sheet with the album for the first time in his career. "I thought it was a good idea because the lyrics are, like, really complex in there," he said. "It would be asking too much for somebody to take 'gilt-edged polymorphous urban' and get that—and not only that, but get the pun on 'gilt.' That's a little much. Hence, the lyric sheet."

And hence this portrait of the artist as a man extricating himself from a tormented past, and moving toward a new vision of his future.

15

JUST AN AVERAGE GUY

REED'S NEXT ALBUM, THE *Blue Mask,* came out on February 23, 1982, a week before his fortieth birthday. That last point is relevant because *The Blue Mask* introduces a determinedly— and self-consciously—grown-up Lou Reed, a figure his fans had not met before. Significantly, while Reed had been drawing on older material and collaborating with cowriters since *Street Hassle,* the ten songs on *The Blue Mask* are credited to Reed alone. While getting clean, he had gone for a long period without writing or picking up a guitar. Now he was playing again, and his struggle with writer's block had ended.

In the opening track, "My House," the ordinarily splenetic singer calmly declares, "I've really got a lucky life / My writing, my motorcycle, and my wife." The "stone and wood" house mentioned in the song isn't another rented Manhattan apartment but a home in rural New Jersey ("the middle of nowhere," in Reed's description) that he and Sylvia, who had been married for two years at the time of the album's release, had purchased. The house, Reed sings, is "very beautiful at night," and Sylvia is mentioned by name. Reed describes geese flying above the trees on his property, as well as the mist that hangs over the lake nearby.

The strange turn in "My House" comes when he asserts that the house is haunted by the ghost of Delmore Schwartz, Reed's "friend and teacher" from his days at Syracuse University, who died in 1966 and was buried in, of all places, New Jersey. In case anyone believed that Reed was inventing a metaphoric haunting, he took great pains to make it clear that he meant the song to be taken literally. "It happened more than once. And continues to happen," he said of the haunting. "I mean, this includes things like footsteps upstairs when no one's there. Those kind of really weird things. I mean, real footsteps, real obvious footsteps. And you turn the light on and you go upstairs and it's gone. You think, well, maybe it's a tree, maybe it's a rat..."

After the release of *Growing Up in Public,* Reed had entered rehab, another development in which Sylvia played a significant role. He now got up early and liked to begin his studio sessions at around two in the afternoon and wrap them up at around ten, or midnight at the latest. Reed's reimagining of himself included, of all unlikely things, his cooperation in the publication of a 1981 *People* magazine profile that celebrated him as healthy, calm, and newly domesticated. "You have to be as close as I've been to the drug scene to be as repelled as I am" by it, he told David Fricke. Drugs, Reed explained, "interfere with my writing." He married Sylvia, he said, because "if you meet the perfect woman, you should pick her up in your arms and dash off with her." The story concludes with Reed's determination to not allow his image or his audience to destroy him. His fans, he said, "would be far happier if I died. That would have completed the Lou Reed myth perfectly. But I'm not about to kill him off just yet."

Reed saw himself as having no alternative but to clean up. Drugs and alcohol were destroying his career, and threatening his life. Looking back on the seventies, he said, "There were a lot of drugs going on during that period. It ruined a lot of careers. . . . Speaking for myself, I could not continue that way. . . . So I had to set about starting at square [one] again." That meant withdrawing from the world he had moved in. "He set me up as a gatekeeper," Sylvia said, "the person to say, 'No, he'll call you back,' sometimes to evade whatever person he was trying to evade. Sometimes those reasons were for health, for a desire not to be involved in a certain scene. Other times it was for business. I think he did that his whole life. He tended to eventually just shut the door on people, sort of like they're in the past. He didn't really make any qualms about that. I think there's a whole litany of people who eventually were surprised, like, 'Oh, I've known you this many years, and there's no longer any communication or access?'"

Starting from square one also meant getting a new band. According to Michael Fonfara, Reed called him after *Growing Up in Public* was completed and said, "'I can't have another drink or do another shot of speed. My doctor says my liver is going to explode. So I'm calling the band off. I'm disbanding it temporarily.' He said, 'I'll call you if I ever get it back together again.'" After that, "our relationship tapered off into almost total evaporation, except for a call once a year," Fonfara said. "There was no dramatic falling out — or if there was, he kept it from me. I mean, I counted him as a very good friend, and I still do. I want to always remember it that way."

Reed may have had other reasons for seeking out a new band. Fonfara and the other musicians in what had come to be called the Everyman Band were all well-trained players who valued technique as much as the Hunter-Wagner *Rock n Roll Animal* band had. Reed valued it as well, but he was beginning to move beyond that phase. "Lou's a poet, but I never did think he could play great guitar," Fonfara said. "I told him that once and I never wanted to say it again because it made him so upset that he didn't talk to me for weeks. See, he imagined himself as a great rock-and-roll guitar player. He had the soul and heart of one, but he just didn't have the chops."

The Blue Mask's cover, which Sylvia designed, is another recasting. It features the Mick Rock portrait used on the cover of *Transformer,* the solo album for which Reed was still best known, and it's shaded in soulful blue tones. That coloring suits the stringent emotional honesty of the album, but the choice of the cover photo also suggests Reed's commercial ambitions for *The Blue Mask. Transformer* was his first hit, and he clearly hoped that *The Blue Mask* would be more than an artistic comeback.

The sound that Reed's new band fashioned for him recalled both the thunder and the delicacy of the Velvet Underground. Guitarist Robert Quine, a brilliant player, had followed the Velvets on tour as a fan, recording their shows and studying their music with a scholar's intensity. He had met Reed back then, but Reed did not remember him when Sylvia reintroduced them. Quine had been the lead guitarist in Richard Hell and the Voidoids, and Sylvia took Reed to see the band at CBGB precisely so that Reed, who was searching for a new direction, could hear him. Reed was mightily impressed and called on Quine when he was ready to record. For Quine, it was a creative dream come true. The Voidoids' songs did not provide him with the canvas that Reed's did, and Quine had an extraordinary ability to render in sonic terms the jarring extremes of Reed's lyrics. And since the Velvet Underground was Quine's primary inspiration, Reed was able to step into a musical frame that he himself had invented.

Quine, of course, had a much different perception of Reed as a guitarist than Fonfara did. "Lou Reed became such a big influence on my playing," Quine said. "He was a true innovator on the guitar and was never appreciated at the time.... I completely absorbed his style." As far as Quine was concerned, Reed had to play guitar on *The Blue Mask*. "I bullied him into playing guitar," Quine said. "I told him straight up if he doesn't play guitar, I'm not working with him, so he played guitar again for the first time in a long time. I would force him to take solos." Quine's encouragement squared perfectly with Reed's own assessment of what he needed to do with *The Blue Mask*. "For the last few years, I was working with musicians who were into funk and jazz," he said of the Everyman Band at around the time *The Blue Mask* came out. "I wasn't playing the guitar on my records because I couldn't really play with those guys, being a simple rock-and-roll player. I thought it would be interesting to explore that direction, but there was a gap between me and them. You can hear it on the records. I heard it one day when some radio station was being brave and played one of my albums. And I said, 'You've carried this experiment far enough. It's not working. The ideas are there and then they disappear. The music isn't consistent. You seem isolated. There's a certain confidence that's not there because you're not really in control.' So I dissolved the band."

Bassist Fernando Saunders provided a perfect balance to Quine's and Reed's guitars. "When I first heard Fernando play, I went over to him and said, 'You are the best bass player I've ever heard,'" Reed said. "And I don't say things like that, generally speaking. Most musicians I run into have lots of technique; they can play scales and their solos sound like that. It doesn't mean anything. You can get a buzz out of it the first listen, maybe even the second, but not after that. And I'm in it for the long run. That's why I work with Fernando." Saunders would remain a regular collaborator until the end of Reed's life. Because Reed wanted as few overdubs as possible on *The Blue Mask,* it was essential that he have players with great skill and originality, but who could also play together seamlessly and support his vocals with finesse, finding sounds that underscored his meanings. As always with Reed, the words were the most important element of the song. Quine, Saunders, and drummer Doane Perry fit the bill in every regard.

Describing the recording of the album, Quine said,

"We did *The Blue Mask* under very unusual circumstances. Lou gave everyone in the band a cassette of him just strumming these songs on an acoustic guitar, and I was free to come up with whatever I came up with. Total freedom. We went in with no rehearsals. None of us had ever played together before, but it just clicked immediately. What you hear on the record is totally live. There are no overdubs, except on one track....Any mistakes that happen are on the record. If I take a solo, I stop playing rhythm. There is no rhythm guitar fill going underneath. It's the way they used to do things in the fifties. I'm especially proud of that record."

THE WILD, AMBISEXUAL NIGHT crawler of the early seventies may have settled down, but, like the seemingly idyllic home in "My House," his newfound peace is haunted. Reed went to extreme lengths to assert the normalcy of his new life — to a degree that sometimes makes it impossible to determine if he was being ironic. The song that follows "My House" is "Women," whose chorus endlessly repeats the declaration "I love women." Presaging the political correctness of the years to come, the singer sheepishly apologizes for having looked at pornographic images of women in magazines. It was "sexist," he confesses, but offers the excuse that "I was in my teens." Still, he slings the macho boast that "I couldn't keep my hands off women / And I won't until I die." One additional odd moment in the song is the singer's wish that he could hire "a choir of castrati to serenade my love" as a kind of foreplay to their love-making. In one sense, it's an innocent enough image, but the notion of castration will reappear in much more disturbing terms on the album. That unsettling echo and the introduction of the notion of castration in a song (and on an album) so gripped by the redemptive power of heterosexual love makes the image worth noting.

Perhaps just as startling is Reed's repeated insistence in "Average Guy" that he is precisely what that title denotes: "just your average guy, trying to do what's right." Because it's a more up-tempo track than "My House" or "Women," it's easier to read the tone of the song as playful. Given Reed's lifelong conviction about his own specialness, it's difficult to take the song seriously. But "Average Guy" also corresponds to the twelve-step code of disowning your sense of specialness, of accepting that you are no different from anybody else and that the rules that apply to everyone apply to you as well. A sense of personal exceptionalism is part of the illness of addiction, according to the twelve steps, and Reed is obviously so grateful for the stability he has found that he is willing to deny his ego to preserve it.

"Only a woman can love a man," Reed sings on "Heavenly Arms," the ballad that concludes *The Blue Mask*. On that song, Reed reaches back once again to the overwhelming romance of the doo-wop songs he loved so much growing up. The singer is helpless, but his lover's heavenly arms come to his rescue. As the Cadillacs did in their 1954 hit "Gloria," Reed repeatedly chants his woman's name as if it were an incantation and Sylvia were a magic force who could protect him from all harm. In a world filled with hate, threatened by an "impending storm," Sylvia is his deliverance.

No one can rely on someone else to that degree without dreading the possibility that the other person might leave. That is certainly the subtheme of "The Heroine," whose title puns on that notorious song from the first Velvet Underground album. Both songs, ultimately, are explorations of addiction and dependency, whether to drugs or to a lover. After all, as Reed sang of heroin in the VU song, "It's my wife and it's my life." Reed would later write that "The Heroine" is about "Jackie Kennedy trying to claw her way out of that car," a reference that ties the song to *The Blue Mask*'s "The Day John Kennedy Died," as well as to one of Andy Warhol's great silkscreen subjects, the mourning Jackie as Pietà.

Unlike the vast majority of Reed's songs, particularly during this period in which he was continually paring his lyrics to the bone, "The Heroine" works primarily in metaphoric terms. In an elaborate allegory, the song describes a ship that is battered in a storm; its crew is waging war against itself, and no one can bring the vessel under control except "the heroine." The helpless crew members are all male; the heroine, of course, is female. In an extraordinary parallel story line, Reed describes a baby in a "box," or crib, also male, also helpless and fearful, desperately waiting for the saving hands—or, perhaps, the heavenly arms—of his mother, the heroine, "who transcends all the men." For Reed, the song was about the "overwhelmingly intense desire for this woman. . . . There's a ship that can't be steered; there's a storm, nobody can control it, the men are down below fighting with one another . . . and where's the heroine?" He acknowledged the "phallic and Freudian imagery" not only in this song, but throughout *The Blue Mask*.

The song does not end happily. The heroine, a symbol of purity in "a virgin white dress"—like the dress Morales wore for her wedding to Reed not long before—is strapped to the mast of the ship, helpless to calm the storm and rescue the crew. Reed himself described this vision of the impeccably pure heroine as "naive" and "childlike." If the heroine had remained a fantasy, Reed said, hope could persist that if she were to appear, salvation might be possible. But when she does enter the scene and is "immobilized," incapable of saving the ship and the men, the terrifying conclusion is that "things are going to continue on as they were, which is terrible."

"Underneath the Bottle" describes the process of hitting bottom as an alcoholic, or possibly relapsing—that feeling when "you get so down, you can't get any lower." However, the tone of the song isn't harrowing, even though the singer describes falling down stairs and finding bruises on his body but not remembering how they got there. He talks about the "shakes inside me," losing his pride, being unable to work, and his desire for another drink, but his delivery is detached and matter-of-fact, even humorous at times. Reed and Quine's guitars establish a seductive, easygoing groove that also lightens the song's mood. Still, "Underneath the Bottle" is the flip side of "The Power of Positive Drinking": it tells of a life that has gone from "bad to weird" and might not be able to turn itself around again.

Epitomizing the phallic imagery running through *The Blue Mask*, "The Gun" describes a character who hides behind his weapon, controlling everyone and everything around him because of the firearm he is holding. As his and Quine's guitars intertwine in a hypnotic, sonic dance, Reed delivers the lyrics as if he's narrating a dream, or as if he were Travis Bickle speaking to himself in the mirror in *Taxi Driver*. (Reed recorded an alternate version of the song with lyrics so revoltingly explicit that he decided that he had pushed the boundaries too far, and he went with the somewhat tamer version for the album.) After the song ends, the album explodes into the roar of the title track, a psychosexual phantasmagoria of fear, violence, and sadomasochism. Explicit references to Oedipus, to incest and patricide, to castration, and to childhood abuse link the song to all the themes underlying the idyllic portrait of domestic bliss the album celebrates. It's as if the blue mask is the brilliant, elegant disguise concealing the horrors inside "My House," the inferno burning within the "Average Guy." Even Reed was spooked by the song and found it difficult to listen to. "'The Blue Mask' as a song is really devastating," he said. "I don't anticipate doing any more of that"—though, of course, he would.

The final word on this disturbing aspect of *The Blue Mask* is "Waves of Fear," a song that in its very title distills all the terror that getting straight, in all senses of the term, was meant to keep at bay. Again, Reed's and Quine's guitars howl as the singer details a catalog of suffering that culminates in the line, "I must be in hell." He is out of both alcohol and pills, and, even more frightening, he is out of control. Beyond its significant role in *The Blue Mask,* the song stands as something like a definitive statement from the core of Reed's heart of darkness. "Waves of Fear" would become a blistering staple of his live shows for many years.

The outlier on *The Blue Mask* is "The Day John Kennedy Died," a song unlike any other that Reed had ever written. The song has two narratives: a dream the singer has that he is the president of the United States and his recollections of November 22, 1963, the day President John F. Kennedy was assassinated in Dallas by Lee Harvey Oswald. Reed recalls hearing the news of the shooting while watching his college football team play on television "upstate in a bar," obviously in Syracuse, whose college team was a football powerhouse in those years. Reed wrote his memories as he actually recalled them. The only problem is that Kennedy was shot on a Friday, and Syracuse University did not have a game scheduled that day.

It's likely—or at least possible—that Reed was unconsciously conflating the murders of John Kennedy and John Lennon, who was shot to death in New York on December 8, 1980. In "The Day John Kennedy Died," Reed recalls the football game he was watching being interrupted by the announcement that the president had been shot. While that did not happen, many millions of people, possibly including Reed, who was an ardent football fan, learned about John Lennon's death when legendary sports announcer Howard Cosell interrupted his *Monday Night Football* broadcast to report that Lennon had been shot and was dead by the time he reached the hospital. For the baby boomer generation, of which Reed was a charter member, "Where were you when John Lennon was shot?" soon stood beside "Where were you when Kennedy was killed?" as a generational milestone. Their sharing a first name reinforces that connection.

Lennon may well have been on Reed's mind; Lennon's final album, *Double Fantasy,* shares many aspects with *The Blue Mask,* most notably a song called "Woman" (recalled by Reed's "Women"), which offers praise to Lennon's wife, Yoko Ono, in much the same way that Reed was doing with Sylvia. Lennon had ended a life of wild excess to reunite with his love in quiet domesticity, much as Reed had done with Sylvia. The men were nearly the same age (Lennon was less than two years older), and Lennon's life was cut short just at the moment when Reed decided that he needed to get clean in order to avoid his own premature demise. And in another similarity, a song like *Double Fantasy's* "I'm Losing You" displays the same desperate fear of abandonment that runs throughout *The Blue Mask*. Reed had met John and Yoko in the back room at Max's, and the parallels between his and Lennon's experiences would not have escaped him.

In "The Day John Kennedy Died," Reed replaces John Kennedy, as if he had been able to live the life that the president could not because he was gunned down. "I dreamed I was the president of these United

States," Reed sings, and then imagines that he had been able to accomplish all the good things that he believes Kennedy would have, had he lived. He was "young and smart" and had overcome "ignorance" and "hate" in the course of creating a "perfect union." But reality intrudes, the dream ends, and the song concludes on a mournful note of lost possibility.

Essentially, the song takes a boomer trope — the Kennedy assassination, the "seven seconds that broke the back of the American century," in novelist Don DeLillo's phrase, as the end of the innocence — and personalizes it. Now cleaned up and married, Reed looks back and imagines an American future that was similarly cleaned up, with him as the charismatic, aggressively masculine young pioneer of the new frontier, not the "fucking faggot junkie" he had once been and was now embarrassed by. "Some people like to think I'm just this black-leather-clad person in sunglasses," he said after *The Blue Mask* came out. "And there's certainly that side of me; I wouldn't want to deny my heritage. But while I have my share of street smarts, I'm not a rat from the streets by any means. I always wanted to be a writer, and I went to college to prepare myself for it." He would later say more bluntly, "I think of myself as a writer. I operate through a rock-and-roll format."

It was relatively rare in those days for rock musicians to have college degrees, so Reed's pride has some justification. But his praise for himself in that regard could be ham-fisted and off-putting. "I took a major in English and a minor in philosophy; I was very into Hegel, Sartre, Kierkegaard," he told the *New York Times* at around the time of *The Blue Mask*'s release. "After you finish reading Kierkegaard, you feel like something horrible has happened to you: Fear and Nothing. See, that's where I'm coming from. If you have my interests and my kind of academic background, then what I'm doing is not really an unlikely thing to do. And now that I've made this album, I'm very, very happy....I feel like I'm just starting to peak, and I want to feel like I've got plenty of time."

Indeed, it was at this point in his career that Reed, who had been shockingly open about his life in both his music and his interviews, began to rigorously guard his privacy and his past. Asked about "Walk on the Wild Side" being regarded as "a kind of national anthem in homosexual circles," Reed snapped at a *New York Times* reporter in a 1982 interview. "I didn't write anybody's national anthem when I wrote 'Walk on the Wild Side,'" he said. "I wrote a character study of four people who hung around Andy Warhol's studio. My past is my past, and it's my business." More privately, he told a friend who offered to return some manuscripts and letters that Reed had sent him years before, "I want nothing to do with that faggot."

In addition, Reed had been a studiously apolitical

figure up to that point in his life and career — "Gimme an issue and I'll give you a tissue — you can wipe my ass with it," he had spat at his audience on *Take No Prisoners*. So "The Day John Kennedy Died" is a curious song from that perspective as well. Reed, in fact, denied the political implications of the song. "I really have no feeling about politics one way or the other," he said. "I just felt bad and I wrote a song about him." Sylvia, however, was more worldly in that regard, and with the fog of drugs and alcohol lifted, Reed could begin looking outward a bit, a development that she encouraged and that would become more pronounced later in his life. His public praise for Sylvia continued in his interviews following the release of *The Blue Mask*. Sylvia, he said, "helped me so much in bringing things together and getting rid of certain things that were bad for me, certain people. I don't know what I would have done without her. She's very, very smart, so I have a realistic person I can ask about things: 'Hey, what do you think of this song?' I've got help, for the first time in my life."

The Blue Mask has come to be regarded as one of the strongest albums of Reed's solo career, and its reception was no less enthusiastic, beginning with Reed's own immodest assessment of it. "I'm not above appreciating my own work," he said at the time. "And I don't think *The Blue Mask* is just a good album. It's way better than that." Robert Palmer declared in the

New York Times that *The Blue Mask* was "the most outstanding rock album of 1982," adding that it had taken Reed "fifteen years to match" the songs on the first Velvet Underground album. Critic Brian Cullman, writing in *Musician,* called *The Blue Mask* "the best album of 1982. It's the record I'd given up all hope of Lou Reed ever making: musically, emotionally, and spiritually. . . . After years of fitfulness and sleepwalking, Lou Reed has begun to dream again." Robert Christgau gave *The Blue Mask* an A — the first he'd ever assigned to one of Reed's albums — and called it Reed's "most controlled, plainspoken, deeply felt, and uninhibited album." *Rolling Stone* was similarly rhapsodic. "Lou Reed's *The Blue Mask* is a great record," the lead review in the magazine begins, "and its genius is at once so simple and unusual that the only appropriate reaction is wonder. Who expected anything like this from Reed at this late stage of the game? . . . Grace has never sounded so tough-minded."

Reed himself saw *The Blue Mask* as "the end of something, the absolute end of everything from the Velvet Underground on. *The Blue Mask* was the final ending and *Legendary Hearts* like a coda."

THE ENTHUSIASTIC RESPONSE TO *The Blue Mask* buoyed Reed. But one aspect of it troubled him: the focus many of those positive responses (justifiably) placed on the role that Robert Quine played in his musical resurgence. While no evidence exists that Reed read Brian Cullman's review of the album in *Musician*—though, given Reed's obsession with his critical reception, he very likely did—one sentence summarizes the source of his disturbance. Cullman wrote, "If the late poet Delmore Schwartz, Reed's mentor and friend, is at the spiritual center of the record, Quine is clearly at the musical center." It was fine, of course, for Cullman to emphasize the significance of Schwartz in *The Blue Mask,* not only because of Reed's admiration for him but also because such notions flattered Reed's sense of himself as a writer. But even though Reed himself had recruited Quine to play on the album, the credit Quine was garnering for the album's success and, eventually, for the renewed power of Reed's live shows began to eat at him. As with Andy Warhol, John Cale, and David Bowie, Reed was happy to collaborate until the goal of the collaboration was achieved. Then every collaborator became a competitor and needed to be cast aside. All those critical statements expressing surprise, even shock, that Reed had managed to make a great album carried the implication that he could not have done it without Quine. That may well have been true. Nonetheless, it became clear to Reed that Quine had to go.

Ostensibly, Reed maintained the same band as on

The Blue Mask, other than replacing drummer Doane Perry with Fred Maher, to whom Quine had introduced him. So Quine's execution was not immediate. But it began with the fact that Quine had become good friends with Reed's onetime critical champion and eventual nemesis, Lester Bangs. Quine became something like the third element in an emotional triangle that took shape between himself, Reed, and Bangs. While Bangs had done everything possible to damage his own relationship with Reed, he grew jealous of the closeness that had developed between Reed and Quine during the recording of *The Blue Mask.* Before it was released, Quine played the album for Bangs, evidently with Reed's permission, and Bangs responded that he liked it, though he thought the lyrics were "weak," information that, incredibly, Quine relayed to Reed. "It was probably the worst thing I could have done," Quine said. "I was just so infatuated with being able to hang around with this guy, my hero."

Quine may have been infatuated with Reed, but conveying Bangs's critique of the album to him was also a means of keeping Reed in his place, a way to express his own reservations about the album using Bangs's comments as a vehicle. Quine could therefore maintain his status with Reed but still get his points across. The strategy did not work. Quine believed that

Reed had softened "The Blue Mask" by paring back the more extreme lyrics he had written for the track. Reed had also rerecorded the vocals he had done live with the band in the studio, and Quine compared the vocals Reed ultimately used on the album to crooning. Whether or not Quine expressed these opinions, Reed, with his acute sensitivity to criticism, certainly would have sensed Quine's less-than-total approval of an album that Reed believed to be among the strongest he had ever made. Reed also had enough of a history with Bangs by this point to see Quine's delivering Bangs's views as evidence of Quine's agreement with them — and he may well have been right about that.

That Bangs died of a drug overdose shortly after *The Blue Mask* was released made matters worse. Quine was devastated by his friend's death, while Reed distanced himself from it. When Quine brought the news to Reed the day after Bangs's death, Reed responded, "That's too bad about your friend," and tore into a lengthy denunciation of Bangs. Quine concluded that his "friendship with Lou ended with Lester's death.... He's an egomaniac and that's why he has no friends. If you're not a yes-man, you're not his friend. He respected the fact that I wasn't a yes-man, but ultimately I had to go."

Reed's first step in the process of pushing Quine out was to minimize Quine's contributions to his next album. "He mixed me off *Legendary Hearts,*" Quine said. "I'm barely audible on it." He particularly noted Reed's treatment of a guitar part on "Home of the Brave," an elegiac ballad in which Quine hoped to express his feelings about the death of Lester Bangs with a coruscating solo. He described his playing on the track as "naked and brutal," but complained that Reed added echo to it and blunted its impact. In Quine's view, Reed had grown jealous of his guitar playing, or, more likely, of the recognition Quine got for it. After Quine had encouraged Reed to begin playing again, Reed got his confidence back. At that point, Quine said, "he turned it into a competitive thing. If there is a competitive thing, there is no way I am going to win. Not when he is telling the guitar guy to mix me out, when people can't hear me taking guitar solos. When he keeps me out of a mix to make sure I'm not being heard. He's an asshole."

As Reed put it, *Legendary Hearts,* which came out in March of 1983, was something of a coda to *The Blue Mask.* The album's cover featured another kind of mask, one that didn't simply shade Reed's face but completely obscured it. That mask was a motorcycle helmet, which he held in the black leather gloves he wore when riding. It was the first Lou Reed album cover that didn't show his face, and the imagery, quite brilliantly, cut several ways. Motorcycles, of course, are about as butch an image as you can find, dating back at least to Marlon Brando's 1953 film classic *The*

Wild One, and the helmet's smooth, cold surface recalls the dehumanizing objectification of bondage masks. But riding his motorcycle had also become an essential element of Reed's newfound country life in New Jersey, an extension of his domesticity in that regard, and he specifically refers to it in the album's lyrics. Similarly, the black leather gloves evoke the "black-leather-clad person" that epitomized Reed's image, but they, too, were part of the safety gear for what could now be seen as his weekend warrior hobby. Beyond that, it's a strikingly impersonal cover for an album titled *Legendary Hearts,* as if Reed had raised his guard again against the painful intimacies of his previous album.

The title track, which opens the album, pulls back from the idealized romantic imagery of *The Blue Mask.* It's an affecting description of how our human flaws — our fears, our anger, our insecurities — prevent us from achieving the love we strive for. The honeymoon is over and reality has set in. In the unforgiving light of the real world, those idealized images transform from shimmering goals into taunting proofs of our inadequacies. As eloquent as the song's melody is, Reed characteristically pushes his theme to an unsettling extreme, suggesting that an essential flaw, a kind of original sin ("His basic soul was stained"), renders the singer incapable of true love. Reed evokes the quintessential Shakespearean lover ("Wherefore art thou Romeo?"), except this gallant is numbing himself with alcohol or drugs and fading into oblivion, "seemingly lost forever." The couple in the song is fighting—an unsettlingly recurrent image on the album—and, in a brilliant bit of Reed wordplay, come to understand that they've got to "fight to keep [their] legendary love."

The fighting imagery continues on one of the strongest tracks on *Legendary Hearts*: "Martial Law." An irresistible guitar groove propels the song, which quickly became a highlight of Reed's live shows. With great humor, the song describes two law enforcement officers, the singer and his friend Ace, who are called to quell a domestic disturbance. They quiet down the battling couple and declare "martial law"—another pun, this time visual, which rests on the close relationship between the words "martial" and "marital." Reed understands how love and war not only exist side by side but are sometimes inextricable, even indistinguishable. In "Bottoming Out," the singer describes taking a spill on his motorcycle—a ride he took because "if I hadn't left, I would have struck you dead."

"Home of the Brave," the song in which Quine had hoped to express his feelings about the death of Lester Bangs, takes a proud image from "The Star-Spangled Banner" and explores the vulnerability and fear running through the lives of the people living with nothing left to lose in the land of the all too free. For each person who has found someone to hold on to ("Micky's got a wife"), others, like the singer, are "shaking in [their] boots." Those people, like Reed's old friend Lincoln Swados ("a friend who jumped in front of a train"), are the ones who are "not saved." They're "the daughters and the sons / Lost in the home of the brave." Domestic violence emerges in this song as well ("A man's kicking a woman"), loneliness, fear, and abandonment erupting in brutal anger. In a move that is both lovely and tense, Reed ends the song quoting lyrics from the 1965 country-soul hit "Every Day I Have to Cry Some." Like Reed, Arthur Alexander, who wrote the song, understood that everybody has to cry some— and die some.

Legendary Hearts ends with a lovely, understated ballad, "Rooftop Garden." The literal reference for the song is the rooftop garden at the West Village apartment Reed shared with Sylvia, here presented as an oasis of tranquility and peace amid the violence and mayhem of the New York that Reed spent so many years chronicling. It is a touch of their rural New Jersey retreat in the heart of New York street life. As he was on *The Blue Mask,* John Lennon was again on Reed's mind. Reed adapts a line from "I Am the Walrus," substituting "rooftop" for "English" in Lennon's lyric "Sitting in my English garden, waiting for the sun." For all the images of strife on *Legendary Hearts,* "Rooftop Garden" ends the album on a serene note. "What a lovely couple are you and I," Reed sings, and the couple shuts out the world for a moment of connection—avoiding the phone, not answering letters, pretending they're not at home. Once again, Reed brings a song to a close with an allusion to an R & B classic, in this case the Drifters' 1962 hit "Up on the Roof," a suggestion on Reed's part, as David Fricke noted in *Rolling Stone,* that "while there are no legendary loves, legendary love songs are a wonderful inspiration."

Despite merely being a coda to *The Blue Mask, Legendary Hearts* garnered reviews nearly as enthusiastic as those for its predecessor, Fricke's notable among them. The album, he wrote in his four-star review, is one of Reed's "most powerful solo statements—or, if you will, understatements. The gray nakedness of the performances and frayed lyrical nerves of the songs underline the familial tension, romantic hurt, and emotional desperation pumping through *Legendary Hearts.* This is Reed's own *Scenes from a Marriage* (no doubt drawn from his own, at least in part), an extended play of the heart in which he savages the myth of moon/June/croon-type love." As he did with *The Blue Mask,* Robert Christgau awarded the album an A, noting that "his great new band is just a way for [Reed] to write great new songs."

However much the relationship between Reed and Quine had deteriorated, Reed felt strongly enough about the band he had assembled to take it on the road for a brief European tour and fully document it in the marketplace. Long-form VHS videos were beginning to make an impact on a music world in the process of being reshaped by MTV, and Reed had a February 1983 Bottom Line concert filmed and released as *A Night with Lou Reed*. In 1984, he released a double LP in Europe titled *Live in Italy,* which was recorded at shows in Verona and Rome. Reed may not have wanted the album released in the United States for fear that it might have distracted listeners from the studio album he would release that year—which it would have. Even as an import, *Live in Italy* garnered significant attention because the Reed-Quine guitar interplay excited critics and fans. The two guitarists lock in and roar on tracks like "White Light/White Heat," "Kill Your Sons," and "Sister Ray." On "Rock and Roll," the band's adrenaline rushes so high that, rather than ground the group, bassist Fernando Saunders and drummer Fred Maher are swept along in the fury. They're playing the song in what sounds like double time, with Reed screaming his vocals (while quoting verses from Stevie Wonder's "Uptight") in order to be heard. It's thrilling to hear him being pushed so hard, all the tension within the band channeled into visceral, exultant expression.

16

NEW SENSATIONS

B Y THE END OF 1983, when Reed went into the studio to record his next album, his attitude had undergone a significant transformation. His sobriety and the stability of his personal life no doubt made this possible. Though he was an artist of enormous international importance, Reed had led somewhat of a sheltered life. Despite his proximity to New York City during his childhood, Reed's family life had not exposed him to a larger world, and while it seems counterintuitive, the presumably sophisticated New York underworld where he had spent so much of his young life was — and continues to be — a very insular community. While Reed had occasionally invited friends to tour his late-night haunts as a kind of emotional initiation, those clubs and their denizens did not typically welcome outsiders or scrutiny of any kind. And though it was beginning to achieve societal legitimacy, homosexuality was still a subculture at the time, particularly the more extreme outposts of it, where Reed tended to venture. The loneliness and isolation of life on the road is as durable a rock-and-roll trope as exists. Cities blend indistinguishably, and the repetitive trek from airports to hotels to venues and back again creates a nowheresville of motion. And whether you're in Paris, Texas, or Paris, France, it makes no difference if all you're trying to do is score.

Despite its cosmopolitan airs, New York manufactures its own distinctive brand of high-IQ hicks: people, Reed very much among them, whose comprehension of the world beyond the Hudson River is willfully nonexistent. Drug addiction, too, creates hard boundaries between users and anyone who might be shocked or disapproving of their activities. Particularly with methedrine, paranoia and the threat of arrest necessarily limit the addict's contact with the outside world. And quite simply, being high does not facilitate honest communication with other people. Finally, Reed's own deep insecurities and desire for control narrowed his world considerably. "Loneliness" is a word that comes up frequently when people speak of him. "I never felt that Lou was running from anything, hiding from anything," guitarist Jeffrey Ross said. "I felt like he was just sort of walking around, going, 'Jesus, where's the door? How do I get out of here? Leave me alone.' That kind of thing."

Now that he was fit, however, and no longer using drugs, Reed began to take the outside world more responsibly into account. Though Sylvia was much younger than Reed, her own travels as a military child, her grounded personality, her intelligence and her ambitions provided her with a confidence that she was able to instill in him. Buying a house in Blairstown, New Jersey, and learning to appreciate it was not something that Reed would have been able to do without her. She was creative, politically aware, and knowledgeable about the music scene, and Reed increasingly involved her in all aspects of his professional life. "Sylvia is one hundred percent for Lou," Reed's manager Eric Kronfeld said at the time. "She's supportive. He relies on her a lot. He's certainly happy." Little did Kronfeld know that before too long Sylvia would replace him at his job.

REED ENTERED THE STUDIO again in December of 1983 to begin work on the album that would become *New Sensations*. Despite still playing with Reed onstage, Robert Quine was not invited to the sessions. Fred Maher, whom Quine had brought into the band, felt funny about working with Lou without Quine being involved, and he asked Quine if he felt okay about it.

Quine encouraged Maher to go ahead. Maher himself had thought about moving in a new direction and had enrolled at Cooper Union in New York City to study architecture. In a touching sign of respect, Reed scheduled the sessions for *New Sensations* to coincide with Maher's Christmas break from school.

Reed claimed that he didn't involve Quine in recording *New Sensations* because he wanted to play all the guitar parts himself. "I've been practicing and practicing, and I knew exactly what I wanted to do in the studio. I didn't need a translator," Reed responded when asked about recording without Quine. Fernando Saunders and Fred Maher were back as the rhythm section, but Reed expanded his sound for the album, a reflection of his relatively buoyant mood at the time. Peter Wood played keyboards, and a horn section that included Randy and Michael Brecker also joined the sessions. With a quartet of background singers, Reed once again tapped into his love of R & B. Most significantly, along with the generally positive emotions chronicled on the album's eleven songs, Reed made a determined effort to engage the music and media world as it existed in the early and mideighties. Working with engineer John Jansen, who received a coproducer credit, Reed crafted a bright, crisp sound for *New Sensations,* one that was not only well suited to radio but something like the sonic equivalent of the bold pastel colors that MTV was establishing as the visual signa-

ture of the decade. It was not a period geared for artists who dressed exclusively in black leather. Reed did
not change his look, but he did change his point of
view.

"This is a positive album, looking at things positively," Reed said about *New Sensations* at the time.
"And I think that's the direction I'm interested in."
The album took him longer to make than usual, but
only because "I was capable of longer concentration."
The song "New Sensations" details these emotions,
and earns its place as the title track of this most outward-
looking of Reed's albums. The song describes a recov-
ered protagonist whose new sensations include a
heightened appreciation of the everyday world around
him. Over a beautifully articulated guitar groove that
is simultaneously propulsive and introspective — not
to mention Saunders's jaw-dropping bass riffs — Reed
declares his desire not to be "stoned or stupid" and
laments that "two years ago today" he'd been arrested on
Christmas Eve. Though that was not true, Reed had
once been arrested on Long Island on Christmas Eve
while trying to pass a fake prescription at a pharmacy.
The word "today" suggests that Reed is recording the
song on Christmas Eve, which gives it the feeling of a
Christmas promise to reform, a Christmas gift to
himself of a new life.

He sings about the desire to "eradicate my negative
views" and the wish to get rid of the people around

him "who are always on a down." He treasures his new life, insisting that "I want to stay married / I ain't no dog tied to a parked car," that latter line recalling Jake LaMotta's desperate declaration in Martin Scorsese's *Raging Bull,* a film Reed mentions elsewhere on the album: "I'm not an animal!" That LaMotta's statement occurs within a prison cell lends resonance to Reed's allusion to his own arrest. The prison cell, in this case, is the prison of the self, and Reed is determined to escape and engage with others. In concert, Reed described writing "New Sensations" immediately after a police officer let him off after stopping him for speeding. The cop recognized him and couldn't believe that Lou Reed, the king of the underground, was out riding a motorcycle near the Delaware Water Gap. The song, then, is in part about finding yourself on the right side of the law—or, better yet, being forgiven for a transgression.

Reed's motorcycle and New Jersey house emerge once again as the means of his transformation. He takes his "GPZ out for a ride"—Reed rode a Kawasaki GPZ900—and exults in the beauty of his surroundings, the sensuality of his bike ("The engine felt good between my thighs... / I love that GPZ so much you know that I could kiss her"), and the bracing speed (this time not the drug) of his ride. He stops at a roadside diner for a burger and a Coke and feels a warm connection to the locals inside who are talking about football and neighbors who got married or recently died.

With the possible exception of "Coney Island Baby," in which the singer's point of view is more internal and complicated, "New Sensations" marks perhaps the only time that Reed expressed such a profound empathy for people so different from himself. He is, of course, rightly revered for portraying characters from the demimonde with respect, but so often that vision seemed accompanied by a contempt for the kind of characters he encountered in that diner, people whose ordinary concerns are seldom the stuff of avant-rock songs. That is far from the case here, and the song infuses a moving sweetness into the album.

The scenes Reed describes in "New Sensations" correspond to the life he was living with Sylvia in Blairstown. They would spend three days in the city and four in New Jersey, and the contrast could not have been more pronounced. Reed's childhood friend Richard Sigal taught sociology at a New Jersey college and lived about a forty-five-minute drive from Reed's house. They became friendly again in the eighties and would often visit each other's homes. One of Sigal's professional specialties was deviant behavior, and he was always threatening to bring Reed to his class as "my classic deviant."

"Their house was in a very rural area," said Sigal of Reed's New Jersey home. "It was impossible to find unless you had very specific directions. It was a large piece of property. Once through the big farm gate, I passed a small caretaker's cottage, a private pond, and got to the house, which looked like a hunting lodge. Dark wood inside and out. Lou loved toys, and he had a snowmobile, a pool table, a Ping-Pong table, a beautiful old jukebox filled with doo-wop 45s, lots of cutting-edge electronics—and a gun. Scary. You'd have to know Lou the way I did, but I never felt putting a loaded pistol in Lou's hand was a very good idea. He proved me right later, when he told me he'd put a round through the living room floor when the gun went off accidentally. I asked him how that happened, and he said, 'I didn't think there was one in the chamber.' Famous last words."

Sylvia got involved with a local environmental group, and their house had an earth toilet, which turned human waste into compost, rather than a septic system. Reed, Sigal, and their wives would go bowling together—and, as with his tennis playing back in high school, "he didn't like losing," Sigal said. Reed explained that he could no longer drink hard liquor, but when they would have dinner together, he would occasionally drink wine. And he would smoke pot. "Lou actually brought some dope out for me," Sigal recalled. "Lou the drug dealer from the city! I don't remember how it came up, but he said, 'I'll bring you something to smoke.' I remember we were at a bowling alley in Sparta, which is where I was living, and we were in the parking lot. All of a sudden he nervously shoved a bag in my pocket, and I paid him for it. And he took the money, too!"

Reed was always gracious to Sigal's children, who were young adolescents at the time. "We would all skate on Lou's pond," Sigal said, "and he was always a technophile, so he would show them all the newest, latest stuff. If it was brand-new, Lou had it. He had an Atari, and we didn't even know what Atari was. He taught the kids how to play, and they were ecstatic. They couldn't get enough of it." One time, Sigal brought his friend a copy of the first record Reed ever made, the Jades' "So Blue" backed with "Leave Her for Me." He had found it in a long-forgotten box hidden away in one of his closets. Reed did not have a copy himself. "I gave it to him," Sigal said, "and he said, 'You know, you shouldn't just give this to me. This might be worth something someday.' I said, 'You're my friend. It's your record. Take it.' So I gave him that 45, and he put it on his jukebox."

Lenny Kaye, the guitarist in the Patti Smith Group and a friend of Reed's, had a house near the Delaware Water Gap in northeastern Pennsylvania, not far from Reed's country home. He shared Reed's love of motorcycles. "One day, he came over on his bike, with Sylvia on the back," Kaye said, "and we took off. It really was a beautiful day, one of the most memorable days ever. I'm driving in back of him, and he's wagging his rear, showing off for me. It was really great to see him at play. I also remember swimming in his pond with him and John Cale. I'm thinking, 'Yeah, man, this is my Velvet Underground dream come true!' And then Lou was showing my daughter how to fish. In a weird way, I used to call him and Sylvia the paranormals, because he seemed so normal, but you know that it was like some strange planetary conjunction!"

ON THE ORIGINAL VINYL version of *New Sensations*, which came out in April of 1984, the title track closes the first side and is followed on the top of the second side by another masterpiece, "Doin' the Things That We Want To." The song captures a split imperative Reed felt at this time. Even as he was attempting to engage the realities of the eighties music industry, he was also becoming more conscious of his status and ambitions as a writer. His sobriety and stability gave him the confidence to move forward on these two seemingly disparate fronts: the increasingly youth-oriented music scene and the more elevated world of his literary ambitions.

Reed once said, "My expectations are high . . . to be the greatest writer that ever lived on God's earth. In other words, I'm talking about Shakespeare, Dostoyevsky." He would later walk that statement back, explaining, "That was just me shooting my mouth off, but it is a real dream. To do something that's not disposable, that could really hold its own forever... whether it's on record or on the printed page." Nonetheless, his open desire for a lasting legacy as a literary figure was understandable and, after all, given his interests and the stature he had already attained, relatively reasonable.

"Doin' the Things That We Want To" floats on a hypnotic guitar riff and a gorgeous, atmospheric violin part by L. Shankar. Reed's vocal is deadpan but intense, as he describes how inspired he felt by a production of Sam Shepard's play *Fool for Love,* which was staged in New York in 1983. The play, which centers on the tangled relationship between a man and a woman, trades on themes straight out of Reed's playbook: sexual jealousy, violence, incest, substance abuse, and the crushing weight of the past. As Reed describes the characters and their actions ("The man was bullish, the woman was a tease"), Shepard's talent, and the impact both had on him as a viewer, the background singers chant variations on the song's title. The characters, Shepard, and Reed are all doing the things that they want to.

Reed then describes how the play reminded him of "the movies Marty made about New York / Those frank and brutal movies that are so brilliant." He rightly draws the connection between *Fool for Love* and Scorsese's *Raging Bull,* which came out in 1980 and is regarded as among the greatest films of that decade. Like *Fool for Love, Raging Bull* deals with violence, jealousy, family tensions, and painfully destructive psychological obsessions. Reed clearly identifies with both Shepard and Scorsese and the characters in their work, the way they do the things they want to do, regardless of the taboos they violate or the more conventional sensibilities they outrage. But Reed also sounds envious of the freedom Scorsese and Shepard enjoy. He often said about the controversies that erupted over his work that if he were writing books or plays or making films, no one would have been concerned. He must have felt that far more acutely as the insurgent energy of punk and the general outrageousness of the seventies receded, and the mainstream blockbuster culture of the eighties took shape. Through the rest of the decade, Reed would make the case that in order to truly understand what he was trying to achieve, the listener had to think of him outside the context of rock and roll.

With his life under control, Reed was also making his play for commercial success. "I really think I have it more together than I ever have in my whole life," he said. "I have more of my powers and abilities to reason, function, and to take a thought, carry it through, complete it, and accomplish what I set out to do over a long span. I personally would love to have commercial success because I know what I'm doing is good." At shows at around this time, he would tell audiences how happy he was to play "Walk on the Wild Side" for them. The song had paid his rent for years, he explained, and if people wanted to hear it, well, Lou was only too pleased to perform it for them.

In what was likely his most emphatic commercial gesture, he not only wrote a fun, upbeat, radio-friendly pop single: he made a textbook MTV video for it. Reed had made videos before, and each attempted, to one degree or another, to present a vision of him that suited both the times and the style of MTV. The video he made for "Legendary Hearts" was misconceived — the song is entirely too complicated to lend itself to a treacly visual treatment. More interesting is his video for "Women," from *The Blue Mask,* which shows him fronting his band in a shirt open to the middle of his chest, his short hair and sculpted features presenting him as the ideal vehicle for the song's ardent hetero-sexuality, a harbinger in its own odd way of the family values that would become such a centerpiece of eight-ies culture. Similarly, the video for "Don't Talk to Me About Work," from *Legendary Hearts,* features Reed, wearing a stylish suit, his collar open and the knot of his tie fashionably pulled down a few inches from his neck, as a harried yuppie, another stereotype entirely in tune with the burgeoning eighties cult of work and success.

But the video for "I Love You, Suzanne," the first single from *New Sensations,* goes the furthest in its attempt to endear Reed to the MTV generation. The song itself is a straight-ahead pop-rock song of a type that Reed really had never written before. Over a propulsive, melodic guitar riff, Reed opens the song by loosely quoting lyrics from the Contours' anarchic 1962 hit "Do You Love Me," in which the singer, whose girlfriend dumped him because of his ineptness on the dance floor, implores her to come back "now that I can dance." Reed's song is a simpler, more direct declaration of love, but the video takes the Contours' theme as its tongue-in-cheek subject. It begins with Reed in familiar territory: on a darkened street at night, making a call from a public telephone. Trying to reach a drug dealer, perhaps, or arrange an illicit tryst? Hardly. He's attempting to reach his cute, much younger, pixieish blonde girlfriend, who, like the girl in the Contours song, had grown weary of his reluctance to dance. He's had a change of heart, it seems, and wants her to come see his band. They're onstage at a club, and after she arrives, men are trying to get her to dance, but she's determined to see if Reed will be willing to step up and show her what he's got. And indeed he is! Reed's body double leaps off the stage and unleashes a series of moves that combine Jewish soul-boy attitude and martial arts athleticism. He twirls, kicks, and even does a somersault. The end of the video shows Reed still on the phone, waiting for his girlfriend to answer, suggesting that the dance floor scene was a fantasy. The video's cheerfulness came across to a new generation of fans who helped make *New Sensations* Reed's most successful album since *Coney Island Baby*.

The video for "I Love You, Suzanne" bears some resemblance to Bruce Springsteen's video for "Dancing in the Dark," which came out at roughly the same time. MTV had altered the terrain of the music industry and attracted a new cadre of young fans, which presented a challenge to older artists—meaning artists like Springsteen, who was then in his midthirties, and certainly Reed, who was in his early forties, which seemed ancient at the time. The vast majority of those younger viewers were entirely unaware of the Velvet Underground, and for that matter, they likely knew very little even about a classic Springsteen album like *Born to Run,* which had come out nearly a decade earlier. Radio remained an important promotional outlet, but video was now the most direct—and, even more important, the hippest—way to reach this new audience. That both Reed and Springsteen had physically transformed themselves into recognizable eighties types—Reed looked like a harried banker, while a newly buff Springsteen resembled a health-conscious gym rat—and were shown cavorting with younger women in their videos played into a conscious strategy to make them relevant in this new era.

Springsteen's anguished tales of vanishing working-class communities—forget Reed's sagas of underground urban decadence—were never going to be the means of introducing these veteran artists to younger listeners. Springsteen's manager Jon Landau specifically requested that Springsteen try to write a radio hit for his *Born in the U.S.A.* album, and Springsteen came up with "Dancing in the Dark." Reed, no doubt, was thinking in similar terms with "I Love You, Suzanne." Springsteen's song helped make *Born in the U.S.A.* one of the best-selling albums in history. While "I Love You, Suzanne" did nothing remotely like that for Reed, it did expand his audience and make him seem contemporary. Even the album's cover, which showed Reed sitting on the floor playing a video game while watching himself on a television screen, mimicked the viewing and gaming habits of a younger generation. The man who had established a credo of making music for adults was now portrayed as just one of the kids.

Predictably, the overall sunniness and pop feel of "I Love You, Suzanne" and *New Sensations* as a whole alienated some longtime Reed fans who continued to measure his every move by the standards of the Velvet Underground. "There seem to be people who only like it when I write—in quotes—'depressive' things," Reed said. "It's not that I resent it, but I can't pay any attention to that. I mean, there's got to be more to life and more to me than that. And I'm not about to sit down and write a song about angel dust or cocaine. Somebody else will have to do that for this generation. I already did it. Faulkner's world was the swamp, James Jones had the war, but Lou Reed is not going to just have dope. That was just me passing through, describing as I go. And I would really hope that there's more to come from my life than to be stuck over there someplace, staring at a wall, and describing in intimate terms every negative thing that's going down."

Others, however, were pleased to see Reed alive and kicking—and, for once, seeming to enjoy himself. In *Rolling Stone,* Kurt Loder first decried that Reed had "stumbled through one of the most self-indulgent and self-defeating solo careers in the annals of rock," but then announced that *New Sensations* had ended that trend. "Never before," Loder wrote, "has Reed seemed so completely and joyfully human as he does on *New Sensations*."

Against all odds, Reed convinced Robert Quine to tour with him to promote *New Sensations,* and the shows garnered rave reviews. Once again, Reed felt sufficiently good about the band to document it, this time with *Coney Island Baby: Live in Jersey,* a VHS release of a concert recorded at the Capitol Theatre in Passaic in 1984.

While he was carrying out his strategic efforts to reach a younger audience, the power of Reed's early work began to inspire a younger generation of artists. When local musicians in Athens, Georgia, referred to R.E.M. as a "pop band" because of the group's relative accessibility, the band's guitarist, Peter Buck, suggested that they cover the Velvet Underground's "There She Goes Again" to demonstrate their artistic credentials. R.E.M. released its version of the song on the flip side of its 1983 single "Radio Free Europe," and it was Eno's remark about the first Velvet Underground album—"I think everyone who bought one of those thirty thousand copies started a band!"—all over again. "Radio Free Europe" was not a huge hit, but it was an enormous succès d'estime, and its B side brought the Velvet Underground closer to precisely the young audience that were likely to become lifelong fans. R.E.M. would go on to perform and record a number of other Velvet Underground songs, but it was hardly the only young progeny of Reed and the Velvets. U2, the Dream Syndicate, the Violent Femmes, and Eurythmics, among many other artists, were also cut, at least in part, from the Velvets' cloth.

ANOTHER PART OF REED'S effort to expand his audience was his participation in a 1985 ad for Honda scooters. Through the seventies, the notion that any company looking for anything remotely like mainstream acceptance would use rock music—let alone a song associated with someone as controversial as Lou Reed—to promote its products would have been regarded as ludicrous. But the generation that had grown up with rock and roll was suddenly successful and affluent. In the age of Reagan, business and commercialism were no longer bad words to the generation that had previously regarded itself as a counterculture. Indeed, rock and roll itself increasingly came to be seen as a business. In a milestone moment for marketing, the Rolling Stones' 1981 tour of America was underwritten by the fragrance company Jōvan to the tune of $1 million, a substantial amount of money at the time. That the Stones, whose reputation for a period rivaled Reed's own for outrageousness, could be regarded as a safe bet for a perfume company broke open the floodgates for corporate sponsorship. The rock press energetically debated the issue of whether or not this was a fatal compromise for rock and roll, and many artists, including Bruce Springsteen and R.E.M., refused to play along. But the advertising community and the vast majority of fans simply regarded corporate sponsorship as good business.

For Honda, Reed typically went further than other artists had. Rather than simply license a song for an ad, have a company name printed on concert tickets, or permit corporate signage at a performance venue,

Reed actually appeared in the Honda ad. As the music (though not the lyrics) for "Walk on the Wild Side" played, images of Reed in a black leather jacket and shades were interspersed with raw depictions of New York street life—hookers, graffiti, squeegee men, buskers—that made the city look at once edgy and glamorous. At the end of the spot, Reed, leaning on the seat of a red scooter, removes his sunglasses and says in his best New York accent, "Hey, don't settle for walkin'."

The spot represented a dramatic break from the clichéd formulas that governed advertising—and, particularly, television advertising—at the time. For one thing, the product being advertised was not even mentioned until the very end of the spot—a radical gesture at the time. That Reed in real life would not be caught dead riding a scooter seemed beside the point. At times he appeared defensive about the ad—"Who else could make a scooter hip?" he asked one journalist. But he also cited more pragmatic reasons for his decision, and mentioned Andy Warhol as a model for his thinking. "I can't live in an ivory tower like people would like me to," he said. "I've got to grab money here and there so that my albums can maintain a certain integrity and purity. My records, except for the fluke of 'Walk on the Wild Side,' have never been very successful commercially."

"I got that from Andy a long time ago," Reed continued. "It's just one more tool to use. I don't think of it in terms of bullshit like 'He's selling out.' I used to watch Andy do something for *TV Guide* or Absolut Vodka so that we could put on our Plastic Exploding Inevitable [*sic*] show. When our equipment broke, that's how it got replaced. We didn't turn around and tell Andy we can't touch that money because it came from doing a commercial. I don't think that occurred to anybody. I'm just interested in putting out my vision as purely as possible, and anything legal I can do to facilitate that is fair game." At shows, Reed began to wryly introduce "Walk on the Wild Side" as the "Honda commercial." But even as he dismissed it, the notion that he had in any way "sold out" wounded him; he felt that he had made every conceivable effort never to do that. That was the sin Delmore Schwartz had warned him about, after all, and he had no desire to be haunted by that ghost. Reed was much more cautious about commercials for many years, though he always would gratefully believe that "ad people play fair with you."

NOW THAT HE WAS sober, Reed also stepped into the political arena, with his wife's encouragement. Characteristically, once he made the decision to publicly engage issues in the world around him, he went at it with conviction. The mideighties were a time of renewed energy at the intersection of rock music and politics. The policies of Ronald Reagan in America and Margaret Thatcher in England had pushed both countries far to the right, and musicians began to push back. In England in 1984, Bob Geldof and Midge Ure organized a group of artists to record the single "Do They Know It's Christmas?" to raise money to combat famine in Ethiopia. To follow that up in the United States, an extraordinary collection of superstars recorded a single called "We Are the World" and then put together all-star concerts in Philadelphia and London to raise even more money for the same cause. As he performed at the closing set of the Philadelphia concert, Bob Dylan mentioned from the stage that he wished a similar event could be organized to help farmers in the United States, who were facing their own economic challenges. That led to the formation of Farm Aid, which was organized by John Mellencamp, Willie Nelson, and Neil Young, and which staged its first benefit concert in Champaign, Illinois, on September 22, 1985. Along with such artists as Kenny Rogers, the Charlie Daniels Band, and John Denver, Lou Reed performed.

By any measure, Reed, perhaps the most definitively city-identified artist of the age, was an unlikely choice to play such an event. Other than at the 1972 Save the Whale benefit in London, to which David Bowie had invited him, Reed had never performed at a show like this. Apart from whatever reservations he had about getting politically involved, his desire for control rendered the notion of sharing the stage with dozens of other acts, many of which had nothing to do with his style of music, extremely unattractive. But Bob Dylan had personally invited him, and once again, his new life with Sylvia played a significant role in his agreeing to perform. Reed's life in Blairstown had acquainted him with some of the issues that rural people face. Having gotten involved in local politics there, Sylvia had encouraged him to accept Dylan's invitation.

Reed's performance went so well that he became something of a Farm Aid regular, returning to perform in both 1987, in Lincoln, Nebraska, and in 1990, in Indianapolis. For the 1987 show, Reed and Sylvia stayed at Mellencamp's guesthouse in Bloomington, Indiana, and Reed performed with Mellencamp's crack band backing him. To calm Reed's nerves about the gig, Mellencamp arranged for the two of them to play an unannounced show at the Bluebird, a small Bloomington club. Everyone had a great time, though Mellencamp recalled that his band had a hard time getting used to Reed's noisy and idiosyncratic guitar playing. Consequently, they repeatedly turned his amp down behind his back. "Lou kept going, 'My amp's fucked up!'" Mellencamp recalled, laughing. "He didn't like it, but he didn't say much. He just turned it back up."

At Mellencamp's recommendation, Reed also agreed to visit and answer questions at a history of rock-and-roll class taught by Glenn Gass, a prominent scholar and composer, at Indiana University's famed School of Music.

Initially, Mellencamp, who was a great fan of both Reed and the Velvet Underground, was surprised by the Lou Reed he met. "He was very personable," Mellencamp said. "He was a lot more interested in sports than one would imagine. He liked basketball and football, and he actually asked me if I knew how to play golf. I do, and I taught him how to swing a golf club. And he didn't want to just take a couple of swings. He was interested in the way you would be if someone was teaching you how to play guitar. He wanted instructions: how do you hold your hands, things like that." At one of his Farm Aid appearances, Reed addressed the audience, stating that he hoped his showing up in support of American farmers meant that the audience would be equally supportive of him when his lyrics came under attack from moral guardians. It was a bold gesture and a challenge, but one that, in its own way, emphasized the possibility of connection.

Reed's relationship with Farm Aid followed a typical pattern for him — that is, having begun with great enthusiasm and promise, it ended with an unfortunate falling out, which was foreshadowed for Mellencamp by a strange exchange he had with Reed. As one of the organizers of Farm Aid, Mellencamp checked in on Reed backstage to make sure that everything was okay with him. "It was peculiar," Mellencamp said. "I looked in on him and said, 'Well, Lou, just let me know if there's anything I can do for you.' And he kind of snapped back at me—and, you know, I'm not used to people snapping at me. He said, 'What do you think you could do for me?' I said, 'Lou, it was just a pleasantry.' And he said, 'Oh, I was just wondering what the hell you thought you could do for me.' It was very Lou Reed."

For the 1990 Farm Aid concert in Indianapolis, Mellencamp invited Guns N' Roses to headline, which proved to be a controversial decision. Guns N' Roses was the biggest band in the world at the time, and the band's lead singer, Axl Rose, and rhythm guitarist, Izzy Stradlin, had grown up in Indiana. But the band's song "One in a Million" included a line complaining about "immigrants and faggots" and claimed that gay people spread disease—a clear reference to AIDS, which was ravaging the gay community at the time. Many people did not want Guns N' Roses to play the show, but Mellencamp would not back down. "Everybody was mad about it, even at Farm Aid," Mellencamp said. "It pissed me off. I was like, 'Are you kidding me? This is the biggest band in the country right now, and you don't want them to come?' It's their song—it made no difference to me. Everything I like doesn't have to be politically correct, and every band that plays here doesn't have to be politically correct. But Lou came into my dressing room and jumped my shit. He was worked up about it. I said, 'Lou, this is a funny conversation coming from a guy who wrote a song named "Heroin."' He just walked out, and I don't think I ever spoke to him again."

ON ANOTHER POLITICAL FRONT, Reed agreed to participate in Steven Van Zandt's antiapartheid protest culminating in the song "Sun City" in 1985. The Sun City resort in South Africa would offer performers exorbitant fees in an effort to get them to violate the African National Congress's request—supported by the United Nations—that artists refuse to play in South Africa as long as apartheid was the law of the land. Many artists had violated that boycott, including Elton John, Linda Ronstadt, and Queen, as well as such black artists as Ray Charles, Dionne Warwick, and Tina Turner. Performances in South Africa by artists of that visibility and stature allowed the country's government to perpetuate the myth that conditions there were not as bad as the Western media portrayed them.

After he left Bruce Springsteen's E Street Band, which he would eventually rejoin, Van Zandt became

an outspoken political activist. He wanted to highlight an issue that, unlike charity events like "We Are
the World" and Farm Aid, actually forced artists to
take a stand. It was an effort at consciousness-raising
and genuine social change: American audiences would
get educated about the horrors of apartheid, and participating artists would take a pledge not to play Sun
City. "I ain't gonna play Sun City," constituted the
song's chorus. With Sylvia's active encouragement,
Reed performed on the "Sun City" single, singing a
solo line, and he appeared in the song's video, along
with such artists as Bruce Springsteen, Run-D.M.C.,
Peter Gabriel, and Ringo Starr. In the video, Reed
strolls along a New York street flanked by Rubén
Blades and John Oates, his arms around the shoulders
of the two men.

Most dramatically, Reed hopped on board the Conspiracy of Hope tour in support of Amnesty International in June of 1986. Along with U2, Sting, Peter
Gabriel, Bryan Adams, and a number of other performers, Reed traveled to six U.S. cities, playing in arenas
and stadiums to call attention to human rights crises
around the world. At press conferences, Reed and the
other artists discussed the plight of political prisoners,
highlighting specific cases and urging audiences to
write letters demanding their release. It was a two-week
commitment that required Reed to be public about his
beliefs in a way he had never been in the past.

*   *   *

AMID ALL THIS ACTIVITY, Reed found the time to record a new album: *Mistrial,* which was released in May of 1986. Sylvia designed the album's cover, which shows a standing, unsmiling Reed wearing a black leather jacket and holding a guitar. Through his dark sunglasses he stares directly at the viewer. This clearly is not the upbeat, optimistic Reed of *New Sensations,* but it is also not the Reed of the seventies indulging in a kind of store-bought decadence. The guitar emphasizes that he is a musician, an artist, and it also provides an indication that, as on *New Sensations,* Reed would be playing all the lead guitar parts on the album. His look is serious and intense, not degenerate.

The title track gets at some of those distinctions. Over a roaring guitar riff—one of the signatures of the songs on the album—Reed runs through a wry catalog of his past misdeeds: sex at six years old, his first drink at eight, a "bad" attitude at thirty, an education earned in the streets. The bridge includes a classic Lou Reed up-in-your-face challenge—"Don't you point your finger at me"—but the song's chorus demands a reconsideration. "I want a mistrial to clear my name," Reed declares, adding that he means to make his case to the "people of New York City." The song is funny and its groove is relentless, but it gets at Reed's conviction that he is in a new frame of mind and needs to be reevaluated.

Some pedantic commentators have pointed out that Reed is misusing the term "mistrial" in the song. A mistrial occurs when either a jury is unable to reach a verdict or a serious error occurs during the trial's proceedings that in the judge's view makes it impossible for the trial to continue. A mistrial, then, does not clear the defendant's name; it simply invalidates the trial. For the purposes of the song, all that is beside the point. Reed's poetic license gives the word a more intuitive meaning — "mistrial" is a way of saying that the charges brought against him were a mistake (note the prefix), even as he admits them in the song. "What's interesting is that after I wrote the song 'Mistrial,' someone asked in an interview, 'Lou, do you feel guilty?' " Reed said. "And I realized I'm going to have a problem with this 'Mistrial' thing."

Reed claimed that the line about finger-pointing was the heart of the song for him, a view that was confirmed for him by, of all people, his mother. "I was listening to a tape of the album over at my parents' house and my mother said, 'What song is that?' and I said, 'It's called "Mistrial." ' And later she had some friends over and she came out and said something I consider interesting. She said, 'Would you play that song about "Don't you point your finger at me"?' She didn't say 'Mistrial.' And that's what I figured the song must really be about, 'cause that's what both Mom and I keyed into."

Both thematically and in terms of its sound, *Mistrial* constitutes another example of Reed's attempt to engage the world around him. He coproduced the album with Fernando Saunders, who programmed drum tracks for six of the album's ten songs, a clear nod to the eighties' radio-friendly move away from live drummers. Reed also takes on the video culture that took shape in the eighties in "Video Violence," one of the album's strongest songs. In 1985, the Parents Music Resource Center (PMRC), cofounded by Tipper Gore, the wife of then-senator Al Gore, and Susan Baker, the wife of then–treasury secretary James Baker, had begun turning the heat on the music industry for the violent and sexual content in song lyrics and videos. Congressional hearings were called to discuss the impact of so-called porn rock on young people, inaugurating an intense five-year culture war fixated on rock and roll and hip-hop. The whiff of censorship and McCarthyism was decidedly in the air.

Understandably, artists and record companies began to circle the wagons, an attack from outside their precincts causing them, for once, to recognize and act in their common interests. As a means of fending off further Congressional interference, record labels agreed to print "Explicit lyrics" warning labels on albums that contained songs thought to be unsuitable for children. Reed, needless to say, was near the top of the list of artists who most required freedom of speech protections. For him to release a song called "Video Vio-lence" was a distinct provocation. That title could easily have served as the subject of one of the Congressional hearings, which, of course, proceeded despite the record companies' agreement to the request to post advisory stickers. But Reed's song, one of his best, was, unsur-prisingly, not a lament over the violence portrayed in music videos. It was a cold-eyed examination of it, and a smart, penetrating one at that.

In the song, Reed describes how the emergence of video culture, the home VCR machine, and available VHS tapes enabled people to enjoy otherwise forbid-den pleasures in the comfort of their living rooms — in a sense, domesticating their most extreme fantasies: "Up in the morning drinking his coffee / Turns on the TV to some slasher movie / Cartoonlike women, tied up and sweaty / Panting and screaming, thank you, have a nice day." Perhaps more significantly, the "age of video violence" made it possible for companies to exploit such desires for profit — and, in the process, trivialize them even further. Slasher movies and cor-porate, saccharine Disney films exist side by side in a "twisted alliance," as Reed's song indicates.

It's a brilliant point. In the age of video violence, the tawdriness and superficiality of the depictions of sex (a Madonna song provides the soundtrack for a stripper) and the treacliness of the slick, prepackaged, soulless art presented to children are two sides of the same profitable coin, just like the "redneck evangelist" exploiting his fearful, desperate congregation. All are betrayals of trust, empty versions of activities that are meant to communicate, however disturbingly, to audiences on the deepest level. People, and particularly young music and movie fans, understand on some level how they are being manipulated, and that is the reason for their nihilism and hair-trigger anger, not the lame content of what they're listening to or looking at. The PMRC might bemoan the sex and violence of pop culture, but it's the insidious, for-profit channeling of those raging currents within us that is the real problem. That is the violence being done to us and to the culture. The "age of video violence" is "no age of reason," Reed sings.

On "The Original Wrapper," Reed puns on the hip-hop music that was becoming one of the definitive sounds of the decade and, with the help of Saunders's programming, fashions a driving beat to carry his funny jeremiad on conditions in the modern world. The song is a rap in itself, and Reed implicitly credits his word-heavy song-speech as a rap precursor. "I wanted to do a rap song—my version," Reed said. "It's just me singing the same way I always do." In the song, he mentions AIDS, the Middle East, President Reagan, Jerry Falwell, and, once again, music videos ("The baby sits in front of MTV / Watching violent fantasies"). Interestingly, Reed made a terrifying video of his own for

"No Money Down," an innocuous, upbeat pop song about the importance of trust in love relationships. In the video, which was directed by the English duo Godley and Crème, an animatronic version of Lou Reed rips the flesh off his own face. Exactly what this had to do with the relatively benign song it accompanied is a mystery, but the video attracted considerable attention, not all of it favorable. Notably, Beavis and Butt-Head, the hilariously stupid cartoon characters that MTV invented to spoof the notion that the network was damaging young minds, later praised the video with their ultimate compliment: "Cool."

The peppy "Outside" is ostensibly about the problems and complexities of the external world set in opposition to the simplicity of a couple's life at home. The world is a "mindless child," the song begins, unable to control its impulses, and, consequently, it's destructive. But the punning references to unprotected sex ("When we come inside") and the song's odd last line ("A baby's what you want inside") suggest that in the back of Reed's mind was Sylvia's desire for a child, one of the issues that had begun to emerge in their marriage.

The album concludes with "Tell It to Your Heart," one of Reed's most eloquent ballads. It celebrates the singer and his partner as "New York City lovers," even as it hints at a nameless anxiety that creates sleepless nights. The singer sees his lover in the lights of the sky at night, as well as in advertisements and other city landmarks. It's a deeply affecting song that relies on none of the classic overwrought imagery of love. Instead, the singer's love resides and manifests itself in the city that surrounds him. It is no more or less beautiful than that, and is all the more meaningful for its tangibility and immediacy. When the singer declares, "We're no teenage movie that ends in tragedy," it's the expression of an adult love that is meant to survive. It's also Reed draining the dark side of any romantic mystique. For all his past fascination with the abyss, its allure is dismissed in this song as merely the easy melancholic indulgence of a teen fling.

17

NEW YORK

I'VE BECOME COMPLETELY WELL-ADJUSTED to being a cult figure," Lou Reed said in 1989, and just about as soon as he spoke those words, it looked as if he might enjoy a commercial breakthrough. His album *New York*, released in January of 1989, received nearly universal critical praise, broke into the Top 40, and performed well enough to qualify for a gold record: it sold more than half a million copies, Reed's only studio album to do so.

Mistrial had been the last of Reed's five-album deal with RCA, and while he had not emerged as a commercial powerhouse during that time, an artist like Reed will always muster a certain amount of attention at record companies. He had sold enough records to create the enduring impression that additional success was just around the corner. Because he was a critics' darling, signing Reed would inevitably generate extensive buzz, which is helpful to any label. Finally, difficult artists like Reed can sometimes appeal to the competitiveness of record executives. If you imagine yourself to be the sort of executive who understands and works well with artists, it's possible to convince yourself that the musician's previous labels simply did not understand or were not creative enough to form a meaningful relationship with him or her. To some extent, Clive Davis had thought that way when he signed Reed to Arista, and now Seymour Stein thought similarly when he signed Reed to his label, Sire.

Stein had cofounded Sire Records in 1966, and in the seventies and eighties, it had earned a reputation for its progressive tastes and its ability to translate those tastes for mainstream audiences. Sire had signed the Ramones, Talking Heads, the Smiths, the Pretenders, the Cure, and Depeche Mode. Most notably, the label had signed an underground dance artist from New York named Madonna and launched her into superstardom. Many of the artists on Sire were Reed's aesthetic heirs, so the label made sense as his home. In addition, Sire was owned by Warner Bros. Records, a company famous for its willingness to work closely with artists and allow them as much creative freedom as possible.

Stein was a man known for his musical enthusiasms, so his signing Reed was hardly a shock to his staff. Still, given Reed's recent track record, not everyone saw signing Reed as a brilliant move. "Lou obviously was a great artist and had great stature, but it wasn't like Seymour had signed a superstar," said Steven Baker, who worked for Warner Bros. in Los Angeles and was Reed's "product manager" at the company—meaning he was something like an in-house advocate for Reed, his representative to the marketing, sales, advertising, and publicity staffs. "It's not as if Seymour was bringing a commercial juggernaut to the label. There were a lot of doubts. 'Why are we signing Lou Reed?'" But when Baker heard the advance cassette tape of *New York* that Stein had given him, he got enthused, and he began to get the rest of the company keyed up. This was something the label would be able to work with.

Reed and Sylvia flew out to Los Angeles for a series of meetings with the relevant people on the Warner Bros. staff. Stein, too, flew in from New York, and Baker and Howie Klein, Sire's general manager, were there as well. Making nice with record executives was never Reed's idea of a good time. However artist-friendly Warners may have been, it was a large record company, and it survived on hits. "It was like Lou was going to meet the players," Baker said. "Some of these people were going to be like, 'Wow, Lou Reed!' Some of them were going to be like, 'Who?'" But Lou was on his best behavior, according to Baker. "I'm sure he and Sylvia were thinking, 'This is the new label. Let's get off on the right foot.' Lou must have thought that he'd delivered one of his career-defining records, so it's important that everybody get along and understand what he's accomplished."

REED DID THINK OF his new album that way, and justifiably so. *New York* is raw and hard-hitting, in both its sound and its subject matter. Reed himself said, "Generally speaking, I have to say that with most of my albums, I've felt that I was behind myself, that the albums didn't represent where I really was when they came out. But on *New York*, I'm not behind myself—that's where I am, that's what I'm capable of doing. . . . I gave it my best shot."

The band consisted of Reed, guitarist Mike Rathke, bassist Rob Wasserman, and drummer Fred Maher, who coproduced the album with Reed. It was a bold choice. Since playing with Reed on *New Sensations*, Maher had joined the British New Wave band Scritti Politti and had lived in London for a year. Reed called him up and asked if he would play on the sessions for *New York*. He also asked Maher (because he was "the young guy," in Maher's view) for recommendations for a producer. "I rattled off a list of the usual names, and I guess people weren't interested in Lou at that point," Maher said. "Full of beans, full of probably too much confidence, I said, 'Well, Lou, how about me?' He said, 'What do you know about recording guitars? All you do is that synth-pop crap.' I said, 'Let's just get one day in the studio. Trust me.'" Reed agreed, and according to Maher, he was knocked out by the results. On that first day, Maher said, "we actually recorded the opening song on *New York,* 'Romeo Had Juliette.' He called me the next day, and he said, 'Fred, it's Lou. I sound like Lou Reed again for the first time in however many years. Let's do this.'"

Despite his trepidations, Maher reported that Reed was easy to produce—relatively speaking, of course. "Strangely, I was uniquely qualified to be his producer, because I had watched other engineers and producers try to make 'hits' with Lou and make him try to sing—'Sing, Lou, sing!' Lou doesn't sing. He's Lou. But I knew that I was heading into new territory. I was going to be in the studio with Lou, long days for a long time. So I psychologically prepared myself....'This is going to be brutal.' And it wasn't.... It was magical. He was in really good form. He was really comfortable.... It was done in six weeks, soup to nuts, basics to mixed. Done." As for Reed's health, Maher said that he was "in great shape. He was very funny about the alcohol stuff. I remember him holding up a big bottle of Evian as he was about to record a vocal and going, 'Mm, vodka!,' and chug[ging] it."

*　　*　　*

THE RAW, STRIPPED-DOWN, GUITAR-BASED sound of *New York* was not to everyone's taste. The singer-songwriter James McMurtry recalled discussing the album with John Mellencamp, who said, "It sounds like it was produced by an eighth grader, but I like it." But the rawness of the production suits the rawness of the album's themes: it's an unflinching look at a city under siege, an era in which more than two thousand murders a year routinely occurred in New York's five boroughs. The AIDS epidemic was also raging, decimating many communities to which Reed had long-standing ties—communities of gays, intravenous drug users, and artists.

AIDS provides the melancholic backdrop to "Halloween Parade," one of the most moving songs on the album. The city's Halloween parade is something like an official holiday for the gay community, an opportunity to celebrate all the theatricality, artifice, outrageousness, sexual adventurism, liberation, and creativity for which the scene is justly famous. The song begins very much in that vein, as Reed casts an affectionate eye on characters dressed like Greta Garbo and Alfred Hitchcock down where "the docks and the badlands meet." In that regard, the song is something like a nearly two-decade-later update on "Walk on the Wild Side." But Reed is no longer capable of maintaining the coolness and detachment of that original song. The political consciousness that began taking shape in him a few years earlier, along with the disease that was ravaging the gay community, force him to break out of his characteristic stoicism. The Halloween parade, with its many thousands of participants, only makes him aware of those who are "not around" because they're too sick to participate or have already died. He insists on "no consolations" but feels the past weighing on him. The "See you next year" that concludes the song sounds casual and offhand, but it is something between a wish and a prayer.

Part of *New York*'s power and appeal is its conceptual boldness and simplicity—beginning with its title. In a sense, virtually all of Reed's recorded work is about New York, so calling a particular album *New York* is a challenge to both himself and the listener. As Reed himself said, "Faulkner had the South, Joyce had Dublin. I've got New York—and its environs." How was this portrait of the city supposed to differ from his previous ones?

For one thing, Reed believed that, having overcome his drug and alcohol problems, he had both the stamina and the concentration to construct a focused concept album—one he viewed in literary terms, as if it were a novel or a collection of short stories. In his liner notes for *New York,* Reed told listeners that the album was meant to be heard straight through, as if it were a book. Of course, he took criticism for the "pretension" of that demand, as well as its implication that somehow making a rock-and-roll album was inherently a less serious aesthetic undertaking than filmmaking or writing. Regardless, Reed was increasingly thinking of himself as a writer and distancing himself from what he saw as the childishness of rock and roll. The man who had talked for years about making rock and roll for adults was now consciously doing so and letting it be known in no uncertain terms. When he toured in support of *New York,* Reed shaped his show like a theatrical performance, including six nights at the St. James Theatre, a Broadway showcase in the heart of New York's theater district. For the first half of the show, he performed the album straight through; then, after an intermission, he performed a set of his other songs. However, rock-and-roll audiences—and Reed's audience, in particular—are not inclined to follow rules. At a show in Los Angeles, Reed carefully explained the format of the show, and then the band kicked into "Dirty Blvd." When the song ended and a voice from the crowd shouted, " 'Walk on the Wild Side'!" Reed was apoplectic.

Though Reed insisted that the songs be listened to in order both on record and live, the sequencing of the album was hardly scientific. "We had tried to put the songs in order, to tell the story moodwise and emotionally," Reed said. "And when it didn't work, it was so bad it was unbelievable. Then Victor [Deyglio], one of the engineers, said, 'There's a trick I've learned over the years. Why not put it in the order that it was recorded in?' And there it was. Wow!"

New York was also a departure in that Reed turned the focus of his writing away from himself and, with the exception of "Halloween Parade," away from the worlds he had moved in. "For a while, I felt a little self-impelled to write Lou Reed kind of songs," Reed said. "I should have understood that a Lou Reed was anything I wanted to write about." That new understanding allowed for a new directness. "In *New York,* the Lou Reed image doesn't exist, as far as I'm concerned," he said. "This is me speaking as directly as I possibly can to whoever hopefully wants to listen to it." Songs like "Romeo Had Juliette," "Hold On," and "Dirty Blvd." explore the lives of New York street characters, but not the doomed and glamorous, sexually ambiguous underground figures that populated his songs previously. These are the New Yorkers whose ships failed to rise with the tides that lifted the affluent to even greater heights during the Reagan-Bush years. "It really is the eight years of Reagan," Reed said. "I'm trying to make you feel the situation we're in....That's what this album is all about." His subjects' drug of choice is crack, which has destroyed their communities. They are the junkies who die anonymously in alleys, not the ones who would have dropped by Andy Warhol's Factory or frequented the after-hours bars that had consumed so much of Reed's life and artistic focus. Indeed, at the time, they would not have occupied much space in the media at all. That many of them are Hispanic—Romeo Rodriguez in "Romeo Had Juliette"; Pedro, the young, abused boy in "Dirty Blvd."—may well have had to do with Sylvia's Mexican American heritage, as well as her class-oriented political consciousness. Reed presents their lives with sympathy and dignity, as well as a keen awareness of the daily struggles they face. The term "Statue of Bigotry," repeated on *New York,* is Reed's telegraphic rendering of how the American dream has been betrayed with devastating consequences.

Perhaps what most sets apart *New York* is that the city, so often treated by Reed as an isolated world of its own, is portrayed on the album as a microcosm of America itself. "We're in this terrible morass of people absolutely not giving a shit about anybody but themselves," Reed said. "And a mean-spirited government that is essentially attacking people that can't defend themselves. That's the weakest people—the kids, the sick, the elderly. And I think we should fight back." With *New York,* Reed was living up to the statement he had made in 1986 at the time of the Amnesty International Conspiracy of Hope tour: "The days of me being aloof about certain things are over."

On "Dirty Blvd.," Reed brought in one of his musical idols: Dion DiMucci, the famed lead singer of Dion and the Belmonts. (Reed appeared on Dion's own album, sang background for him at a Madison Square Garden benefit, and, in early 1989, inducted Dion into the Rock and Roll Hall of Fame.) Reed also invited Moe Tucker to play drums on two of *New York*'s tracks. He planned to have John Cale play on the album, but Maher inadvertently sabotaged that possibility when he mentioned to Cale that Tucker would be coming in as well. Reed had not informed Cale, who said to Maher, "What is this, some sort of Velvet Underground reunion?" That was the end of that—at least for a while.

"Last Great American Whale" indicts America's ecological failings, while "There Is No Time," "Sick of You," and "Busload of Faith" all evoke the urgency of then-current political conditions, the desperate need for action to overcome the nation's crisis. Interestingly, "Endless Cycle" takes a much more psychological view of social conditions. It describes how violence and child abuse pass from generation to generation, with alcohol and drugs blunting people's ability to rise against their circumstances and change them. The song ends with a stark conclusion about a couple doomed to repeat their parents' bitter histories: "The truth is they're happier when they're in pain / In fact, that's why they got married." The only percussion on the track is a metronome that Maher sampled, its regular ticktock underscoring the song's main theme: the passage of time and its repetition.

Perhaps the most complicated song on *New York* is "Good Evening Mr. Waldheim," which, among other things, highlights the degree to which Reed's awareness of himself as a Jew grew stronger with his sobriety. Throughout his life, Reed had either ignored or spoken dismissively—even disparagingly—of his Jewish background. His parents were not observant, and he bitterly rejected the stereotypical suburban aspiration that he become a doctor, lawyer, or businessman. He went through a period of being fascinated by Nazi imagery and, as part of the Warhol crowd, represented a cultural movement that couldn't have been further removed from the self-seriousness of the New York Jewish intellectual world. In conversation, he'd been known to use anti-Semitic slurs.

"Good Evening Mr. Waldheim" takes its title from Kurt Waldheim, the Austrian diplomat and politician who had served as secretary general of the United Nations and was revealed in the mideighties, when he was president of Austria, to have been aware of Nazi atrocities during World War II, when he was in the German Army. Reed also refers to "Pontiff" in the song, an apparent allusion to Pope John Paul II, whose boyhood in Poland had begun to be explored for his possible youthful connection to, or at least passive acceptance of, Nazi war crimes. But the real target of the song is Jesse Jackson, who, in an interview with a *Washington Post* reporter during his 1984 presidential run, had used the term "Hymie" to refer to Jews and called New York "Hymietown." Jackson had believed the comments to be off the record, but the reporter published them and completely derailed Jackson's campaign. He ended up formally apologizing to a group of national Jewish leaders at a synagogue in New Hampshire.

As a presidential candidate once again in 1988, Jackson had given a speech at the Democratic National Convention that took the term "common ground" as its conceit—a space where all Americans could come together regardless of their differences. At the time, Jackson represented the most progressive wing of the Democratic Party. He had run a campaign that pointedly addressed class as well as race inequality, and he had energized many African American voters. In fact, Jackson was by far the only candidate to make serious issues of all the problems Reed identified in the songs on *New York*. Reed admitted how powerfully Jackson's speech had affected him. "I saw the speech Jesse made about 'common ground,' and it was amazing, emotionally moving," Reed said. "He should have been elected on the spot, on the basis of that speech. Except for one problem. Does that 'common ground' include me, Jesse? If I met the man, that's what I would ask him."

In "Good Evening Mr. Waldheim," however, Reed

focuses on Jackson's seeming bias against Jews and his refusal to disown his relationship with Louis Farrakhan, the leader of the Nation of Islam. The song's title implies that Jackson's racial slur puts him in the same moral category as a Nazi sympathizer. Reed also draws a comparison between the Nation of Islam and the Ku Klux Klan. Such sentiments were a reflection of how Reed's feelings about his own Jewishness — and his relationship to the state of Israel — had changed. "He could take a conservative stance on the pro-Israel side," Sylvia said, contrasting that position to Reed's leftist views on most other issues. "Somebody wrote very eloquently on that subject that if you're a Jew, you're a Jew. You can't escape it. You can't change it. That's who you are, and it marks you. And Lou would often define himself that way, sometimes really irreverently, like, this is what Jewish culture represents. You want a lawyer, you get a smart Jew. You want a doctor, get the Jew. On and on and on. That was part of him, part of who he was."

"Beginning of a Great Adventure" touches, once again, on Sylvia's desire to have children. The title evokes a phrase that many people use when embarking on parenthood, which Reed attributes to Sylvia: "I hope it's true what my wife said to me / She says, 'Baby, it's the beginning of a great adventure.'" But the song ultimately treats the idea of having children humorously. Over a jazzy guitar riff, Reed first imagines that it might be fun "to have a kid that I could kick around." Then, in a shift from the connection he felt to his rural New Jersey neighbors in "New Sensations," he imagines having enough children to "breed a little liberal army in the woods / Just like these redneck lunatics I see at the local bar / With their tribe of mutant inbred piglets with cloven hooves." While Reed's anxieties about what he perceived as the traumas of his own childhood ultimately prevented him from agreeing to become a father, the song's jauntiness and sense of fun suggest that the idea still remained a possibility in his mind. The song ends with Reed alluding to "Love Is Strange," the classic 1956 hit by Mickey and Sylvia (note the female name), as he sings, "Sylvia, what do you call your lover man?" It's a sexy close to a song about a sexy subject that had been treated quite unsexily up to that point.

New York concludes, oddly, on a spiritual note, one far removed from the social issues that preoccupy the rest of the record. "Dime Store Mystery" begins with a meditation on Jesus Christ's last moments alive. Reed was inspired by hearing Martin Scorsese on a television news show discussing his film *The Last Temptation of Christ,* which came out in 1988 and had been virulently attacked for blasphemy. "I was watching Marty Scorsese on *Nightline,*" Reed recalled, "trying to explain to these fundamentalists and Ted Koppel his take on Christ. I was writing down the things he

was saying: human nature, godly nature, the dichot-
omy. It reminded me of when I was in college, philosophy classes." The singer notes that he could imagine
that Christ "might question his beliefs"—that is, his
divine origins—given the horrors of his crucifixion.
Reed continues to explore this duality, how "godly
nature, human nature / Splits the soul." Which brings
him, in the song's concluding verse, to pondering the
passing of Andy Warhol, who died in 1987. Reed seems
to wonder if Warhol had at any point rethought his
studied superficiality. Warhol may also have come to
mind because of his staunch Catholicism (the faith in
which Scorsese was also raised), emphasized by Reed's
alluding to Warhol's memorial service at St. Patrick's
Cathedral. "What must you have been thinking," Reed
asks, "when you realized the time had come for you? /
I wish I hadn't thrown away my time / On so much
human and so much less divine."

The reviews for *New York* were very strong. In *Musician,* Bill Flanagan wrote that the album "sounds like
the best thing Lou Reed's ever done." In a four-star
lead review for *Rolling Stone,* I wrote, "In whatever
future there is, whenever anyone wants to hear the
sound of the eighties collapsing into the nineties in
the city of dreams, *New York* is where they'll have to
go." But as troubled as Reed's hometown was, he did
not read his own fate into it. "I'm not going to let that

be my future," he said, still grateful for his recovery. "If the town has to go down, it can go down without me." Reed was feeling at the absolute height of his powers, and he was about to enter one of the most transformative periods of both his life and his work.

18

I HATE LOU REED

O N FEBRUARY 20, 1987, Andy Warhol entered New York Hospital (now New York–Presbyterian) on the Upper East Side of Manhattan under the pseudonym Bob Roberts for gallbladder surgery. He had complained to his dermatologist about pains in his right side that were diagnosed as gallbladder attacks, but surgical treatment had been put off because of Warhol's fear of hospitals. (He evidently had a premonition that he would die in one.) Finally, after second opinions were sought, it was agreed that Warhol's gallbladder would have to be removed. The three-and-a-half-hour surgery, which removed his gangrenous gallbladder, took place the following day, February 21, and seemed to have gone well. On February 22, a

Sunday, Warhol died. It was stunning news that no one expected.

The quality of the care—or lack of it—that Warhol received at New York Hospital became the subject of a wrongful death lawsuit more than four years later, and, in a sealed agreement, the hospital paid an undisclosed sum described as "substantial" (the hospital also called it "fair and equitable") to the heirs of the Warhol estate. (The settlement was later reported to be $3 million.) Warhol, who was five foot eleven, weighed a mere 128 pounds when he checked into New York Hospital, and despite having been described as in "good" health on the hospital's admission report, he was, according to the estate's attorney, anemic and undernourished. The hospital "negligently pumped more than twice the required volume of fluids" into Warhol (a doctor at his autopsy indicated his weight then as 150 pounds), according to Bruce Clark, the lawyer for the estate, and then it had failed to monitor his condition, causing the heart attack that killed him.

In a chilling statement that underscores the loneliness that seemed to be so much at the heart of Warhol's life, Clark said, "No doctor looked in on him. The floor nurses never looked in. The only one to inquire about Andy Warhol's condition after his surgery was a resident in training who called the private duty nurse on the phone." The nurse, who had been reading her Bible at the time, noticed that Warhol had turned blue and that his pulse was weak. When she couldn't wake him, she called the floor nurse, who, in turn, summoned an emergency cardiac team. Warhol could not be revived and was pronounced dead at 6:31 a.m. That a figure of Warhol's fame and stature would receive such shoddy treatment—and seemingly be so alone at a time of acute crisis—was as shocking as his premature death. He was fifty-eight years old.

After he was shot in 1968, Warhol told Reed that he felt as if he may have already died. His actual death triggered an enormous response in the media and, needless to say, among the thousands of people who had known, worked with, socialized with, or simply met him. By 1987, Warhol had achieved the affectionate status of a New York tabloid staple—indeed, it seemed as if he had held that station forever. Arguments about the quality and importance of his art, once eagerly— often heatedly—debated, had long ago fallen to the experts to adjudicate. For New Yorkers, it seemed that not a day could go by without a mention in the gossip pages or on the local television news regarding where Warhol had gone the night before and with whom. Drifting through the media landscape like a benignly smiling specter, invariably positioned next to someone well-known or socially prominent, he seemed to have achieved the kind of ubiquitous anonymity, or famous invisibility, that he had always sought. Warhol was a member of the city's media family—the dotty uncle who hobnobbed with the rich and famous—and his death struck a nerve. Suddenly everyone remembered that the eccentric character they'd long taken for granted was an important and influential artist, one of the essential architects of the postmodern age.

Warhol's obituary in the *New York Times* was dutiful, even respectful, though not extravagant in its praise, noting that "Mr. Warhol's keenest talents were for attracting publicity, for uttering the unforgettable quote, and for finding the single visual image that would most shock and endure." The Velvet Underground went unmentioned.

Of course, those who knew Warhol responded far more viscerally to the shock of his death. A complicated figure—sweet and manipulative, generous and withholding—Warhol left his survivors to untangle the knot of their often contradictory feelings. For Lou Reed, whose encounters with him ran the full emotional gamut from loving to resentful, Warhol's death actually simplified matters. "Lou was always very wary of Andy, always a bit guarded," Sylvia said. But once Warhol was no longer present to remind him of past grudges or incite feelings of guilt, Reed could more easily access the genuine love that he felt for one of his earliest benefactors, the man who played the most significant role of anyone in putting the Velvet Underground on the map. Warhol was no longer there to cast his long shadow, so Reed did not have to diminish him in order to be free of it and stand on his own. "He may be *the* American artist — period," he said of Warhol in 2006.

Warhol was waked, in the Catholic tradition, at the Thomas P. Kunsak Funeral Home in his hometown of Pittsburgh, and after his funeral, which was attended by family members and a smattering of Factory stalwarts (no one was sure if nonfamily would be welcome), he was buried in St. John the Baptist Byzantine Cemetery in Bethel Park, Pennsylvania, just outside Pittsburgh, next to his mother and father. On April 1, however, a memorial service was held for Warhol at St. Patrick's Cathedral in Manhattan, attended by two thousand people and avidly covered by the media. The guest list was vintage Warhol, including the likes of Raquel Welch, Claes Oldenburg, the prince and princess of Greece, Grace Jones, Tom Wolfe, Sophia Loren, Robert Mapplethorpe, Calvin Klein, Ric Ocasek, Jean-Michel Basquiat, and, of course, Lou Reed and John Cale. "This day was, in many ways, Andy's masterpiece," said photographer Christophe von Hohenberg, whose photographs outside the cathedral eventually became the book *Andy Warhol: The Day the Factory Died*. "He encapsulated pop, and this day celebrated that.... There was more laughter than crying that day. I don't mean that in a bad way. Of course, the way he died was a tragedy. But I just mean that it was an Andy

Warhol event. Inside the cathedral was more solemn, but outside was like a celebration. Andy would have loved that."

The Reverend Anthony Dalla Villa, the celebrant at St. Patrick's, delivered a eulogy in which he described Warhol as "a simple, humble, modest person, a child of God who in his own life cherished others." Yoko Ono spoke as well and expressed gratitude to Warhol for the kindness he had showed to Sean, her son with John Lennon, after Lennon was murdered. Clearly, despite his famed detachment, Warhol, the victim of an assassination attempt himself, would have understood the emotional impact of such a horrific event on a young boy. Indeed, art critic John Richardson, in his comments that day, addressed that very point, refuting the notion that Warhol was "cool to the point of callousness." Warhol was "a recording angel," Richardson said, and the "distance he established between the world and himself was above all a matter of innocence and of art." Against the charge that Warhol had exploited the Factory's vulnerable lost boys and girls and watched impassively as they spiraled downward, Richardson asserted that some Factory "hangers-on" were "hell-bent on destroying themselves." Richardson put it simply: Warhol "was not cut out to be his brother's keeper" because detachment "was his special gift." That, no doubt, was true, even insightful, though in citing the Biblical question that led to the curse of

Cain, Richardson was making an odd statement during a service devoted to a dead person in a cathedral.

After the ceremony, which ran for an hour, four hundred guests gathered for a luncheon in the basement nightclub at the Paramount Century Hotel on West Forty-Sixth Street, a few blocks from St. Patrick's. The hotel had recently been purchased by Ian Schrager, who had co-run Studio 54, one of Warhol's favorite stops, and the club where the luncheon took place had been the site of Billy Rose's Diamond Horseshoe, a forties hot spot that became the glamorous subject of a 1945 musical starring Betty Grable. Obviously, it was as perfect a choice for the final Warhol celebration as St. Patrick's had been for his memorial. The music of the Velvet Underground provided the soundtrack for the Paramount event, and at one point, Reed remarked, "It's hard to believe Andy's not going to be around. I was hoping he'd turn up and say, 'April Fool!'"

Singer-songwriter Eric Andersen, who had been part of the Greenwich Village folk scene in the sixties and had starred in the 1965 Warhol film *Space* with Edie Sedgwick, came to the luncheon with the actress and Warhol superstar Viva. Andersen had seen the Exploding Plastic Inevitable and admired Reed as a writer, so he thought he might introduce himself. "I noticed Lou was just standing alone, so I walked over to him," Andersen said. "He didn't say 'Hello' or 'Hi' or anything. He just said, 'Andy Warhol was the only person in the music business who didn't try to fuck me or cheat me.' That was his opening shot."

As guests ate, drank, and mingled, one of the subjects that kept coming up was the notion of a tribute to Warhol involving music. The artist Julian Schnabel brought up the subject with Cale. "He said, 'Look, you got to do something for Andy,'" Cale recalled. "I replied it would be a bit tough to do anything now. 'No, no, let's you and me get together and write something.' Then he said, 'Let's get Lou over here.' I thought, what the hell is Julian doing?" The photographer Billy Name also drew Reed and Cale into a conversation together, helping to break the ice between them. The two men had not been in touch, at least in part, Cale believed, because he was still drinking and Lou had gotten sober, though he also pointed out that, in his relations with Reed, it was always "three steps forward, two steps back."

But once the idea of a Warhol tribute had been broached, it was only a few days before Cale contacted Reed, and "Lou and I started to discuss doing a collaboration." Cale told Reed, "Look, I've got these few songs and I'm stuck with them. I thought maybe you'd be interested." Things moved quickly from there. Reed may have been surprised to hear from Cale, but "I think he was more surprised how easy it was to get back into working than anything else—just as I was that things started off in one direction and rapidly grew in strength. The ideas were really good."

That was the start of *Songs for Drella,* Reed and Cale's tribute (or, as Reed might put it, epitaph) to their departed friend. Drella, a conflation of "Cinderella" and "Dracula," was a nickname coined years before by Ronnie Cutrone, an artist and Factory stalwart, to capture the contradictory halves of Warhol's personality. From the outset, Reed and Cale had a specific idea in mind. "First of all, we wanted to see if anyone anywhere had done a rock album that teaches you something about the life of whomever, and there wasn't any," Reed said. "We thought what an amazing learning tool this would be....I was thinking there must be an album to tell you about Malcolm X, for instance, or Martin Luther King...and then you can play it in school and make learning fun....I think John had the idea, 'Why don't we do an album about Andy's life that's really positive?' because we felt very positive towards Andy, to say the least, and there were all these terrible negative things. We thought it would be great to do the Andy we knew."

St. Ann's Warehouse in Brooklyn Heights, which three years earlier had hosted the American premiere of Cale's *The Falklands Suite,* teamed up with the Brooklyn Academy of Music and commissioned Reed and Cale to perform *Songs for Drella.* Reed described their work as "a hundred percent collaboration. John and I just rented out a small rehearsal studio for three weeks and locked ourselves in."

Though he and Warhol had not stayed in close touch, Cale had never experienced the deep ambivalence toward him that Reed had. "I don't think Lou could have had a clue how I felt about Andy," Cale said. "I had always felt emotionally close to Andy—always. And he always welcomed me whenever I showed up at the Factory." The process of working on *Songs for Drella* brought some realizations to Cale about his own history. Reed had pushed Cale out of the Velvets at roughly the same time he got rid of Warhol as the group's manager. Consequently, Cale was unaware of much that had gone on between Warhol and Reed. "There were a lot of things I didn't know until we came to write *Drella* twenty years later about how Lou had treated Andy," Cale recalled. For his part, Reed, speaking about the Factory at around the time of Warhol's death, said, "I watched Andy. I watched Andy, watching everybody. You've got to understand. I was never part of it. I was not a great friend of Andy's."

Reed's and Cale's differing perspectives on the past created an underlying tension in *Songs for Drella*. The presence of Cale, a partial witness to Reed's rejection of Warhol (not to mention a person who had experienced a similar fate at Reed's hands), made it impossible for Reed to simply flip the script and claim an undying devotion to Warhol, as he might otherwise have done. Instead, Reed was forced to grapple with the consequences of his own behavior, and that is the most gripping aspect of *Songs for Drella*. Nor was that process a one-way street. *The Andy Warhol Diaries* were published in May of 1989, two years after his death and four months after Reed and Cale first performed *Songs for Drella* at St. Ann's in Brooklyn Heights. The diary's passages about Reed expressed precisely the passive-aggressive ambivalence that Reed felt about Warhol.

After seeing Reed at the Bottom Line in March of 1978, Warhol described himself as "*proud* of him. For once, finally he's himself, he's not copying anybody. Finally he's got his own style. Now everything he does works, he dances better. Because when John Cale and Lou were the Velvets, they really had a style, but when Lou went solo he got bad and was copying people like Mick Jagger." Warhol's visit to Reed's rent-controlled Christopher Street apartment (six rooms, $485 per month) later that year prompted this reflection: "And oh, Lou's life is everything I want my life to be. I mean, every room has every electronic gadget in it—a big big big big TV, a phone answerer that you hear when the phone rings, tapes, TVs, Betamaxes, and he's so sweet and so funny at the same time, so together, it's just incredible. And his house is very neat. He had a maid come in...well, I guess it does smell a little of dog shit, but…" At a dinner celebrating Warhol's fif-tieth birthday in August of 1978, Reed gave him "a great present, a one-inch TV, and he was so adorable, so sober."

In 1981, after reading an article about Reed in *People,* Warhol wondered why he hadn't been invited to Reed's wedding to Sylvia Morales the previous year. "They had a big reception and everything," he wrote. The next month, he saw Lou and his new bride on the street in Greenwich Village. "She's nothing special," Warhol wrote of Sylvia, "just a little sexy girl. I told him that I'd just been reading about him in *People* and I asked him why he doesn't come over and see us, and he said it's because he doesn't know any of the people anymore, and then he asked if Ronnie was still around, and I said yes, and then if Vincent was still around, and I said yes, and if PH was still around, and I said yes, so it was funny." Warhol ran into Reed at a party for Ronnie Cutrone and described him as look-ing "so glum, so peculiar. His wife looks more Puerto Rican every time I see her. I don't know if Lou is big or not. *Rolling Stone* gave his album [*Legendary Hearts*] four stars, but was it a hit? Ronnie said Lou's in AA so I guess he's not drinking. But Sam the next night was telling me that he saw Lou at the Ninth Circle drink-ing, but maybe he was just there picking up boys. But then he lived in that neighborhood, anyway, so maybe he was just hanging out. Ronnie says that when he goes to visit Lou in the country that he's always just bought another motorcycle and another piece of land."

Warhol sat in the same row as Reed at the MTV awards in 1984 but reported that Reed "never even looked over. I don't understand Lou, why he doesn't talk to me now." The following year, Warhol complained, "I just don't understand why I have never gotten a penny from that first Velvet Underground record. That record really sells and I was the producer! Shouldn't I get something? I mean, shouldn't I? And what I can't figure out is when Lou stopped liking me. I mean, he even went out and got himself two dachshunds like I had and then after that he started not liking me, but I don't know exactly why or when. Maybe it was when he married this last wife, maybe he decided that he didn't want to see peculiar people. I'm surprised he hasn't had kids, you know?" Finally, in September of 1986: "I hate Lou Reed more and more, I really do, because he's not giving us any video work."

No question, Warhol was equally catty—or worse— about many people in his diaries, but his comments got under Reed's skin. Just as he had begun to revise his hostile feelings toward Warhol, Warhol's own anger toward Reed had come into public view. In a musical response, Reed and Cale wrote "A Dream," a haunting recitation by Cale of many of the passages from Warhol's diaries about him and Reed. The words about

Cale are positive ("He's been looking really great / He's been coming by the office to exercise with me"), while his comments about Reed ("You know I hate Lou") are often stinging. The "hate" line was particularly important to Reed. "When John was doing the reading," he said, "I kept telling him that when we get to that line, 'I hate Lou,' you gotta say it like a kid. It's like the way a little kid would say it." The swirling, hallucinogenic roar that Reed and Cale, on guitar and keyboards, respectively, conjure to accompany those words gives the song a surreal atmosphere.

Perhaps the two incidents that haunted Reed the most were when Warhol called him a "rat" ("The worst thing he could think of to call me") when Reed fired him as the Velvets' manager, and the time years later when Warhol asked him why he hadn't phoned or visited the hospital after he was shot. " 'Why didn't you visit me? Where were you?' " Reed remembered Warhol asking. "Which was something that's bothered me over the years. But he said it more than once."

According to Reed, the song "A Dream" was "John's idea. He had said, 'Why don't we do a short story like "The Gift"?' But then he went away to Europe. He goes off to Europe saying, 'Hey Lou, go write a short story.' But I thought, no, not a short story; let's make it a dream. That way, we can have Andy do anything we want. Time and dimension and reality won't matter. Let me tell you, man, it was really hard to do. But once I got into Andy's tone of voice, I was able to write for a long time that way." In "Hello It's Me," which concludes *Songs for Drella,* Reed addresses Warhol directly, speaking in his own voice. He admits his remorse ("I'm sorry that I doubted your good heart"), acknowledges his sense of loss ("I really miss you"), but finally, characteristically, can't entirely relinquish his own sense of injury: "But I have some resentments that can never be unmade / You hit me where it hurt, I didn't laugh / Your diaries are not a worthy epitaph."

The implication of that last line is that *Songs for Drella* would provide the epitaph that Warhol deserved. "It's emotionally honest, which is something I've tried to be on all my records," Reed said. "I mean, if there's a thing that is negative toward me, I don't take it out. If it works in the context of the project and if it's true in the context of the project, I leave it in." Cale explained, "Lou comes to terms with himself in songs. I wouldn't be surprised if he's most satisfied when he's written a song 'cause it's worked out all these tensions that are in his head. . . . It's like somebody discovering their identity."

Reed gave *Songs for Drella* the subtitle *A Fiction* precisely to grant himself some emotional and thematic leeway in writing the lyrics, "so that if I decided to take poetic license with certain facts — like, did it happen on Eighty-First Street or was it actually Seventy-

Third Street?—I wouldn't have to be called into account for it."

Having the character of Warhol speak in his own voice from his own perspective in the song successfully humanizes him, but significantly, Reed and Cale also had him address the issue that John Richardson had raised in his eulogy: the notion that Warhol was somehow morally responsible for the self-destructive actions of so many of the Factory regulars, most notably Edie Sedgwick, who died at twenty-eight of an accidental drug overdose in 1971. When *Edie: An American Biography,* a gripping oral history of Sedgwick's life by Jean Stein and edited with George Plimpton, appeared in 1982, it was a massive best seller and became a central text in the indictment of Warhol as a callous manipulator. In "It Wasn't Me," which Reed sings, the character of Warhol responds to such charges. "The problems you had were there before you met me," Reed sings. "I know she's dead, it wasn't me." The song is powerfully emotional, with Reed playing a stately theme on guitar and Cale providing texture in a variety of keyboard voicings, including church organ. No doubt those particular attacks on Warhol resonated deeply with Reed, who endured similar charges for his morally neutral depictions of drug use in his music, particularly in "Heroin." Speaking about "It Wasn't Me," Reed said, "You'd have to be in Andy's shoes before casting the first stone.... What was he supposed to do? Have a little counseling session for thirty people? I mean, like, everybody was free, white, and twenty-one. If they had been looking for counseling, they wouldn't have been there, right? Anyway, he *did* make suggestions. Suppose I say to you, 'Oh, don't do that. That's really bad,' and you don't listen to me. Have I fulfilled my obligation? Well, he did that a lot. I don't think it's fair to put such a burden on him."

Songs for Drella's arrangements are necessarily spare, relying on only Reed's electric guitar and Cale's keyboards and electric viola; plans to orchestrate the songs had been abandoned. "I was really excited by the amount of power just two people could do without needing drums," Cale said. "When we started work, I was always, in the back of my mind, wondering, 'Where the hell does the backbeat go?' And by the time we finished it, I was saying, 'Thank God we don't have one!'" While the music certainly gets noisy at points, the absence of a rhythm section put the emphasis squarely on the words, which is exactly where Reed and Cale wanted it: it was essential that the audience be able to make out the lyrics. "In this particular show, we're throwing an amazing amount of information at you," Reed said. "Usually, when people go to rock-and-roll shows, they expect to hear songs they already know, and the lyrics aren't really that important. In my case... there is no show without the lyrics, and no one's heard them before. It's really like going to a *concert*."

Songs for Drella was performed twice at St. Ann's Church in January of 1989, as a work in progress, and then for four nights in November and December at the Brooklyn Academy of Music (BAM), as part of the Next Wave Festival. *The Andy Warhol Diaries* had not been published by the time of the St. Ann's dates, and "A Dream" was written between the two sets of shows. At the performances, Cale and Reed sat on opposite sides of the stage, and images and text were projected onto a large screen behind them. That was it. (While very different in tone, the format nodded to Warhol's multimedia Exploding Plastic Inevitable, during which the Velvet Underground would perform as films and images were projected onto them.) The performance was about an hour long. The goal, Reed explained, was "to get you as close to the music and the words as possible, with as little showbizzy glitz going on as there could be, and to introduce you to our friend Andy."

During one of the performances at BAM, a heckler yelled out, "Tell us something we don't know." It was the sort of incident that, ordinarily, would have pro-voked a scathing outburst from Reed—and, very likely, that's what it was designed to do. Instead, Reed and Cale simply carried on with their performance. "The thing about that comment," Reed said later, "is that if the guy had really been listening, I'm, like, *telling* him something he doesn't know. I'm giving him a side of Andy that *nobody* knows. But I was concentrating too much to respond."

Much as they were meant as a celebration of Warhol, the performances had a serious, funereal air, if that term can be used in a positive sense, particularly at St. Ann's, which was a beautiful, atmospheric, Gothic church as well as a performance space, with stained glass windows well over a century old. The audience sat in wooden pews and in the choir loft, and Reed and Cale performed in front of an altar. In their invocations of the dead, their no-nonsense presentation, and the silent concentration of the audience, the shows there had very much the feeling of a service. The death obsession that runs through Warhol's work has often been attributed to his Catholicism, and Reed and Cale believed that the religious environment of St. Ann's brought that element of his life to the fore. Reed said that the church "was a very powerful part of the thing. We didn't realize during sound checks and dress rehearsals that when there were people in it and we were up there with the stained windows...you suddenly felt this incredible surge that this house devoted to belief can generate." It's relevant, Reed added, that "Andy always went to church, which was something that a lot of people either didn't know, or didn't associate with him even though they'd heard about it. Every Sunday he went to church."

Reed and Cale filmed a version of *Songs for Drella* at BAM but without an audience present, for release on VHS. Then they went into the studio to record an album of the songs, which was released in 1990. When the album appeared, the rock world was thrilled by the notion of half a VU reunion, though Reed had gone out of his way to dismiss any hope of that prospect. People had failed to appreciate the Velvet Underground when it existed, he said, "so here's a little second shot for them. People have been moaning about, 'Gee, I didn't see it then,' or 'Why isn't there a Velvet Underground reunion?'—which there isn't going to be. But there is this particular thing. And we wanted to present it in as pure a state as possible." At the performances at St. Ann's and BAM, Reed and Cale played only material from *Songs for Drella*—nothing from the Velvets' catalog.

Though the project brought Reed and Cale back together, in the course of it, they essentially replicated their entire previous relationship, moving from initial enthusiasm to tense collaboration to frustration and distance. In the liner notes for the album, Cale wrote, "*Songs for Drella* is a collaboration, the second Lou and I have completed since 1965, and I must say that although I think he did most of the work, he has allowed me to keep a position of dignity in the process." In its way, it was a pointed comment, especially from a musician as accomplished as Cale. It speaks to his desire to work with Reed and take a pragmatic approach to his idiosyncrasies, but it also has a passive-aggressive element. True collaborators don't worry too much about who is doing "most of the work," and allowing your partner a "position of dignity" would seem to be a bare-minimum requirement for any project involving an artist of Cale's stature. As with the Velvet Underground, there is no question that Cale's contributions to *Drella* are just as important as Reed's. By making it public that he felt the need to acknowledge Reed's generosity in this regard—or that Reed, at least implicitly, required such an acknowledgment—Cale slyly revealed the difficulties in their working together. Reed seemed to understand this and didn't appreciate it. After telling a journalist, "You can just say that John Cale was the easygoing one and Lou was the prick," he refused to respond to Cale's comments in the liner notes. "That thing he wrote says what it says: it says Lou did the majority of the work," Reed said. "That's that."

As for the album, in a four-star review, *Rolling Stone* called *Songs for Drella* "a shining, tense merger of visions. Reed's edgy guitar, fullness of heart, and clipped, journalistic poetry bring into sculptural relief Cale's elegant keyboards and brainy lyricism. As their subject,

Warhol is both immediate and mythic. The idea entrepreneur who produced the Velvets, he provokes an homage that's romantic yet casual—and Cale and Reed pay their debt with an offhand pop epic." *Songs for Drella,* the review concludes, is a "sweet and knowing tribute to these men's mentor, prod—and friend."

Significantly, Drella was a sobriquet that Warhol hated. Though meant as an endearment in the context of the album, its usage had a sharp edge. Like Warhol himself, and like Reed's relationship with him, and like Reed and Cale's relationship, *Songs for Drella* is full of contradictory emotions; praise, respect, affection, and even love are inextricable from bitterness, envy, jealousy, and resentment. In that sense, just as Reed promised, Warhol got the epitaph he deserved.

19

MAGIC AND LOSS

IN THE MID- TO late eighties, vast political changes swept across the Soviet Union and its satellite countries in Eastern Europe, behind what had been termed the Iron Curtain in the West. Uprisings by workers and students in Czechoslovakia toppled the Communist government there in 1989, and by the end of that year, playwright and activist Václav Havel had been installed as the country's president. In 1990, he was elected president in Czechoslovakia's first open elections since the end of World War II. Havel was an internationally acclaimed literary figure, and his activism, for which he was jailed many times, included support for the psychedelic rock band the Plastic People of the Universe, which was inspired by the Velvet Underground and whose long hair, bohemian lifestyle, and outspokenness incurred the wrath of Communist leaders. Havel himself was a fan of the Velvet Underground, whose music he had first heard when he visited the United States for six weeks in 1968. While exploring Greenwich Village and the East Village with his friend the filmmaker Miloš Forman, Havel bought one of the first two Velvet Underground albums. The Velvets' music and Reed's solo work remained inspirational to dissidents in Czechoslovakia throughout the gray decades of Communist rule there. The movement that brought Havel to power had come to be called the Velvet Revolution because of its aspirations to nonviolence, but the pun would not have been lost on anyone as sensitive to language as he.

After Havel won election to the presidency, *Rolling Stone* approached Reed about going to Czechoslovakia to interview Havel. It seemed like a perfect story for the magazine, which had always combined its coverage of the music scene with progressive political stories. Reed had just appeared on the cover of the magazine for the first time, and Havel's interest in the Velvet Underground and rock music in general had already become part of his myth. That Reed's music could somehow have played a significant role in history surpassed even the artist's most grandiose notions about himself. He was understandably flattered and accepted the assignment. Havel was delighted that Reed, one of his musical heroes, would be interviewing him.

When publications make an assignment like this, it's essentially an act of faith — faith that if you get two people of such significance in one room, whatever they talk about, whatever happens between them, will be more interesting than if a seasoned reporter had been sent to do the job. A complication is that, because both people involved in doing the story are notable in their own right, it's not easy to provide direction or even make suggestions about what topics their conversation should take on — especially true in this case, given Reed's prickliness, insecurities, and desire for control. So off he went to interview Havel in Prague.

Reed flew to Prague after participating in Nelson Mandela: An International Tribute for a Free South Africa, a concert at Wembley Stadium in London on April 16, 1990, to celebrate Mandela's release from the South African prison in which he had been held for twenty-seven years because of his efforts to bring down that country's apartheid regime. Despite the fact that he was about to interview a political and cultural figure of enormous significance, Reed treated all the preliminary steps as if he were going to do a concert date in a region with which he wasn't familiar. He did not relax his desire for control a whit. He displayed no comprehension that he was dealing with a newly liberated country, some of whose citizens, however shockingly, might not even have been aware of who Lou Reed was. All requests that diverged from his ordinary travel routine—would he consider performing at a small club?—were flatly denied.

The original transcript Reed turned in to *Rolling Stone* reflected a similar myopia. While Havel would occasionally attempt to explore some larger issues, particularly how the counterculture in the United States had made a strong impact on him, Reed continually nudged the conversation toward his own preoccupations—which is to say himself and his world. Pressed for time and eager to get to the substantive issues he wanted to discuss with Reed, Havel spoke affectingly about the history of the dissident movement in Czechoslovakia, emphasizing its musical and cultural aspects—most notably, the rise of Charter 77, which emerged, in part, in opposition to the government's persecution of the Plastic People of the Universe. "By this I mean to say," Havel said, "the music, underground music, in particular one record by a band called Velvet Underground, played a rather significant role in the development of our country, and I don't think that many people in the United States have noticed this." Reed's response? "Joan Baez says hello."

When Havel described at length his visit to the United States in 1968 and his participation in the historic student uprising that year at Columbia University, Reed responded, "Did you go to CBGB's?"—which, of course, did not exist in 1968. Havel's remarks on all these matters were nuanced and insightful, but Reed reduced them to a truism: "You obviously feel and prove that music can change the world?" Havel's response was characteristically thoughtful: "Not in itself, it's not sufficient in itself. But it can contribute to that significantly in being a part of the awakening of the human spirit."

Reed, as it happens, intentionally set out not to do the type of interview a journalist would do. "I don't like it when the interview's so cleaned up that the interviewer and subject sound like the same person," he said. "I like to keep the real rhythm of the way the person talks." What journalists know and Reed didn't understand is that spoken words and words on a page are two different things. Some cleaning up is always necessary. Reed also spoke about how nervous he had been to interview Havel, which makes some of its awkwardness more understandable. It's not surprising that his seeming offhandedness and brusque attitude masked insecurities. "With Hubert Selby," Reed said, referring to an interview he'd done with one of his literary idols, "I came in with typed questions, because I was sure I'd be nerve-racked and I didn't want to forget anything. Same with Havel.... It's just really hard work. I'd much rather go out for a drink with them."

What Reed turned in to the magazine was not what *Rolling Stone* was looking for. The assignment had not been made by a music editor, but by Robert Vare, who handled much of the magazine's political coverage. He was taken aback and asked me to have a look at the piece. I, too, was surprised by how one-dimensional it was. My suggestion was to see if Reed, whom I had not yet met at that time, might be willing to write something longer — or perhaps something shorter — in which the best material from the interview could play a part. Given that working with him up to that point had not exactly been a joyride, the feeling at the magazine was that he was unlikely to want to do that. Finally, it was decided to simply give the piece back to Reed and let him do what he wanted with it somewhere else. (The publication that had commissioned Reed to interview Hubert Selby also turned down the resulting interview.)

Reed was livid. In a smart move, he showed the piece to Rob Bowman, a critic and professor of musicology who was producing and writing liner notes for *Between Thought and Expression,* a three-CD anthology of Reed's solo work with RCA and Arista. Wisely concealing his own estimation of the piece — "It was definitely terrible," Bowman said later; "I could see why *Rolling Stone* rejected it" — he suggested that Reed contact Bill Flanagan at *Musician.* Flanagan had interviewed Reed a number of times and was one of his staunchest supporters. *Musician* was a smaller magazine than *Rolling Stone,* and while it was highly regarded in the music industry, it did not have anything like *Rolling Stone*'s reputation for political reporting to live up to. Having a Lou Reed interview with Václav Havel would be a coup for *Musician* regardless of its quality. Flying a bit under the media radar ultimately freed *Musician* to turn the piece into something idiosyncratic and quite readable. Perhaps chastened by *Rolling Stone*'s rejection, Reed did write a longer piece of which the interview was just a part. A few moments remain cringeworthy, but at many other points, Reed seems genuinely stirred by Havel and wonder-struck by the role his songs had played in such a monumental historical moment. Even in its difficult spots, the story reveals — consciously or unconsciously — aspects of Reed that he ordinarily took great pains to conceal.

In the piece, Reed complains that arranging to get to recently liberated Czechoslovakia was "Kafkaesque" because "It was hard to get clear answers to the most basic requests." Beyond that, his Czech facilitators "wanted me to play. At a club." The horror. But as Reed spends some time with Havel, he seems increasingly to become aware of what the situation requires of him. As Havel is ending their conversation, he asks Reed, referring to a Prague performance space, "Is it true or not that you will play at the Gallery tonight?" Reed demurs. "It was never true that I would play at the Gallery," he says, explaining that he is a "private person" and prefers "controlled situations." As a compromise, he offers to play for Havel in private. Havel gracefully deflects that offer and gently attempts to educate Reed on why it would be important for him to perform publicly in the newly liberated country. "I think it would be sort of embarrassing for me if only I could enjoy it and tens of my friends who would like to be there as well could not be there," Havel says. He had earlier explained to Reed how many musicians and activists had risked imprisonment simply by listening to bands like the Velvet Underground and their progeny. He tells Reed, "The bands that I was talking about would be there, and people who had been arrested for listening to this kind of music, and friends." Reed continues to hem and haw — "I'm not aware of the circumstances, and it's difficult for me" — until, after endless reassurances from Havel and his interpreter, he finally relents, graciously saying what he should have said in the first place: "If this is something you would like, it would be an honor to do it for you and your people."

When Reed and Sylvia arrived at the Gallery, he marveled at the band onstage, which was "playing Velvet Underground songs — beautiful, heartfelt, impeccable versions of my songs. I couldn't believe it. This was not something they could have gotten together overnight. The music grew stronger and louder as I listened. . . . It was as though I was in a time warp and had returned to hear myself play. . . . It was as though they had absorbed the very heart and soul of the VU." As for Reed's irrational fears about who was going to be at the club and how many of them, the three hundred people there primarily consisted of former dissidents who were thrilled to be in the presence of the man who had created music that inspired them so much. Eventually, after he got word that Havel had arrived at the club, Reed went onstage and played songs from *New York,* as he had done at the Nelson Mandela concert. When he was finished, he was asked if the band that had been onstage earlier could join him to perform some Velvet Underground songs, and he agreed. As Reed wrote, "we blazed through some old VU numbers. Any song I called, they knew. It was as if Moe, John, and Sterl were right there behind me, and it was a glorious feeling."

When he came offstage, Reed went to sit at a table with Havel, who had removed his jacket and loosened his tie. Havel introduced Reed to some of the people who were in the audience that night, and Reed finally came to understand the value and significance of his willingness to visit the club and perform. Havel, Reed wrote, "introduced me to an astonishing array of people, all dissidents, all of whom had been jailed. Some had been jailed for playing my music. Many told me of reciting my lyrics for inspiration and comfort when in jail. Some had remembered a line I had written in an essay fifteen years ago: 'Everybody should die for the music.' It was very much a dream for me and well beyond my wildest expectations. When I had gotten out of college and helped form the VU, I had been concerned with, among other things, demonstrating how much more a song could be about than what was currently being written. So the VU albums and my own are implicitly about freedom of expression — freedom to write about what you please in any way you please. And the music had found a home here in Czechoslovakia."

After a while, Havel got up to leave. Late as it was — he had arrived at the club after 11 p.m., just before Reed's set — he still had affairs of state to attend to. "Oh, you must have this," he said to Reed as he handed him a "small black book about the size of a diary" just before he headed out. "These are your lyrics hand-printed and translated into Czechoslovakian. There were only two hundred of them. They were very dangerous to have. People went to jail, and now you have one. Keep your fingers crossed for us."

At the end of his report, Reed returned to the question that had most puzzled him about Havel: why didn't he leave Czechoslovakia when, as an important literary figure, he had the opportunity to do so? Havel's answer was characteristically straightforward. "I stayed because I live here," he explained. "I never doubted that we would succeed. All I ever wanted to do was the right thing."

REED'S PROFOUND EXPERIENCE IN Czechoslovakia occurred amid a series of events that caused him to examine his life, his work, and their meaning more deeply. Consequently, his next album, *Magic and Loss,* extended his run of strong, provocative albums on serious subjects. In a sense, the album's emotional source went back to the death of Andy Warhol in 1987 and the track "Dime Store Mystery" on *New York.* That song's philosophical exploration of life and death expanded into *Songs for Drella,* which looked at Warhol as a person and an artist, and became a meditation on the impact of a life devoted to surfaces. "Halloween Parade" on *New York* responded to the holocaust of deaths resulting from the AIDS epidemic, which devastated the gay community, the arts community, and intravenous drug users—three realms in which Reed was or had been deeply involved. Many of his friends and acquaintances had died. He himself had been diagnosed with hepatitis C, and he must have felt that he had dodged a bullet in not becoming infected with HIV. Reed turned fifty not long after *Magic and Loss* came out in January of 1992, and thoughts of mortality and the meaning of his life clearly were on his mind. "I do consider myself even lucky to be here," he said.

Nineteen ninety-one brought two deaths, both from cancer, that intensely affected Reed. One was Kenneth Rapp, more commonly known as Rotten Rita, an amphetamine maven and drag queen on the Warhol Factory scene who was so popular among that crowd that he was dubbed "The Mayor." Reed and Rita were among a group of speed freaks known as the Moles because of their nocturnal habits, and Rita was among the lost characters Reed mentioned in "Halloween Parade." The other inspiration for *Magic and Loss* was the legendary songwriter Doc Pomus, who had written the lyrics for such indelible hits as "Save the Last Dance for Me," "This Magic Moment," and "A Teenager in Love." Like Reed, Pomus, whose birth name was Jerome Felder, had been born in Brooklyn to Jewish parents and had fallen in love with the music he heard on the radio, particularly R & B. A bout with polio as a young boy had left Pomus disabled. He could walk only with crutches and eventually required a wheelchair—a reality that made the lyrics of a song like "Save the Last Dance for Me" especially poignant. "Between two Aprils I lost two friends," Reed wrote in the liner notes to the album. "Between two Aprils magic and loss." He dedicated the album "to Doc and especially to Rita."

Pomus's daughter, Sharyn Felder, remembered Reed and her father becoming close friends in the late seventies or early eighties, though Reed recalled their friendship developing later. Pomus was precisely the sort of person Reed was drawn to: urban, articulate, well-read, musically knowledgeable, streetwise, and, like Reed himself, crusty around the edges but sentimental at the core. That Pomus was nearly seventeen years older than Reed allowed the songwriter to serve as something of a father figure to him. While it was difficult for Reed's own father to show any genuine appreciation for Reed's accomplishments—and for Reed to accept it if he ever did—Reed viewed Pomus's regard for him as a kind of benediction. Pomus was like a rock-and-roll Delmore Schwartz to Reed. In Pomus's presence, Reed could be an unabashed fan— one of his most endearing qualities. "I couldn't even believe your father knew who I was," he told Felder at one point. Pomus taught classes for young songwriters at his impossibly cluttered apartment on West Seventy-Second Street—the singer Joan Osborne was among his students—and Reed would sometimes visit as a guest, proud to sit at the feet of the master as well as offer his own advice and suggestions. Reed and Pomus would also watch videos of boxing matches together; despite his illness, Pomus had dreamed of being a fighter, and Reed was fascinated by both the violence and the theater of the fights. When Pomus died, Reed inherited those tapes, Pomus's pipe, and the decks of cards Pomus had used during tough times, when he had hosted nights of illegal gambling at his apartment in order to make a living.

For his part, Pomus, who had enjoyed his greatest successes in the late fifties and the sixties, often felt overlooked by the contemporary music world. He was flattered that Reed, at the height of his creative powers and perhaps the most daring member of the rock scene that had taken shape after Pomus's own peak, regarded him with such undisguised respect. When Reed wrote "What's Good," one of the strongest tracks on what would become *Magic and Loss,* after Pomus was diagnosed with lung cancer, Pomus said to his daughter, "Can you believe that Lou Reed wrote a song for me?"

Reed was devastated when he learned about Pomus's cancer diagnosis, and while "What's Good" reflected its impact, Pomus was shielded—or perhaps shielded himself—from the song's true meaning. "I don't think he really could hear the lyrics on some level, because we were still trying to be optimistic," Felder said. Reed stayed close to Pomus throughout the course of his illness, and he chronicled the arc of that emotional journey on *Magic and Loss*. As writers do, Reed was mining the experience for material, and producing some of his best work. But that process took nothing away from the devotion he showed to Pomus and his family during that difficult time. Equally important, Reed allowed himself to feel the disturbing emotions that Pomus's steady decline evoked in him, and he openly expressed them, though not in any way directly to Pomus in order not to upset him.

"When my father got sick, Lou came to the hospital every day," Felder recalled. "I remember going out with him, and he just said, 'Doc can't leave the planet—he's like the sun.'" No doubt unconsciously, Reed's remark was a pun straight out of *Hamlet*. Pomus may have been the metaphorical sun, but Reed was his metaphorical son, and Pomus's impending death made Reed feel as if he were being orphaned—cast into a black abyss, as the imagery of "Cremation" on *Magic and Loss* described it. "Lou's relationship with my father was not like songwriter to songwriter," Felder said. "It was much more paternal. Their friendship was always about my father's advice. Lou was always going through something. A lot of drama. A lot of lawsuits. He was really vexed by that stuff. My father would listen and help him find a way through, because, as Lou would always say, there was no college at the time that could teach you about those things. Lou seemed to be looking for someone who could navigate the way for him, because he seemed a bit lost." Felder also had the sense that at around that time, "maybe Lou's marriage to Sylvia was shifting a bit. She was still managing him, and they were still living on West End Avenue, but I think their marriage was fading out."

When Pomus died, Reed spoke at his funeral, ending his remarks with the wish that Doc, wherever he was, would save the last dance for him. On *Till the Night Is Gone,* a tribute album devoted to Pomus's songs that was released in 1995, Reed performed a passionate version of "This Magic Moment," and it is possible to see the "magic" in the title *Magic and Loss* as deriving from that song's simple, eloquent description of falling in love. The title might also derive from a line in Thomas Wolfe's *Look Homeward, Angel* ("O, the wonder, the magic, and the loss!") that additionally inspired the title of *The Magic and the Loss,* a play by Julian Funt that ran on Broadway for a few weeks in 1954.

All the songs on *Magic and Loss* have subtitles; there's "Dorita: The Spirit," "What's Good: The Thesis," and so on. ("Dorita" is a conflation of "Doc" and "Rita"; it also derives from the Greek word meaning "gift.") That was part of Reed's ongoing effort to frame his writing in literary as much as musical terms—"like a novel," is how he explained it, "at the head of each chapter a little phrase explaining what it is." The album's cover features a photo of Reed placed within a design that suggests both flames and a forest, as if he were a character out of Dante's *Inferno,* lost in a dark wood and searching for meaning. On each corner of the cover is an alchemical image. They also appear throughout the lyric booklet accompanying the album.

Alchemy was a medieval science, a predecessor of chemistry, which attempted to transform base metals into gold. At its heart lay the belief that all matter is somehow perfectible, which, in turn, made alchemy a potent metaphor for the transformation of the physical into the spiritual. It's a particularly resonant concept for a man whose best-known album is titled *Transformer*—and whose work rested on the assumption that even the most degraded human beings could somehow be redeemed. According to Spencer Drate, who, along with his partner, Judith Salavetz, codesigned the album's cover with Sylvia, the alchemical symbols were consciously chosen by Reed and his wife. Reed specifically refers to one of alchemy's central goals—"gold being made from lead"—in "Power and Glory: The Situation," a song on *Magic and Loss*. That sense of transformation is central to the album. Pomus, a physically enormous man, wastes away from cancer, his booming voice growing quiet, and Rita loses her youth and beauty as death approaches. Finally, both figures pass "through the fire" of life and perhaps, Reed speculates, hopes, ultimately dissolve into spirit—some magic, possibly, to compensate for the desolation of loss.

Reed's direct, profoundly personal lyrics on *Magic and Loss* show us a man examining his own life in the deepest ways. The most powerful example of that comes on the title track and the album's closing song, "Magic and Loss: The Summation." In it, Reed takes the image of passing through fire and uses it as an image of purification, as if the flames of all the struggles one faces in life were a kiln in which one forged one's perfection. However, like the radiation treatments that Doc Pomus underwent (and which Reed mentions in "Power and Glory"), the same heat that can cure you can kill you. Describing the passages of his own life in "Magic and Loss," Reed indicts his insecurities ("a maze of self-doubt"), "arrogance," "anger," and "caustic dread"— all of which will "never help you out." He looks honestly at his own soaring ambitions and seeks to divine a direction through them: "They say no one person can do it all / But you want to in your head / But you can't be Shakespeare and you can't be Joyce / So what is left instead?" The only possibility of deliverance lies in acceptance, "the strength to acknowledge it all." When that happens, you can "survive your own war," and "You find that that fire is passion / And there's a door up ahead, not a wall."

Magic and Loss, Reed said, "is the culmination of everything I've tried to achieve, all the mistakes I've made." Death, he concludes, is only one part of life, not the entire story: "There's a bit of magic in everything," he sings, "and then some loss to even things out." The meaning of the album, he said, is "the magic of art transforming meaningless loss into something else."

*　　*　　*

ONE INTRIGUING RESULT OF Reed's friendship with Doc Pomus was his discovery of the jazz singer Little Jimmy Scott, who was himself a close friend of Doc's and one of Doc's favorite vocalists. Scott had a strong commercial run in the forties and fifties, but then his career stalled. He suffered from Kallmann syndrome, a hereditary hormonal condition that, along with other effects, forestalls the onset of puberty. In Scott's case, the disease left him with an extraordinary voice that seemed neither male nor female—without question, one of the reasons Reed became so taken with him. Scott's voice was high, delicate, and expressive—Billie Holiday was one of his biggest fans—but somehow informed by a masculine intelligence and perspective, a combination that made his vocals extremely distinctive. At Pomus's request, Scott sang a soulful version of "Someone to Watch Over Me" at his funeral. That performance—and Reed's relentless importuning—led Seymour Stein to sign Scott to Sire Records, sparking a strong career revival. Scott also sang a haunting vocal on "Power and Glory," and he and Reed would perform together many times.

Reed was understandably proud of *Magic and Loss,* and as usual, he was not shy about saying so. "I don't think of my records as disposable," he said. "I'm always in there trying to make the one that will really live, that you go back to ten years from now, two hundred years from now, that is not encompassed or attenuated by some fad or circumstance that's purely temporal."

As he had on *New York* and *Songs for Drella,* Reed looked outside himself and the subterranean world that had been the focus of his work for years. "I'm not interested in 'Lou Reed' the character now," he said. "I'm interested in Doc and Rita and how you deal with something like their loss, and giving that to the listener." That desire to look outward derived from an increasing understanding of his own connection to other people, his growing belief that, his talent aside, he was no different from anyone else. "The people who I would keep at bay are the people who approach me as 'Lou Reed.' That 'Lou Reed.' That makes me very uncomfortable. I can't really function in that situation. Because of the expectations they bring or because they're looking for the feet of clay. Well, I'm just a person, too. I'm not on any pedestal. Read my stuff to verify that. I'm as human as the next person. I make the exact same mistakes that I write about."

Because of its seriousness and depth — not to mention the stature of its creator — *Magic and Loss* was the sort of album that made critics stretch in their own writing, attempting to match Reed's eloquence with their own. In the *New York Times,* Stephen Holden wrote that Reed's "pose of cultivated cool, of someone who has not only seen it all but experienced it, has always masked an incendiary rage that can be sensed in the quiver that ruffles his monotone. And in these songs about final things, the tension between his affectless attitude and his suppressed fury is as palpable and as gripping as it has ever been."

20

BETWEEN THOUGHT AND EXPRESSION

I N APRIL OF 1992, about four months after the release of *Magic and Loss,* Reed put out *Between Thought and Expression: The Lou Reed Anthology,* a three-CD overview of his solo career with RCA and Arista—which is to say everything before he moved to Sire Records for *New York* in 1989. The original idea for the box set came from Rob Bowman, a professor of musicology at York University in Canada who had assembled highly regarded box sets devoted to Stax/Volt singles and Otis Redding. When *New York* came out, Bowman got an assignment to interview Reed. Given Reed's obsession with soul music—and his unspoken regard for academic credentials—the two men hit it off immediately. Reed even used Bowman's Otis Redding box set as the house music before he came onstage at some of the shows on his tour in support of *New York.*

So when Bowman proposed a box set of Reed's solo work, Reed expressed interest. "He immediately gave me his phone number," Bowman said, "which shocked me. He said, 'Look, start putting together what you think a track list should be, and let's start talking about this.'" Bowman had a carefully worked-out concept for what the set should be, and he presented it to Reed in great detail. "I saw it as a celebration and summation of his art up to that point," Bowman said. "If you think about the way Lou talked about Delmore Schwartz and other artists he respected, he really had a sense of those people being recognized and their art being appreciated with a dignity, richness, grace, and depth that the art merits. He was really excited that this was going to happen with his catalog. He was excited about his music being treated as art and given this high-class treatment, if you will."

By the early nineties, box sets had become a kind of artistic gold standard in the music industry; Bob Dylan's *Biograph* and Eric Clapton's *Crossroads* were both critically acclaimed and commercially successful. The CD format generally, with its precious jewel case, book-size presentation, and higher price point, had already begun to transform albums into status objects. Box sets were the inevitable next step. The original assumption was that only artists, movements, and labels of great artistic significance would warrant the box set treatment. Of course, once the format proved commercially successful, everyone with enough material to fill three or more discs eventually got a box set. But at their best, with their aspirations to definitiveness, elaborate artwork, remastering for state-of-the-art sound, and hefty price tags, box sets epitomized connoisseurship. They suggested seriousness — and sometimes achieved it — and flattered their purchasers, frequently baby boomers, many of whom had considerable disposable income to spend on their youthful passions. Record companies loved box sets because, just as the transition from vinyl to CD had done, they enabled labels to sell music that they already owned yet another time.

Bowman was nothing if not meticulous, and he quickly set out to uncover the kind of rarities — alternate versions of familiar Lou Reed songs, neglected gems, distinctive live tracks, revealing demos — that deepen and add texture to such collections. "I spent somewhere between six weeks and two months locating and listening to reams and reams of material — live recordings, studio takes," Bowman recalled, "trying to put together what I thought really represented his work in the strongest way — including a significant number of outtakes that would blow people's minds.

"Meanwhile, Lou would call me virtually every day. To be honest, it seemed to me that he was kind of lonely. It was like he didn't have other friends to call. I realize that he must have, but it was surprising. Sometimes he'd call me at two in the morning to tell me what he and Sylvia had done that day. He'd tell me about some spa they'd gone to. He'd say, 'You should bring your wife down here and go to that spa. It would be great. You guys would love it!' On the box, I dealt with Lou directly on everything. It was like we were becoming close friends."

In the course of their lengthy and frequent conversations, Reed would occasionally express opinions about other artists. When Bowman compared the guitar interplay on a live version of "Sister Ray" that Reed had performed with the Tots to the Rolling Stones, Reed dismissed the idea, saying, "The only thing I ever liked about that band was Keith Richards." He also told Bowman that he would find listening to a full album by Muddy Waters "boring."

Yet Bowman knew enough not to read too much into the closeness that seemed to have developed between him and Reed. "I was told by somebody that worked closely with him for many years that Lou eventually x-ed out everybody in his life," Bowman said. "At a certain point, people would cross him or he'd feel they crossed him in some way, and he would just cut them off. They'd be gone. And this person said, 'This will happen to you, too, eventually. Be prepared. But in the meantime, if he likes you, he'll be your best friend.' And that's exactly what happened."

The first significant point of contention had to do with the track listing Bowman assembled. Bowman understood that, in order to generate the kind of excitement that was essential to motivate fans to purchase an expensive box set, it needed rarities to make it more than a greatest hits collection. Then fans could justifiably feel that they were purchasing new material, not simply remastered tracks that they already owned or that were already available. Rarities also helped generate the sort of reviews that would push the box commercially, as well as further establish the notion of Reed as a serious artist worthy of such elaborate treatment. Just as albums like *Rock n Roll Animal* and the Velvet Underground's *1969* had done, this box set could, ideally, excite interest in Reed's catalog. And from a purely aesthetic standpoint, rarities deepen and add texture to fans' understanding of an artist.

Bowman was well aware of all this. "I put together cassettes of what I thought the CDs in the set should look like, including all the outtakes," he said. "I sequenced everything. Lou phoned me back and he was pretty excited, but he said, 'You know, I'm not sure I want all these outtakes on here.' His basic attitude was that if they were good enough to come out in the first place, he would have put them out. I tried to explain that I understood that he had made choices and that those choices say a lot about his artistic vision at any given moment.... I said, 'This is a celebration of your work. This is like looking at Bach manuscripts that are not the final version of a given fugue but are close, and show the kind of genius where Bach took something that was already really good and made it something fucking unbelievable.'

"Lou had a very hard time getting to that place. He felt that he had been mistreated and fucked over by various people in the music industry. And by the time the Velvets were over, if not before, he had become a control freak. So the idea of allowing these things out of the vault went against that instinct. His gut told him his original decision had to be right and no alternative version should be presented."

The two men went back and forth on the issue. Finally, Reed agreed that of the forty-five tracks on the three-CD set, five rarities could be included. The irony is that Reed himself loved to hear rarities by the artists he was interested in and valued the deeper understanding such tracks brought. He just could not allow himself to be similarly revealing. "I was pretty disappointed," Bowman said. "I thought he'd compromised the box pretty heavily, but I did the best I could. We were still going ahead with the project and there were still some cool things on there."

Once the track listing was set, Bowman needed to arrange an interview with Reed for his liner notes. Bowman had been awarded a Grammy for his liner notes for the Stax/Volt box set, and he had earned a reputation for the accuracy, thoroughness, and carefulness of his writing. Indeed, the quality of Bowman's work was one reason Reed had agreed to move forward with the project in the first place. It was agreed that Bowman would fly to New York and interview Reed at the West End Avenue apartment that Reed and Sylvia lived in and used as a work space. Bowman asked Reed who else he thought should be interviewed for his liner notes essay. Reed responded, "No one. Everyone I worked with was an asshole or else I'd still be working with them." Bowman grew exasperated. "Come on, Lou," he said. "Every musician, every producer, every engineer was an asshole?" According to Bowman, "Lou said, 'Yes. Or else I'd still be working with them.' And he got that Lou Reed aggressive tone." Eventually, Bowman was permitted to interview Bob Ezrin, Michael Fonfara, and Clive Davis, along with Reed himself.

When Bowman came to New York, he and Reed initially met at a restaurant for breakfast to do the interview. Bowman began his first question, "I want to start by talking about when you were growing up," and Reed interrupted him. "Rob, I don't talk about anything personal," he said. "You know that." Bowman was taken aback. "I wasn't going to ask you anything personal," he responded. "I wanted to ask about musical experiences: what you're hearing on the radio, what records you're buying." Bowman reported that "you could see him physically calm down and relax. It was interesting because, despite our relationship at that point, which consisted of nearly daily conversations for four months, the interview really had him uptight. At the first question, he was immediately ready to pounce." Once Reed relaxed, the interview went smoothly. After a while, the two men decided to continue their conversation in the West End Avenue apartment.

"On the way there, we stop to buy cigarettes for Lou, and then we go to the bank because Lou needs to use the ATM," Bowman said. "It was kind of funny lining up with Lou Reed at an ATM behind three or four other people. Nobody takes notice of him, but he's pissed off that there's a line. Meanwhile, there's a homeless person sleeping in the vestibule where the ATM is. Lou goes, 'That's disgusting!' I said, 'What?' Lou gestured toward the homeless person. I didn't say anything, but I felt like, 'Fuck, Lou, it's cold out. This poor guy—what's wrong with him being here?' Lou was fuming. Finally, he says, 'Come on,' and he grabs me and we go into the branch. Lou wants to see the manager. He tells the manager that there's a homeless guy in the vestibule and he wants him kicked out immediately. I'm stunned. This is Lou Reed doing this to this person. For what reason? It wasn't the most pleasant thing, he smelled a bit — big fucking deal. Especially given that Lou Reed chronicles the underbelly of New York, right? Anyway, security comes along, shuffles the poor homeless guy out of there, we get back on line at the ATM, Lou gets his money, and we start walking to his apartment. And I'm still a little bit stunned."

There has long been a homeless population in New York, and Reed's response, while far more extreme than most people's, was not incomprehensible. No question: the image of Lou Reed, of all people, kicking a needy person out of a bank into the freezing cold is like something out of Dickens — just so that he could have a more pleasant experience as he waited to withdraw his money. It's as potent a symbol of 1 percent selfishness as can be conjured, and a reflection of the distance — emotional, psychological, financial — that Reed had traveled since his years as a junkie. It's certainly possible to speculate that his outsize response to the sight — and smell — of the homeless man was generated by the specter of a fate that he had come too close to suffering and that he needed to have immediately removed from his presence. Also striking is that Reed either had no idea how his actions would look to somebody else or didn't care. This was, after all, the man who wrote in "Dirty Blvd.," "Give me your hungry, your tired, your poor, I'll piss on 'em / That's what the Statue of Bigotry says"—a fierce indictment of how our society has abandoned the ideals expressed on the Statue of Liberty. Regardless of whether they might have shared Reed's feelings about the homeless man, most artists would have been too savvy and image-conscious to behave as he had in public, let alone in front of a writer. It's another example of Reed's inability or unwillingness to play by anyone else's rules—or of his lack of a clear sense of how he was being perceived.

On the way back to Reed's apartment, Bowman couldn't contain his feelings, but because he was in the middle of interviewing Reed and needed to complete the box set project, he couldn't be as direct as he might otherwise have been. As they were walking, Bowman asked Reed, "So, ten years ago, would you have gone to the bank manager and had that guy removed?" Reed spat back, "That's a stupid question." Bowman remained calm. "Well, I don't know if it was a stupid question," he said, "but I'm just curious. Given your lyrics and the things you've talked about, it might not have bothered you at a certain point." Next, Bowman recalled, "Lou started going on about how somebody had been shot a day or two ago in New York for seventeen cents, which shows you how cheap life is in the city, blah, blah, blah. It was clear that he was pissed off that I brought it up. It was probably a mistake on my part and I tried to do it gingerly, but I still just couldn't believe it. Whatever."

When they arrived at Reed's apartment, Reed showed Bowman the bedroom in which he had set up a small home studio. Then they sat down at the dining room table to continue their interview. Bowman was drinking Coca-Cola—a choice that Reed disapproved of for health reasons—and Reed drank water and tea. Bowman had a hard time leading Reed into the sort of conversation that would make for a strong liner notes essay. Reed's reluctance to credit others was very much on display. "Lou was cooperative but occasionally short," Bowman recalled. "I remember talking about *Transformer* and some of the incredible arrangements that Mick Ronson had done. Lou said, 'Well, I'm sure Mick would be happy to hear you say that. You got a question?'" Reed then began to respond with one-word or yes-or-no answers. This was standard Reed behavior with journalists, but with Bowman? The guy who was collaborating with him on what was meant to be—and what Reed had seemingly wanted to be—a major career statement? It was very much in Reed's interest to speak as compellingly as possible about his own work. After about ninety minutes of resistance, Bowman said, "Lou, you don't really seem like you're into this. Would it be better if we picked this up another time? We've spent months on this project, so let's do it right." According to Bowman, Reed's reply was, " 'Rob, you know I hate doing interviews. Let's get it done.' I said, 'All right, but it would be helpful if sometimes you wouldn't just say "Yes" or "No." ' "

The interview ended up lasting six hours, from late morning to late afternoon, no doubt a record for Reed, who was squeezing a stress ball throughout the conversation. At one point, Reed left for half an hour to run an errand. Bowman recalled, "I remember when he left thinking, 'Thank God.' I really needed a break, because it was agony. By the time I left there, I was more exhausted than I've ever been in my life from an interview. I had a splitting headache. He was so fucking difficult." Oddly, Reed did not share that assessment. About three or four hours into their conversation, Reed said, "Rob, thank God this is you and you're so organized. With anybody else, this would be beyond excruciating." In fact, the interview proved substantive and revealing. Bowman had more than enough material to work with for his essay. "I knew I got great stuff," Bowman said, "but it felt like our relationship was rocked a little bit compared to what it had been."

As Bowman prepared to leave, the gentler Lou Reed emerged, as if on cue. It was pouring rain and Bowman was headed downtown to try to score a ticket to see the Grateful Dead at Madison Square Garden. Earlier in the day, Reed had grabbed Bowman around the chest and physically pulled him back as he attempted to cross the street against the light. "You don't know New York drivers," Reed said. "You're going to get killed!" He was similarly protective of Bowman as he set off (unsuccessfully, as it happened) in search of a miracle. Reed was concerned about the rain—would Bowman be able to get a cab? Should Lou come downstairs with him to help hail one? "He was really sweet, really kind," Bowman said.

Bowman returned home to Toronto, and after a few days, the calls from Reed resumed once again. "We were best friends again," Bowman said. "He would talk about what he had done that day, ask what I had done. We would talk about the set, but he'd always want to know how soon he could see the liner notes." Bowman was known for lengthy, thorough essays, and along with going through the six-hour interview he had done with Reed, he needed to complete the secondary interviews that Reed had finally sanctioned. The liner notes for *Between Thought and Expression* ended up being more than twenty thousand words— after Reed's extensive edits. The idea that Bowman would have something to show Reed after a few days was not rational. When Bowman completed the essay, he promptly sent Reed a copy by Federal Express. Reed read it immediately.

"That's when things went to hell," Bowman recalled. "He phoned me and just started yelling. He was angry because of a couple of things that Michael Fonfara had told me. One was about Lou leaving for vacation and giving him the tapes for what would become *Take No Prisoners* and telling him to turn it into an album. When Lou came back, he didn't like what Fonfara had done and made him do it over again. That story pretty much stayed in the notes.

"The other thing was about a violinist Lou had hired while Fonfara was leading the band. They'd gone through rehearsals, and the violinist would often show up on a unicycle, which to Lou was like, 'What the fuck is this?' They were about to go on tour and were at the airport in New York, ready to fly overseas. As the flight starts to board, Lou goes up to the violinist and says, 'You're not coming.' The guy's got his boarding pass, his luggage was on the plane, but Lou decided the guy wasn't coming. I realize that story doesn't make Lou look good, but my idea was, here was a man that had absolute confidence in his decisions and would make them no matter what the cost. But Lou wanted that story out, and it's not in the notes."

At this point, Reed also returned to the issue of the track listing for the box, which he had already approved after much debate. He noticed that the set did not include a single track from *The Bells*—"I think it's a terrible record," Bowman said—and he wanted that emended. "The idea of having one album in the whole body of work that's not included is kind of odd," Bowman admitted. "But I came to that conclusion, and it never came up in my conversations with Lou. Fonfara told me about the sessions for *The Bells* and *Growing Up in Public*—that they were chaotic and Lou was hammered the whole time. I included stuff in the notes to the effect that it was not a great time. To me, that doesn't diminish Lou as a great artist. It explains a moment in his career. Lou was furious about that, too. It was midnight, one in the morning, and he was yelling. He had never yelled at me before. He said, 'Typical. I didn't think you'd be this way, but it's, oh, yeah, let's paint a picture of big bad Lou.' He was really flipping out. He also said, '*The Bells* is the best record I've ever made.' As a result, 'The Bells' is now on the set."

Bowman attempted to calm Reed down. Privately, he had sent his draft of the notes to Bill Bentley, who had worked closely with Reed for many years, and to M. C. Kostek, who ran the Velvet Underground Appreciation Society and was deeply knowledgeable about Reed. Both men had told Bowman that his notes were perhaps the best writing they'd ever read about Reed. But Reed's paranoia had kicked in hard. At one point, Reed heard a sound on the phone line and accused Bowman of recording their call. Reed insisted that

Sylvia was the only person he trusted and that he would have her read the notes and he'd call Bowman back. At 7 a.m., Bowman's phone rang. "Lou wakes me up, and he says, 'Guess what? Sylvia hates them.' He just started ranting and raving again. This is, like, six hours after we last spoke. So Sylvia read the notes between one a.m. and seven a.m.? Maybe, but I'm suspicious."

Technically, Reed did not have final approval over either the track listing or the liner notes. Record companies, however, try to accommodate artists as much as possible on such projects, out of regard for the artist's wishes about his own work and to avoid creating bad blood. In this case, even though Reed was no longer signed to RCA, the company no doubt believed there would be more catalog projects down the road, and they also would have wanted Reed to help promote *Between Thought and Expression*. Bowman had acquiesced to Reed on the track listing, but he resisted making all the changes Reed demanded on the liner notes. His feeling was that the music was Lou's, but the liner notes were his. Soon after, Bowman got a call from the record company, explaining that Reed had offered to take a lower royalty rate on the box set in exchange for control over both the track listing and the liner notes. In order to keep Reed happy, the company agreed to the deal. "Ultimately, Lou edited the liner notes and took out all sorts of stuff he didn't want in there," Bowman said.

Reed finally saw the box set as a means of getting greater recognition for work that had already been released but that, in his view, had been overlooked or had never gotten its due. For example, six tracks from *Berlin* appear on the set. "If the box was going to be representative," Reed told *Rolling Stone,* "I wanted to maintain a level of integrity with it and not just have this plethora of unreleased garbage on there." If not out of print, much of Reed's solo work was difficult to find in the early nineties. His great admiration for it aside, Reed himself did not own a copy of *The Bells.* Despite his difficulties with Bowman, Reed called him up to ask if he could borrow Bowman's copy. (Realizing that he would likely never get the album back if he loaned it to Reed, Bowman suggested that Reed scout around New York's many used record stores for it. Reed did, eventually finding a copy.)

At the time of its release, however, *Between Thought and Expression* did not make much of an impression, either commercially or critically. "The goal of the album was not just to do a greatest hits," Reed said. "I was trying to put down stuff in a way that was representative and that would really be meaningful to a collector." But that is precisely what he didn't do. Collectors would primarily be interested in exactly the sort of material that Reed pulled out of the set. As for critics, they are more inclined to write about an anthology when it significantly deepens their understanding of a major artist, or offers a meaningful look at his creative process. *Between Thought and Expression* did neither. As a result, it was not so much attacked as ignored. There really wasn't much to say about it. As for its taking its place alongside groundbreaking collections like Dylan's *Biograph* and Eric Clapton's *Crossroads,* that did not remotely happen. In his effort to control what the set would be, Reed blunted whatever impact it might have had.

SOME MONTHS BEFORE THE release of the box set, Reed published a book of his lyrics, titled *Between Thought and Expression: Selected Lyrics of Lou Reed.* Rob Bowman was miffed that Reed had used the title of the box set — it's a line from the Velvet Underground song "Some Kinda Love" — for the book. (Bowman had suggested the box set title to Reed after conferring with another writer and Reed fan, Jeffrey Morgan.) Reed clearly saw the book as part of the same effort as the box set: to shape and define his achievement up to that point. Published by Hyperion in hardcover, the book is handsome and consciously literary. The black-and-white cover photo by Matt Mahurin shows Reed in profile against a black background, out of focus, softly lit, his eyes closed. The cover design by Sylvia and Spencer Drate features elegant gold-and-black type, and the back cover features half a dozen quotes from Reed's lyrics. It was another effort on Reed's part to move away from his identity as a rock star and define himself as a writer. "It isn't a rock star's compilation," he said of the book. "There's no pictures of my house or of the band. I didn't bring in some Belgian to paint the cover. It was serious.... The songs are like my diary. If I want to know where I was, the book gives me a good idea."

In his brief introduction to the book, Reed wrote, "Over the last few years I have done occasional 'poetry' readings, always using my lyrics as the basis. I was continually struck by the different voices that emerged when the words were heard without music, and those experiences encouraged me to consider the possibility of publishing them naked." Along with the selection of lyrics from his Velvet Underground and solo material, Reed included two previously published poems as well as his interviews with Hubert Selby and Václav Havel. Intermittently, Reed offers comments on the origins of his songs, and while sparing, they're among the most revealing remarks he made since he cleaned up in the early eighties and began refusing to discuss "personal" matters in interviews. The book also reflects Reed's deepening understanding of himself as a writer, as well as his weary comprehension that "drugs and liquor did not do me any good." In fact, Reed created much of his greatest work when he was using drugs and alcohol, but the toll those excesses exacted on him finally proved unsustainable and certainly would have killed him. Sobriety was key to his continuing ability to make strong records, to appreciate and nourish his gift. "I know more about writing now than when I was a lunatic," he said. "I'm very respectful of it now and I try to do everything in my power not to impede the process. I've been around a long time, and I know things that do impede it: drugs impede it; getting in a fight with a friend impedes it; tension impedes it." His sobriety also allowed for a focus and precision that had been a nearly impossible struggle for him to achieve before. "Once you get past the first inspiration, which is always great fun, then comes the real business at hand: how do we make this say exactly what we want it to say—not almost, not close, not sort of, not, well, I can't explain that, it's poetry—but how can we put it exactly in the least words possible? I spend the bulk of my time taking things out. I'm always trying to get a visual image you can get really quickly. When you hear the record, it shoots by, so I want you to get the image quick. And if you didn't, then it's bad writing."

Perhaps the most striking aspect of the book is its dedication: "For Sid, Toby, Bunny / And most of all /

For Sylvia." Including his parents and his sister like this in a book devoted to his most prized vision of himself—that is, as a writer—suggests an ongoing effort on Reed's part to come to terms with his upbringing and his past. And simply having a book that consists solely of his own words, that defined him as a writer, was incalculably important to him. Bill Bentley, who handled Reed's publicity at Sire, accompanied him to a book signing for *Between Thought and Expression* at Book Soup in Los Angeles. "Lou built a real toughness around himself," Bentley said. "He could be rude—let's face it. But he wasn't at all a hard person. At that signing, everybody was telling him their stories. One guy had him sign a banana—that was funny. But one lady said, 'My sister had cancer, and *Magic and Loss* really got me through it.'

"Lou would never show a whole lot. He would be polite, sign everything. But afterwards he went into a private room in the back of the store, and just sat down, fell into Sylvia's arms, and started to weep. That image has always stuck with me. He'd been so touched by what people said. This wasn't like a record release party—these were his words. I'll never forget that. I remember looking at him and thinking, 'That's a Lou Reed that very few people have ever seen.' I would always think of that when another side of him would come out. It made me really appreciate the depth of his feeling for other people. There are people who live by Lou's lyrics. He's written things that inspire you, give you hope, fuel your dreams. He's one of a handful of rockers who did that over and over, forever, as long as they created. That showed me he knew the power of his music. He was no fool."

21

ME BURGER WITH I SAUCE

I F *NEW YORK* GOT Reed off on the right foot with his new label, Sire Records, *Magic and Loss* began the perhaps inevitable fraying of that relationship. With *New York,* Reed had brought Sire an album that both got strong critical attention and sold well. Its spare production and high-powered playing suggested that Reed was reenergized — exactly the message a new label wants to convey about an iconic artist it has just signed. The album was also ambitious and serious-minded, which made it a worthy addition to the Lou Reed oeuvre — another positive point, as far as Sire was concerned. Many critics thought it was the best work of Reed's solo career.

"The fact is, *New York* had great tracks and a strong first single in 'Dirty Blvd.,'" said Steven Baker, Reed's product manager at Warner Bros., Sire's corporate home. "We did right by it and did a good job of promoting it. The song was an alternative radio hit, and even though Lou wasn't exactly MTV material, the video got a certain amount of play on MTV. We sold more than half a million records. When records go that well, there's not a lot of friction." While Sire was excited about *Songs for Drella* and saw its appeal to serious music fans, the label still regarded it as a niche project. From Sire's standpoint, *Magic and Loss* was the true follow-up to *New York*.

When Reed delivered *Magic and Loss,* the label recognized its quality and understood its personal importance for Reed. But there was still a sense of disappointment. "I listened to *Magic and Loss* and thought, 'Well, someone is really going to like this record, and that someone is going to be writers,'" said Baker. "When you're working at a record company, you're always really focused on, 'How is this record going to be marketed compared to the one before it, which did quite well? What are our options for singles?' All that stuff. If someone sent me *Magic and Loss* now, I could just sit back, enjoy its brilliance, and not worry. But then I was thinking, 'The first track is good, but it's not a single.' And I kept hoping the next track would be the one. Then you get to the last track, and you think, 'Well, there you go—it's not going to emerge.' *Magic and Loss* was a great record, but nothing on it was as obvious a single as 'Dirty Blvd.' "

Reed's stature ensured that Sire would support *Magic and Loss* regardless of its commercial potential, but, as with Reed's experiences at both RCA and Arista, the problem was convincing him to have realistic expectations for both sales and promotion of the album. A key ally in any such effort would typically be the artist's manager—in Reed's case, his wife. Managers, of course, advocate for their artists as strongly as possible, but "client control" is also one of their responsibilities. While artists are thought to be in need of constant ego massaging, record company executives assume that they can speak candidly to managers about their sense of what's possible with a particular project and what the most effective marketing strategies would be. But even under optimal circumstances, Reed would be hard to handle. As usual, his hopes for the album far exceeded what could reasonably be expected to happen. And he was not the sort of artist who would agree to do extensive interviews, for example, or visit radio stations. With record companies as well as fellow musicians, he was not an ideal collaborator.

"George Clinton used to have this expression: he would talk about somebody being a 'Me burger with I sauce,' " said Jeff Gold, who was senior vice president of creative services at Warner Bros. "That was my experience with Lou. It was all about Lou. Lou did what Lou wanted to do on Lou's timetable, and fuck the rest of it. And I have no objection to artists being that way. They just have to put that into the calculus of how successful their record is going to be."

Unfortunately, Sylvia was in no position to convey that reality to Reed—though whether anyone else could have is a fair question. Sire came to believe that she was essentially useless in serving as an intermediary between Reed and the company. In a diplomatic understatement, Steven Baker observed that Sylvia "was probably not that well versed in the mechanics of Warner Bros. Records at that point." Ultimately, he said, "my only impression of Sylvia is that she was nice. She was very easy to deal with. She was looking out for Lou's interests. I have to say, though, that she wasn't a seasoned manager, so she was naive about how things get done. There was a big difference between Sylvia Reed and dealing with someone like Cliff Bernstein [who managed Metallica and Def Leppard] or John Silva [who managed Nirvana and Nine Inch Nails], people whom I would respect as a manager. Not that I didn't respect her, but she wasn't bringing a lot of creative energy to the table. She was basically supporting her husband and client."

"Whenever you would hear something from Sylvia, my expectation was that Lou had said to her, 'Call Warner Bros. and ask them for this or get them to do that,'" Jeff Gold said. "That's perfectly fine, and she was a pleasant person. But I don't think she contributed anything to the marketing of Lou's records."

To be fair, Sylvia was in an impossible position, even if it was one she voluntarily accepted. When she first met Reed in her early twenties, she knew very little about him. Sylvia had come to New York on a scholarship to Pratt Institute, where she studied fine arts and filmmaking. The arts meant everything to her, and as she fell in love with Reed, his work loomed as something like a noble mission—as did relieving the desperate neediness that manifested itself in all his love relationships. "I felt that I had to fill this role," she said. "There's a lot of need there, the side of him that's very fragile, very vulnerable. Here's Lou the great artist in this misunderstanding world. 'You understand me. Help me with this.'" Early on, he would bring Sylvia to meetings, sit her in a corner, and not introduce her to anyone. "It was key for him to have me there," she said. "He'd never speak to me. But later he'd ask, 'Okay, who said what? Who did this? What did you think? What's your impression of this person?'" She was eager to impress him and passed all the tests he put her through. When Reed left his manager Eric Kronfield, he put Sylvia in charge as an interim decision that inevitably became permanent. He trusted her implicitly, and her role grew and grew. There was virtually no aspect of Reed's life in which Sylvia, as a wife and business partner, did not play a significant role.

"It snuck up on me," she said. "I cannot believe how much he was having me handle. It ended up where all the requests, all the things that would normally go to a business manager, I'm handling. I'm making sure that the tours and the recording sessions are set up right in every aspect — the musicians, the transportation. I'm also dealing with the huge number of daily requests: 'Are we allowed to print the lyrics?' 'Can we use this song for a benefit?' 'Will you make an appearance here?' Endless, endless. It was a huge amount of work.

"That's the importance it had for him. Every single thing that came in, all of it had to be vetted by someone he trusted and presented to him for a final yes or no. And then the worm turns. 'How do I know your point of view is right on this? You're the only one telling me this.' He'd want to pull away and get on with his own creative process, but then he would feel, 'No, I need to be in control.' He became sober, and as with many people who clean up and get dry, there's that underlying alcoholic thing about control. And that was difficult, a very difficult time. He was an absolute control freak, and I don't think it would have bothered him to be called that at all. I think he would think of it as a point of pride.... But I will say this. I don't believe, even at the end, that he ever let go of trusting me."

Finally, both Sire and Sylvia were up against what may well have been an immovable force: Lou Reed himself. Said Jeff Gold: "You can do all this stuff around the release of an album: take out provocative advertising, make the most of whatever video the artist is willing to do, create special packages—a lot of hoopla. But ultimately, nothing can compete with the artist getting in there and doing something himself. A writer doing an article about what Warner Bros. is doing to support a Lou Reed album is not nearly as exciting as the writer talking to Lou Reed. There's nothing you can do for the key buyer of a retail chain that can compete with bringing Lou Reed in and having him meet the guy. Same with radio programmers. Lou had negative interest in doing any of that."

Reed developed strategies for dealing with the various people at his record company, though the degree to which he was in control of his behavior is unclear. For the most part, he felt fully justified expressing his dissatisfaction directly—and personally. Information that would typically come from a manager often came straight from Reed himself. Jeff Gold came to Warner Bros. at around the time of *Magic and Loss,* and as a fan of Reed and the Velvet Underground, he found himself in a complicated position. "I think Lou had pissed off enough people in the sales department, the publicity department, the advertising and marketing departments that a phone call from Lou Reed wasn't good news," Gold said. "It would be like, 'Uh-oh, what's wrong? What's he going to yell at me about? Jesus Christ, I don't want to talk to this guy.' And he didn't have a real manager who could help you. So I was kind of fresh meat — like, 'Wow, a call from Lou Reed? Great, put him on.' You figure, 'I can talk to this guy. How bad can he be?'"

Gold would eventually learn the answer to that question. At around the time of *Magic and Loss,* he also discovered one of Reed's strategies for avoiding personal conversations and discussions about the meaning of his songs: his retreat into the subject of sound technology. "I remember going to meet Lou at his house with Steven Baker," Gold recalled. "I was thinking, 'Wow, what a trip — going to Lou Reed's house!' Lou had a bunch of instruments set up, maybe some drums and guitars, and he had a guitar that was rectangular and he was going on and on about the sonics of it. I remember thinking, 'It seems like he's more obsessed with the sound he can get from his guitar than the songs.' ... This is the guy who's the visionary behind the Velvet Underground, who was so far ahead of the pack, and all he wants to talk about is some new amp he's found. He was obsessed with it. That was my take-away from going to Lou Reed's house. It was so mind-bogglingly uninteresting. It's like you're going to the Messiah to get the answer and all he wants to talk about is the lunch menu."

Without question, Reed's obsession with sonic niceties was a way of avoiding the personal questions that his style of songwriting, self-presentation, and lurid history inevitably generated. But in his defense, he had clearly come to believe that sound was the primary means of how songs communicated. For someone as obsessed with lyrics as Reed was, that's saying something. Fans and many critics hear music solely in emotional terms, but for Reed, that emotional effect can come only when sound has been properly deployed. Critic Simon Reynolds called it Reed's "science of magic." Reed told him, "I know how much the magic disappears when the technical stuff is wrong."

With Baker, Reed conveyed his disappointed expectations in a different way. "He never screamed at me," Baker said. "He would make me feel guilty. He would call and say, 'I was in a record store in'—pick your city—'and there weren't any posters up in the store.' I would be thinking, 'There's no way Lou went to that record store. Maybe one of his roadies did.' But I'd get this call at eight in the morning. That's what I remember—you'd get this call and Lou's upset. He's not yelling. He's telling you what he's seen, and he's disappointed. The way I would react to that is to feel incredibly guilty, that we weren't coming through for

Lou. He understood that that was a great way of pressing my buttons. I never remember a barrage of anger, that kind of energy coming from Lou. More like a constant sense of disappointment."

As REED'S SOLO CAREER proceeded, interest in the Velvet Underground seemed only to gain momentum. From June 14 to September 9, 1990, the Cartier Foundation for Contemporary Art presented an exhibition devoted to Andy Warhol, titled *Andy Warhol System: Pub-Pop-Rock,* in Jouy-en-Josas, about sixteen miles outside Paris. All four original members of the Velvet Underground were invited to and attended the opening, which took place on a gorgeous summer day, and Reed and Cale agreed to perform five selections from *Songs for Drella* on a simple outdoor stage arranged in a woodland setting. Some people, of course, were hoping the Velvets would play together, but word of bickering at their table during lunch spread through the crowd, and those hopes diminished.

But when Reed and Cale finished their short set, Reed called Sterling Morrison and Maureen Tucker to join them onstage. To enthusiastic cheers, they took their places, and edged into "Heroin." This reunion was not planned, or at least was not a foregone conclusion. Morrison had not even brought a guitar. But the performance was riveting—stunning, really, for the relatively small crowd of a few hundred insiders and notables who witnessed it. Cale's viola was a mesmerizing drone, and Tucker's drumming was tribal and intense. Reed and Morrison locked in on guitar, and Reed's singing was simultaneously impassioned and coolly detached. Reed got lost in the song once or twice and dropped lyrics, but all in all, the performance was everything anyone could have wanted from such an event. This particular VU lineup had not been onstage together in twenty-two years, and they sounded better than they had in their heyday. Their conviction and sense of the historical importance of what they were doing lent their performance a weight it never could have had back when they were desperately struggling for recognition. And for all their maturity and intelligence, they had lost none of their rawness. The audience was ecstatic. "That would be an amazing one for the bootleggers," Reed joked to a friend backstage, and, of course, it was. At that moment, something that would have seemed unthinkable emerged as a possibility: a genuine Velvet Underground reunion.

For years, Reed, Cale, Morrison, and Tucker had been circling one another warily. In addition to participating in the Cartier performance, Tucker appeared on Reed's album *New York*. Reed, Cale, and Morrison all performed on Tucker's 1991 solo album, *I Spent a Week There the Other Night*. That same year, Reed and Morrison joined Cale onstage during a solo gig of his at New York University. That this degree of inter-action had not already led to a VU reunion suggests how much distrust still permeated their relations. In 1992, the group did some rehearsals, still unsure if they could successfully perform together. Finally, the group made the decision to proceed.

Tremendous excitement surrounded the announce-ment of the band's European tour, which was set to begin with two shows in Edinburgh at the beginning of June. Morrison wanted Doug Yule to join the band on the road, but Reed and Cale nixed the idea. Cale wanted the band to write new material for the tour; his oft-repeated watchword was that the purpose of the tour was to "remythologize" the band, not "demy-thologize" it. He was overruled by the other members. According to Cale, Reed believed that he was doing the band an "enormous favor" by participating in the reunion at all. Sylvia, who designed the stage lighting for the tour, also very much wanted the reunion to happen, and Cale suspected that Reed's agreeing to do it was part of his strategy to negotiate the divorce that seemed to be in his future. Reed and Sylvia were in the process of breaking up, though they were still working together—an untenable situation.

Still, Reed understood what was at stake. "We're confronting the myth head-on," he said while the band was in rehearsals before the tour began. "I'm sure there will be people who will say afterward, 'Oh, it would have been better if they didn't play. The memory of it is so much better than the reality of it.'" Morrison, perhaps, had the best attitude about the band's determination to perform again. "Should we stay in hiding just because a myth is loose in the land?" he asked. The rock press, which had spent the previous quarter century or so praising the band to the skies, remained skeptical, of course. In the *Times of London,* critic David Sinclair wrote that the Velvets' "unique godhead status will begin to diminish almost from the moment they start their first number." The problem was that the Velvets were not competing with actual memories— relatively few people had ever seen the band, and for that matter, the Velvets had never performed outside the United States. Few recordings of their live performances were available at the time, as legitimate releases or even as bootlegs, and few people had heard any of those. Reed, Cale, Morrison, and Tucker were competing with the *idea* of the Velvet Underground, the symbolic importance that the band had come to assume, and that, understandably, must have been a little bit frightening. It was brave of them to proceed in the face of that challenge.

As it happens, the band inevitably did not match the exalted expectations generated by its storied past. In part because of Reed's desire to exert as much control over the reunion as possible, the group often sounded like former members of the Velvet Underground backing Lou Reed in a set of Velvet Underground classics. Reed simply could not relax into allowing the group to explore the musical outer limits of what the band had done in the past — and could still do. That experimental urge was largely Cale's province, and Reed was not going to yield to him on it. Still, the band performed at a high level, and critics were respectful of both its gifts and its legend. David Sinclair, who had assumed that the reunited group's first notes would tarnish the Velvets' standing, concluded that one of the Scotland shows "did not produce a feeling of déjà vu, more an impression that, after twenty-five years, the rest of the world has only just caught up with them." The sheer excitement of seeing the foursome onstage performing a body of work that ranks among the most significant in the history of rock and roll no doubt affected the reactions of both critics and fans.

Among the people who were most enthusiastic about a Velvets reunion were the executives at Reed's label, Sire Records. While it was unlikely ever to be a massive commercial success, the Velvets reunion had the potential to generate a great deal of interest in Reed and his solo work. A live album from the tour was the least of it. Very quickly, the possibility of the band making an appearance on *MTV Unplugged* emerged, an event that would expose Reed and the Velvets to an entire generation of younger fans. An *Unplugged* album would no doubt follow, and after that, who knew? Perhaps a new Velvet Underground album. Of course, the team at Sire was under no illusions about how sturdy the Velvets' reunion was. When the tour was announced, Jeff Gold jokingly told Steven Baker, "We've got to go to the first show in Edinburgh, because there might not be a second one." But that did not diminish the thrill of seeing the legendary band perform live. "We went backstage before the show," Gold recalled. "It was almost an intellectual disconnect for me, this band I loved so much, and here they are in one room and I'm meeting them and they're about to play. It was really overwhelming, almost beyond belief." That the shows themselves did not rise to the level of what the Velvets were capable of was almost a secondary consideration. "It seemed like Lou was running things. He was doing all the talking and he was calling the shots onstage," Gold recalled. "That said, I was really happy I went. It was a bucket list moment, the closest I was going to get. But it wasn't what it could have been."

Everyone's assumption was that the European shows were a run-up to a U.S. tour. It was inconceivable that the band would reunite for a few weeks in Europe and then not perform in America. But that's precisely what happened. The reason? As Gold put it, Lou "was really being Lou." The band insisted that Reed not produce the Velvets' live album, which ended up being titled *Live MCMXCIII*—the Roman numerals for 1993 and a nod, playful or not, to the monumental nature of the Velvets reunion. As far as the production went, Reed settled for, in his view, the next best thing to a compromise. He brought in Mike Rathke, who had worked with Reed and Fred Maher on *New York*. Reed said, "You don't want me to do it? Okay. I'll make this happen. Mike is my right-hand man. He will do what I would have done. And he did. He did a brilliant job of it."

Because of the tensions that arose—primarily between Reed and Cale, though also between Reed and Morrison—the notion that the band would do some dates in the United States was scuttled. Finally, the *MTV Unplugged* performance was also abandoned because Reed insisted on producing—and receiving an additional fee for—the album that would result from that appearance. For Reed, the issue was completely straightforward. "The reason the Velvet Underground did not play in the United States—and obviously never will—is twofold. It was a volatile brew; I was happy it made it through Europe in the first place. Two, I wanted to produce and be paid for the production of any albums we were going to do. The other members of the group, led by John Cale, didn't want me to." To anyone who cared about the Velvet Underground, Reed's decision seemed mind-bogglingly petty.

"I was in the middle of that whole situation," said Steven Baker, who had come up with the idea of the Velvets doing *MTV Unplugged*. "I just recall taking calls, ping-ponging back and forth between John and Lou, and feeling like, 'This thing is falling apart,' and it's ridiculous because that really could have been a moment. It fell apart because nobody from their side could help them rationalize a way to get it done."

Once again, the most likely person to perform that key role was Sylvia. During rehearsals for the tour, when an issue about song publishing came up, Reed immediately called Sylvia and insisted that she drop whatever she was doing and come down to deal with Cale. When she arrived, Cale informed her that, while she might manage Lou Reed, she did not manage the Velvet Underground, and he had no interest in discussing the matter with her. "Sylvia couldn't possibly have brokered the peace between them," Baker said. "There was nobody who could have brought them together and said, 'We should look at this as in the best interests of the Velvet Underground,' and also say to Lou, 'This is good for you, for whatever you do solo after this, because this just brings more attention to your accomplishments with the Velvet Underground.'

"The *Unplugged* would have brought the Velvet Underground to the forefront of MTV viewers' imaginations. Even those kids who may have heard the *New York* album on alternative radio might not have had a clue what group Lou came from. Look, this record was not going to do what Eric Clapton's or Nirvana's *Unplugged* did. I'm not suggesting that. The simple fact is they could have put an album into their catalog that might have sold better than any previous Velvet Underground record."

According to Cale, the final decision about the *Unplugged* album and the tour was made during a band meeting on Long Island for which Reed arrived in a white limousine. Reed sat by the pool "draped in white towels, looking like an outpatient or an old-age pensioner," as Cale put it, and insisted that he was the only person who could produce the Velvet Underground. "I saw immediately what that was about— everybody would be taking orders from Lou Reed," Cale wrote afterward. Cale suggested alternatives: George Martin, Chris Thomas, or "any producer we wanted." Reed's response: "I must produce." Cale's position: "Absolutely not."

Cale was, needless to say, at least as well established a producer as Reed. Along with his own estimable solo work, Cale had produced groundbreaking albums for the Stooges, Patti Smith, Jonathan Richman and the Modern Lovers, and Nico. That, of course, was a piece of the problem. Part of Reed's mission was to demonstrate that he was the most important figure in the Velvet Underground, and Cale was his most significant rival in that regard. The band's reunion shows took on the character they did for that reason. The two men had shared the production credit for *Songs for Drella,* but that was a side project. In the same way the other band members were contained onstage for the reunion shows, there was no way Reed would let the production of a VU album, live or not, seem like a communal process—or the result of anyone's decisions but his. Even the back of the *Live MCMXCIII* CD booklet reads "ALL SONGS WRITTEN BY LOU REED," in all caps and in a typeface much larger than the titles of the songs themselves. In infinitely smaller type appears the parenthetical "except where indicated."

22

FOURTEENTH CHANCE

IN 1992, JOHN ZORN, a saxophonist and charter
member of New York's downtown music scene,
curated the Munich Art Projekt, an annual festival devoted to new music. The rubric Zorn chose to
explore was what he called radical Jewish culture.
Zorn had recently become interested in both his Jewish identity and the role of Jewish musicians in the
most adventurous quarters of the New York music
scene. He had composed a piece commemorating
Kristallnacht, the "night of broken glass," the attack
on the Jewish community in Germany and Austria in
1938 that signaled the beginning of the systematic
genocide that would evolve into the Holocaust. It was
the first of his pieces to explore this aspect of his history and identity. As part of his curator's role in the

festival, Zorn invited Lou Reed to perform. That's where Reed met Laurie Anderson, another of the artists Zorn had invited.

Like Zorn, Anderson had been a fixture on the avant-garde scene in New York, and like him, she moved in circles that occasionally grazed against the world of popular music. Unlike Zorn, however, Anderson had actually enjoyed a hit. Her 1981 song "O Superman (for Massenet)" rose to number two on the UK singles chart and created a sufficient impression in the United States to land her a multialbum deal with Warner Bros. (Jules Massenet was a French opera composer of the late nineteenth and early twentieth century.) Essentially, then, Reed and Anderson were labelmates. Trained as a classical violinist, Anderson combined an array of styles in her work. As a performance artist, she often treated her voice in a way that blurred or even erased gender. Even Anderson's looks refused a commitment to gender. Her face was pretty and fine-boned, with expressive eyes, but her cropped hair and inevitable pants made her appear boyish. She was fascinated by electronics and invented several instruments that explore the interface between acoustic and synthetic sound. Musically adventurous, her songs often include vocal parts that are not so much sung as intoned. Her cadences are musical but more like spoken-word recitations than like songs. They are delivered with a studied lack of affect, as if she were an anthropologist describing a realm she had never seen before and to which she had no emotional connection.

Not only was she not blown over by meeting Lou Reed; she barely knew who he was. That had to have made an impression on him. When Reed invited her to perform with him in Munich, Anderson wondered to herself why he didn't have an English accent: she had thought the Velvet Underground was from England. Only five years younger than Reed, she was hardly in the position of looking up to him as a more famous and established figure. On the other hand, she was extremely intelligent, and Reed's gifts and accomplishments— not to mention his charm and wit—would not have been lost on her.

Reed was taken by her performance in Munich and suggested that they get together again when they were both back in New York. "Yes! Absolutely!" she said. "I'm on tour, but when I get back—let's see, about four months from now—let's *definitely* get together." That she was in no hurry to cement her connection with Reed would not have slipped by him. It would have tugged at his insecurities, for one thing, but also circumvented his paranoia regarding the agenda, expectations, and intentions of anyone who tried to get close to him. According to Anderson, they solidified their relationship while attending the Audio Engineering Society convention. "The AES convention is the greatest and biggest place to geek out on new equipment, and we spent a happy afternoon looking at amps and cables and shop-talking electronics," Anderson later wrote. She claimed that she had no idea they were on a date, but when Reed suggested a movie and dinner afterward, it became clear where they were headed. Their true relationship began on that day.

As HIS MARRIAGE TO Sylvia was falling apart, Reed had begun to seek out other prospects. Before he set his sights on Laurie Anderson, this made for some awkward times, given that Sylvia still managed him and they still socialized. Suzanne Vega recalled Sylvia calling her up and inviting her to dinner with her and Lou; the singer-songwriter Victoria Williams would also be there. Vega had asked if she could bring along the producer Mitchell Froom, whom she had begun to date and would later marry. When Froom left the table for a few minutes, Reed moved into his chair. "Lou grabbed my hand and started stroking it, saying, 'You and I really need to get together and have lunch,'" Vega recalled. "I started laughing because Sylvia's sitting right there. I'm thinking, 'You're kidding, right?' And he keeps on: 'We really need to get together.' So I say, 'Sure, call me up. We'll have lunch. Whatever.' So Mitchell comes back to the table, and Lou's holding my hand and stroking my arm. I'm still laughing, and Mitchell is like, 'What's going on here?' I'm like, 'Nothing. Lou's being mischievous. He's being flirtatious.' Obviously, this was a piece of theater. I'd been procured by Sylvia to come to this dinner, so I didn't take it that seriously. And Lou never called." The next time she saw Reed was in early 1994, when they were both performing at a songwriters' evening at the Bottom Line. Vega was pregnant with Froom's child, Sylvia was backstage with Reed, and Laurie Anderson was in the audience.

Also during this period, Reed's friend Erin Clermont thought that something deeper might be developing between her and Reed. "We had been getting very close," she said. "Sylvia had left him, and there was a new element in the relationship. He was being so nice and caring. I didn't know where it was going, but it was fun. And then he called me and said he had gotten involved with someone. I said, 'Oh, who?' He said, 'Laurie Anderson.' My jaw dropped. I had no idea. I felt that he treated me quite shabbily."

Reed and Sylvia divorced in 1994, at which point Sylvia no longer managed him. The stresses of their personal and business relationships, as well as Reed's refusal to have children, which Sylvia very much wanted, eventually took a fatal toll. In the divorce, Sylvia got the couple's home in Blairstown, New Jersey, which on *The Blue Mask* and elsewhere had seemed such a symbol of the life they had created together.

Characteristically, Reed dove headfirst into his new relationship. Apart from their affection for each other, Reed and Anderson brought valuable qualities to each other's lives. By the midnineties, Reed was past fifty and was in danger of becoming a rock-and-roll elder statesman. He was creating strong work, but, as had happened with punk fifteen years earlier, his own successors seemed to push him from the edge into the mainstream. The so-called grunge movement had brought a corrosive version of punk back into prominence, and even to the top of the charts. Bands like Nirvana, Pearl Jam, and Screaming Trees owed a considerable debt to Reed and the Velvet Underground, but the fans of those bands had little idea of that lineage. Gangsta rap, too, had introduced elements of violence, sexual provocation, linguistic shock value, and abrasive noise into popular music that made Reed at his most extreme seem quaint—all while selling millions of records. Though Anderson was no help in that regard, her impeccable avant-garde credentials sharpened the edge of Reed's stature. He was now not merely an aging rocker but someone with direct ties to the still-roiling New York underground scene. Her aesthetic credibility and the seriousness with which her work was regarded functioned for Reed as something like the literary standing that he so ardently sought. If Reed wanted to distance himself somewhat from rock and roll in order to be perceived as a Serious Artist, his involvement with Anderson advanced that cause.

As for Anderson, disturbing as some of the themes of her work could be, it generally had a genial quality that made her more accessible to mainstream audiences than other, more abrasive experimental artists. *People* magazine, for example, ran a feature in which Anderson, monologist Spalding Gray, and director Jonathan Demme, all of whom had worked on the film version of Gray's *Swimming to Cambodia,* went bowling—partly just for a fun setting for the story and partly to show *People*'s readership that it need not be put off by their arty backgrounds. That Anderson would agree to such a stunt—indeed, that she would agree to be in *People* at all—shows that she saw herself as an artist whose work could reach a wide audience. R.E.M. guitarist Peter Buck once described his band's relationship to the rock underground as being "the acceptable edge of the unacceptable stuff." Anderson occupied that spot in relation to New York's underground art scene. While Reed was hardly a household name, he was vastly more well-known than Anderson and helped to refresh awareness of her among the more adventurous rock fans who would be receptive to her brand of performance art, which combined elements of music, video, and spoken-word recitations. Reed and Anderson would soon become, as Bob Neuwirth put it, "the Ma and Pa Kettle" of the New York underground.

WHEN WORD OF REED and Anderson's involvement began to spread, the reaction mingled delight and surprise. They seemed an intriguing match, the sort of union that could only make sense in New York. They seemed to go everywhere together—galleries, movies, concerts, events of all sorts having to do with the arts. Sightings of them walking on the street or dining in downtown restaurants took on the quality of definitive New York experiences, much as seeing Woody Allen or John Lennon and Yoko Ono had been a couple of decades earlier. In public, Reed was unusually deferential to Anderson, almost boyish in his efforts to be pleasing, like a high school kid trying to learn how to properly behave with his first girlfriend. People who met them together and expected to encounter the fearsome Lou Reed were struck by how puppyish he could be around her. Anderson, meanwhile, routinely maintained her air of friendly, benign detachment, almost as if she were as much observing the situation as participating in it. She clearly felt affection for Reed, and somehow seemed to understand how fragile he was beneath his protective armor. She received his attentions not so much as her due, but as if unsurprised by them, maybe even a little amused. Chatty as she could be in her work, she was far more reserved around him, and seemed perfectly willing to let him do most of the talking.

For all their seeming closeness, they never fully lived together. Anderson kept her Canal Street loft, while Reed maintained an apartment on West Eleventh Street. They eventually purchased a weekend home in East Hampton that they regarded as "theirs"—"a house that was separate from our own places," is how Anderson described it.

That they often lived apart was painful for Reed; it was a subject he complained about, sometimes tearfully, to the people closest to him. But Anderson seemed to require such distance in order to maintain her own equilibrium in relation to Reed and not be overwhelmed by him. Reed's tempestuousness and hair-trigger temper could not have been more different from Anderson's firm but gentle determination and desire to avoid confrontation. Every couple needs to work out its own rhythm of individuality and union, and Reed and Anderson were no exception. It wasn't as if they were a young couple just starting out and establishing a home together. They were older, and each had a demanding career that required frequent travel. The time they spent apart was likely essential to their successfully remaining together.

They were so different that many people reacted to their getting together with something like shock. Jeff Gold had occasion to work with both Reed and Anderson at Warner Bros. "There's no explanation for relationships," he said, "but everybody at Warners was trying to do the math on this. We knew Laurie as a highly motivated and interesting artist, but as friendly as could be. And Lou seemed like a changed man around her: docile and pleasant, deferential, pulling her chair out when she was about to sit down. I'm sure she was the best thing ever to happen to him."

Steven Baker felt similarly. "I was just so amazed that Lou and Laurie found each other," he said. "I just saw her bringing out the best in Lou." On one occasion, Reed and Anderson invited Steven and his wife to dinner at a friend's apartment on the Upper West Side: "That night, Lou would tell me that if I ate this particular food, it would be really good for me—almost like somebody who was looking out for me. Laurie was this conceptual artist, and my expectation was that she was going to be like one of these famous intellectual people. She is very brilliant, but she's also the nicest person in the world, so wonderful to be around. And all of a sudden, Lou, who could be the polar opposite of that, is now spending time with her, and every time I'm with Lou and Laurie, it's fantastic. I kept thinking of how lucky Lou was to have met Laurie."

REED'S NEXT ALBUM ADDRESSED both his divorce and his new relationship with Anderson. Released in February of

1996, just before Reed's fifty-fourth birthday, *Set the Twilight Reeling* provided a thematic break from the albums that had immediately preceded it. *Songs for Drella* and *Magic and Loss* both explored mortality, *New York* took a hard look at social conditions, and the Velvet Underground's *Live MCMXCIII* was a journey through the past, an attempt to see what the most significant episode in Reed's creative life might mean in the present day. They were all, in their way, rigorously organized concept albums.

Set the Twilight Reeling is a unified statement as well, though it feels more relaxed than those earlier projects. "I wanted to make a record that would take you on a trip of passion," Reed explained. "I was having a good old time when I made the record. And I'm having an even better time now." Even in his interviews to promote the album, Reed seemed in an uncharacteristically easygoing mood. In his conversation with a reporter for the *Philadelphia Inquirer,* for example, Reed genially chatted about the New York Knicks, whom he was about to go see play against Philly's hometown team, the 76ers. He complained like any fan about how coddled sports superstars are ("It's not like we can all go to arbitration when we're unhappy.... Boy, that would be nice to live like that. But this is the real world") and explained that he hadn't smoked in nearly a year. "I feel like I conquered the world," he said. "I do smoke cigars, but I'm like Clinton: I don't inhale." He even responded in a friendly way to a direct question regarding his relationship with Anderson, the sort of "personal" inquiry that would have typically set him off. Asked if "wedding bells are ready to ring," Reed responded, "I would never answer a question like that, but the minute any plans are set, I will probably make a public announcement from Mount Everest. If I ever get that lucky."

What *Set the Twilight Reeling* does share with its predecessors is that it's an album about transformation. Reed clearly saw his relationship with Anderson as an essential new beginning, and the promise that relationship held—and the challenge that Anderson presented to him as a person—suggested a future that he was excited about. He had felt that way about the start of his relationship with Sylvia as well, of course, as documented on *The Blue Mask* and *Legendary Hearts*. But it's a lot harder to resist cynicism in your midfifties than it is at forty. Reed saw his horizons expanding in all directions at a time when others might have been feeling the first chill of mortality. "I'd like to think I'm capable of growing," he said. "That's part of what this album is about. Change is the only constant. Without getting all New Agey and dewy-eyed about it, I do truly believe that if you practice the guitar, you play better. If you spend enough time with the recording process, you record better. And certainly I believe that I've learned things about writing over the years that allow me to write better. So for me, the best is yet to come."

"Set the twilight reeling": it almost seems as if it could be a line from the national anthem, the sound of a new country being born. And if the image of twilight recalls the concern with mortality of Reed's earlier work, the title suggests that his discovery of Anderson upended that preoccupation. Rather than meditating on the sense of an ending, he is gripped by the idea of a new beginning. As he sings on the title track, which closes the album, "I accept the newfound man and set the twilight reeling." That song begins softly, as Reed prays for acceptance—and self-acceptance—as, a bit frightened, he faces the changes to come. Once again, new love has him at his most vulnerable. "A new self is borne," he sings, "the other self dead." That use of "borne" rather than "born" is striking. This being rock and roll, it's possible that it was simply spelled incorrectly on the album's lyric sheet, though "borne" remains the spelling in the book of lyrics Reed published afterward. Regardless, even as an unintended homophone pun, it's lovely. The "new self" is not merely being born, coming into being, but must be borne, like a weight or a responsibility. It's as if Reed understood that the person he was could not survive in his relationship with Anderson, that she would not tolerate the man whose behavior may well have undermined his previous relationships. The song ends with the image of a soul singer onstage, dropping to his knees, the horn section "unrelenting" as he belts out his lover's prayer. Finally, as he gazes into the microphone, his lover's face appears, and "I lose all my regrets." The writing there, like the singing, is both restrained and powerful, Reed at his finest.

The song "Trade In," a ballad distinguished by a melodic bass line by Fernando Saunders, also addresses the theme of Reed shedding an old, abrasive self ("such an obvious schmuck") in order to transform into someone new. That is the "trade in" of the title. He insists that he now desires a "fourteenth chance at this life." In a telling image, Reed credits Anderson as the source of his willingness to change. "I met a woman with a thousand faces," he sings, "and I want to make her my wife." The "faces" Reed is referring to are the many characters Anderson assumes in her work, her own transformations that blur gender, and the shifting nature of reality in her art. Reed has also described the character of "Lou Reed" as ever-changing. Those changes pertain to his life as well as his art. Many people have pointed out that dealing with Reed was complicated because no one could ever be sure which version of him was going to appear in any situation. Anderson's own mutability held an allure for Reed because of the control she was capable of exerting over it. It would not be surprising if Reed himself had occasionally been shaken by his unpredictable responses to people and situations. Anderson's placid demeanor, her Buddhist detachment, served as a kind of model for him, something to aspire to.

Anderson is also the subject of "Adventurer," the title a reference to not only her intellectual daring but her willingness to put herself in physically dangerous situations in pursuit of spiritual knowledge. The song moves forward with rapid rhythmic propulsion and a profusion of words, as if Reed is racing both to say everything he wants to say about Anderson and also to quell his anxiety over her behavior. He admires her adventurousness, but fears for her physical safety and feels abandoned by her. He recognizes that, artistically, he is an adventurer as well, and that her travel, like his own, is, in an unusual phrase for a song lyric, "a necessary adjunct to what we both do." But he is afraid of losing her. Her leaving is like "splitting up the atom, splitting up what once was, splitting up the essence." A woman with her own serious ambitions and goals, Anderson was the least compliant of any of Reed's lovers. She met Reed as an equal and steadfastly maintained that status, regardless of whatever fears of abandonment that might awaken in him. Her independence was not designed or intended to unsettle him, but if it occasionally did, that did not dissuade her from exercising it.

The anxiety underlying Reed's love for Anderson manifests itself in other songs on *Set the Twilight Reel-*

ing. On "NYC Man," Reed assumes the tough guy posture of the New York native, but turns the song into a kind of plea for honesty and directness. If his new lover doesn't want him, she doesn't need to lie or pretend, the song says. As a "New York City man," the singer wants her to tell it like it is. All she has to do is "say 'Go' and I am gone," he asserts. But as always with Reed, vulnerability underlies the hard posture of the song. A quick, uncomplicated ending is preferable only because dragging it out would make it even more painful. "Hang On to Your Emotions" echoes "Hang On to Your Ego," the early title of the Beach Boys song "I Know There's an Answer," cowritten by Brian Wilson, one of Reed's idols. Reed's song seems to be addressed to Anderson, who sings background on the track. He confesses the deep self-loathing within him, the "demagogue" inside his head, the feral "cat" and rabid "rat" who occupy his mind and tear him apart for his "litany of failures." Only the sound of his "lover's breath" allows him to free himself from those feelings and "let go." It's a powerful statement of how Reed looked to his lovers—specifically Anderson, in this case—for a kind of salvation, for the absolution of his sins.

Reed treats his romance with Anderson again on "Hookywooky." His desire to "hookywooky" with her means exactly what you think it does, and it's hilarious to hear Reed, who never backed off from describing the most extreme sex acts in unvarnished detail, use a childish euphemism to describe sex with his girl-friend. The song's upbeat rock-and-roll groove under-scores its playful tone, as Reed once again compares his black-and-white thinking to Anderson's open-mindedness. He describes how "civilized" she is, how she remains friends with all her former lovers — as opposed to him ("When things / End for me, they end"). He allows that he could "learn a lot" from her about "people, plants, and relationships" and "how not to get hurt." Finally, he wonders if, should he adopt Anderson's easygoing approach to life, he wouldn't so much want to throw her ex-lovers off the roof of her building and watch them be crushed "under the wheels of a car on Canal Street."

The outlier on the album is "Sex with Your Parents (Motherfucker) Part II," which Reed recorded live in the studio. It's a furious, obscenity-laced screed against right-wing moralizing that mentions Robert Dole, the Republican candidate for the presidency in 1996, by name. Understandably, Reed took the culture wars of the late eighties and nineties personally. He viewed them as driven by the basest hypocrisy, and that's the explicit tone of "Sex with Your Parents." The song posits that Republicans' hatred of sexuality in art derives from their own Oedipal desires and crimes. It's not a subtle critique, but Reed was writing out of fury and perhaps fear that his own work would, once again, be targeted by the Right. As if to start that fight rather than wait for his opponents to attack, Reed unleashed a song that he was certain would incite controversy. The only problem was that no one noticed.

Rolling Stone dependably awarded the album four stars. But typically, it did not sell well, and typically, Reed blamed his record company. Warner Bros. released "Adventurer," Reed's hymn to Laurie Anderson, as the first promotional track to radio, and it failed to perform. Reed was fired up by "Sex with Your Parents" and was determined to have it released both as a way to reshape the conversation about the Republican Right and to ignite interest in *Set the Twilight Reeling*. The suggestion did not go over well. "I was talking to Lou somewhat regularly on the phone at the time," Jeff Gold recalled, "and I had made the big mistake of giving him my home number, which record executives typically don't do because you want to have some semblance of a homelife. In 1996, I had an eight-year-old daughter and a four-year-old daughter, and, to the degree that I could, my weekends were devoted to hanging out with them. I vividly remember my wife coming into the backyard where I was playing with my daughters and saying, 'Lou Reed is on the phone for you.' My reaction was, 'Oh, fuck! Why is he calling me on a Sunday afternoon?' At that point, we were six years into working with him, so I knew it couldn't be good news."

It turned out that Reed had a promotional idea for

his album that could not wait until Monday. "He was pissed off because radio wasn't embracing his record, and he wanted us to send out 'Sex with Your Parents' to all of radio with a copy of the First Amendment," Gold said. "He might have wanted to have that song released first, and we had said, 'Look, nobody's going to play that.' So Lou's pushback was, 'Fuck them, I'm going to give them the real message of this record.' There was no scenario where radio was going to get behind that record, and rubbing shit in their face is not a way to advance your cause. He was really fucking pissed. And I don't think he thought for a quarter of a second, 'I'm calling this guy at home on a Sunday. Maybe that's not the right time.' Unfortunately, those experiences become the ones you remember about an artist."

LOU REED DEDICATED THE song "Finish Line" on *Set the Twilight Reeling* to Sterling Morrison, who died of non-Hodgkin's lymphoma on August 30, 1995, one day after his fifty-third birthday; he had been diagnosed with the disease in 1994. The song does not explicitly refer to Morrison, but the notion of "heading for the finish line" suggests the approach of mortality, the subject that, understandably, would always come to Reed's creative mind whenever someone who had been close to him died. Reed had trouble viewing virtually any experience except in terms of himself, and death, in particular, was difficult for him to see in any objective way. He understood that, given his self-destructive habits over many years, luck alone had shielded him from an early death ("I should have been dead a thousand times," he said when discussing the song at one point), so the passing of others affected him powerfully. And the more complicated his relationship had been during the dead person's lifetime, the more his ambivalent emotions transformed into openhearted generosity.

According to Martha Morrison, Sterling's wife, Reed stayed alert to Sterling's condition once he was diagnosed, and kept in close touch. "Lou was tuned in the whole time Sterling was sick," Martha said. "He came to the house, and Sterling was at the Albany Medical Center for a long time, and Lou sent him flowers there, and they talked on the phone." In a tribute to Morrison that he wrote for the *New York Times* at the end of 1995, Reed warmly recalled his friend and bandmate. He talked about visiting Morrison in Poughkeepsie, traveling there by train, and meeting up with Maureen Tucker at the Morrisons' home. Morrison's health had deteriorated, and Reed described the "extreme gauntness of his once-muscular physique. He was bald, with nothing but skin over bone. But his eyes. His eyes were as alert and clear as any eyes I've seen in this world." Reed held Morrison's hand as they spoke. They did not discuss Morrison's condition. In his conclusion, Reed called Morrison "the warrior heart of the Velvet Underground."

A MONTH BEFORE THE release of *Set the Twilight Reeling,* the Velvet Underground was inducted into the Rock and Roll Hall of Fame in a ceremony held at the Waldorf Astoria in New York. It was an outrage, of course, that the Velvets had not been inducted when they had first become eligible, in 1992, but the journalists, musicians, producers, and record company executives who constituted the voting rolls of the Rock Hall took a while to move beyond the more obvious classic rock heroes that had entered earlier. Though it meant a great deal to the group's members to be inducted, Reed, in particular, assumed a don't-give-a-fuck posture as they took the stage to accept their induction. Reed spoke first, saying only, "I'd like to thank all the people who worked so hard to get us in. And I just wanted to say how much we regret that our friend and fellow musician Sterling Morrison couldn't be with us." Maureen Tucker said that she was "proud and honored," and she, too, expressed her sadness over Morrison's death.

Only Cale took the opportunity to try to make a statement and to find a larger meaning in the honor the band was receiving. First, he pointedly mentioned the contributions made by two of the band's collaborators who had gone unmentioned by Reed and Tucker. "This, of course, is shared by three other people," he began, as he held the award in his hand: "Sterling, Nico, and Andy." Then he went on to say, "This event makes an astonishing point to all the young musicians in the world: that sales are not the be-all and end-all of rock and roll. And everyone should be encouraged.... Inspiration and artistic freedom is the cornerstone of rock and roll." Martha Morrison accepted on Sterling's behalf and sweetly acknowledged that he very much "wanted to be in the Hall—and I know he would have loved this party."

The band members did not seem especially comfortable with one another, and, the sour taste of their European reunion still in their mouths, they performed only one song together. Taking advantage of their last bit of emotional common ground, they had composed a ballad in honor of Sterling Morrison titled "Last Night I Said Goodbye to My Friend." It has almost a doo-wop feel, though Cale's eloquent piano part elevates the song above any specific genre. Reed, Cale, and Tucker all share the vocals, but despite the sincerity of the feelings behind it, the song is a throwaway. But that was the best the trio could do under the circumstances. It was the last song the Velvet Underground would ever play together.

23

SADLY LISTENING

IN 1996, LOU REED embarked on a collaboration with avant-garde director and set designer Robert Wilson and novelist and playwright Darryl Pinckney. Titled *Time Rocker,* the production was the third in a trilogy that Wilson had begun with songwriter Tom Waits; the first two productions were *The Black Rider: The Casting of the Magic Bullets* (with a text by William Burroughs), based on a nineteenth-century German ghost story, and *Alice,* based on Lewis Carroll's *Alice's Adventures in Wonderland. Time Rocker* is based, very loosely, on H. G. Wells's *The Time Machine,* which, when it was published in 1895, introduced the concept of the time machine and popularized the notion of time travel.

Collaborating with Wilson, a highly prestigious figure in the world of experimental theater, was another important step in Reed's refinement of his identity as an artist. Best known for his work with Philip Glass on the groundbreaking 1976 opera *Einstein on the Beach,* Wilson had also worked with Laurie Anderson, deepening Reed's connection to the celebrated underground art scene in which she was a central figure. Reed wrote new songs for *Time Rocker,* some of which, like "Turning Time Around," appeared on his own albums later, and he also repurposed songs, like "Cremation" from *Magic and Loss.* Though their collaboration would continue and they worked together without the cataclysmic disruptions that so often afflicted Reed's partnerships, he and Wilson were not an ideal match. Whereas Wilson was a surrealist whose work strived for a nonlinear associative power, Reed was at his best when he was as direct and concise as possible. In *Time Rocker,* Wilson took the opportunity to unhinge Wells's characters from chronology, exploring not so much the trajectories of their lives as the mysteries of time itself, both in the external world and in the depths of our consciousness. While Reed's songs have their own beauty and power, they work toward entirely different ends.

After its debut at the Thalia Theater in Hamburg, which had commissioned it, *Time Rocker* ran for ten performances at Brooklyn Academy of Music, where it was staged by the same theater company that had performed it in Germany. The performers spoke German, with translations provided in superscript, though Reed's songs were sung in English. Reviewing the show in the *New York Times,* Jon Pareles offered a smart critique that surely took the self-consciously avant-garde collaborators by surprise. He deftly pointed out that "with straightforward rock songs backing brief, abstract scenes, *Time Rocker* bumps into unexpected competition: music video. Mr. Wilson's style of theater, once startling, is now available day and night on cable. *Time Rocker* ends up uncomfortably close to late-night MTV: an entertaining miscellany with striking effects and a sentimental heart."

REED'S NEXT ALBUM, *ECSTASY,* released on April 4, 2000, would turn out to be his last major solo effort without collaborators. By this point, Reed's commercial fortunes had dwindled, and as one consequence, he continued to explore artistic outlets outside rock and roll. That, of course, corresponded nicely with the conception of himself that he had forged in the late eighties, when his ambitions were primarily literary and his means were concept albums. Now, with his relationship with Laurie Anderson and collaboration with Robert Wilson, his artistic identity had expanded. It would expand further in the years to come.

Ecstasy hit with uncompromising power. Reed and Mike Rathke cranked up their guitars and flooded the album with roaring distortion and feedback. The horns that played on a number of tracks, along with Jane Scarpantoni's cello and Laurie Anderson's electric violin, provided even deeper levels of texture. The horn arrangements recall Reed's fascination with Otis Redding and the Stax/Volt sound, adding melodic punch and soulfulness to the hurricane of noise on the album.

The album's cover art — photographic self-portraits from the shoulders up — portrays Reed with facial expressions that recall Mantegna's portraits of St. Sebastian or Bernini's sculpture *The Ecstasy of St. Teresa* (note its title). As in those classic works, Reed looks as if he is undergoing an exquisite, orgasmic torture, a mixture of love and pain. (Another possible inspiration is Andy Warhol's 1964 silent film *Blow Job,* in which the camera focuses on a young man's face, presumably, given the title, as someone off camera performs oral sex on him.) The assumption in those works that the agony has both a spiritual source and a spiritual goal corresponds nicely with Reed's vision of the interplay between forbidden lust and transcendence.

Ecstasy explores the torrent of feelings — jealousy, boredom, dependence, lust for others — that arise in nearly every long-standing relationship. Gone are the sweet hymns to Anderson as the epitome of female perfection. Replacing that sweetness, in a song like "Paranoia Key of E," is a mutual wariness, a desperate puzzling out of why things have gotten so complicated and never seem to resolve. The "E" of the title recalls the first letter of the album's title, a reference to both the drug ecstasy and the feeling of exultation that true love is expected to deliver. The conflation of those two notions suggests that the euphoric effects of love may be no more reliable—and may last no longer—than the speedy psychedelic high that the drug provides. "It's all downhill after the first kiss," Reed sings on "Modern Dance," a song that registers confusion at the contemporary ways of love, in which couples drift together and then apart, unmoored from the certainties that grounded relationships in the past. Given Reed's dependency issues, such laissez-faire attitudes—far more characteristic of Anderson than of him—were deeply unsettling. The title track explores that theme further. Ecstasy comes and goes, raising the singer's hopes but then disappearing. It continually eludes the singer, who, like Reed, harbors a fear of abandonment and who, in desperate need of connection, laments, "I couldn't hold you close... / I couldn't become you."

Two songs on the album return Reed to the back alleys, after-hours clubs, and dockside trysts that had been part of his life for so long. "Rock Minuet" sounds as if it could have appeared on *Street Hassle,* the contrasting words of its title telegraphing the song's cool elevation of the grim sexual tableaux it describes. Its arrangement is eerily formal, guitars wailing and feeding back over a simple, elegant melody enhanced by Anderson's electric violin. Even more so than usual, Reed's vocal is a dispassionate recitative as he chronicles a Boschean world of anonymous, sadomasochistic sex and thrill-seeking violence. As is so often true when Reed enters this subterranean realm, Oedipal desires and rivalries occupy the ninth circle of his forbidden erotic phantasmagoria. He conjures a charged primal scene with "his mother on all fours and his father behind," while fantasizing that "if he murdered his father he thought he'd become whole." A gay pickup turns ugly as one man draws a knife and "thought of his father" as he slices the other man's throat. As the album posits the potential disintegration of a marriage, "Rock Minuet" limns the netherworld that waits as an alternative, as alluring as it is terrifying.

"Like a Possum" is one of the most compelling tracks that Reed ever recorded. At more than eighteen minutes, it's certainly the longest, outstripping even the Velvet Underground's epic studio version of "Sister Ray" by half a minute or so. The title suggests the expression "playing possum," a reference to that animal's strategy of lying low, playing dead, to confuse predators and avoid attacks. But the possum is perfectly capable of coming to life and striking back, as the mature, settled Lou is capable of exploding into the thunder of *Ecstasy* and this song in particular. Two lines occupy the emotional center of the song: "I got a hole in my heart the size of a truck / It won't be filled by a one-night fuck." That yearning for stability, and the hope that love can somehow help to fill the void within him, is accompanied, as always with Reed, by the fear that he will be abandoned, that his lover will forsake him for another. He mentions his ever-shifting sense of who he is, the "different selves who cancel out one another," and refers, however obliquely, to his bisexuality: "One likes muscles, oil, and dirt / And the other likes the women with the butt that hurts." The oil and dirt refer to the rawness of the sexual playground into which the docks and the empty trucks parked there transform overnight, as well as the motorcycles he loved. Smoking crack, used condoms, whores, shooting drugs, and anonymous blow jobs all make appearances in the song—a roaring, nightmarish inferno of what awaits him if he cannot manage to fill that hole in his heart.

Ecstasy stands as a searing examination of life in an unnervingly complex, adult relationship—particularly for someone whose fears and insecurities lay as deep as Reed's. Typically, Reed stayed away from such subjects when discussing the album, retreating, as always, into talking about its sound. Speaking about "Like a Possum," he said, "Every night, when the recording sessions were over and everybody would leave the studio, I'd grab the tapes with the guitars we'd recorded and listen to them at home. For hours at night, I'd listen to those guitars in all their eternal beauty. Of course, I listened to them loud. As loud as it can get. And I found peace." The one personal point he conceded was in response to a question about his line that he was "the only one left standing"—which he admitted alluded, in part, to the AIDS crisis. "I've put my dick in every hole available," he said. "But in a way, I haven't lived a different life compared to many others. I mean, most of us have experiences with drugs, many of us smoke and drink too much. I am no different except for the fact that I have always been in the limelight."

Ecstasy ended Reed's solo career on an extremely strong note, even if it failed to generate much attention, either critically or commercially. Despite the visibility he enjoyed with Laurie Anderson as part of New York's cultural elite, he had become something of a museum piece, more admired than listened to. It was a confusing time for him. His only regret, he said, was that he had to promote his work personally—"Album after album, year after year. Maybe for my next record I should record one interview that you could access only via a phone number: 'For questions about the new album, press one. For questions about the Velvet

Underground and Nico, press two. For questions about my private life and other gossip, press three—and hang the fuck up.'"

Hal Willner, who coproduced *Ecstasy* with Reed, was jolted by the album's commercial failure. "To this day, I have never worked harder on a record," Willner said. "He wrote those songs and he woodshedded. We did that whole thing where we went and listened to eighteen guitars and changed the pickups and changed the amps. I just love that record. And it got a great reaction. And then nothing. Nothing. It freaked me out, and I think it broke his heart because he never really wrote another record after that. That was the last, shall we say, proper Lou Reed record."

Willner would go on to become, in his description, Tonto to Reed's Lone Ranger. They developed a working relationship—and a personal closeness—that Willner thought of as a traditional artist-producer bond, though it was much deeper than that. They had come a long way from when Willner first approached Reed years earlier about contributing to one of the conceptual projects he was a master at organizing, this one devoted to the music of Kurt Weill. Titled *Lost in the Stars,* the compilation came out in 1985 and features performances by Sting, Van Dyke Parks, Marianne Faithfull, and Carla Bley, along with Reed's sprightly reading of "September Song." When, in their first telephone conversation, Willner suggested that Reed perform the song, Reed slammed the phone down. But Reed thought about it and, a short while later, called Willner back, and the two men began discussing how Reed's participation in the project—and his performance of the song—might work. "So you're a real producer," Reed joked at the end of the conversation, a compliment that forged a connection between the two men that would last until the end of Reed's life.

Of course, the relationship was not always smooth sailing. As Reed had in the past, Willner had serious problems with substance abuse. At one point, he had accidentally set fire to his apartment, and Reed paid to send his possessions to storage. Reed had asked Willner to do some work on *Set the Twilight Reeling,* but Willner was in no condition to do it. "I was at the end of my chemical era," he said. He did go see Reed perform at the Beacon in 1997, and the two men hung out together and had a great time. Later, Willner joined Reed as Reed was working on some songs, and afterward, Reed called him. "You're not right," Reed said, implying that Willner was still using drugs and that, as a consequence, Reed couldn't be around him. "He kind of wrote me off," Willner said. "He talked about the money he had invested in me, and he was totally right. I wasn't right. I don't know how he picked that up—that I was still going to have some adventures. I was freaked out. I went and paid him the money he had invested in me. Then we didn't talk for two years."

As Reed began working on *Ecstasy*, he thought about Willner again. Fernando Saunders, Reed's bassist, called Willner and told him that Reed had been asking about him. Willner ran into Reed at the Knitting Factory, a downtown club, and "he was just hugs. He looked at me and said, 'You're great. You know, I don't like many people. Please, let's stay friends.' That probably has a lot to do with how I got through that difficult time. Then he asked me to work with him on *Ecstasy*." The two men would be in continual contact, working together professionally and socializing constantly. Like so many of the people close to Reed, Willner noted his friend's fear of isolation. "It's weird not getting those phone calls," Willner said after Reed's death. "He hated being alone, so he would always be in touch. Sometimes it would be scary, because you'd come back from a trip, and I would wait a few days before calling him, because the minute you did, he'd be like, 'Coming out to the movie at eleven tonight? What else are you doing?' He would go do anything with you — movies, restaurants."

Willner understood the complaint about Reed's brusqueness — recall that Reed slammed the phone down on their first conversation. "Look, Lou could be short with people," Willner said. But he believed that Reed's behavior had to be seen in the context of the amount of contact that artists like him have coming at them every day, particularly since Reed made a point of living his life in New York as openly as possible. That made him seem accessible, even though he wasn't. "People would go, 'I saw Lou Reed on the street when I went to New York, and I went up to him and he was an asshole,'" Willner said. "I would say, 'Was he a bigger asshole than Bob Dylan was to you?' 'Oh, I've never seen Bob Dylan.' Right. 'What about Miles Davis—was he nice to you?' Lou was just out there; he was on the street. How would you like people coming up to you going, 'Oh, Lou, you changed my life'? What the fuck do you tell them?...Who knows what it's like to be Lou Reed?"

"Lou was difficult," Willner concluded. "Any artist is difficult to live with....But if he liked you, I've never met a more generous person. He was sentimental about birthdays. If you were sick, he'd come see you every fucking day. He protected all his friends. It was a small circle that saw that side of him, but it was just unbelievable."

LIKE MANY WHO WERE so geographically close to what would become known as Ground Zero—Reed lived perhaps a mile uptown from the World Trade Center—on the morning of September 11, 2001, he watched the towers burn and crumble from the roof of his building, and witnessed people leaping off to their deaths. Afterward, he struggled to make sense of the attacks and, as many people did, succumbed to some of the urban legends that quickly sprang up after the events of that day. He told me that he had heard about a Muslim family on Long Island that had warned its neighbors to stay out of Manhattan that Tuesday. After issuing their warning, Reed said, the family members mysteriously abandoned their home, never to be heard from again. There were many versions of that story, an expression of the fear that repeatedly surfaces in America that outsiders among us are secretly plotting our destruction while simultaneously enjoying the pleasures of suburban life. Reed delivered the story, however, with characteristic intensity, his eyes blazing. He clearly had no doubt that the story was true. He also described a tense confrontation he and a friend had had with a Muslim cabdriver as they dropped off donations of clothing for the victims and responders at Ground Zero.

In another sign of Reed's growing prominence on the New York cultural scene, he was asked to contribute to a theme issue of the *New York Times Magazine* titled "Beginnings: An Issue About the Next New York." The issue appeared in the November 11, 2001, Sunday *New York Times,* and it consisted of contributions from prominent New Yorkers about the state of the city and the direction of its future in the wake of the 9/11 attacks. Other contributors included Oliver

Sacks, Robert Frank, and Paul Auster. Reed contributed a poem titled "Laurie Sadly Listening," about his
watching the towers burn from his rooftop without
her. He describes the scene as a kind of holocaust
("Incinerated flesh repelling") and his sense that the
world's possibilities had suddenly evaporated: "And I
had thought a beautiful / Season was / Upon us." On
9/11, he and Anderson had been unable to communicate because phones didn't work after the attacks, and
as would so often be the case, her absence became the
subject of his writing. He imagines her "sadly listening" to what he is describing, though he is unable to
reach her. Like everyone who was separated from loved
ones on that grim day, he wants her to know how
much he missed her: "Laurie if you're sadly listening /
Know one thing above all others / You were all I really
thought of / As the TV blared the screaming / The
deathlike snowflakes / Sirens screaming / All I wished
was you to be holding."

In 2000, Reed had begun his second collaboration
with Robert Wilson. Once again commissioned by and
originally staged at the Thalia Theater in Hamburg,
POEtry was devoted to the work of Edgar Allan Poe, a
writer singularly appropriate for Reed. Billed as a rock
opera, the show made its New York debut at the Brooklyn Academy of Music in December of 2001, three
months after 9/11. As devastating as the attacks were,

in aesthetic terms, it seemed a perfect moment for both Reed and Poe. The city was reeling, balanced precariously on a razor's edge, and the sense of dread that permeates so much of Poe's writing simply felt like the psychic waters that all New Yorkers were swimming in, as Reed understood. But beyond its thematic relationship to 9/11, Poe's writing lives in the same emotional terrain as Reed's. Stylistically, the two men could not have been more different. Poe loved elaborate, Latinate words, many of them archaic even at the time he was using them, almost as if he were translating English into another highly personal, emotionally charged language. His rolling rhythms and relentless repetitions channel an intense musicality, but they were designed to make his words seem strange, even frightening, like the incantations of a dark religion. Reed, on the other hand, aspired to a hard-boiled concision, a language that yields nothing to the extreme behavior he often described. His words were meant to be as stoic and nonjudgmental as his singing, cool, intractable, and removed, a challenge to the listener to sustain a similar posture in the face of such outrages.

But in the themes Reed and Poe explored, the two men could hardly have been more alike. Guilt, obsession, violence, and self-destruction run through the veins of both bodies of work. Predictably, Reed was especially gripped by the 1845 short story "The Imp of the Perverse," in which Poe wonders why we are drawn to actions that are damaging to us—not despite the fact that they're damaging but precisely *because* they are. It's what Joseph Conrad later called the "fascination of the abomination," a phrase that could arguably sum up the entirety of Reed's work. Writing about his attraction to Poe and his appropriateness to the turn of the twenty-first century, Reed said, "Obsessions, paranoia, willful acts of self-destruction surround us constantly. Though we age, we still hear the cries of those for whom the attraction to mournful chaos is monumental. . . . Who am I? Why am I drawn to do what I should not? I have wrestled with this thought innumerable times: the impulse of destructive desire—the desire for self-mortification." A fascination with decay—the source of the term "decadence"—is another obsession Poe and Reed shared. The belief that there is some kind of original sin, some corruption at life's core, haunted both men, and rendered Poe an ideal subject for Reed.

Just over a year after the performance at BAM, Reed released *The Raven,* an audio version of the theater performance, as a double CD. (A single-CD version was also available for less hearty fans.) Here was one of Reed's strategies for avoiding what Willner called a "proper Lou Reed record" after the heartbreaking experience of *Ecstasy.* Still, *The Raven* is an extraordinary collection. It includes readings of Poe's work and Reed's songs, notably a somber reworking of "The Bed" from

Berlin and a strangulated performance of "Perfect Day" by the sexually ambiguous singer Antony Hegarty, whom Reed had taken under his wing, like a younger version of Little Jimmy Scott. David Bowie, Willem Dafoe, Elizabeth Ashley, Amanda Plummer, Ornette Coleman, Steve Buscemi, Kate and Anna McGarrigle, and, of course, Laurie Anderson are just a few of the artists who participated in the project.

Perhaps the most controversial aspect of *The Raven* was Reed's decision to rewrite some of Poe's work and add his own words to it. It seems like a shockingly arrogant move—and, in part, it was—but Reed did it with a kind of modesty, if with mixed results. As he was working on *POEtry,* he was struck by how often Poe's ornate word choices sent him to the dictionary, and he was concerned that audiences wouldn't be able to properly follow the language without some help. In that sense, the desire to adapt Poe was a pop decision, though Reed never would have thought of it in these terms. In this relatively high art context of a classic American writer reinterpreted by world-class actors and musicians, Reed could allow himself to do to Poe what he would never permit to be done to his own songs, despite decades of urgings by record executives.

"I saw it as a can't-win situation," Reed told the *New York Times.* "I knew people would say, 'How dare he rewrite Poe?' But I thought, here's the opportunity of a lifetime for real fun: to combine the kind of lyricism that he has into a flexible rock format. I really like my version of it. It's accessible, among other things. And I felt I was in league with the master.... Particularly now, with the anxiety and everything else that's permeating our lives right now." In that same conversation, Reed offered one of his more articulate, least defensive and evasive explanations for his obsession with sound and technology. "I've spent the better part of my life, the way a great saxophonist will try to find the perfect reed or a violinist will look for the perfect violin," attempting to identify "the best tube, the best speaker, the cone, the wood, the string, the pickup, on and on and on." If sound was Reed's chosen method of conveying meaning, then the sound had to be perfect.

24

THIS IS TODAY

REED HAD BEEN PRACTICING tai chi since the early eighties with a master known as Leung Shum, with whom he worked for fifteen years, until Shum retired. It was part of Reed's recovery, a way for him to integrate his physical, emotional, and spiritual health. It tied in nicely with some of the spiritual concerns that had always been part of his life, including his interest in the possibility of the world beyond. Even as Reed's writing concentrated so fiercely on the here and now, the impulse toward redemption always wove through it. Spiritual discipline provided a focus strong enough to keep his attention away from more dangerous attractions.

Tai chi works on the principle of balance, but most of the practitioners in the United States concentrate on the more sensitive side of the discipline. However, Ren GuangYi, the tai chi master with whom Reed began studying after Shum retired, specialized in the Chen style, which is far more explosive and which, for a time, was thought to have become extinct, part of a knowledge system that had been lost. For Reed, encountering Master Ren was a revelation. In Ren's practice, Reed's rock-and-roll side—his love of noise and feedback, his affection for motorcycles and speed, his fascination with brutality and violence—found expression, and he became a devoted practitioner and a student of Ren's. Tai chi is about the relationship of polarities and extremes, and in Master Ren, Reed found an ideal guide to a wild side he had never realized existed in the discipline.

"He combines the very beautiful form, the great control, the focus, and a really, truly remarkable *fajing* [explosive power]," Reed said about Master Ren. "When I saw that combination of grace and power, the fast and the soft, the yin and the yang, that's what I'd been looking for.... From the minute I saw Master Ren do *fajing*, I thought, I will study this forever." When one thinks about the contradictions that battled within Reed his entire life, the appeal of a discipline that allowed profound expression to all of it—as rock and roll did—becomes apparent.

When Reed first approached him, Master Ren, a bit like Laurie Anderson in this way, had no idea who he was. "At the beginning, I didn't know his music," Ren said. "I was talking to a friend and I said I was teaching a musician now, his name was Reed. Later he came and said to me, 'Do you mean Lou Reed?' I said yes. He said, 'Are you kidding?' I said, 'I'm not kidding.' He says, 'Wow, he's very, very famous!' . . . After I tell people I teach Lou Reed tai chi, they don't believe me."

Reed took Master Ren on the road with him, exposing audiences across the United States and Europe to the master's deft movements as Reed and his band performed, lending his songs an extraordinary interpretive element, an intense physicality, and an even more complex spiritual dimension. Reed also performed a riveting version of "Sunday Morning" on *Late Night with David Letterman* accompanied by Master Ren.

For his own practice, or "bodywork," as he liked to call it, Reed composed music that he eventually released in 2007 as *Hudson River Wind Meditations*. "I had made it for myself," Reed explained. "Just for a number of different uses and meditation bodywork, tai chi. And I would also just leave it on all day . . . because it absorbs the outside sounds that might be irritating otherwise. . . . People started saying to me, 'Can I have a copy of that?' 'Can you put that music on?' . . . We just put the music out on the theory that you probably have your own meditation you're doing, and this is a great music to do it to, rather than me putting the voice on it."

Reed and Laurie Anderson also studied meditation with Yongey Mingyur Rinpoche, a renowned master of Tibetan Buddhism. Rinpoche was born in Nepal and directed the Tergar Meditation Community, an international network of meditation groups. He was a successful author and a quiet evangelist for the benefits of meditation. He encouraged his students to accept the essential nature of suffering in every life, but to achieve a detachment from it as well. That's a central tenet of Buddhism, of course, but Rinpoche expressed it with an intelligence and casualness that both charmed and encouraged his followers. Anderson, in particular, became an ardent devotee of Rinpoche. She would often quote his recommendation that in difficult times, it is important to feel sad without being sad. Such koan-like expressions are similar to the detached observations Anderson would make in the surreal narrative monologues that were such a central element of her work. But Reed, too, was quite taken by Rinpoche. No doubt Rinpoche's easy ability to relinquish control of experience held a compelling allure for Reed, who, for better or worse, always gripped his life so tightly. Reed jumped in feetfirst after meeting Rinpoche, and looked up to him uncritically, as he did with all the various guides who came into — and eventually left —

his life. "He's just wonderful and I love him," Reed said. "I think of him as a friend who, for whatever reason, teaches me things. If I could learn one-thousandth of what he knows in my time left, that's what I want." Rinpoche's teachings, like those of Master Ren, would remain an important aspect of Reed's life until his death.

SUSAN FELDMAN, THE ARTISTIC director of St. Ann's Warehouse, had been approaching Reed over the years about staging a version of *Berlin*, but Reed had never consented. Friends, too, including Julian Schnabel, had also encouraged him to do it, professing that *Berlin* was his favorite of Reed's albums. "This record was the embodiment of love's dark sisters: jealousy, rage, and loss," Schnabel said. "It may be the most romantic record ever made." Reed always resisted the suggestions, however. He preferred to move on to new projects, and the prospect of revisiting *Berlin* was painful. The failure of his and producer Bob Ezrin's plan for some kind of dramatic staging of *Berlin*, their "movie for the mind," had been a signal disappointment decades earlier. The negative reviews didn't help.

As 2006 approached, however, and he did not have any major new projects lined up, Reed decided to pursue Feldman's suggestion. Before he heard her urgings, "I couldn't imagine that anyone would want to do it," Reed said. "I had put *Berlin* out of my mind. It was disappointing, what happened to it, and I didn't want to go through all that again." In December of 2006, Reed performed *Berlin* in full for five nights at St. Ann's Warehouse. He had assembled an extraordinary band for the performances, including Steve Hunter (who played on the original album) on guitar, Fernando Saunders on bass, Rob Wasserman on double bass, Rupert Christie on keyboards, Tony "Thunder" Smith on drums, and Sharon Jones and Antony Hegarty on backing vocals. In addition, a horn and string section joined the group, along with a choir, Brooklyn Youth Chorus. Hal Willner oversaw musical direction on the project, along with Bob Ezrin. Ezrin appeared onstage conducting the musicians while wearing a white lab coat with "Berlin" written vertically on the back in large capital letters. Julian Schnabel, who had previously told Reed he wanted to make a movie of *Berlin,* designed sets for the shows and filmed them. During the performances, Reed fully inhabited the songs, creating intense emotional drama out of the grim, destructive story of Jim and Caroline, the two doomed speed addicts at the heart of the album.

The more than three decades that had passed since its original release served the album well. No one was shocked any longer by the descent of Jim and Caroline into violence and suicide; debates about lyrical content and the extremes that hip-hop and heavy metal had gone on to explore made the hand-wringing over *Berlin* seem silly. Reed, too, had continued to push boundaries in his own work, and the stature that he had achieved since the early seventies made the revival of *Berlin* seem like just another honor that a great artist deserved as he neared old age. At around this time, veteran artists began to explore their back catalogs for albums that fans would like to see performed in their entirety. That had rarely been done in the past, though of course Reed had done it with both *New York* and *Songs for Drella*. For many artists, it had become a way to freshen up their live performances, which had increasingly become economically important as CD sales began to decline. Also, as rock artists entered their sixties, an age at which it had once seemed inconceivable that they would still be performing, they became concerned about their legacy. Despite his protestations to the contrary, Reed had been thinking about his legacy from the time of the first Velvet Underground album. The commercial failures of *Set the Twilight Reeling* and *Ecstasy* made the prospect of a new album less enticing. For all those reasons, performing *Berlin* was something of an ideal project.

While he would never admit it, Reed regarded the renewed interest in the album as a vindication. When one writer asked him about *Rolling Stone*'s positive review of the Brooklyn shows ("The triumph was all

Reed's, and too long in coming"), Reed brushed it aside. "*Rolling Stone*? Who cares?" he said. "That's not who I'm writing for." In another interview, he even downplayed the personal importance of *Berlin*. "It was just another of my albums that didn't sell," he said. Hal Willner had a sense of Reed's true feelings. Reed took *Berlin* on tour, and one stop was the Royal Albert Hall in London. Reed asked Willner to go on stage first to say a few words. "I go out and I was like, 'Turn your cell phones off, please, and no flash photography,'" Willner recalled. "But then I just look around and it's the Royal Albert Hall. It was like one of those old Max Fleischer cartoons: you look out into the audience and everybody's famous. There's Peter Gabriel. There's Annie Lennox. There's Rachel Weisz and Daniel Craig. So out of nowhere I say, 'Here's some words none of us ever thought we'd hear, and I get to say them: ladies and gentlemen, now at Royal Albert Hall, Lou Reed's *Berlin*.' And Lou just bounded onto that stage. What a moment of validation. It was just encouraging in every way that he got to see that."

For the shows, Julian Schnabel designed a set that evoked the "greenish walls" that Reed mentions when describing Caroline's room in the song "Lady Day." Green also evokes the jealousy at the heart of the album's songs—it was the album's central theme, in Reed's view—as well as the cirrhotic tinge that alcohol and methedrine use can lead to. Video projected onto the wall included footage shot by Schnabel's daughter Lola, who was twenty-five at the time. Lola's scenes featured the French actress Emmanuelle Seigner in the role of Caroline, though the footage is more impressionistic than literal, designed to convey the unsettling feel of the album rather than simply depict the scenarios the songs describe.

In addition to the entire *Berlin* album, Reed performed three other songs: "Sweet Jane," "Candy Says," and "Rock Minuet," selections than can be read as commentaries on the themes of *Berlin*. The couple in "Sweet Jane" reflect an alternate reality, one as idealistic as *Berlin* is nihilistic. Like Caroline, Candy in "Candy Says"—based on Candy Darling, the most gorgeous drag queen on the Warhol Factory scene—lives in an environment that is going to destroy her. Her profound alienation from herself ("I've come to hate my body / And all that it requires in this world") is one source of her anguish. What would now be called her gender dysphoria results in a self-loathing that makes her desperate to escape her life. Antony Hegarty provided the lead vocal on "Candy Says," and his otherworldly voice, simultaneously haunting and somehow reassuring, beautifully evokes Candy's yearning for a more accepting world. Hegarty's voice rises on "What do you think I'd see / If I could walk away from me?" and that eerie sense of emotional disassociation comes across chillingly, as does the poignancy of the feelings that motivate it. It's a spellbinding performance. (Hegarty would eventually identify as female and take the name Anohni.)

Reed performed "Rock Minuet" at the specific request of Schnabel; it is one of Reed's last bloodcurdling documentations of New York's sexual demimonde and one of Schnabel's favorite songs. In the unlikely event that anyone present might miss the connection, images of Reed from the midseventies, blond and skeletal, appeared in the video playing behind him, an eloquent evocation of a man haunted by his own past. Among the song's most explicit lyrics are Reed's descriptions of a Freudian primal scene and his patricidal rage. What rendered the lyrics particularly trenchant at this performance was the fact that Reed's mother was in the audience. As with all the other songs he sang that evening, Reed delivered "Rock Minuet" with steely, matter-of-fact conviction, conjuring the scenes of violence and depravity with bone-chilling clarity, passing absolutely no judgment.

Reed obviously relished bringing *Berlin* to life onstage, and took the opportunity to deliver the songs as if they were scenes from a play, realizing in that sense the original vision that he and Ezrin had created. It's not that his *Berlin* performances were theatrical. If anything, they were more minimalist than was typical for even Reed. By this time, his voice had lost some of its range, a condition that he made a virtue of by doing more with less. Every one of his gestures—a glance, a movement of his hands—seemed meaningful. Reed would often close his eyes, as if he were interpreting the songs in images within his own mind, an effect lent even more force by the video accompaniment. Rarely has an album achieved such a degree of artistic integrity onstage. All these years later, *Berlin* had fully delivered on its promise, made real all its terrible beauty.

BEYOND THEIR PHYSICAL AND spiritual benefits, Reed's studies with Master Ren led to a fertile musical connection with Sarth Calhoun, a Brooklyn-based experimental musician who had become gripped by the possibilities of computers and the electronic processing of sound. Like Reed, Calhoun had been drawn to Ren because of a fascination with the Chen style of tai chi. Ren taught classes on Sunday mornings and Tuesday evenings, and along with his private lessons, Reed would typically attend the Sunday class, though sometimes he would go to both.

Calhoun knew who Reed was, but had never been particularly drawn to his music. "I'd never listened to the Velvet Underground," he said. "Not only did I not care about them, but I also didn't care about all the music that was vaguely in their category. Despite that, I was still intimidated. He's a really strong personality. I would have been intimidated even if he wasn't a famous guy, just by the wealth of his knowledge."

Reed would join members of the class when they went out to brunch after their training, and at first the conversations were general, not music-related. Calhoun recalled that in one of their first talks, he and Reed argued about a *Star Wars* movie that Reed loved and insisted that Calhoun go see. Calhoun had already given up on the franchise. "It was really acrimonious," Calhoun recalled. "I was like, 'George Lucas gave us our childhood and then he took it away'—which is not even my line. Lou just looked at me and said, 'Nobody can hit it out of the park every time, Sarth.'" When Reed learned that Calhoun created electronic music, his interest was piqued. Calhoun's medium necessarily involved considerable technological know-how—always an attraction for Reed. As Reed was beginning to explore alternatives to rock and roll, someone like Calhoun—young, hip, from Brooklyn, conversant with rock and roll but working on the periphery of it—was inherently intriguing to him. Calhoun invited Reed to come see his band, Lucibel Crater, and Reed did, bringing Master Ren along with him.

"We didn't play live that often, but on two occasions, Lou and Master Ren pulled up chairs right in front of the stage and nodded their heads significantly to the music," recalled Paul Chuffo, the drummer in Lucibel Crater and an occasional practitioner of tai chi. "I thought it was a good sign, even if it was strange that they looked like two oddball mafioso goons waiting to get their hands on us after the show. No clapping, no smiling, dead serious. And they had the only chairs in the room. I remember Lou wearing sunglasses through one of them. After the show, a grunting hello from Lou. We also had a record release party where Lou came up onstage for a solo on the continuum fingerboard, and I finally got a smile and a handshake from him."

Reed "was very complimentary about the band," said Calhoun. Reed had begun to work on the music for a training DVD that Ren was making, and he enlisted Calhoun to help him with it. "I was running live electronics, and Lou was really interested in what that was about," Calhoun recalled. "He came to my house and played some guitar and I processed it. We connected right away. He came out again, and then we did more work in his studio. It was all about him playing guitar and me processing it, either starting from drones or compositions that I already had, or from him improvising something and me processing it in real time and then editing it afterwards."

The two men got along brilliantly. "I learned a ton

from him," Calhoun said. "He was very good at picking something as being important and really focusing on it. Partly from working with him, I started to develop the theory that that's what makes an artist, in a way: being able to say, 'This is the important thing. All that other stuff—no. This is the thing.'" As Lucibel Crater began working on *The Family Album*, which was released in 2008, Reed expressed interest in helping out. "Basically, I think he was just looking for stuff to do that was new," Calhoun said. "Our guitar player had quit, and Lou was always saying, 'If you need a guitar player, you should look to me.' So I was like, 'All right, cool. Come out and jam.' And he really did follow through on that. He played on the track 'Threadbare Funeral.' Lou had this idea that when you play music with someone, either it connects or it doesn't. It's just that feeling you have, and the first time I played with him, I felt that kind of love-at-first-sight feeling. I think we both felt that way."

In search of new approaches to his music, Reed wanted to explore further ways of involving Calhoun in his work. "One day, he called me up and said, 'I'm doing this U.S. tour. Do you want to come along and do your processing thing with my rock band?' That was so cool because I had this dream of processing a whole live band through my rig for years, and it was just so weird to actually get an opportunity to do it on that level—and then that it happened in front of fifty thousand people at Lollapalooza."

Calhoun experienced Reed's legendarily grueling sound checks, but he also came to understand the reasons behind them. "One of the first things I learned from him was that there's a lot of validity in his obsession," Calhoun said. "I remember once we were recording at his house, and we spent so long positioning the guitar mic. I'm like, 'Come on, really?' But he might spend forty-five minutes positioning the guitar mic and then play one take and be like, 'That's good.' And he was right. Get the sound exactly right. It was like a clear-off-your-desk kind of thing. He was really into that. His space was always really neat. His studio was always really neat. His office was always neat. The whole principle is making sure your work space is in order so there's nothing between you and what you're trying to do. I learned from him how valid it is to take that kind of thing seriously."

By this point in his life and career, Reed had grown more relaxed in how he interacted with his band. The explosive anger he used to show when a band member made a mistake was much less apparent—and even when it was, Reed would now wait before bringing down the lash. "The band would go out with Lou to dinner every night, pretty much, after the show," Calhoun said. "It was extremely rare that he would be critical on the night after a show—only if he was really pissed or if something had gone dreadfully wrong. Usually he would hold his criticisms until the next day." Even then, "it wasn't like this long critique—more like, 'What was that crazy sound I heard during the second song?' Generally, if he said something was a problem, something had really gone wrong."

Calhoun also noticed and admired Reed's "rock-and-roll attitude"—his determination to "keep it fresh" all the time. "He was really improvisational onstage. He was always trying to change the orchestration or do something different, always keep it alive. Look, it could be frustrating, too, you know? You might think, 'Here we are doing this song, and we did it this way six months ago on the last tour, so I'm all set up and I have my sound and I know what to do.' But Lou would be like, 'What is that horrible sound you're using?' And you'd say, 'It's the sound I used last tour.' And he'd say, 'Don't tell me what you did last tour.' You learned really quickly that he never wanted to hear 'But this is what we agreed yesterday.' 'This is today.' He would say, 'Today, as of four twenty-three, I want you to play a solo there.'"

CALHOUN'S SENSE THAT REED was "just looking for stuff to do that was new" was exactly right. At one point, as the digital dismantling of the music business was fully under way, Reed wondered if it might be somehow possible to sell music the way a painter would sell a painting: create one copy that a collector could buy and own. Like so many of Reed's wilder notions, it seemed preposterous until 2015, when the Wu-Tang Clan sold its double album *Once Upon a Time in Shaolin* to hedge fund manager and pharmaceutical entrepreneur Martin Shkreli for a reported $2 million. Reed was looking for new outlets for his creativity, and he soon found an exciting one.

As Reed's friendship with Calhoun developed and deepened, he also remained in regular contact with Ulrich Krieger, the experimental composer who, much to Reed's delight and amazement, had transcribed and staged *Metal Machine Music*. Krieger and Reed had discussed the idea of performing improvised music together onstage, and they finally got the opportunity to do so. From his position as a professor at CalArts, Krieger arranged to play two nights of completely improvised music with Reed at REDCAT, the university-affiliated performance space designed by Frank Gehry. The theater was small—its maximum capacity was 240—and because the two scheduled shows on October 2, 2008, sold out immediately, a third was added for the next night. The show was advertised as Unclassified: Lou Reed and Ulrich Krieger. No doubt recalling the outraged reactions of his rock fans to *Metal Machine Music,* Reed made sure that the promotion for the show made it as clear as possible that the performances would include "no songs" and no singing by Reed. Instead, the show would be a "venture into deep acoustic space, drawing on new music, free jazz, avant-rock, noise, and ambient." Pushing the idea of improvisation to its furthest point, Reed pulled Calhoun into the performance at the last minute. "I think initially Ulrich was like, 'Why are you bringing some random dude into this?' But Ulrich and I wound up getting along really well. I love playing with him. I think he's brilliant. The group really connected."

At REDCAT, Reed played various guitars, Krieger primarily played saxophone, and Calhoun processed everything through his banks of computers. The performances ran for about an hour and were well received. Though hardly a bastion of avant-garde aesthetics, *Billboard* ran a smart, insightful paean to the show by Jeffrey Overwood. "Krieger's saxophone was heavily processed into rich, electronic, glacial sweeps, while Reed's thick distorted guitar chords took on the various characters of the effects pedals around him. Calhoun, seated behind a desk with computers and mixers, added chunky layers of subfrequency bass vibrations to the mix, which reached near-deafening volumes at various points. The performers shared minimal interaction onstage, but when their eyes locked, it provided the performance with welcome jolts of humanity." No doubt to Reed's delight, some audience members walked out. After all, what would be the point of doing such a show if no one was pushed beyond his or her limits? The audience might not have heard "Satellite of Love," Overwood concluded, "but if they paid attention, they surely felt the cosmic heft of three deeply creative spirits."

The three musicians found the shows deeply gratifying, and a double CD of the concerts titled *The Creation of the Universe* was released in December of 2008 on a label Reed founded, Best Seat in the House. The album's title evoked Reed's conviction that the work he was doing with Krieger and Calhoun was somehow elemental, a kind of pure, primal sound that resided at the heart of all his musical efforts, indeed at the very heart of sound itself. Reed proposed a tour. But what to call the group? Based on the original billing at REDCAT, they considered Reed Krieger Calhoun but quickly rejected it. Reed came up with the idea of calling it Metal Machine Trio, often abbreviated MM3. That would make it a lot easier — and, in very relative terms, more lucrative — to book a tour. The irony can't have been lost on Reed that, after nearly ending his career, *Metal Machine Music* had somehow become a commercial asset three decades later. Still, with the group's name, Reed had a larger point to make. For Reed, "MM3 came as a late artistic confirmation,"

Krieger declared. "He had been right all along. *Metal Machine Music* had come home. Completely unexpected by him, a younger generation of musicians now got it." Once again, Reed's most extreme sounds had found their proper place and their true audience.

25

METALLICA

WHILE REED WAS WORKING with Metal Machine Trio, the Rock and Roll Hall of Fame was planning to celebrate its twenty-fifth anniversary. Despite his resistance to pretty much everything the Hall of Fame represented, Reed frequently participated in its events. He delivered a scorching performance of "Sweet Jane" backed by Soul Asylum at the concert at Cleveland Stadium honoring the opening of the Hall in that city in 1995. He gave speeches inducting Dion, Leonard Cohen, and even Frank Zappa, whom he had publicly disparaged early in his career, into the Hall at the organization's swanky induction dinners. Reed also appeared and performed, of course, when the Velvet Underground was inducted in 1996. No doubt he admired the artists he inducted, but he also had one eye on his legacy, possibly believing that cooperating with the Rock Hall's powers that be might somehow ease his own induction.

To celebrate its twenty-fifth anniversary, the Rock Hall organized two nights of concerts at Madison Square Garden in New York, to take place on October 29 and 30, 2009. It was a characteristically grandiose evening, with artists like Bruce Springsteen, U2, Stevie Wonder, and Crosby, Stills, and Nash serving as house bands, performing their own songs, and playing with special guests. Somehow it was determined that Reed would perform during the hard rock portion of the second night, backed by Metallica, who would also support Ray Davies and Ozzy Osbourne. While Osbourne's collaboration with Metallica made perfect sense, Reed's (and Davies's, for that matter) was more problematic. It rested on the assumption that the noise extravaganzas of the Velvet Underground, the guitar orchestrations of Reed's *Rock n Roll Animal* band, and the sonic blitzkrieg of *Metal Machine Music* all contributed to the development of heavy metal — or, in its upscale version, hard rock — that Metallica was part of. That's a stretch, but Reed certainly deserved a place in the two concerts' retrospective look at the history of rock and roll, and that's where he ended up. And to be fair, the idea wasn't entirely indefensible. Metallica's lead guitarist, Kirk Hammett, told *Rolling*

Stone that year, "I can clearly draw a line from Ray and Lou to what we're doing now."

To their mutual credit, both Reed and Metallica fully committed to the collaboration. Metallica's drummer, Lars Ulrich, said that the group told Reed, "We're your backing band. We can go this way. We can go that way. Tell us what you would like." Reed took them up on that offer. During rehearsals, Reed listened to Metallica's heavied-up arrangement of "Sweet Jane" and told the band that it sounded "too militaristic." "You need the hop in there," he explained. On the other hand, Reed also encouraged Hammett to solo more freely on the song, no doubt having the extended *Rock n Roll Animal* version in mind. Reed and the band performed two songs at the concert — "Sweet Jane" and "White Light/White Heat" — and leaned into them hard. Reed deeply believed in sonic impact, and having a band with Metallica's hurricane force behind him clearly was a thrill. "They're as powerful as you can get," Reed said of the band. Metallica, meanwhile, took a kind of filial pride in performing with Reed. Within the context of the sixties-oriented Rock and Roll Hall of Fame, metal was still regarded as an outlier, a slightly embarrassing misfit son. To be part of such a visible event — let alone to back one of the most lauded critical darlings in rock history — was a form of validation for Metallica. Ulrich declared, "It says a lot about the Hall of Fame that in 2009 there's a place for what we represent at this kind of party." The members of Metallica obviously had one eye on their own legacy — and understandably so.

Responses to the performance were mixed. The more adventurous wing of Reed's fans, the ones inclined to reward him for any step outside the realm of what he actually did best, praised him for working with a younger band across genres. Even so, they tended to applaud the intention more than the music. Reed's more conservative fans found the performances leaden and unmelodic. Metallica's audience, to the degree that it paid attention to the Rock Hall show, seemed mystified. Why were their idols playing behind this old guy who couldn't sing?

By their own lights, however, Reed and the band were satisfied. When their performance ended, they were sweaty and beaming. Their embraces were hearty and genuinely affectionate. Reed retained some reservations. "If you watch the Rock and Roll Hall of Fame thing, 'Sweet Jane,' it's off," Hal Willner said. "No one else was acknowledging this, but Lou and I did. It doesn't work like that rhythmically." Still, both Reed and Metallica were unwilling to let the partnership end. "We knew from then that we were made for each other," Reed said. Reed was determined to record with the band, and discussions soon began about extending the collaboration. As willing as he had been to experiment, Reed never gave up on the notion that he could build on his cult following and find a new audience. Metallica had sold more than a hundred million albums. Even if a tiny portion of those fans came on board for a Reed-Metallica collaboration, that would be hugely significant. Not that Reed was desperate for money or sales, though he endlessly complained about both. But making a commercial impact with a band like Metallica would demonstrate that he was still an essential part of the contemporary cultural conversation. That was the appeal for him.

Reed's initial idea was to record a set of some of his older songs, giving them the pulverizing treatment Metallica had dished out to "Sweet Jane" and "White Light/White Heat." But rather than do his classics, the band would instead tackle, in Reed's words, "fallen jewels that no one remembered." But Reed had also built up a body of songs he had recorded with Sarth Calhoun for a project Robert Wilson had brought to him about the work of German expressionist playwright Frank Wedekind titled *Lulu,* after the sexually adventurous female character in two of Wedekind's plays, *Earth Spirit* and *Pandora's Box.* (Presumably, it was purely a wry coincidence that Reed's girly nickname at the Factory had been Lulu.) Calhoun and Reed came up with soundscapes along the lines of the meditation music they had done, and Reed improvised lyrics over them, which were then edited down to manageable lengths. Reed invited Calhoun to come to Berlin to help him and Wilson incorporate the music into Wilson's play. However, most of it ended up never being used, and it has never been released.

"It was extremely difficult for the live band to interpret the material, and it was unworkable just to play back the recordings," Calhoun said. "The actors very diligently learned Lou's phrasings and microtonal pitches, but the stuff was so strong that it just kind of stood on its own. It didn't really work with the stage production. I think Robert Wilson had already envisioned the play working with more typical Lou Reed songs, so he'd planned the whole thing with that element in mind. And now he had something that couldn't be more different: long eight-minute, ten-minute abstract pieces. Beautiful, heartbreaking stuff, but he'd set everything up with something else."

The Wilson piece was performed in Berlin in April of 2011 using some of Reed's material and was well reviewed. But Reed still had plenty of music and songs left, and he was pondering what to do with them. Calhoun suggested that Reed bring the songs to Metallica. "In stark contrast to my initial views on Lou Reed, I'm of an age where Metallica was a really big deal," Calhoun said. "I wanted an excuse to be involved in that gig, but there really was no reason why I should be. What would I do, exactly? So I just said, 'What would be crazy is if you took these abstract pieces with all these electronic sounds and contrasted that with intense metal riffs and mind-blowing lyrics. You could do it. It would work. You could do *Lulu* with heavy metal guitars over it and contrast the two elements.' Lou said, 'I would have to hear what you're talking about.' So I arranged some of the pieces as songs and played different metal riffs over them. I don't really play guitar—they were just horrible mock-ups."

One day, Calhoun accompanied Reed and Laurie Anderson to Dia:Beacon, the art foundation in Beacon, New York, about an hour north of Manhattan. On the car ride, Calhoun played the mock-ups he had done for Reed on his phone. "I said, 'This is what it could sound like if you had Metallica doing this material with you,'" Calhoun recalled. Reed said, "That's exactly what I want to do." So a week before Reed was to fly to San Francisco to begin working with Metallica in their studio, he sent them the demos and suggested that they scrap the previous idea of working on earlier songs of his and attack this new material.

Initially—and understandably—Metallica was stunned by the songs Reed had sent them. Wedekind was a writer obsessed with sexuality and the interface of erotic obsession and self-destruction, and such themes were hardly foreign to Reed. They were not, however, Metallica's typical fare, to say the least. In many ways, Reed's lyrics were the least of the problem. In signing on to work with Reed on his earlier songs, the members of Metallica knew what they were likely to be getting. But this music was another matter entirely. By the standards of Metallica's brutally formulated thrash metal, these tracks were drifting and formless. "Lars and I listened to the stuff," vocalist James Hetfield said, "and it was like, 'Wow, this is very different.' It was scary at first, because the music was so open. But then I thought, 'This could go anywhere.'"

"He was defensive, ready to roll his eyes," Ulrich said of Hetfield's initial reaction. "Then you could see this weight lifted off his shoulders. He felt a connection. He had not expected that." Reed also made it clear that he was not treating Metallica as if its members were hired hands. He wanted the band to bring the firepower that had made its reputation, and to help shape the arrangements to the band's own strengths. "It's so easy, because we're not trying to change anyone," Reed said of the collaboration. Ulrich agreed: "It wasn't 'This is my shit, do as you're told.' Lou understood we were going to give him something nobody else would...almost like two languages. We have m-e-t-a-l in our name. But we can go fucking anywhere and do anything." Meanwhile, Calhoun got his wish.

Reed brought him out to the sessions to help communicate their musical ideas to the band. Hal Willner also joined them as one of the album's coproducers, along with Reed, Metallica, and engineer Greg Fidelman, who had previously worked with Metallica. "It was crazy," Calhoun said, "because, like, now I'm showing James Hetfield a riff I wrote. I mean, ninety-nine percent of the riffs on the record were written by Metallica, but even if for half an hour I'm teaching him a riff I wrote, like, how is that even happening?"

As they had at the Hall of Fame concert, Reed and Metallica locked in relentlessly. "They were so into the project," Calhoun said of Metallica. "They completely rose to the challenge. They're, like, one of the greatest bands that has ever been. If you're going to try to do something crazy, why not? It's Metallica. It was an insane experience, because it was this huge meeting of two totally different working aesthetics, two totally different ideas about what music is. But they connected in the same place: power, clarity, intent.

"Metallica, they're a thoroughly composed band, by and large. Their live shows sound very much like their records. Whereas Lou would never want to do that. When Metallica makes records, they spend a long time, do a lot of overdubs, a lot of getting everything perfect. That's part of why they're so amazing. But what's crazy about them is that they could walk into a room, pick up their instruments, and just start playing whatever, and Metallica comes out. It sounds just perfect. And Lou capitalized on that, because he's a first take–best take kind of guy. So a lot of the songs on the album were literally first takes. It was, like, improvised metal. They could do that. You would think that would be impossible because metal's all about these precise changes, but I think they were really into this idea of, 'Whoa, we can just make a record in four weeks instead of a year? We can just let it flow out?' I remember James saying, 'I don't know how I'd go back to making records the old way now that I've done this.' They were really affected and willing to follow Lou's lead. They were super respectful of him as this great genius who was leading the charge."

Of course, issues arose in the studio resulting from the different work styles of Reed and the band. Reed's instinctiveness and go-from-the-gut impulses proved a stark contrast to Metallica's far more methodical approach. It wasn't a tussle, really; ever deferential to the master, Metallica just wanted more direction. As they were recording "The View," Hetfield was having trouble with the countervocal he was doing to complement Reed's characteristically deadpan narration. More specifically, he was having a hard time getting inside Reed's telegraphic lyrics ("I am the root / I am the progress / I'm the aggressor / I am the tablet") — their meaning, as well as their cadences, which, as Reed's lyrics often do, ignore the beat and move haphazardly across bars. There was another complexity as well. "I think Lou and Metallica met equally, but, if anything, Metallica seemed a bit cowed by Lou," said Lenny Kaye. "Which really makes me chuckle. And Lou probably chuckled inwardly, too, because he knew he had the goods, that no matter how dark *Master of Puppets* is, it's not as dark as 'Sister Ray.'"

"You gotta mean it," was Reed's direction to Hetfield about his vocal on "The View," as the two men stared each other down. "Give me a clue," Hetfield said. "What do you want me to mean? And these lines don't rhyme. There's five syllables in this, two in there." Still, at the end of the stark, black-and-white video for the song made by Darren Aronofsky, who directed the films *Black Swan* and *The Wrestler,* one can see Reed applauding Metallica's performance. "Bravo, bravo!" he says. "Encore!" That a major director was hired to do a video and that Reed agreed to edits that would keep it under four minutes indicate the degree of commercial expectations everyone held for the album.

Whatever other problems arose seemed to be taken in good spirits. Lars Ulrich said of Reed, "One time, I had to point something out to him...and he got hot and bothered. He challenged me to a street fight, which is a pretty daunting proposition because he's an expert in martial arts and is never too far from a sword. The good thing about me is I can do the hundred-meter dash faster than most forty-eight-year-old musicians."

But the sessions included moments of profound connection. "Things just kept falling into place," Calhoun said. "If you want to be mystical, that's when you feel like you're tapping into something. You see weird coincidences, and you know you're on the right path. Those sessions had that quality to them."

Lulu concludes with "Junior Dad," a nineteen-minute track that's easily one of the strongest songs on the album and, in some ways, one of Reed's great moments. The music moves at a glacial pace and retains the beautiful, melodic quality of the original tracks Reed had done with Calhoun. Metallica adds a note of grandeur. As the song's title suggests, Reed's lyrics explore the complex Oedipal dance in which fathers and sons inevitably engage. As he neared seventy, perhaps it seemed pointless to Reed to continue to rail against his father in his music, though in other contexts, he continued to do so. Perhaps it made more sense to explore the extent to which he had become a "Junior Dad," a reflection of his own father, standing in judgment of himself.

The song begins with the image of a man drowning and pleading to be saved—a son, presumably, begging his father to rescue him. "Pull me up," Reed sings. "Would you be my lord and savior? / Pull me up by my hair / Now would you kiss me on my lips?" The father responds cruelly: "I will teach you meanness, fear and blindness / No social redeeming kindness or state of grace." By the end of the song, Reed sings, "The greatest disappointment / Age withered him and changed him / Into junior dad." As Reed's own father neared death, the song suggests, he seemed an object of pity, a mighty, fearsome man reduced to a juvenile version of himself. But age had withered and changed Reed as well, and not relieved the fear that he was in fact the "greatest disappointment" that he believed his father believed him to be. The horror he had always felt about his father's imagined vengefulness was there, along with an unnerving empathy. When Hammett, whose father had died a few months earlier, and Hetfield first heard the playback of the completed track, they wept. "After that," Hammett said, "anything Lou wanted, he had me. I'd play it."

Reed's own father had died of cancer in 2005 at the age of ninety-one. Reed would occasionally visit him when he was in a hospice in the Bronx, but they never truly reconciled. At the service after he died, Merrill delivered a eulogy. Reed did not speak, and he did not stay long. His mother, too, had entered a hospice on Long Island, and Reed was closer to her. He would visit her more frequently but, as with his father, only if his sister was there. Merrill had to assume the primary responsibility of caring for their parents, given Reed's complicated relationship with them. Toby, as Reed would always refer to his mother, would light up when her son came to visit, and they would eat lox and bagels with Merrill. Reed would speak calmly to Toby and try to make her feel better. He could be playful with her. If she felt she was not being treated well at the hospice, he would speak to her in a soothing voice. "Why are you angry with people, Toby?" he'd ask, smiling gently. "You can't take out a machine gun and kill them just because you're angry!" Toby never lost her insecurities, her feeling that, because of the shock treatments, she and her husband had done something terribly wrong, something that made their son resent them so. Reed was incapable of being around either of his parents for extended periods, but, particularly with his mother, he could occasionally locate feelings of something like love.

THE GOOD FEELINGS, OPTIMISM, and high expectations of the *Lulu* sessions began to wither as word spread about the project. "The record got bad reviews before it was even recorded," Willner said. "Metallica's fans went nuts." When the album was released for streaming in October of 2011, the response grew only more vicious. While Reed's fans, for the most part, had no use for Metallica, they were accustomed to his frequent left turns and were content to ignore the album. Age had something to do with that as well. Much as

Reed's fans revered him, they were well past the point of living and dying with every one of his releases. Not so Metallica's fans. The band members themselves may have been well into their forties, but many of their fans were still in their teens, and they regarded *Lulu* as a betrayal of the worst kind. "It was more spiteful than anyone was prepared for," Ulrich said. "Especially against Lou. He is such a sweet man. But when Metallica do impulsive riffing and Lou Reed is reciting abstract poetry about German bohemians from a hundred fifty years ago, it can be difficult to embrace."

That Reed's lyrics deviated so dramatically from Metallica's postadolescent apocalyptic pronouncements and veered into deeply disturbing sexual territory only made matters worse. Asked if the band had reservations about some of Reed's lyrics, like "I swallow your sharpest cutter / Like a colored man's dick," from "Pumping Blood," Ulrich responded, "I understand that to some thirteen-year-old in Cape Girardeau, Missouri, it can all seem a little cringeworthy, but to someone raised in an art community in Copenhagen in the late sixties, that was expected." To the band's credit, Metallica never stopped defending *Lulu* or turned on Reed. A couple of years after its release, Ulrich wrote, "I played the record for my kids yesterday in the car, and it sounded as relevant and more intense than ever; it sounded incredibly potent, very alive, and impulsive.... Twenty-five years from now, you're going to have millions of people claiming they owned the record or loved it when it came out. Of course, neither will be true....In some ways, it's almost cooler that people didn't embrace it, because it makes it more ours, it's our project, our record, and this was never made for the masses, and the masses didn't take to it. It makes it more precious for those who were involved."

Of course, it didn't feel like that at the time. Both Reed and Metallica were stung by the response. Plans to tour in support of the album were scrapped. It clearly was not a fight Reed and Metallica were going to win, so the best strategy seemed to be to back away from the project. Calhoun said that he and Reed had discussed releasing their original version of *Lulu* once the Metallica version was out. "Maybe that would have served the material better," Calhoun said. "Who knows? I think we all had such high hopes. We expected there to be criticism, but maybe not monolithic criticism. I know Lou was disappointed not to be able to tour it." For Reed, it seemed like another setback—just as *Set the Twilight Reeling* and *Ecstasy* had been. If he couldn't make something happen with a band that had sold a hundred million records, what hope was there to make an impact?

The album attracted some notable fans, however. According to Laurie Anderson, "David Bowie made a big point of saying to me, 'Listen, this is Lou's greatest work. This is his masterpiece. Just wait: it will be like *Berlin*. It will take everyone a while to catch up.' I've been reading the lyrics and it is so fierce. It's written by a man who understood fear and rage and venom and terror and revenge and love. And it is raging."

26

THE MEASURE OF A MAN

A S THE BLOWBACK FROM the Metallica collaboration eased, Reed returned to the regularity of his life with Anderson. If it was not the perfectly idyllic romance that it was often portrayed to be, it had all the sustaining qualities of a solid marriage. Indeed, in the spring of 2008, it had become a marriage in fact. Anderson was speaking to Reed by phone from California when she began enumerating things that she had always wanted to do but had never done. "I never learned German," she said. "I never studied physics, I never got married." Ever impulsive, Reed immediately suggested that they get married the next day. "I'll meet you halfway," he said. "I'll come to Colorado" —where Anderson had a show the following night. They got married in a friend's back-yard in Boulder wearing their "old Saturday clothes."

"I guess there are lots of ways to get married," Anderson later wrote. "Some people marry someone they hardly know—which can work out, too. When you marry your best friend of many years, there should be another name for it. But the thing that surprised me about getting married was the way it altered time. And also the way it added a tenderness that was somehow completely new." Of course, marriage did not ameliorate the tensions in their relationship. "Like many couples, we constructed ways to be—strategies, and sometimes compromises, that would enable us to be part of a pair," she wrote. "Sometimes we lost a bit more than we were able to give, or gave up way too much, or felt abandoned. Sometimes we got really angry. But even when I was mad, I was never bored. We learned to forgive each other." Of course, it was Reed's fears of abandonment, and his anger when he felt Anderson's distance, and her anger as a result of that. Reed spent many hours on the telephone and in conversation lamenting Anderson's peripatetic ways with people close to him. When Anderson wrote that she and Reed "shared a house that was separate from our own places," she was referring to their Hamptons home—and to the fact that they often lived apart in New York. Without a doubt, her independence was not simply her natural inclination as an artist, but a strategy for helping their relationship survive. Reed's tendency to subsume whomever he was involved with and then resent her for living in his shadow was a fate that Anderson had no interest in enduring. Her detachment both drove Reed mad and made him value and respect her.

Reed was out constantly, often with Anderson, frequently with Hal Willner. I personally ran into him outside a Buena Vista Social Club concert at Carnegie Hall, leaving a performance by Antony and the Johnsons at Joe's Pub, waiting outside Town Hall to see Joanna Newsom, at a reception for Amnesty International, and many other times. He frequently had lunch at the French bistro Les Deux Gamins, near Sheridan Square, and would sit there reading quietly after his meal. Alone and together, Reed and Anderson had become ubiquitous, accessible, and friendly while somehow still managing to maintain their subversive edge. In 2010, they served as King Neptune and Queen Mermaid in the Mermaid Parade in Coney Island, a zany, low-rent, faux Mardi Gras event that featured old-school Brooklynites, seminude hipsters, and all-purpose revelers who gathered to kick off the summer season at the famous beach community. Dressed in blue and green robes, they rode along in a rickety float, protected themselves from the sun with a parasol, wore beads and necklaces, and waved to the crowd. Reed wore a white T-shirt, black shorts, a white baseball cap, and sunglasses. Reed and Willner cohosted a radio show titled *New York Shuffle* that aired on the Loft, a channel on SiriusXM satellite radio. The two men chatted about music in the most relaxed way possible, their topics ranging seamlessly from a Leadbelly song to the Angels' "My Boyfriend's Back" to a Jimmy Durante track to an obscure reggae song to a Staple Singers' classic to the most current music that had caught their ears. While Willner, a music obsessive, was clearly the show's talent spotter and archivist, Reed enjoyed himself as he evoked both the radio shows he had loved as a boy and his own free jazz rantings while at Syracuse University. Reed even crossed the line into writing criticism. He reviewed Kanye West's album *Yeezus* on the website the Talkhouse, and while his piece is rambling and unfocused, it's riveting to witness him tangle with one of the thorniest artists of the new millennium.

On another note, Keith Richards encountered Reed, who was vacationing with Anderson in the Caribbean, and Reed asked if Richards could provide him with some weed. Richards happily obliged. How did Reed respond? "Well," Richards said with a catarrhal laugh, "I didn't hear any complaints!" The idea of these two reprobates in winter—men who had spent decades battling each other for the top spot on the list of the rock stars most likely to croak—sharing weed while on vacation says so much about the quotidian joys survival can make possible.

Sarth Calhoun toured with Reed and Anderson and experienced the uncanny connection that the two very different people had developed. "It was intense hanging out with them every day, going to lunch with them and then being onstage between them," he said. "Onstage, it couldn't have been more different from the Metal Machine Trio. It was so delicate, where the slightest breath would affect the music. They understood each other very well, and they both had this great ability to be succinct, so in conversations with them I would always feel like I was rambling on. It was like hanging out with two poets. Everything they said was like a perfect koan, and I'm just like, 'Blah blah blah.'"

"Some people marry themselves, but they brought different worlds together," Willner said about the contrast between Reed and Anderson. "You've got Laurie, who's in the art world, very edgy and experimental, and she brought Lou into that world. Laurie became close friends with David Bowie and other of Lou's rock friends. And as artists they're very different. Lou doesn't throw anything out, and some of Laurie's best stuff we will never hear. But they brought their two worlds together, and it was just magic."

Suzanne Vega was a downtown neighbor of Anderson's as well as a friend of Reed's, and she took note when the two became a couple. "To a certain extent, I wasn't surprised because I knew Lou had broken up with Sylvia and was looking around," she said, "and Laurie's beautiful and clever and a New York icon. Love works in unpredictable ways. There was a transcendent thing going on when you would see them together, but that's not what I would have predicted. I would have predicted that they would each be somewhat defensive or ironic, you know? I mean, when I was around Lou, I never let my guard down, so I would only imagine that others would do the same. I knew that Lou could turn on you. But the way Laurie describes what happened between them is that they started talking and they never stopped, and there didn't seem to be this ironic shield. They were both so clever that you would think that they would be like two shells banging against each other rather than the beautiful thing that it was."

Often when Reed and Anderson were together, it seemed as if Reed was doting on her and she maintained a certain distance, a bit of emotional remove that was certain to keep Reed alert. However, Vega noted that that dynamic worked both ways. "Lou could be flirtatious," Vega said. "Just because he was madly in love with Laurie didn't mean that he wouldn't occasionally flirt with some blonde or some this-or-that. And Laurie would just walk over and tap him on the shoulder and say, 'Hey, let's go sit down.' Or she would just go over and play with him until his face turned around to hers again. He would sort of joust with her, and she would defend herself or just slip out of the grip of it, transcend it." Reed's own way of handling such situations was typically more blunt and frontal. At a birthday dinner for the novelist A. M. Homes at the Greenwich Village restaurant Il Cantinori, Reed noticed Anderson, seated across the table from him, enjoying a conversation with writer Lee Smith. Reed leaned across the table, glared at Smith, and challenged Anderson. "Who the fuck is this guy?" he asked. A devoted fan of Reed's, Smith defused Reed's anger by asking him about Delmore Schwartz.

"Lou and Laurie's relationship was like this beautiful, shimmering thing that seemed to be directed at each other very much," Vega said. "But it wasn't exclusive. I still felt very comfortable, even if it was just the three of us there. I never felt like, 'Oh, I should leave.' I felt friendly with both and included in whatever dynamic was going on. But the relationship between them had its own life, and that's nothing I could have predicted."

Michael Dorf, who ran the Knitting Factory and later established the high-end club City Winery, came to know Reed and Anderson quite well. As a young man, he had come to New York enamored of Warhol and the Factory scene, and viewed the outpouring of creativity of that time as embodying "the appeal of wanting to do something in the live arts in New York. Even the name Knitting Factory had its odd connection to the Factory. So getting a chance to meet Lou was as high up on my check-off list as possible." Dorf was present in the early days of Reed and Anderson's courtship, and he was continually struck by the quality of Reed's behavior around her. "I never saw anything but absolute reverence," he said. "I don't know how anyone can do that with their lover. He would act like her bodyguard and handler, always monitoring to make sure that she was being taken care of. He really put her on a pedestal in a way that was special. They were a cute couple and you saw them together all the time. You could see the incredible love he had for her." Like Willner, Dorf spoke of Reed's kindness and affection. "I've heard the stories of him yelling, being angry with people," he said. "I never had that. My memory of him was soft skin, very soft skin, his being very physical, giving me a kiss every single time I saw him. The last time he was onstage at City Winery, he kind of pushed my head down to kiss me on the forehead. It was fatherly, just very warm."

The Reed who had shaved a swastika into his hair in the seventies and had not hesitated to sling anti-Semitic comments altered his relationship to Judaism as he got older. Dorf organized alternative public Seders to celebrate Passover at the Knitting Factory, City Winery, the Museum of Jewish Heritage, and Lincoln Center, and Reed was a regular participant, typically playing the role of the Wise Child, one of the four children (Wise, Wicked, Simple, and the One Who Does Not Know How to Ask) who reside within all of us and who have complex, overlapping relationships with one another. Philip Glass and John Zorn were two other notable musicians who participated. One year, Reed brought his sister, Merrill, and an aunt to the Seder, an example of his warming toward his family. "We had this interesting bond," Dorf said of Reed's participation in the Seders. "It was a cool relationship that started around not so much exploring his Jewishness but his willingness to identify as Jewish. I still feel very much like a cultural Jew, and I think Lou connected in that way, that there was a way to express yourself and be connected to your identity and feel more Jewish without its having a religious focus." For his texts, Reed read from Poe's "The Raven" and from Bob Marley's aptly titled "Exodus."

Reed, who had relatives in Haifa, visited Israel a number of times and performed there with Anderson in 2008. Rabbi Levi Weiman-Kelman, a progressive spiritual leader based in Jerusalem, guided Reed and Anderson on a tour of the old city in 2011 and described him as having a "Jewish soul." Rabbi Weiman-Kelman also described how, during their first meeting, he and Reed had "quite a long, complicated discussion about the origins of circumcision." Reed also connected with his family and his Jewish roots in the sweet documentary he made about his father's cousin Shirley Novick in 2010, as she was about to celebrate her hundredth birthday. Titled *Red Shirley* and directed by Ralph Gibson, the film captures Reed in conversation with Shirley, who fled Poland during World War II and became a socialist, union organizer, and civil rights activist in New York. The Nazis had murdered her parents and all the Jewish residents of her village. "This was an act of love," Reed said. "I realized if I didn't do this, a connection of a lot of things would be lost forever. So there was a great impetus to do this."

Dorf and Reed also forged a friendship based on a mutual love of good wine—a surprising interest for Reed, given his rehab experience and his struggles with both diabetes and hepatitis C, which he contracted from shooting drugs. The first time Reed played at the Knitting Factory, he and Dorf enjoyed a bottle of Domaine Drouhin Willamette Pinot Noir that photographer Timothy Greenfield-Sanders provided. Next door to the Knitting Factory was the restaurant Montrachet, which, according to Dorf, "had one of the best Burgundy collections in the world." It became a tradition for Dorf to treat Reed and his band to dinner at Montrachet after his Knitting Factory shows. "That was rare for me, because we didn't have enough money to do it," Dorf said. "We were struggling at the Knitting Factory. But these shows were so successful for us that I was willing to take a chunk of the money and go to Montrachet. We really enjoyed our Burgundy indulgence."

Dorf recalled going with his wife, Sarah, to Reed and Anderson's apartment on West Eleventh Street, ostensibly for dinner. "This was going to be a big Pinot Noir evening," Dorf said, so he brought a magnum of Domaine Drouhin. Reed also contributed a magnum of the wine. Sarah was pregnant at the time, but she and Dorf had not yet told anyone, so they agreed that she would sneak her glasses to him. Anderson did not drink much, but she was dancing around the room, celebrating the feeling of the apartment's radiant heat on her feet. They decided not to eat dinner at the apartment and instead brought the wine with them to the Spotted Pig, a nearby celebrity hangout. Reed and Dorf drank most of the wine, and, thrilled by the evening—and drunk enough—Dorf finally raised the topic he had always wanted to with Reed. "Wow," Dorf said, "you were really in the Velvet Underground!" Reed seemed amused but simply said, "Michael..." and muttered some kind of response. "What was he going to say at that point?" Dorf wondered later. The moment was awkward in the way that drunken conversations between friends can sometimes be, but it was another marker of the connection between them.

Reed brought Václav Havel to the Knitting Factory to see John Zorn's band Masada. Then the staff of

Secretary of State Madeleine Albright contacted Dorf and said that Albright wanted to attend the show with Havel. Dorf closed off the club's balcony and provided food and drinks. Masada was playing as all the dignitaries arrived with their security details, and lots of noise ensued as everyone greeted one another and tried to get settled. Zorn was not amused. He looked up at the balcony and said, "Shut the fuck up!" "All the Secret Service folks were about to draw their weapons," Dorf recalled. "Havel and Albright stopped talking, and Lou, who was standing with me off to the side, looked at me, and we both started laughing very quietly. He put his arm around me to shield both our laughter and also not have Zorn get madder at us. It was a highlight of my life. The band continued and everyone was quiet. Lou had a smirk and twinkle in his eye for the rest of the night, and we had a new bond."

Strangely, this was not the first time that Secretary Albright had socialized with Reed. She was also present when Reed played a thirty-five-minute set at the White House in 1998, when President and Mrs. Clinton hosted a state dinner for Václav Havel. Reed had tangled with the Clintons' social secretary that night about the volume at which he should play, but the evening came off without a hitch. Among the other attendees that night were Kurt Vonnegut, Mia Farrow, Henry Kissinger, and Stevie Wonder. Reed's appearance came less than a week after special prosecutor Ken Starr issued his report about the Monica Lewinsky affair, and the White House was engulfed in scandal. The president, however, seemed in an excellent mood. After Reed's set, Clinton said, "If you had as much fun as I did just now, you should give President Havel all the credit." Speaking to a reporter from the *Washington Post,* Reed offered a strong defense of the president. "I think what's being done to him is terrible," Reed said. "Your private life should be your private life. I think it's a smear campaign."

Reed's private life provided quiet moments of pleasure that complemented the more public life that he and Anderson lived. Writer Brian Cullman described watching Reed search through the box of old 45s that Cullman had brought to a birthday party for Reed's friend the singer-songwriter Jenni Muldaur. Cullman recalled Reed's pausing to admire his copy of the Jaynetts' haunting "Sally Go 'Round the Roses," a number two single in 1963. Whatever else was happening in his life, Reed never stopped loving the music of that era. At a party in a West Village gallery to celebrate the publication of his disturbingly surreal book of photos, *Emotions in Action*—a stark collection of images that plunge beneath the surface of their subjects, whether human or landscape, into the realm of suppressed feelings—Reed stood with Anderson and their dog Lolabelle and reached to light a cigarette. "I can smoke in here, right?" Reed asked his publicist. The answer to his question was, of course, no: smoking had been banned in all public places in New York City. Reed didn't wait for an answer. He leaned against the wall, lit his cigarette, and wryly said, "It's my party..." I happened to be there and completed his reference to Lesley Gore's classic hit: "And I'll smoke if I want to." Reed smiled and put his hand on my arm. "There's not many of us who remember that stuff," he said.

The title of Reed's photo book recalls Ernest Hemingway's line about the goal of his writing being to provide "the sequence of motion and fact which made the emotion." That's an apt description of Reed's photos as well as his lyrics, his gift for describing events as simply and directly as possible and letting the listener's emotional response emerge from the stated facts at hand. In addition to *Emotions in Action,* Reed published two other books of photos: 2006's *Lou Reed's New York* and 2009's *Romanticism,* a collection of photos he took while traveling in Europe, Asia, California, and other locales. As with his music, Reed approached photography in rigorously technical terms, and he would often discuss his pictures in regard to how they were shot and printed rather than their evocative, impressionistic subjects. Reed's photography was another example of Anderson's influence on him, his adoption of her willingness to cross aesthetic boundaries and assume that her sensibility would lead her in a productive direction. It was also another expression of his desire to establish himself as an artist beyond the realm of rock and roll.

In 2009, Reed and Anderson bought their house on Old Stone Highway in East Hampton, near Amagansett. It was not a gaudy showplace—just under two thousand square feet with a pool and a small guesthouse. It was in a swank area, but it also represented something like a return to Reed's roots. For all the vitriol he had spewed over the years about Long Island, he was now returning to it as a retreat from his life in New York, much as his house in New Jersey had been when he was married to Sylvia. Reed and Anderson frequently entertained guests in East Hampton, and Reed would occasionally go there on his own when Anderson was traveling. Suzanne Vega had a home nearby, and she frequently socialized with the couple. When she first learned that Anderson and Reed had a home there, she contacted them. "Laurie was super engaging," Vega said. "She was like, 'Oh, come on by! We'll go for bike rides!' I was like, really? It just seemed like such a healthy, all-American thing to do with, like, Laurie Anderson and Lou Reed. So I was like, I'm in! I called them, and I started to see this other side to Lou. We'd have chats at his lunch table about all kinds of things. Lou was complaining that Laurie was going away and he had nobody to eat with, so my brother Matt, the hermit of all hermits, invited him over to our house for dinner." Reed came with Jenni Muldaur, and, according to Vega, they ate "so much and so fast that it was like having locusts in the house." After Reed left, Matt surrounded the place where he was sitting with copies of Reed's work and memorialized it with a photograph. "This is where he ate," Matt said. Reed stayed in touch with Vega by text and invited her to his house. He liked to travel in a group, and if he was invited to someone's home, he would sometimes invite Vega along. "He would complain about other people's diva behavior," Vega said. "He'd been invited to Donna Karan's house and he felt that he hadn't been treated well. I guess Donna was having some kind of private tête-à-tête with Barbra Streisand or something. He was kept waiting, and Lou was not happy about it."

Among the many honors that began to come to Reed as he got older was the George Arents Pioneer Medal for excellence, the highest alumni honor offered by Reed's alma mater, Syracuse University; other recipients have included Joyce Carol Oates, Ted Koppel, William Safire, Dick Clark, and Joe Biden. The presentation of the award took place at the W Hotel in Manhattan. Anderson accompanied Reed, and Bono, David Bowie, novelist Oscar Hijuelos, and writer Mary Karr also attended. "We have an alchemist in our company tonight," Bono said to those gathered to honor Reed. "Lou has turned the cosmic litter of this city into gold." The university took the occasion to announce the creation of the Lou Reed/Delmore Schwartz scholarship in creative writing. Karr presented Reed with an autographed first edition of Schwartz's classic collection of short stories and poems, *In Dreams Begin Responsibilities,* and on violin, Anderson offered interpretations of two of Schwartz's poems, "The Heavy Bear Who Goes with Me" and "All of Us Turning Away for Solace." Reed would write a lovely, poetic introduction for a new edition of *In Dreams Begin Responsibilities* in 2012.

Given Reed's checkered history at the university, he began his acceptance speech by glancing at his sister, Merrill, and asking, "Who would've believed this one?" But he devoted most of his remarks to his regard for Schwartz, and how much getting to know the writer at Syracuse meant to him. "I will always love the university for giving me the opportunity to study with him," Reed said. "Delmore inspired me to write, and to this day, I draw inspiration from his stories, poems, and essays. His titles alone were a writer's dream." In conclusion, Reed said, "I hope, Delmore, if you're listening, you are finally proud as well. My name is finally linked to yours in that part of heaven reserved for Brooklyn poets."

*　　*　　*

As Reed was living this life of public events and private moments, few people beyond his tightest inner circle were aware of how ill he was becoming. The hepatitis C he had contracted as a young man was damaging his liver, and the interferon treatments he was undergoing to rid himself of the virus were taking their toll as well. In addition, he was suffering from diabetes. News items were popping up here and there about Reed nodding off at public events or performances. It was a source of mirth: Lou Reed, the eternal enfant terrible, evidently so old or out of it that he could barely stay awake. Or maybe he was nodding out on drugs? His fatigue, however, was the result of his illness.

"I look back on *Lulu* pretty favorably, except Lou was ill and I couldn't really tell the Metallica guys that," Willner said. "I called them all afterwards to explain. I was just trying to help him through it. He'd get very tired and he'd fall asleep at times. It was like knowing when he needed to push and when not.... That was my job on that project—watching him, being protective of him." Reed canceled live performances, including at Coachella and Lollapalooza, but still kept word of his health problems quiet. "I didn't understand why he canceled the Coachella tour, and he canceled a tour before that," Sarth Calhoun said. "I knew he had health problems, but he always seemed so indestructible. Even though, given that he was Lou Reed, you could say, 'This dude must have one foot in the grave,' when you hung out with him, that's not what it felt like. He felt indomitable."

Nonetheless, Reed's condition continued to deteriorate. The situation proved especially difficult for Anderson. "She took care of him, and she canceled everything," Willner said, speaking of Anderson's many ongoing projects. Her love for Reed was unquestionable, but such selflessness did not come naturally to her. Her ability to travel and disappear into her work was not simply important to her as an artist; it was an essential strategy to her survival in a relationship with someone as thorny as Reed. Anderson hated to stay still, and Reed hated being alone — a potentially combustible combination of traits under the best of circumstances. As his health began to deteriorate, he became more dependent on Anderson and more frightened about what was happening to him. It put a strain on their marriage, and as Reed grew angrier, Anderson sometimes felt that she had no choice but to leave at times. Various caretakers stepped in to help — Sharyn Felder; Jenni Muldaur; Reed's sister, Merrill — and friends like Willner were always available. But it was a difficult, frightening time.

It was finally determined that intermediate measures would not work and that Reed required a liver transplant, which took place at the Cleveland Clinic in May of 2013. The clinic has one of the largest transplant programs in the United States; in 2013 alone it performed 143 liver transplants. Strangely, Anderson announced that the operation had taken place in an interview with the *Times of London* that ran on June 1, 2013. Of the operation, Anderson said, "It's as serious as it gets. He was dying. You don't get it for fun." Once the news was announced, the reaction was widespread. Fans were relieved, first of all, that Reed had survived. While not downplaying how perilous Reed's condition had been, Anderson described him as steadily recovering—doing tai chi and hoping to be back at work in a few months. While Reed was hospitalized, Paul Simon sent him R & B albums from the fifties, along with works by the composers Harry Partch and Lou Harrison. "I figured that covered the spectrum with Lou, as it did with me," Simon said. As often happens when a prominent person receives a new liver, there was some speculation about whether or not Reed had somehow used his influence to jump the line.

The logistics of the operation were complicated, according to Anderson. "You send out two planes—one for the donor, one for the recipient—at the same time," she explained. "You bring the donor in live, you take him off life support. It's a technological feat. . . . I was completely awestruck. I find certain things about technology truly, deeply inspiring." While Reed was in the process of recovering, Anderson stated that, in terms of the operation's emotional impact, "I don't think he'll ever totally recover from this."

Reed's surgeon, Dr. Charles Miller, described how Reed handled his illness and the surgery it required. Reed was extremely ill, Miller said, when he came to Cleveland, and as he failed to respond to therapies, he got "crabbier and crabbier" as he waited for a liver to materialize. Miller attributed Reed's foul mood to the side effects of liver disease, not to his personality, though the two were likely a tough combination. Reed was desperate to leave the hospital and get back to New York, but just when he was at his worst, a suitable liver arrived. Miller described Reed as eager for the surgery, with "not a fear in his eyes." That bravery characterized Reed's response to the entire experience, Miller said: "This operation takes the measure of a man, and Lou measured up in every way and more." Miller performed the operation while listening to Reed's music, and stated that "sewing to 'Walk on the Wild Side' ain't too bad. It was a beautiful operation." The operation was successful, and afterward, Reed and Miller became friends and socialized in the Hamptons. Deeply grateful for having been provided a chance to live, Reed described Miller as a "new old friend," and they always ended their conversations by saying "I love you."

After Anderson's interview in the *Times of London*, Reed posted a statement on his website: "I would like to thank the Cleveland Clinic and all of you around the world who have lifted me with prayer and wishes of love. Your support has buoyed me forever and I am deeply grateful. I am also really up and strong. Thanks to your spirit." He described himself as "a triumph of modern medicine, physics, and chemistry" and, in language that was almost childlike, said that he was "bigger and stronger than ever." Anderson was equally optimistic. "Lou is in the best physical shape in years—strong and energetic," she said. "He has a wonderful new life now."

Like many people who pass through the ordeal of something like a liver operation, Reed came out of it determined to live his life to the fullest. To say he was optimistic about his chances of survival is a vast understatement. He was determined to survive, and believed that he had snatched his life from the jaws of death. "What people often don't get about Lou is his love of life," Hal Willner said. "We've all seen plenty of people commit suicide, and because of the kind of people we've chosen to be around, we've known way too many people who have died. We've chosen to be around people who don't take life on life's terms and who flirt with the devil. But I never saw anybody fight as hard to live as he did. He didn't want to die, not one iota. He wanted to live."

But it was a hard struggle for Reed. Even before the operation, at the annual Passover Seder he had arranged, Michael Dorf noticed how weak Reed had become.

Reed insisted on participating. "I had to help him up on the stage," Dorf recalled. "He paused a little, and I was actually a little nervous. But then he made a barb about not having received any preparatory notes from me, a little personal jab, so I was like, 'Okay, he's coming alive.' He read Bob Marley's 'Exodus' as his part, and he did it in this incredible Lou Reed manner, where he had these annotated comments throughout the reading. Once he got going, his voice went from weak to strong. He had a fire in him. And that was wonderful to see. But I did know that something had overtaken his body."

Even during the difficult period after his operation, Reed's reputation remained unchanged. *The Onion* could not resist a satirical take on his illness. "New Liver Complains of Difficulty Working with Lou Reed" was the headline for a short piece that ran a couple of days after Anderson revealed that the transplant had taken place. "It's really hard to get along with Lou," the liver was quoted as saying about the "temperamental rock legend." Their relationship, the liver said, was "strained at best," because with Reed, "one minute he's your best friend and the next he's outright abusive." The liver was frustrated and considering simply letting Reed "synthesize proteins and digestive biochemicals on his own."

Suzanne Vega described attending a party at a Hamptons mansion by the ocean with Reed. A steep flight of stairs led to the beach from the house. "I have trouble seeing in the dark," Reed told her. "Would you help me down these stairs?" She used her iPhone flashlight app to guide them as Reed leaned on her to make his way down. "Thank you," he said simply when they arrived at the beach. That "little scene moved me, and still does," Vega recalled. Reed told her that "rock and roll is a young man's game. And the critics, for some reason, have decided that this new project with Metallica isn't any good. And my health isn't what it was." Vega "always felt privileged to be part of his group of friends, whenever I was invited." On another occasion, Vega wore a pair of enormous white sunglasses when she went to visit Reed's home in East Hampton. "Oh, those are interview sunglasses," Reed said, a notion that would never have occurred to Vega; "I wore them more as a joke," she said. Reed's dog Little Will snatched the glasses and chewed them up. "Lou was mortified," Vega said. "He was like, 'I'll go get them fixed right now. I'll take them over to Main Street.' Meanwhile, I was like, 'It's your puppy!' I was worried that he had a mouthful of glass. But I was really touched by his being so freaked out. The idea that I had lost my shield, that his dog had come and crunched up my scary sunglasses—that was meaningful to him."

Reed enjoyed giving Vega business advice, and one time he discussed the concept of branding with her. "He was really enthused about it, because he'd gone to a branding convention," she recalled. "We talked about how Burberry had switched its brand, and he talked about Warhol and that one has to keep one's brand up to date and give it a twist from time to time. I don't always think that way and it's not my lifestyle, but I thought it was really brilliant that he was still thinking in that super-aggressive, modern way. He never let that go." In August of 2013, Vega visited Anderson and Reed for lunch at their home. Reed's body was scarred from his operation, but he was lying on a lounge chair in his backyard. At lunch, Reed asked Vega if she would prefer that he put his shirt on. "Only if it brings you comfort," she replied. "At that point I wasn't even really thinking of him as a person," she said later. "He was sort of like a spirit in a body. That's how I felt when I was there with him. His body was changing. His face was changing. He was changing. I felt that we were so beyond social niceties. There was a tableful of people, so for him to ask me if he needed to put a shirt on, I found that really touching."

IN SEPTEMBER OF 2013, Reed flew to London to accept the Inspiration award from the British edition of *GQ* magazine at its Men of the Year awards presentation. The magazine was concerned that Reed might not be able to attend. When the editors learned about his liver transplant, and when he was hospitalized again, for "dehydration," they checked with Reed's handlers. Both times they were assured that Reed very much wanted to go and would certainly be there. The magazine was lavish in its praise of the artist. "When we first thought about who we wanted to give our Inspiration award to, there was only one name we spoke of: Lou Reed," writer Stuart McGurk stated. "Some people inspire movements, some inspire generations. But Lou Reed inspired almost every generation—from punk in the seventies, to glam in the eighties, to alternative rock in the nineties. Hell, his halting delivery was even sometimes credited with inventing rap." Iggy Pop wrote a brief tribute to Reed, which credited him as "the bedrock beneath my feet and a beacon shining through the black night of crap. . . . I think he's one of the few guys or gals who's been in this biz a long time and still has a feeling for the world around him. Most of the others just end up singing to the mirror." Ron Wood of the Rolling Stones presented Reed with the award.

When Reed appeared at the event, at the Covent Garden Opera House, on September 3, he appeared frail. Accepting the award required climbing three or four steps to the stage, and Reed had insisted that a handrail be installed to assist him, which was hastily done at the last minute. Still, Reed's presence inspired awe in a room that was filled with boldfaced names, Pharrell Williams, Arctic Monkeys, Noel Gallagher,

Emma Watson, Michael Douglas, and Justin Timberlake among them. He was the person everyone there wanted to meet, if only to shake his hand and pay deserved respect. Reed, dressed entirely in black, ascended to the stage to the sound of "Romeo Had Juliette" and rapturous applause. He gathered strength as he stepped up to the mic. In his brief acceptance speech, his voice started out hoarse and shaky but found its pitch and conviction quickly. "There's only one great occupation that can change the world: that's real rock and roll," he said. "I believe to the bottom of my heart, the last cell, that rock and roll can change everything. And I'm a graduate of Warhol University, and I believe in the power of punk. To this day, I want to blow it up. Thank you."

On October 3, 2013, Reed appeared with photographer Mick Rock at a book launch event for *Transformer,* a high-end, limited-edition collection of Rock's work with Reed and other artists in their circle, like David Bowie, Mick Jagger, and Andy Warhol. The event took place at the John Varvatos store on the Bowery in downtown Manhattan, the former site of CBGB. The book took its title from the album that had propelled Reed's solo career in 1972, and that album's iconic cover served as the cover of Rock's book as well. Reed fully collaborated with Rock on the book, and they shared the royalties on it. The super-limited-edition version of *Transformer* cost close to $1,000. Reed was in the hospital following the transplant as the book was being completed, and Rock sent him some of its images and pages so he could see how the work was proceeding. After receiving them, Reed emailed Rock. "Beautiful book, Mick," he wrote, "and beautiful price."

When the time came for the October event, at which Reed and Rock were to be interviewed by John Varvatos, Rock offered Reed the opportunity to back out. "He was very sick, and I remember saying to him, 'Lou, you don't have to come and do this,'" Rock said. "He said, 'No, I want to. I want to do it for you. This is your book, Mick. It's not my book.' I remember thinking, 'I'm not sure I need to take that burden on, because I don't think it's helping Lou's health.' But whatever. Nobody could tell Lou what to do. I went to meet him coming in, and it was very difficult. Laurie was helping him along. You could see how weak he was at first, but the minute he got aggravated by people talking, then he perked up. His strength seemed to come for a while. Anger somehow seemed to fuel him. And then I never saw him after that."

27

THE AFTERLIFE

Lou Reed died on October 27, 2013 — poetically enough, a Sunday morning, a beautiful, haunted time eloquently captured in one of his sweetest ballads, "Sunday Morning," on *The Velvet Underground and Nico*. Despite his liver transplant, not to mention the excesses of his early life, his death came to the world as a shock. Reed's declaration that he was a "triumph of modern medicine" after the transplant in May proved to be more an expression of what he needed to believe than a statement of fact. Actually, he had been ill for months after the operation, and growing frailer. As his health faded, Reed returned to the Cleveland Clinic, where the transplant had been performed, for further treatment, but options had run out. Dr. Charles Miller, who had performed the transplant, said, "We all agreed that we did everything we could," and Reed decided that he wanted to return to the Hamptons home that he and Anderson shared. The young rebel who had despised Long Island and spoken about it with the bitterest contempt had come to love his life there, near the ocean, with Anderson. And the defiant reprobate who walked on a ledge for decades had lived to be seventy-one. On a lovely, ironic, and extremely unlikely note, the last song Reed streamed on Spotify was Hall and Oates's sweet 1983 number two hit, "Say It Isn't So."

Reed spent his final days calmly, at peace, with friends and family. "I was with Lou the morning he died, and he knew exactly what was happening," Anderson said later. "He had described this feeling the week before of slipping down through the body, through the inside and out. And that Sunday morning, he said, 'It's happening again now.' And then he had an expression on his face that I had only seen once before, when my mother died. . . . It looked like inexpressible wonder and incredible joy." Hal Willner said that he believed Reed had given up his "battle to live and keep working, to keep going out," only two or three days before his death. Willner and Jenni Muldaur were with Reed on the Friday night before his death. "This is so hard," Reed said, referring to his acceptance of his inevitable death. "Jenni and I were just lying on the floor with him," Willner said. "He asked me to play one of my New York shuffles, but I wasn't prepared, so we just played records. We put on things he loved—Nina Simone, stuff like that. He heard Valerie June, and he started to get excited. He wasn't familiar with her and he could hardly talk, but he said, 'I want to know about her.' Then when Dion came on, his version of the Doc Pomus song 'Troubled Mind,' he grabbed me and said, 'I am so susceptible to beauty.' It was insane. I could still see the goose bumps on him. And at the end of that run of songs, we sat him up and we watched the movie *Naked City*. Perfect. But I think it wasn't until then that he accepted that he was going to die."

Anderson described this experience in a piece she wrote for *Rolling Stone* after Reed's death. "I have never seen an expression as full of wonder as Lou's as he died," she said. "His hands were doing the water-flowing twenty-one form of tai chi. His eyes were wide-open. I was holding in my arms the person I loved the most in the world, and talking to him as he died. His heart stopped. He wasn't afraid. I had gotten to walk with him to the end of the world. Life—so beautiful, painful, and dazzling—does not get better than that."

The night before his death, Reed and Anderson had stayed up talking, and in the morning, Reed asked to be taken outside, onto the porch of the couple's home. "Take me into the light," Reed had requested. Anderson later remarked, "It was only a few days later that I realized that light was his very last word." But all was not beauty and tranquility during those final days. In some ways, Reed remained haunted by his own version of his past. One of Reed's close friends, the painter Julian Schnabel, also visited him in East Hampton that week. "We were in the swimming pool and I was holding him in my arms, and he said to me, 'You know, I was on the beach with my dad, and I put my hand in his hand and he smacked me in the face—and he drew the line right there.' And I thought that was really a crazy thing for a guy who's seventy years old. I mean, he's thinking about that all these years [later]."

We can't know the ultimate truth about Reed's relationship with his father—and people who knew his father describe the idea of his slapping Reed that way as inconceivable—but it is significant that, like Kafka, Reed carried the image of his father as a tyrannical monster to his grave. "My father didn't give me shit," he bluntly declared in his final interview in September of 2013, a little over a month before he died. But justifiably or not, intentionally or not, Reed's father had bequeathed his only son an image of himself as punishing and denying.

PERHAPS THE MOST EXTRAORDINARY consequence of Reed's death was the revelation of how profound and ranging the impact of his life and music had been.

Undoubtedly, Reed's stature had been assured. But even some of his most long-standing and devoted fans were stunned by the deep, lasting, ongoing response his passing evoked. If the importance of the Velvet Underground had been concealed for years, until all those people who had bought the group's first album formed bands, Reed's own importance during the last decade or more of his life had been assumed, but rarely expressed. As he and Anderson made their nightly rounds of art openings, plays, movie premieres, and avant-garde events, it was as if he was hidden in plain sight, a ghost haunting the aesthetic worlds he had so much helped shape, but in which he had ceased to be a vital force. Reed was never elected to the Rock and Roll Hall of Fame as a solo artist during his lifetime, however much he had deserved to be. He had made too many enemies in the industry.

As with every significant rock death, tributes immediately poured in and media coverage abounded. A front-page obituary in the *New York Times* declared that Reed's work with the Velvet Underground "had a major influence on generations of rock musicians," and that as a solo artist, he "remained a powerful if polarizing force" whose "early work assured him a permanent audience." That emphasis on his "early work" would have enraged Reed. *Rolling Stone* put him on its cover—he'd occupied that spot only once before—and in the magazine's extensive coverage, Mick Jagger dubbed him the "Johnny Cash of New York rock: he was always the man in black." Bono, living up to Bruce Springsteen's declaration that "you always want an Irishman" to speak about you at important moments, hailed Reed as "a still figure in the eye of a metallic hurricane, an artist pulling strange shapes out of the formless void that is pop culture, a songwriter pulling melodies out of the dissonance of what Yeats called 'this filthy modern tide.'" David Byrne said that Reed's "work and that of the Velvets was a big reason I moved to New York, and I don't think I'm alone there. We wanted to be in a city that nurtured and fed that kind of talent." Morrissey recorded a gorgeous version of "Satellite of Love" and wrote that he had "no words to express the sadness at the death of Lou Reed. He had been there all my life. He will always be pressed to my heart. Thank God for those, like Lou, who move within their own laws; otherwise, imagine how dull the world would be." Ryan Adams, one of Reed's musical descendants, tweeted, simply and tastefully, "Lou Reed."

Tributes came in from closer to home as well. On his Facebook page, John Cale wrote, "The world has lost a fine songwriter and poet. . . . I've lost my 'school yard buddy.'" Cale also issued a statement saying, "Unlike so many others with similar stories, we have the best of our fury laid out on vinyl, for the world to catch a glimpse. The laughs we shared just a few weeks ago will forever remind me of all that was good between us." Maureen Tucker told a journalist "Lou and I had a special friendship. I loved him very much. He was always encouraging and helpful to me and a good friend." David Bowie termed Reed "a master."

Artists also honored Reed onstage. Playing in Baltimore on the night of Reed's death, Pearl Jam blasted "I'm Waiting for the Man." That same night in Eugene, Oregon, Gov't Mule performed "I'm Waiting for the Man," along with "Walk on the Wild Side" and "Sweet Jane." In Hartford, Connecticut, Phish opened its show with a rollicking ten-minute version of "Rock and Roll." At Neil Young's annual Bridge School benefit concert for disabled children at the Shoreline Amphitheatre in Mountain View, California, Young joined My Morning Jacket, Elvis Costello, and Jenny Lewis to end the evening with a nine-minute version of the Velvet Underground's "Oh! Sweet Nuthin'."

But it soon became clear that's Reed's impact extended much further than former bandmates and rock stars. "noooooooooo nottttttttt LOU REED," tweeted Miley Cyrus, punctuating her lament with a broken heart emoticon. Ricky Gervais wrote, "RIP Lou Reed. One of the greatest artists of our time." Lena Dunham wrote, "We love you Lou. We love you Laurie." Cyndi Lauper declared, "I still can't believe Lou Reed passed away. I'm sorry for his family's loss. greatful [*sic*] for his music and the influence he had on my music." Samuel L. Jackson mourned, "R.I.P. Lou

Reed ... The music of my generation. Still Relevant!"
Said Susan Sarandon, "NY lost one of its originals
with Lou Reed's passing. So sad." Mia Farrow offered,
"Deepest gratitude Lou Reed. Peace." Sarah Silverman,
poignantly, quoted lyrics from "Perfect Day" ("I thought
I was someone else, someone good"), while Kesha confessed that she was "so sad with the loss of Lou Reed —
such an incredible visionary and songwriter, so
inspirational. transformer on repeat."

On Thursday, November 14, a brisk fall day, a public memorial, arranged by Laurie Anderson, was held
for Reed. The outdoor event took place by the Bar-
clays Capital Grove and the Paul Milstein Pool and
Terrace outside Lincoln Center Theater and the Met-
ropolitan Opera House, from one until four in the
afternoon. Along with its obvious cultural relevance,
the site was not far from where Reed had joined an
Occupy Wall Street demonstration a couple of years
earlier — and where he had debuted as a solo artist in
1973. Billed as *New York: Lou Reed at Lincoln Center*,
the memorial was neither widely publicized nor exclusive or secret in any way. It seemed premised on the
assumption that anyone who was likely to want to be
there would find out about it and come. It was
announced on Reed's Facebook page as "a gathering
open to the public — no speeches, no live performances,
just Lou's voice, guitar music, and songs — playing the
recordings selected by his family and friends."

The event adhered precisely to that description, and somewhere between one and two hundred people attended. Reed's music played for three hours through an impeccable sound system overseen by Hal Willner that lived up to Reed's unrelenting sonic standards. The selection of songs kicked off with the roaring guitar feedback alarum of "The Blue Mask," after which the set list, curated by Willner, touched every phase and style of Reed's career, ranging from "Femme Fatale" to "Set the Twilight Reeling," from "Candy Says" to "Waves of Fear." The afternoon finally crashed to a close with an excerpt from *Metal Machine Music*.

At Anderson's insistence, there was no VIP area of any kind, so she mingled with friends like Julian Schnabel, Master Ren, Philip Glass, and Salman Rushdie but also chatted with whatever fans approached her with their condolences and good wishes. A few reporters were present and were under no restrictions. People listened to the music, danced by themselves, chatted with one another, and let their thoughts and emotions run to whatever meaning Lou Reed had brought to their lives. One attendee wrote to a friend that "while 'White Light' played, some odd homeless dude with Down's syndrome was swaying next to Schnabel and Rushdie. As he should be." As David Chiu wrote at rollingstone.com, "The event didn't feature any large signs, banners, photographs of Reed, or any other markers indicating it was a memorial. For three hours, it was just about letting the songs speak for themselves."

FOR A FEW WEEKS, it seemed as if that might be it. And somehow, that felt about right. An important artist who never had an enormous following had died, and he was suitably, movingly honored in his death. He had not produced essential work for some time, but as the media in all its forms reflected on his life, the impact of his most vital contributions had become clear again. People assumed that Laurie Anderson would organize a memorial for family and friends but that, since Reed was such a private person, it would likely be kept small and private. Certainly, Reed would be heralded once again as the year ended and attention turned to notable figures who had died within the last twelve months. As so often was the case throughout his career, Reed would have received something like his due, though nothing more.

All that made perfect sense, except that the grieving for Reed never ended. The real impact had taken place in people's hearts and required time to find expression. Dean Wareham of Dean and Britta, who had recently written songs to accompany some of the screen tests (including Reed's) commissioned by Andy Warhol, recalled that he was on the road when he heard that Reed had died. "I think at first I was like, 'Oh, well, that's not really a shock because I know he's been ill, and I don't think it's going to affect me that much,'" he said. "But driving home, I started listening to some of his older songs, like 'Love Makes You Feel,' and some of the obscure ones. . . . There's a lot of records, a lot of good ones, a lot of bad records, but even the bad ones have gems on them, too." Singer-songwriter Joseph Arthur wrote that six weeks after Reed's death, "I was tired of mourning him and it felt like I was done, but in truth, the real mourning was only just beginning."

That proved to be the case not only for Arthur, who would go on to record an album of Reed's songs titled *Lou,* but for just about everyone else who loved Reed's music. Even staunch admirers were struck by the ongoing public acknowledgments of Reed's significance; the accolades simply never stopped. Tribute concerts were organized in cities around the country, as well as in Canada, the UK, and Australia. Most notably, at the South by Southwest music conference in Austin, the musicians Richard Barone and Alejandro Escovedo put together an evening devoted to Reed's music that featured the likes of Lucinda Williams, Suzanne Vega, and Sean Lennon. Remembrances of Reed by friends, acquaintances, and fans cropped up repeatedly in magazines, newspapers, websites, and blogs. Versions of his songs flooded the Internet. "It was fucking huge. Lou would never have believed it," said his friend Eric Andersen, smiling and shaking his head. Andersen lived in Europe and was stunned to see that "the Norwegian media, the French media, the Italian media, the German media all covered his death. He would not ever have believed that this could be true."

Reed's first wife, Bettye Kronstad, was struck by the depth and complexity of her feelings after hearing about her ex-husband's passing. After their bitter, final breakup, they had not been in touch for forty years. "One of my daughters texted me and said, 'Mom, I don't know if you've seen the news, but I wanted to get ahold of you beforehand: Lewis died,'" she recalled. "My initial reaction was, 'I knew this would happen.' You knew he would go early, and you knew it would have something to do with his liver. Of course, I didn't want to see him go. You know, I loved him. I believed in him. It was a shame. I was very glad to know that the drugs and drinking were gone and he had a good relationship. It settled things for me to a certain extent. Still, it was totally unexpected how much it hurt me to hear that he died, how much it hurt to know that he's no longer walking around on this planet."

LAURIE ANDERSON SAID THAT a minute after Reed stopped breathing, she contacted Mingyur Rinpoche, the couple's Tibetan Buddhist instructor, "to set in motion the forty-nine days of prayers of *powa,* which are prayers translated as 'the practice of conscious dying' or the 'transference of consciousness at the time of death.'" According to Anderson, *The Tibetan Book of the Dead* reveals that "after death, all beings spend forty-nine days in the bardo. And the bardo is a place, or really a process, that lasts forty-nine days as the mind dissolves and, as the Tibetans believe, the spirit or, let's say, the energy prepares to take another life-form." To commemorate that seven-week period of the bardo, Anderson organized a series of memorials at the apartment that she and Reed shared on West Eleventh Street. Each Sunday afternoon, specially invited friends of the couple gathered to discuss Reed's many interests, including technology, photography, film, music, writing, meditation, tai chi, and *New York Shuffle,* the satellite radio show he had cohosted with Hal Willner.

"During the last seven weeks, I've heard literally hundreds of stories, mostly about Lou's kindness and generosity," Anderson said. "'He put me through college,' 'He gave me two cameras,' 'He listened to my problems.' But most of all the stories were, 'He changed my life by making me do whatever it was better—music, writing, planning.'" Indeed, that seemed to have been Reed's most immediate legacy: providing an example and encouragement to people to, as his song put it, do the things that they want to, regardless of anyone else's opinion.

On Monday, December 16, the fiftieth day after Reed's death, Anderson hosted a memorial for him at the Apollo Theater on 125th Street in Harlem, for invited family members and friends. "We wanted to be here at the Apollo near Lexington and One Hundred and Twenty-Fifth because that was a place he really loved," Anderson explained, nodding to the street corner and subway stop cited in "I'm Waiting for the Man." She explained that the event was meant to celebrate the end of the bardo, and that the invitees were there to "join us in this most important moment of all—the liberation into the cosmos and into eternity of [Reed's] power and his sweetness."

The event was structured enough to bear the weight of its meaning and intent, and casual enough to do so without pretension. Performances by the likes of Deborah Harry, Paul Simon, and Patti Smith alternated with spoken remembrances by Hal Willner; Julian Schnabel; Lou's sister, Bunny; and, most affectingly, Anderson herself. Speakers, friends, family members, and some colleagues were casually seated onstage to the left, including Elisabeth Weiss, a dog trainer who was there to tend to Will, Reed and Anderson's beloved rat terrier, who barked in participation from time to time throughout the evening. A number of the people who spoke noted the appropriateness of the setting, given

Reed's lifelong love for black music. Master Ren and some of the friends with whom Reed had practiced tai chi demonstrated the elegance and force of the martial arts discipline that had become such an important part of his life. The lyricism and sheer physical power of their movements echoed both the beauty and brutality of his songs and the vulnerability and ferocity of his personality. "I finally see why tai chi is called a moving meditation, and what tai chi must have really meant to Lou as he studied it with his friends and his beloved teacher," Anderson said.

Understandably, the evening evoked a vision of Reed that, for the most part, smoothed his abrasive edges and offered rationales — the usual ones — for his explosive anger: his perfectionism, the impenetrability of critics and record company executives, the philistinism of others' expectations of him. Anderson came closest to offering a more comprehensive portrait of this most troubling aspect of Reed's personality. "People who knew him also sometimes experienced his anger and his fury," she said. "But in the last few years, each time he was angry, it was followed by an apology, until the anger and the apology got closer and closer, until they were almost on top of each other. Lou knew what he was doing and what he was going for, and his incredible complexity and his anger was one of the biggest parts of his beauty."

Her remarks made a powerful impression. "I don't

think anyone was ready for her speeches at the memorial service," said Reed's friend the musician Richard Barone. "They were just the most touching and beautiful things that I've ever heard. It transcended their own relationship, and really was about relationships in general."

In a moving remembrance that depicted her brother as the pride of a family that both loved and was a little frightened by him, Bunny revealed the strange coincidence that, ten days after Reed's death, their mother, Toby, died at age ninety-three from what an obituary described as "a ravaging, devastating illness." In his will, Reed had left 75 percent of his estate to Anderson, and the other 25 percent to Bunny, with half a million dollars specifically earmarked for the care of his mother until her death. How somehow fitting that Reed and Toby would leave this world so close together.

It later came to light that Reed's estate, including his song publishing, was worth approximately $30 million, an extraordinary sum for an artist who had complained about money throughout his career. The apartment on West Eleventh Street in Greenwich Village was worth $7 million, and their Hamptons home was estimated to be worth $1.5 million.

Anderson spoke twice at the memorial, once at the beginning and once near the end, and performed a beautiful solo violin piece titled "Flow" that she had written for Reed's birthday a few years earlier. "I wasn't really ready for this," she said during her first remarks. "I wasn't ready for all the crazy things that have happened since Lou died. I've learned more in the last fifty days than I have in my whole life, things I could never have predicted or imagined, things about time and energy and transformation, and about love and life and death and compassion. I began to see things as if for the first time, bound together. It's as if the world has suddenly opened and everything is illuminated and transparent and utterly fragile."

Anderson's eulogies, particularly the final one, were very much in the spirit of her performance art pieces: smart, precisely observed, funny, affectionate, gracious, and strangely detached. "Lou and I were meditators," she stated at one point. "We were students of Buddhism and also artists, so we had lots of reasons to try to understand how life and death can illuminate each other."

Understandably and characteristically, she wanted to emphasize the joy she and Reed had experienced together, and the sense of spiritual deliverance that his death represented for them. She claimed that *The Tibetan Book of the Dead* forbade crying when someone dies, "because it's supposedly confusing to the dead, and you don't want to summon them back, because they actually can't come back. So no crying."

True, many eulogies discourage mourning, but Anderson's were notable for their distinct lack of expressed sadness. She mentioned that Mingyur Rinpoche had presented her and Reed with the emotional challenge of attempting to "feel sad without being sad," which, she said, the couple "worked on all our lives." She further claimed that, since her husband's death, she "had the great experience of actually living in the present, a state of the greatest possible happiness that I'm sure will take me the rest of my life to understand and fully realize." Rinpoche had also taught them about grief. According to Anderson, he told them, "Whenever you think of that person you're grieving for, instead of giving in to grief, do something kind or give something away. 'But,' you say, 'grief is terrible and it's constant! I'd be giving things away nonstop.' And he said, 'So?'"

At their most moving, Anderson's remarks emphasized what she and Reed had found in each other and experienced together. "As a partner in both work and love, Lou was true," she said, "and he was completely transparent. I never had a single doubt that we loved each other beyond anything else from the time we first met until the moment he died. And almost every day we said, 'And you, you are the love of my life,' or some version of that in one of our many private and somewhat bizarre languages. We knew exactly what we had, and we were both beyond grateful." In *Rolling Stone,* Anderson wrote after Reed's death, "At the moment, I have only the greatest happiness, and I am so proud of the way he lived and died, of his incredible power and grace.

"And death? I believe that the purpose of death is the release of love."

That "release of love" seems to mean the transformation of a human being into energy. "Living in the present, I see him and the way his life has turned to energy everywhere I look.... I see how people turn into light and into music and eventually into other people, and how fluid the boundaries really are."

AND SO LOU REED and his music continue to find their way out into the world. After his death, it was announced that a Velvet Underground archive was being assembled at Cornell University, and some of his beloved gear was auctioned off to help fund it. Anderson also arranged for Reed's extensive personal archive to be housed at the New York Public Library, where it will eventually be available to the public.

Reed's work with the Velvet Underground remains the most significant music of his career, but his importance in the twenty-first century extends well beyond the songs he wrote either with that band or as a solo artist. As Laurie Anderson suggested in her eulogy, Reed had become a symbol of artistic freedom, the willingness to try anything regardless of what record executives, critics, or even his own fans might think. For thousands of musicians and artists, he had become an avatar of personal freedom as well. His bisexuality and fascination with transsexualism now feel very much a part of the cultural moment, a rejection of gender orthodoxy as stark as his refusal to conform to aesthetic expectations of any kind. In a culture that rewards success above all else, Reed stood for an insistence on succeeding on his own terms or not at all. The violence of his anger — the least attractive aspect of his personality — came to be seen as an expression of frustration with the limited options offered to artists. It can be viewed as cathartic, a necessary purging of the inessential, rather than offensive. If Reed occasionally went too far, personally or artistically, that was just the price that had to be paid for everyone else not going far enough. What Reed attempted was at least as significant as what he accomplished; his failures are marks of his integrity. As time passes, he will increasingly be judged, as all artists are, by the greatness of his best work. By that standard, there is little chance that he will ever be forgotten.

But as always, Reed maintained a pragmatic view of what his legacy would be. Speaking about a track on *Magic and Loss* in 1992, an interviewer said to Reed, "'Cremation' could stand as your elegy. When you die, radio stations will play that."

"When I die," Reed coolly responded, "they'll play 'Walk on the Wild Side.'" And they certainly did.

ACKNOWLEDGMENTS

A village? No way. Not even Greenwich Village, where I was born and grew up and where Lou Reed lived for many years at various points in his life. No, it evidently takes a city to write a biography of Lou Reed, at least for me. In one sense that's literally true. I feel that I should acknowledge my own upbringing and decades spent living in New York, often in environments central to Reed's story. He and I could share jokes ("It's Fleet Week? Hello, sailor! Can I show you the docks?") that would take some time for outsiders to unpack, if they even cared to. A small thing, perhaps, but a kind of emotional shorthand for a mutual understanding. So, as the King of New York, Lou Reed deserves the first acknowledgment for his extraordinary music and, more personally, his frequent graciousness to me.

But it sometimes seemed as if the number of people who helped bring this book to fruition could populate a city. Most obviously due my thanks are the dozens of people who agreed to do interviews and the nearly equal number who spoke to me on background or off the record. All of them helped guide me to a greater understanding of a life filled with secrets and dark corners. Some writers, including Jim Sullivan and, especially, Tom Anderson, went beyond encouragement (as if that weren't enough) to unsolicited generosity, providing transcripts, hard-to-find published stories, leads on potential sources, and valuable perspective. Beyond the insight in his own work, Rob Enslin provided essential assistance in all things regarding Syracuse University. A number of people — Doug Van Buskirk, Merrill Weiner, Sylvia Ramos, John DiPalermo, and Jeff Gold, in particular — provided help themselves, and led me to others who proved equally helpful. Julia Cox did first-rate research that led me in valuable directions. Anne Marie Morrissey and, especially, Chelsey Madden proved eminently trustworthy heroines of transcription. As photo researcher, my friend Ashley Kahn identified and made it possible for me to obtain all the wonderful pictures in this book.

As always, my agent, Sarah Lazin, provided encouragement and support from the conception of this book to its completion, with the smart, capable aid of assistant agent Julia Conrad. When Sarah asked me with whom I'd most like to work on this project, I immediately said Michael Pietsch, whom I'd known and respected for many years. Now the chief executive officer of Hachette Book Group, Michael, in turn, recommended me to John Parsley, who was then an executive editor at Little, Brown. In our first getting-to-know-you meeting, John said so many smart things that stayed with me for days afterward. His keen intelligence, poise, and understated humor made it inevitable that I would want to work with him, and happily he believed sufficiently in the book to share that desire. He was a dream editor—focused, incisive, encouraging, and inspiring. He improved this book in every possible regard.

For all those reasons, I was heartbroken when John left for another job shortly after the primary edit of this book was completed. He assured me, however, that I would be in good hands with Jean Garnett, who had coedited the manuscript with him. As usual, he was right. Jean has been a splendid comrade-in-arms—fun, energizing, sharp, and completely reliable, an absolute pleasure to work with. Indeed, everyone at Little, Brown—from senior production editor Ben Allen to editorial assistant Gabriella Mongelli and proofreader Leslie Cauldwell—has set a standard for both professionalism and grace. I would especially like to thank copyeditor Nell Beram, who, to use a term of art of which I doubt she'd approve, saved my ass more times than it's comfortable for me to remember. Nell, I definitely owe you one!

My psychotherapist, Jim Traub, not only performed his primary task of sorting out my psychological and emotional life with characteristic insight and sensitivity, but he has been a superb teacher in helping me to comprehend everything that comes into play at every moment in a life. His deft interpretive skills are reflected in all that is worthwhile on every page of this book. No book I write would ever be complete without thanking my late father and mother, Ray and Rose Marie DeCurtis, or my sister, Carmela, and my brother, Dom, who helped make me the person who could write it.

Finally, my darling daughter, Francesca, who was eight years old when I began this book. At times, I feared I might never complete it, though, of course, I always tried to put a brave face on for her. But we understand each other too well—deeply, unspokenly— for her to be fooled. She became interested in origami, and one day last year, when I was in the depths of my fears, she casually handed me a small piece she had done. It was a ramshackle desk, sort of like the one I work at in my office, with a folded paper tucked into it that read: "Lou Reed: The Book, by Anthony." I was so moved by her empathy, but I didn't say anything, nor did she. I simply placed that little desk in front of me, beneath my computer screen, and every day it helped me visualize an end to this work. And, eventually, it did end.

So here it is, sweetheart: *Lou Reed: A Life,* by Dad. For you.

May 2017
New York City

NOTES

Chapter 1. *From Brooklyn to the Crotch of Long Island*

9 "beauty pageants": Merrill Reed Weiner, "A Family in Peril: Lou Reed's Sister Sets the Record Straight About His Childhood," *Cuepoint,* April 13, 2015, https://medium.com/cuepoint/a-family-in-peril-lou-reed-s-sister-sets-the-record-straight-about-his-childhood-20e8399f84a3#.cir5z3hsf.

12 "if you walked": Josh Alan Friedman, "Lou Reed: Ugly People Got No Reason to Live," *Soho Weekly News,* March 9–15, 1978, http://joshalanfriedman.blogspot.com/2009/09/lou-reed-ugly-people-got-no-reason-to.html.

13 "I didn't hear nothin'": Friedman, "Lou Reed: Ugly People Got No Reason to Live."

13 "Most of my childhood memories": *Blue in the Face,* directed by Wayne Wang and Paul Auster (Miramax Films, 1995).

14 "thought that the opportunity": Author interview, Allan Hyman.

14 "It was a fantastic place": Author interview, Doug Van Buskirk.

15 "I don't think any of us thought": Author interview, Judy November.

16 "a quiet guy. Very reserved": Author interview, Allan Hyman.

16 "If you wanted to cast": Author interview, Allan Hyman.

16 "I never got to know": Author interview, Richard Sigal.

16 "anxious individual": Weiner, "A Family in Peril."

17 "Hempstead's like the crotch of Long Island": Friedman, "Lou Reed: Ugly People Got No Reason to Live."

17 "He would refer to my father": Author interview, Allan Hyman.

18 "suffered from anxiety and panic attacks": Weiner, "A Family in Peril."

18 "He started being disrespectful early on": Richard Bloom, email to author.

18 "Lou was a good student": Author interview, Judy November.

19 "Lou and I were always reading": Author interview, Richard Sigal.

21 "I saw him practically every day": Author interview, Allan Hyman.

21 "the dusky, musky, mellifluous, liquid sounds": Lou Reed inducts Dion DiMucci into the Rock and Roll Hall of Fame, January 18, 1989, https://www.youtube.com/watch?v=eigDGXduHiU.

22 "made me believe that I could write a song": David Fricke interview with Lou Reed, Maureen Tucker, and Doug Yule, New York Public Library, December 8, 2009, https://www.youtube.com/watch?v=Zrz0kilk8p8.

22 "I was looking for an opportunity": Author interview, Judy November.

22 "We were in many of the same classes": Olivier Landemaine, "So Blue: An Interview with Phil Harris," updated October 26, 2008, http://olivier.landemaine.free.fr/loureed/thejades/jades.html.

23 "I used to ask Bob Shad": Landemaine, "So Blue: An Interview with Phil Harris."

24 "We played openings": Landemaine, "So Blue: An Interview with Phil Harris."

24 "I used to go up to Harlem": David Fricke, "Q&A: Lou Reed," *Rolling Stone,* March 6, 2003.

24 "We started a garage band": Author interview, Richard Sigal.

24 "Jerry had a good voice": Author interview, Richard Sigal.

NOTES

25 "Lou was starting to become enthusiastic": Author interview, Allan Hyman.

25 "Allan was banging away": Author interview, Richard Sigal.

25 "As we got older in high school": Author interview, Allan Hyman.

25 "We all had long-term girlfriends": Author interview, Richard Sigal.

26 "There was a radio station": Author interview, Allan Hyman.

28 "We all knew everything": Author interview, Richard Sigal.

31 "limp and unresponsive": Weiner, "A Family in Peril."

31 "suffered from delusions": Weiner, "A Family in Peril."

31 "My father, controlling and rigid": Weiner, "A Family in Peril."

32 "I watched my brother": Weiner, "A Family in Peril."

32 "My parents were many things": Weiner, "A Family in Peril."

32 "every day until the day they died": Weiner, "A Family in Peril."

Chapter 2. *Corner Table at the Orange*

35 "He thought it was the stupidest idea": Author interview, Allan Hyman.

36 "Lou and I really hit it off": Author interview, Richard Mishkin.

36 "I knew I was in trouble": Dylan Segelbaum and Erik van Rheenan, *"Excursions on a Wobbly Rail:* "Alumna Remembers Lou Reed's Time at WAER," the *Daily Orange,* November 4, 2013, http://dailyorange.com/2013/11/excursions-on-a-wobbly-rail-alumna-remembers-lou-reeds-time-at-waer/.

37 "Lou fashioned himself a rebel" and following: Author interview, Richard Mishkin.

40 "We knocked. No one answered" and following: Author interview, Richard Sigal.

42 "When I would come into a room": Author interview, Shelley Albin.

43 "She was exquisite": Author interview, Richard Sigal.

43 "Lou ended up with this gorgeous": Author interview, Allan Hyman.

43 "I was very struck": Author interview, Erin Clermont.

43 "It's a strange word to use" and following: Author interview, Shelley Albin.

51 "he was invited to John F. Kennedy's 1961 inauguration": James Atlas, *Delmore Schwartz: The Life of an American Poet* (Avon Books, 1977), p. 340.

52 "like Grant taking Richmond": Atlas, *Delmore Schwartz,* p. 346.

53 "I'm not surprised by his friendship": Rob Enslin, "Doin' the Things That He Wants To: Lou Reed '64 Honored for Achievements in Music, Writing, and Artistic Expression," throughthe jungle.com, 2014, http://www.throughthejungle.com/clients/art -sci/loureed.html.

53 "Those gatherings at the Orange Bar": Author interview, Erin Clermont.

54 "Delmore was drunk all the time": Author interview, Richard Mishkin.

54 "I don't drink": Author interview, Shelley Albin.

Chapter 3. *Fellini Squared*

56 "When all is said and done": Author interview, Richard Mishkin.

57 "He wrote to Delmore Schwartz" and following: Lou Reed, letter to Delmore Schwartz, 1965, Beinecke Rare Book and Manuscript Library, Yale University.

57 "Much of my income": Lou Reed, "My First Year in New York: 1965," the *New York Times Magazine,* September 17, 2000.

58 "They would put us in a room and say": Author interview, Lou Reed.

59 "Phillips evidently assumed": Victor Bockris and John Cale, *What's Welsh for Zen: The Autobiography of John Cale* (Bloomsbury, 1999).

60 "It was a period when a lot of new took place": Author interview, Bob Neuwirth.

61 "My first impressions" and following: Bockris and Cale, *What's Welsh for Zen.*

63 "I had a loft on Spring Street": Author interview, Eric Andersen.

64 "before I met Lou" and following: Bockris and Cale, *What's Welsh for Zen.*

69 "secretly I was exhilarated": Bockris and Cale, *What's Welsh for Zen.*

69 "I felt like someone turned a blender on": Author interview, Rob Norris.

71 "At first, before they got to know him": Bockris and Cale, *What's Welsh for Zen.*

73 "I think Andy was afraid of him" and following: Author interview, Danny Fields.

73 "Moe and I were pretty young": Author interview, Martha Morrison.

74 "I couldn't believe what he was living in": Author interview, Richard Mishkin.

76 "We were definitely observed": Author interview, Martha Morrison.

76 "You just felt like you were at the center of things": Author interview, Danny Fields.

78 "Can you imagine doing that to a band?": Author interview, Danny Fields.

78 "I cannot make love to Jews anymore": Bockris and Cale, *What's Welsh for Zen.*

79 "I remember him saying to me": Author interview, Shelley Albin.

80 "black-tied psychiatrists": Grace Glueck, "Syndromes Pop at Delmonico's: Andy Warhol and His Gang Meet the Psychiatrists," the *New York Times,* January 14, 1966.

80 "a famous fashion model and now a singer": Glueck, "Syndromes Pop at Delmonico's."

84 "I don't think we would have been anything" and following: Bockris and Cale, *What's Welsh for Zen.*

84 "I had never been in an environment like that": Author interview, Richard Mishkin.

85 "It wasn't really rock": Author interview, Bob Neuwirth.

Chapter 4. *The Destructive Element*

88 "We were really excited": Victor Bockris and John Cale, *What's Welsh for Zen: The Autobiography of John Cale* (Bloomsbury, 1999).

88 "'Heroin' was an incredible thing": Rob Enslin, "Doin' the Things That He Wants To: Lou Reed '64 Honored for Achievements in Music, Writing, and Artistic Expression," throughthe jungle.com, 2014, http://www.throughthejungle.com/clients/art -sci/loureed.html.

90 "It will replace nothing, except maybe suicide": Andy Warhol and Pat Hackett, *POPism: The Warhol Sixties* (Harcourt Brace Jovanovich, 1980), p. 210.

91 "We were pretty much appalled": Author interview, John Cale.

91 "all very campy and very Greenwich Village sick": Ralph J. Gleason, review of the Velvet Underground, the *San Francisco Chronicle,* May 30, 1966.

91 "I really didn't need Ralph Gleason landing on me": Author interview, Lou Reed.

92 "his body had lain unclaimed at Bellevue Hospital for two days": James Atlas, *Delmore Schwartz: The Life of an American Poet* (Avon Books, 1977), p. 354.

93 "I was one of the first Medicare patients": Lou Reed, *Between Thought and Expression: Selected Lyrics of Lou Reed* (Hyperion, 1991), p. 5.

93 "Into the destructive element": Atlas, *Delmore Schwartz,* p. 356.

95 "*Sgt. Pepper* was a theatrical statement": Author interview, John Cale.

95 "Robert Lowell, up for a poetry prize": Lou Reed, "The View from the Bandstand: Life Among the Poo-bahs," *Aspen Magazine,* Volume 1, No. 3 (December 1966).

97 "So Far 'Underground,' You Get the Bends": David Fricke, liner notes, *The Velvet Underground: 45th Anniversary Super Deluxe Edition* (Polydor).

100 "Warhol's favorite of the Velvets' songs": Reed, *Between Thought and Expression,* p. 10.

101 "The idea here was to string words together": Reed, *Between Thought and Expression,* p. 7.

Chapter 5. *Aggressive, Going to God*

103 "was talking to Lou Reed the other day": Kristine McKenna, "Brian Eno: Lots of Aura, No Airplay," the *Los Angeles Times,* May 23, 1982.

103 "The album's sales were actually not quite that dismal": Jeff Gold, "Lou Reed and Exactly How Many Albums the Velvet Underground Sold," *RecordMecca: Fine Music Collectibles,* November 10, 2013, http://recordmecca.com/news/lou-reed -exactly-many-albums-velvet-underground-sold/.

104 "Mick Jagger said that the song 'Stray Cat Blues'": Nick Kent, *New Musical Express,* June 1977.

104 "Max's at that time was kind of a metaphor": Author interview, Danny Fields.

105 "'Lou Reed' was a character": Author interview, Bob Neuwirth.

106 "That was the worst thing": David Fricke, "Lou Reed: The *Rolling Stone* Interview," *Rolling Stone,* May 4, 1989.

107 "I was always inviting Louie": Author interview, Martha Morrison.

108 "Every time I'd go there" and following: Author interview, Rob Norris.

109 "You'd pay three bucks" and following: Tony Lioce, "When Backstage Was No Big Deal," the *New York Times,* November 2, 2013.

110 "I don't know how Sesnick ended up managing the Velvets": Author interview, Rob Norris.

111 "Our lives were in chaos": David Fricke, liner notes, *White Light/ White Heat: 45th Anniversary Super Deluxe Edition* (Polydor).

111 "very rabid record": David Fricke, liner notes, *Peel Slowly and See* (Polydor Chronicles).

NOTES

112 "I had twenty-four shock treatments": Lou Reed, *Between Thought and Expression: Selected Lyrics of Lou Reed* (Hyperion, 1991), p. 11.

112 "It finally got to the point": Author interview, Lou Reed.

113 "When I think of the many wonderful producers": Victor Bockris and John Cale, *What's Welsh for Zen: The Autobiography of John Cale* (Bloomsbury, 1999).

113 "We used to rehearse, basically, onstage": Fricke, *White Light/White Heat.*

113 "like a finely tuned British racing car" and following: Author interview, Rob Norris.

114 "Live, they were like nothing we'd ever heard": Lioce, "When Backstage Was No Big Deal."

114 "They say rock is life-affirming music": Fricke, *White Light/White Heat.*

115 "Come. Step softly into the inevitable world": Fricke, *White Light/White Heat.*

115 "No one listened to it": Fricke, *White Light/White Heat.*

116 "To Lou...everybody's gay": Bockris and Cale, *What's Welsh for Zen.*

117 "We never had a booking agent": Fricke, *Peel Slowly and See.*

119 "Yule claimed that his astrological sign of Pisces": Andrew Lapointe, "Interview with Doug Yule," *PopMatters,* February 11, 2005, http://www.popmatters.com/feature/yule-doug -021105.

119 "I knew it would make some difference": David Fricke, liner notes, *The Velvet Underground: 45th Anniversary Super Deluxe Edition* (Polydor).

120 "this all-enveloping cloud of heaven music": Richie Unterberger, *White Light/White Heat: The Velvet Underground Day by Day* (Jawbone Press, 2009), p. 230.

120 "The greatest thing about the Velvets was the holes in the music": Fricke, *The Velvet Underground.*

121 "Yeah, it's about Candy Darling": Fricke, *Peel Slowly and See.*

121 "You still don't hear that kind of purity in vocals": Fricke, *Peel Slowly and See.*

121 "missed very much": Reed, *Between Thought and Expression,* p. 23.

122 "I didn't want to hear any of those songs": Author interview, Shelley Albin.

122 "How do you define a group like this": Lester Bangs, review of *The Velvet Underground, Rolling Stone,* May 17, 1969.

123 "I was having fun with words": Reed, *Between Thought and Expression,* p. 25.

124 "Their music is just impure enough": Fricke, *The Velvet Underground.*

125 "I think he thought they were Warhol-esque": David Fricke, liner notes, *Loaded: Fully Loaded Edition* (Rhino/Atlantic).

126 "loaded with hits": Fricke, *Loaded.*

127 "The guy couldn't dance either": Fricke, *Loaded.*

127 "It may seem astounding in retrospect": Bockris and Cale, *What's Welsh for Zen.*

128 "The Velvets played there all summer for no apparent reason": Author interview, Lenny Kaye.

128 "No slur on Doug": Fricke, *Peel Slowly and See.*

129 "It's still called a Velvet Underground record": Fricke, *Peel Slowly and See.*

129 "'Rock and Roll' is about me": Fricke, *Loaded.*

130 "This schmuck, he tried to kill himself": Author interview, Ed McCormack.

Chapter 6. *All the Things That Are Missing*

132 "Oh, I guess they're going to be the Velveteen Underground": Author interview, Danny Fields.

132 "I was still very foreign": David Fricke, liner notes, *Loaded: Fully Loaded Edition* (Rhino/Atlantic).

133 "worked for forty dollars a week": Richie Unterberger, *White Light/White Heat: The Velvet Underground Day by Day* (Jawbone Press, 2009), p. 292.

133 "easily one of the best albums to show up": Lenny Kaye, review of *Loaded, Rolling Stone,* December 24, 1970.

134 "Due to a near-textbook case of management hassles": Kaye, review of *Loaded.*

134 "Interestingly, the English band Squeeze": Jason P. Woodbury, "Squeeze's Chris Difford on England, John Cale, and the Paul McCartney–Produced Record That Never Came to Be," *Phoenix New Times,* April 11, 2012, http://www.phoenixnewtimes. com/music/squeezes-chris-difford-on-england-john-cale-and -the-paul-mccartney-produced-record-that-never-came -to-be-6610763#page-2.

135 "He didn't make the most positive impression" and following: Author interview, Bettye Kronstad.

137 "Lou would tell me how much he loved Bettye" and following: Author interview, Ed McCormack.

138 "there was some thought about going to corporations" and following: Author interview, Lenny Kaye.

139 "When Lou would come into the city": Author interview, Bettye Kronstad.

139 "We made fun of her": Author interview, Danny Fields.

140 "It's just making a rock-and-roll album": Richard Williams, *Melody Maker,* quoted in liner notes to *Lou Reed* (BMG, 2000) by David Fricke.

142 "This is the closest realization": From *Disc and Music Echo,* quoted in liner notes to *Lou Reed.*

142 "Back in London, the consensus is": David Fricke, liner notes, *Lou Reed.*

142 "How successful is an album that keeps you imagining": Greg Shaw, review of *Lou Reed* (RCA), *Phonograph Record,* May 1972.

142 "There's just too many things wrong with it": Mick Rock, "Lou Reed Sees the Future, Darkly," *Rolling Stone*, October 26, 1972.

Chapter 7. *Transformer*

143 "I've not been particularly good": Vic Garbarini, "Lou Reed: Waiting for the Muse," *Musician*, July 1, 1986.

144 "I been in and out of mental institutions": Susan Braudy, "James Taylor: A New Troubadour," the *New York Times Magazine*, February 21, 1971.

145 "he viewed the Velvet Underground as an essential influence": Charles Shaar Murray, "David at the Dorchester: Bowie on Ziggy and Other Matters," *New Musical Express*, July 22, 1972.

145 "had a rule: no blues licks": Garbarini, "Lou Reed: Waiting for the Muse."

147 "I seem to inspire transvestite bands": Mick Rock, "Lou Reed Sees the Future, Darkly," *Rolling Stone*, October 26, 1972.

148 "Lou was going through an incredibly bad patch" and following: Marc Spitz, *Bowie: A Biography* (Crown, 2009), p. 171.

148 "Glam rock, androgyny, polymorphic sex": *Lou Reed: Rock and Roll Heart, American Masters* documentary, directed by Timothy Greenfield-Sanders, 1998.

149 "I wanted to see how he did things in the studio": David Fricke, "Lou Reed," *Rolling Stone*, November 5–December 10, 1987.

149 "The year started out with David Bowie": *Billboard*, quoted in Spitz, *Bowie*, p. 200.

149 "That was a really exciting time": Author interview, Bettye Kronstad.

149 "While Lou's solo debut had been difficult": Lisa Robinson, *There Goes Gravity: A Life in Rock and Roll* (Riverhead Books, 2014), pp. 86–87.

150 "shades and maroon fingernails" and following: Murray, "David at the Dorchester."

150 "I remember David in interviews": Author interview, Mick Rock.

151 "I was petrified that he said yes to working with me" and following: *Lou Reed: Rock and Roll Heart, American Masters* documentary.

151 "I think his new material on the album that we're gonna do": Murray, "David at the Dorchester."

151 "a classic...absolutely brilliant": *Lou Reed: Rock and Roll Heart, American Masters* documentary.

152 "They're just cursory sketches": "Walk on the Wild Side," Lou Reed, *Rolling Stone,* September 8, 1988.

152 "With a name like that it was too good to leave alone": *Classic Albums: Lou Reed, Transformer,* documentary directed by Bob Smeaton (Eagle Rock Entertainment), 2001.

152 "They were the ragtag queens of Max's Kansas City": *Classic Albums: Lou Reed, Transformer,* documentary.

152 "I have always thought it would be kinda fun": Nick Kent, "A Walk on the Wild Side of Lou Reed," *New Musical Express,* June 9, 1973.

153 "Writing songs is like making a play": Richard Witts, *The Velvet Underground* (Equinox Publishing, 2006), p. 44.

154 "Ronson's influence...'was stronger than David's'": Nick Kent, "Lou Reed: The Sinatra of the Seventies," *New Musical Express,* April 28, 1973.

154 "With Ronno and David there was a real simpatico": *Classic Albums: Lou Reed, Transformer,* documentary.

155 "Lou used to say some funny things to me": *Classic Albums: Lou Reed, Transformer,* documentary.

155 "The thing with Ronno is that I could very rarely understand a word he said": *Classic Albums: Lou Reed, Transformer,* documentary.

155 "I actually wasn't aware of it, if it happened": Author interview, Bettye Kronstad.

156 "It's what I thought about Andy being shot": *Classic Albums: Lou Reed, Transformer,* documentary.

157 "Vicious, I hit you with a flower": *Classic Albums: Lou Reed, Transformer,* documentary.

157 "Here is this whole glam thing going on": *Classic Albums: Lou Reed, Transformer,* documentary.

157 "You can't imagine how profound and delirious it was": Don Shewey, Lou Reed in memoriam, loureed.com, http://www .loureed.com/inmemoriam/.

159 "We had plans to meet in the park" and following: Author interview, Bettye Kronstad.

160 "Lou pounced on it": Author interview, Mick Rock.

160 "an effeminate Frankenstein monster": Ed McCormack, "Scotch and Sympathy at Tully Hall," *Rolling Stone,* March 1, 1973.

160 "the degenerate side of glam": Author interview, Mick Rock.

161 "Haven't you seen the cover?": Ray Fox-Cumming, "Lou Reed: The Black Sheep of New York," *Disc and Music Echo,* October 21, 1972.

161 "I could have had a whole new career": *Classic Albums: Lou Reed, Transformer,* documentary.

161 "It's just showbiz": Author interview, Bettye Kronstad.

161 "In the midst of all the make-believe madness, the mock depravity": *Classic Albums: Lou Reed, Transformer,* documentary.

161 "real cockteaser": Nick Tosches, review of *Transformer, Rolling Stone,* January 4, 1973.

162 "This new album is further proof": Robot A. Hull, review of *Transformer, Creem,* February 1973.

162 "the Lou Reed Chic album": Kent, "A Walk on the Wild Side of Lou Reed."

162 "It is his best-ever album": Fox-Cumming, "Lou Reed: The Black Sheep of New York."

NOTES

Chapter 8. *A City's Divided Soul*

163 "The fact is that his association with David Bowie": Richard Williams, "Broken Reed? Lou Reed, Duncan Browne: Sundown Theatre, Edmonton, London," *Melody Maker,* October 7, 1972.

163 "I'm not going in the same direction as David": Ray Fox-Cumming, "Lou Reed: The Black Sheep of New York."

164 "a backlash on *Transformer*": Nick Kent, "A Walk on the Wild Side of Lou Reed," *New Musical Express,* June 9, 1973.

164 "some graffiti genius": Ed McCormack, "Scotch and Sympathy at Tully Hall," *Rolling Stone,* March 1, 1973.

164 "Did you know that both shows are sold out?": McCormack, "Scotch and Sympathy at Tully Hall."

164 "Those who expected the fey Phantom in pancake": McCormack, "Scotch and Sympathy at Tully Hall."

165 "Andy heard the news from the vultures": McCormack, "Scotch and Sympathy at Tully Hall."

165 "His presence is cool and benign": McCormack, "Scotch and Sympathy at Tully Hall."

165 "the kind of rock and roll that stands up to anything": Richard Nusser, *Village Voice,* February 1, 1973.

166 "This is the weirdest party I've ever seen": McCormack, "Scotch and Sympathy at Tully Hall."

166 "somnambulant heart" and following: McCormack, "Scotch and Sympathy at Tully Hall."

166 "In Fred's mind": Author interview, Bettye Kronstad.

166 "Lou's a changed man": Nick Kent, "Lou Reed: The Sinatra of the Seventies," *New Musical Express,* April 28, 1973.

167 "to sag. His chin drops down on his chest": McCormack, "Scotch and Sympathy at Tully Hall."

168 "I still do shoot it": Lester Bangs, "Deaf-Mute in a Telephone Booth," *Let It Rock,* November 1973.

168 "It was like going to see God": Author interview, Bettye Kronstad.

168 "Let's go...Get dressed" and following: Ed McCormack, "A Last Waltz on the Wild Side," *Vanity Fair,* January 13, 2014.

169 "That's my masterpiece": McCormack, "Scotch and Sympathy at Tully Hall."

169 "In the end...he kind of resented the song": Author interview, Bettye Kronstad.

169 "Lou is out of the glitter thing": Stephen Demorest, "Lou Reed Stuns Listeners with the Horrifying Story of *Berlin,*" *Circus,* December 1973.

170 "it was his favorite version that had ever been done on one of his songs": Demorest, "Lou Reed Stuns Listeners with the Horrifying Story of *Berlin.*"

170 "I just found him blazingly smart and challenging": Nick Patch, "Q and A: Bob Ezrin Discusses His Good Friend, Late Musician Lou Reed," the *Canadian Press,* October 28, 2013.

171 "do justice to his sledgehammer images" and following: Larry Sloman, "Lou Reed's New Deco-Disk: Sledgehammer Blow to Glitterbugs," *Rolling Stone,* September 27, 1973.

171 "a top-notch set": "Top Album Picks," *Billboard,* October 13, 1973.

172 "movie without pictures": Demorest, "Lou Reed Stuns Listeners with the Horrifying Story of *Berlin.*"

173 "*Berlin* was real close to home": David Fricke, "Lou Reed: Out of the Darkness," *Rolling Stone,* September 25, 1986.

173 "Lou had become abusive": Bettye Kronstad, "Bettye Kronstad on Lou Reed's *Berlin,*" cloudsandclocks.net, July 20, 2007, http://www.cloudsandclocks.net/features/kronstad_on _berlin_E.html.

173 "might have had something to do with all the fucking drugs and drinking" and following: Author interview, Bettye Kronstad.

174 "I remember the morning I woke up": Kronstad, "Bettye Kronstad on Lou Reed's *Berlin.*"

175 "The other thing...is that he was actually writing" and following: Author interview, Bettye Kronstad.

175 "I love the idea of a divided city": Author interview, Lou Reed.

176 "*Berlin* needed a lyrical approach that was direct": Bruce Pollock, "Lou Reed Does Not Want Anyone to Know How He Writes His Songs," *Modern Hi-Fi and Music,* 1975.

176 "just magnificent, visceral, elemental writing": Patch, "Q and A: Bob Ezrin Discusses His Good Friend, Late Musician Lou Reed."

176 "a nightmare to make" and following: Russell Hall, "Bob Ezrin," *Performing Songwriter,* January/February 2002.

177 "It drove me literally crazy": Demorest, "Lou Reed Stuns Listeners with the Horrifying Story of *Berlin.*"

177 "I dropped fourteen minutes of endings, solos, interstitial material": Sloman, "Lou Reed's New Deco-Disk."

177 "told his seven-year-old son, David": Rob Bowman, liner notes, *Between Thought and Expression: The Lou Reed Anthology* (RCA), 1992.

178 "It was a heroin rebound": Bowman, *Between Thought and Expression.*

178 "Lou doesn't want to talk about it much": Demorest, "Lou Reed Stuns Listeners with the Horrifying Story of *Berlin.*"

178 "I think I've gone as deep as I want to go": Pollock, "Lou Reed Does Not Want Anyone to Know How He Writes His Songs."

178 "I know why he called it *Berlin*": Ron Ross, "The Head Doll Talks About Lou Reed's *Berlin,*" *Phonograph Record,* December 1973.

179 "Just when you think your ex-idol has slumped": Nick Kent, review of *Berlin, New Musical Express,* October 6, 1973.

179 "Lou Reed's *Berlin*... is a disaster": Stephen Davis, review of *Berlin, Rolling Stone,* December 20, 1973.

179 "It's one of the worst reviews I've ever seen of anything": Pollock, "Lou Reed Does Not Want Anyone to Know How He Writes His Songs."

179 "Strikingly and unexpectedly, Lou Reed's *Berlin*": John Rockwell, "Pop: The Glitter Is Gold," the *New York Times,* December 9, 1973.

180 "the most affecting rock effort in recent memory": Demorest, "Lou Reed Stuns Listeners with the Horrifying Story of *Berlin*."

180 "But I fail to see how that makes it a bad record": Timothy Ferris, "The Beauty of Decay," review of *Rock n Roll Animal, Rolling Stone*, March 28, 1974.

180 "I don't think anybody is anybody else's moral compass": David Marchese, "The Spin Interview: Lou Reed," *Spin*, November 1, 2008.

Chapter 9. *Rock n Roll Animal*

181 "That was the bad move": Author interview, Lou Reed.

182 "The expectation was that I was going to do something very commercial with him": Ben Sisario, "Revisiting a Bleak Album to Plumb Its Dark Riches," the *New York Times*, December 13, 2006.

182 "didn't have a radio-friendly single": Russell Hall, "Bob Ezrin," *Performing Songwriter*, January/February 2002.

183 "not for good reasons": Author interview, Lou Reed.

183 "I had heard of Lou because some of my friends" and following: Author interview, Eddie Reynolds.

185 "I know why you're all here": Nick Kent, "Lou Reed: The Sinatra of the Seventies," *New Musical Express*, April 28, 1973.

186 "He ripped me a new one" and following: Author interview, Eddie Reynolds.

187 "I don't think I'm a singer": Chris Charlesworth, "Lou Reed: Man of Few Words," *Melody Maker*, March 9, 1974.

188 "It's just like Lou Reed": Wayne Robins, "Lou Reed: *Rock n Roll Animal*," *Zoo World*, April 25, 1974.

188 "Reed's live music brings the Velvets into the arena": Robert Christgau, Consumer Guide review of *Rock n Roll Animal*, 1974, https://www.robertchristgau.com/get_artist.php?name=Lou+Reed.

188 "mediocre pickup band": Paul Nelson, review of *Lou Reed Live, Rolling Stone*, June 5, 1975.

190 "It was the only thing to do at the time" and following: Lenny Kaye, "Lou Reed," *New Musical Express,* January 24, 1976.

190 "A lot of people, myself included": Author interview, Lou Reed.

190 "that macabre... ah, majestic": Nick Kent, "A Limey in L.A. #1: Hey Man, You with a Gwoop?," *New Musical Express,* March 15, 1975.

191 "so incredible, the most incredible albums ever made": Kaye, "Lou Reed."

191 "When I made my pitch at an A&R meeting": Kevin Avery, *Everything Is an Afterthought: The Life and Writings of Paul Nelson* (Fantagraphics Books, 2011), p. 435.

192 "Do you people have a curfew": Lou Reed, spoken introduction to "I'm Waiting for the Man," *1969: The Velvet Underground Live* (Mercury, 1974).

193 "couldn't wait to hear them": Avery, *Everything Is an Afterthought,* p. 435.

193 "The Velvet Underground must have scared a lot of people": Elliott Murphy, liner notes, *1969: The Velvet Underground Live* (Mercury, 1974).

193 "this very nice boy Lewis Reed called": Avery, *Everything Is an Afterthought,* p. 435.

194 "After the show, all these people came over" and following: Author interview, Bettye Kronstad.

194 "While everyone else was at the show": Bettye Kronstad, "Bettye Kronstad on Lou Reed's *Berlin,*" cloudsandclocks .net, July 20, 2007, http://www.cloudsandclocks.net/features/ kronstad_on_berlin_E.html.

194 "Then things calmed down" and following: Author interview, Bettye Kronstad.

Chapter 10. *One Machine Talking to Another*

198 "Steve left because he thought" and following: Author interview, Michael Fonfara.

200 "This is fantastic: the worse I am, the more it sells": Author interview, Danny Fields.

201 "According to one of the spot's producers": Richard Metzger, "Amusing TV Commercial for Lou Reed's Sleazy *Sally Can't Dance* Album, 1974," dangerousminds.net, February 25, 2014, http://dangerousminds.net/comments/amusing_tv _commercial_for_lou_reeds_sleazy_sally_cant_dance _album_1974.

202 "Oh, I slept through *Sally Can't Dance*": Caroline Coon, "Lou Reed: How Lou Saw the White Light," *Melody Maker,* December 18, 1976.

202 "What a horror. It went Top 10 and it sucks": Lenny Kaye, "Lou Reed," *New Musical Express,* January 24, 1976.

203 "The worse the albums were, the more they apparently sold": Coon, "Lou Reed: How Lou Saw the White Light."

203 "I kept thinking that somehow it would stop": Coon, "Lou Reed: How Lou Saw the White Light."

204 "My goal at the time": Lou Reed, liner notes, *Metal Machine Music: Performed by Zeitkratzer Live* (Asphodel, 2007).

204 "Warhol once said that his ambition was to become a machine": Ken Emerson, "Why Can't America Love New York City's Pop Favorites?," the *New York Times,* Arts and Leisure, September 28, 1975.

204 "It's just one machine talking to another": Anthony O'Grady, "An Afternoon with Lou Reed and *Metal Machine Music,*" *RAM,* August 9, 1975.

205 "pretentious": Rob Bowman, liner notes, *Between Thought and Expression: The Lou Reed Anthology* (RCA).

206 "I did tons of shows with the Velvet Underground": David Fricke, liner notes, *Metal Machine Music* reissue (Buddha/ RCA/BMG, 2000).

207 "you start to hear a certain oblique cohesion": Fricke, *Metal Machine Music* reissue.

207 *"Methedrine Machine Music"*: Kaye, "Lou Reed."

207 "All the specs were a lie": Reed, *Metal Machine Music: Performed by Zeitkratzer Live.*

207 "This record is not for parties/dancing/background/romance" and following: Lou Reed, liner notes, *Metal Machine Music* (RCA, 1975).

207 "a try at a Warholian soundbyte": Reed, *Metal Machine Music: Performed by Zeitkratzer Live.*

208 "onstage image of off-the-wall instability" and following: John Rockwell, "The Pop Life: Lou Reed Turns Up the Volume," the *New York Times,* June 20, 1975.

208 "What's most distressing is the possibility": James Wolcott, review of *Metal Machine Music, Rolling Stone,* August 14, 1975.

208 "In time...it will prove itself": Mikal Gilmore, "Lou Reed's Heart of Darkness," *Rolling Stone,* March 22, 1979.

208 "I run into different musicians": Fricke, *Metal Machine Music* reissue.

209 "as an underground artist again": Kaye, "Lou Reed."

Chapter 11. *A Speed-Addled, Leather-Clad Virgil*

212 "what made it special?": Author interview, Clive Davis.

213 "I saw them the way they wanted to see themselves" and following: Author interview, Mick Rock.

214 "Rock's educated, but I am, too": Mark Beaumont, "Lou Reed: The Last Interview, *New Musical Express,* November 9, 2013.

214 "I had been around interesting clubs in London" and following: Author interview, Mick Rock.

215 "It's very buttoned-up": Author interview, Erin Clermont.

216 "I'd been up for days, as usual": Marc Campbell, "Rachel: Lou Reed's Transsexual Muse," dangerousminds.net, February 6, 2013, http://dangerousminds.net/comments/rachel_lou_reeds _transsexual_muse.

217 "a strange, somewhat female thing" and following: Lester Bangs, "Let Us Now Praise Famous Death Dwarves, or How

I Slugged It Out with Lou Reed and Stayed Awake," *Creem,* March 1975.

218 "Do you understand, Quine? This is a person I was close to": Jim DeRogatis, "Robert Quine: Such a Lovable Genius," *Perfect Sound Forever,* http://www.furious.com/perfect/Quine/quinederogatis.html.

218 "Lou's babysitter" and following: Bangs, "Let Us Now Praise Famous Death Dwarves."

219 "She took care of things for him" and following: Author interview, Erin Clermont.

220 "When Lou walked into a room": Author interview, Michael Fonfara.

220 "It was an amazing picture": Author interview, Clive Davis.

223 "using those kinds of pop doo-wop phrases": Rob Bowman, liner notes, *Between Thought and Expression: The Lou Reed Anthology* (RCA).

223 "a tall, exotic person with cascading hair": Caroline Coon, "Lou Reed: How Lou Saw the White Light," *Melody Maker,* December 18, 1976.

224 "Saying 'I'm a Coney Island baby' at the end of that song": Mikal Gilmore, "Lou Reed's Heart of Darkness," *Rolling Stone,* March 22, 1979.

224 "made it that much harder for *Coney Island Baby*": Lenny Kaye, "Lou Reed," *New Musical Express,* January 24, 1976.

224 "best album in years": John Rockwell, "Lou Reed: Commercial or Defiant," the *New York Times,* February 4, 1976.

224 "he is expressing the profound dream of the damned": Paul Nelson, review of *Coney Island Baby, Rolling Stone,* March 23, 1976.

Chapter 12. *This Gender Business*

226 "complained vituperatively" and following: John Rockwell, "Lou Reed: Commercial or Defiant," the *New York Times,* February 4, 1976.

226 "a chain of racist and anti-Semitic remarks": Timothy Ferris, "Lou Reed's Degenerate Regeneration," *Rolling Stone,* April 8, 1976.

226 "nigger comb": Ed McCormack, "A Last Waltz on the Wild Side," *Vanity Fair,* January 13, 2014.

226 "nigger music—pardon me": John Morthland, "Lou Reed: Say It Again, Lou," *Creem,* December 1976.

226 "live-in boyfriend" and following: Ferris, "Lou Reed's Degenerate Regeneration."

227 "with similar characters, and those do not get published": Author interview, Mick Rock.

227 "glass-coffee-table queen" and following: Ferris, "Lou Reed's Degenerate Regeneration."

227 "You're going to get interviewed": Author interview, Jeffrey Ross.

228 "The critics think I'm that tape": Ferris, "Lou Reed's Degenerate Regeneration."

228 "Well, look, why don't you come back to my hotel with me?" and following: Legs McNeil and Gillian McCain, *Please Kill Me: The Uncensored Oral History of Punk* (Grove Press, 1996), pp. 97–98.

229 "You want me to tell you my real feelings?" and following: Author interview, Jonny Podell.

229 "one had to wonder if his very public relationship with Rachel": McCormack, "A Last Waltz on the Wild Side."

229 "I always thought one way kids had of getting back at their parents": David Fricke, "Lou Reed," *Rolling Stone,* November 5–December 10, 1987.

229 "I never regard other people's relationships as being my business": Author interview, Mick Rock.

229 "We used to have this joke going" and following: Author interview, Michael Fonfara.

230 "very stoned," "beat up and locked out": Author interview, Richard Sassin.

230 "Lou Reed called and that was the drama of the day": Entry for December 19, 1976, *The Andy Warhol Diaries*, edited by Pat Hackett (Warner Books, 1989).

230 "I have these pictures of Lou holding this puppy": Author interview, Mick Rock.

230 "couldn't cook. She tried desperately": Author interview, Michael Fonfara.

231 "I was walking along the shore with my husband": Author interview, Susan Blond.

231 "a marriage made in the emergency room": Author interview, Jonny Podell.

233 "an elegant glass coffee table" and following: Ed McCormack, "A Last Waltz on the Wild Side."

233 "S and M following" and following: Binky Philips, "I Ignore Lou Reed, but My Friend Charlie Winds Up in Lou's Apartment," the *Huffington Post*, November 1, 2013.

235 "infected lung" and following: Caroline Coon, "Lou Reed: How Lou Saw the White Light," *Melody Maker*, December 18, 1976.

235 "as soon as you met Rachel/Richard" and following: Author interview, Jeffrey Ross.

237 "We'll listen to music, we'll relax": Author interview, Clive Davis.

237 "There was just me and Rachel...living at the fucking Gramercy Park Hotel": Mikal Gilmore, "Lou Reed's Heart of Darkness," *Rolling Stone*, March 22, 1979.

238 "Lou doesn't sell albums, but Clive believes in him": Peter Silverton, "Lou Reed in Cloning Sensation," *Sounds*, May 6, 1978.

238 "I didn't make a record because I couldn't have it my way": Coon, "Lou Reed: How Lou Saw the White Light."

238 "Lou had relevance. He wanted mass popularity": Author interview, Jonny Podell.

239 "good ears" and following: Rob Bowman, liner notes, *Between Thought and Expression: The Lou Reed Anthology* (RCA).

239 "Clive is a genius" and following: Author interview, Michael Fonfara.

239 "Every once in a while...Lou would say": Bowman, *Between Thought and Expression*.

239 "If I were a painter" and following: Author interview, Clive Davis.

240 "very danceable, the kind of thing that, if you were sitting in a bar": John Morthland, "Lou Reed Bangs Drum Slowly," *Rolling Stone*, September 23, 1976.

240 "Mr. Reed had paid his debts to Mr. Davis" and following: John Rockwell, "The Pop Life: Review of *Rock and Roll Heart*," the *New York Times*, November 12, 1976.

Chapter 13. *Fucking Faggot Junkie*

241 "There weren't sound systems": Gavin Martin, "Lou Reed: 'I've Lied So Much About the Past That I Can't Tell What Is True Anymore," *Uncut*, March 2003.

241 "Lou always had lots of issues on the road": Author interview, Michael Fonfara.

242 "You said a little while ago that you sing mainly about drugs" and following: Lou Reed press conference, Sydney, Australia, August 19, 1974.

244 "In the middle of that tour, Lou decided": Author interview, Michael Fonfara.

245 "Lou was smashing things": Author interview, Suzanne Vega.

245 "If he didn't do too much, he'd be right on the money" and following: Author interview, Michael Fonfara.

246 "a very, very personal problem that should never have damned well happened": Liam Hyslop, "Top 10 Worst New Zealand Concerts," *Stuff*, February 20, 2015, http://www.stuff.co.nz/entertainment/music/66436599/top-10-worst-new-zealand-concerts.

246 "at Tom Jones's shows would throw roses, panties, and hotel room keys": Author interview, Eric Andersen.

247 "For the most part, the audiences were terrific" and following: Author interview, Michael Fonfara.

248 "the mood was only enhanced" and following: John Rockwell, "Spark Lacking for Lou Reed at Palladium," the *New York Times,* November 14, 1976.

250 "We're playing the Anaheim Convention Center" and following: Author interview, Michael Fonfara.

250 "He was like some ghost": Rob Bowman, liner notes, *Between Thought and Expression: The Lou Reed Anthology* (RCA).

251 "Lou's very, very smart": Legs McNeil and Gillian McCain, *Please Kill Me: The Uncensored Oral History of Punk* (Grove Press, 1996), p. 285.

252 "She was very smart, and she knew when not to talk" and following: Author interview, Michael Fonfara.

252 "I was walking across the street": Author interview, Jeffrey Ross.

253 "The detail was as precise as possible": Bowman, *Between Thought and Expression.*

254 "They're crazy!" and following: Charles Curkin, "He Was Present at the Birth of Punk, and He Took Notes," the *New York Times,* December 26, 2014.

254 "what the Ramones *should* do": John Morthland, "Lou Reed Bangs Drum Slowly," *Rolling Stone,* September 23, 1976.

254 "Shakespeare had a phrase for that": Mikal Gilmore, "Lou Reed's Heart of Darkness," *Rolling Stone,* March 22, 1979.

254 "The kid adopted me": Author interview, Camille O'Grady.

255 "No more bullshit, dyed hair, faggot junkie trip": Lenny Kaye, "Lou Reed," *New Musical Express,* January 24, 1976.

255 "What would happen if Raymond Chandler wrote a rock-and-roll song?": "Radio with Pictures: Lou Reed," TVNZ interview with Lou Reed, 1985, available through NZONSCREEN, https://www.nzonscreen.com/title/radio-with-pictures---lou-reed-1985.

257 "come out funny. And when he did it, it sounded real": David Fricke, "Lou Reed: The *Rolling Stone* Interview," May 4, 1989.

258 "There are some severe little tangent things" and following: Gilmore, "Lou Reed's Heart of Darkness."

260 "as if Mr. Reed were finally beginning to make some sort of productive synthesis": John Rockwell, "Three Faces of New York Rock," the *New York Times,* April 16, 1978.

260 "a stunning incandescent triumph": Tom Carson, "Lou Reed Fights the Law and Wins," *Rolling Stone,* April 6, 1978.

260 "After all this time, he still cares": Carson, "Lou Reed Fights the Law and Wins."

260 "I thought I had a killer group": David Fricke, liner notes, *Take No Prisoners* reissue (Arista/BMG, 2000).

261 "I thank Lou for pronouncing my name right": Robert Christgau, Consumer Guide review of *Take No Prisoners,* 1978, https://www.robertchristgau.com/get_album.php?id=7622.

261 "I thought he was too drunk" and following: Author interview, Michael Fonfara.

261 "When we were in Montreal": Bowman, *Between Thought and Expression.*

262 "I wanted to make a record that wouldn't give an inch": Gilmore, "Lou Reed's Heart of Darkness."

262 "Everybody said, 'You don't talk enough onstage'": Fricke, *Take No Prisoners.*

262 "a barrage of invective": Ken Tucker, review of *Take No Prisoners, Rolling Stone,* February 8, 1979.

262 "I always think of the audiences in New York as friends": Fricke, *Take No Prisoners* reissue (2000).

263 "Why did I do it? Who knows?": Fricke, *Take No Prisoners.*

263 "If you can't play rock and you can't play jazz": Timothy and Karin Greenfield-Sanders, liner notes, *The Bells* reissue (Buddha/Arista/BMG, 2000).

264 "It was released and dropped into a dark well": Bowman, *Between Thought and Expression.*

264 "Where's the money, Clive?": Clive Davis with Anthony DeCurtis, *The Soundtrack of My Life* (Simon and Schuster, 2013), p. 223.

264 "I've always loved Clive": Davis with DeCurtis, *The Soundtrack of My Life,* p. 223.

264 "first-class mail correspondence": Greenfield-Sanders, *The Bells.*

267 "I had rented a fifteen-foot gong": Bowman, *Between Thought and Expression.*

267 "It was a spontaneous piece": Bowman, *Between Thought and Expression.*

267 "Love and the desire for transcendence": Lou Reed, *Pass Through Fire: The Collected Lyrics* (Da Capo Press, 2000), p. xxv.

267 "If he didn't seem so genuinely confused a person": John Rockwell, "More from Patti Smith and Lou Reed," the *New York Times,* May 13, 1979.

267 "the likely keynote for the final year of the seventies": Jon Savage, "Lou Reed: *The Bells,*" *Melody Maker,* May 5, 1979.

267 "*The Bells* isn't merely Lou Reed's best solo LP": Lester Bangs, "Lou Reed's Act of Love," review of *The Bells, Rolling Stone,* June 14, 1979.

Chapter 14. *Growing Up in Public*

270 "I was pleased with that album" and following: Author interview, Michael Fonfara.

270 "I got off on the Beatles": Mikal Gilmore, "Lou Reed's Heart of Darkness," *Rolling Stone,* March 22, 1979.

270 "I never liked the Beatles": "Lou Reed: On Guns and Ammo," *Blank on Blank,* March 20, 1987, http://blankonblank.org/interviews/lou-reed-guns-ammo-the-velvet-underground.

271 "Lou and George got along perfectly": Author interview, Michael Fonfara.

271 "*Growing Up in Public* is one of the great drinking records of all time": Rob Bowman, liner notes, *Between Thought and Expression* (RCA).

271 "This was a studio where they had waiters come by" and following: Author interview, Michael Fonfara.

272 "When I met Lou, he was living with Rachel" and following: Author interview, Sylvia Morales.

272 "Look at that cover": Author interview, Mick Rock.

272 "You do interviews and what they want to know is": Author interview, Lou Reed.

273 "Most of [my] major mistakes were in public": David Fricke, "Lou Reed: The *Rolling Stone* Interview," *Rolling Stone,* May 4, 1989.

274 "Well, actually, my mother's not dead": Dave DiMartino, "Lou Reed Tilts the Machine," *Creem,* September 1980.

275 "I wrote that song specifically for Sylvia": DiMartino, "Lou Reed Tilts the Machine."

276 "I think of the whole thing as being on a very up note": DiMartino, "Lou Reed Tilts the Machine."

276 "I thought it was a good idea": DiMartino, "Lou Reed Tilts the Machine."

Chapter 15. *Just an Average Guy*

278 "It happened more than once": "Lou Reed: A Radio Interview," *The Blue Mask,* track by track promotional interview (RCA), 1982.

278 "You have to be as close as I've been to the drug scene" and following: David Fricke, "A Refugee from Rock's Dark Side, Lou Reed Says Goodbye Excess, Hello New Jersey," *People,* March 30, 1981.

278 "There were a lot of drugs going on during that period": Rob Bowman, liner notes, *Between Thought and Expression: The Lou Reed Anthology* (RCA).

278 "He set me up as a gatekeeper": Author interview, Sylvia Morales.

279 "I can't have another drink or do another shot of speed" and following: Author interview, Michael Fonfara.

280 "Lou Reed became such a big influence on my playing": Robert Quine, from November 1983 *Guitar World* interview, quoted in Bowman, *Between Thought and Expression.*

NOTES

280 "I bullied him into playing guitar": Jim DeRogatis, "Robert Quine: Such a Lovable Genius," *Perfect Sound Forever*, http://www.furious.com/perfect/Quine/quinederogatis.html.

280 "For the last few years, I was working with musicians": Robert Palmer, "The Pop Life," the *New York Times*, March 10, 1982.

281 "When I first heard Fernando play": Vic Garbarini, "Lou Reed: Waiting for the Muse," *Musician*, July 1, 1986.

281 "We did *The Blue Mask* under very unusual circumstances": Quine, quoted in Bowman, *Between Thought and Expression*.

283 "Jackie Kennedy trying to claw her way out of that car": Lou Reed, *Between Thought and Expression: Selected Lyrics of Lou Reed* (Hyperion, 1991), p. 79.

284 "overwhelmingly intense desire for this woman": "Lou Reed: A Radio Interview."

285 " 'The Blue Mask' as a song is really devastating": "Lou Reed: A Radio Interview."

287 "Some people like to think I'm just this black-leather-clad person in sunglasses": Palmer, "The Pop Life."

287 "I think of myself as a writer. I operate through a rock-and-roll format": Scott Isler, "Lou Reed: A Reluctant Legend Doffs His Mask—Briefly," *Musician*, 1984.

287 "I took a major in English and a minor in philosophy": Palmer, "The Pop Life."

288 "a kind of national anthem in homosexual circles": Palmer, "The Pop Life."

288 "I really have no feeling about politics one way or the other" and following: Palmer, "The Pop Life."

289 "the most outstanding rock album of 1982": Robert Palmer, "The Pop Life," review of *The Blue Mask*, the *New York Times*, December 22, 1982.

289 "the best album of 1982": Brian Cullman, review of *The Blue Mask, Musician*, April 1, 1982.

289 "most controlled, plainspoken, deeply felt, and uninhibited album": Robert Christgau, Consumer Guide review of *The*

Blue Mask, 1982, https://www.robertchristgau.com/get_album
.php?id=2150.

289 "Lou Reed's *The Blue Mask* is a great record": Tom Carson,
"Lou Reed Uncorks a Great One," *Rolling Stone,* April 15, 1982.

289 "the end of something, the absolute end of everything from
the Velvet Underground on": "The 100 Best Albums of the
Eighties," *Rolling Stone,* November 16, 1989.

289 "If the late poet Delmore Schwartz": Cullman, review of *The
Blue Mask.*

290 "It was probably the worst thing I could have done" and following: DeRogatis, "Robert Quine: Such a Lovable Genius."

294 "while there are no legendary loves" and following: David
Fricke, review of *Legendary Hearts, Rolling Stone,* April 28,
1983.

294 "his great new band is just a way": Robert Christgau, Consumer Guide review of *Legendary Hearts,* 1983, https://www
.robertchristgau.com/get_album.php?id=2151.

Chapter 16. *New Sensations*

297 "I never felt that Lou was running from anything": Author
interview, Jeffrey Ross.

297 "Sylvia is one hundred percent for Lou": David Fricke, "A
Refugee from Rock's Dark Side, Lou Reed Says Goodbye
Excess, Hello New Jersey," *People,* March 30, 1981.

298 "I've been practicing and practicing, and I knew exactly what
I wanted to do": Scott Isler, "Lou Reed: A Reluctant Legend
Doffs His Mask—Briefly," *Musician,* 1984.

298 "This is a positive album, looking at things positively" and
following: Isler, "Lou Reed: A Reluctant Legend Doffs His
Mask—Briefly."

300 "Their house was in a very rural area" and following: Author
interview, Richard Sigal.

301 "One day, he came over on his bike": Author interview, Lenny
Kaye.

302 "My expectations are high...to be the greatest writer that ever lived on God's earth": Lou Reed, quoted in Simon Reynolds, "Lou Reed: Alchemical Engineering," *The Wire,* February 1992.

302 "That was just me shooting my mouth off": Reynolds, "Lou Reed: Alchemical Engineering."

303 "I really think I have it more together than I ever have in my whole life" and following: Bill Holdship, "Lou Reed: New Rock Sensations," *Creem,* November 1994.

307 "stumbled through one of the most self-indulgent and self-defeating solo careers": Kurt Loder, "Lou Reed Lightens Up His Life and Looks Like a Winner Again," *Rolling Stone,* June 7, 1984.

309 "Who else could make a scooter hip?": Ben Fong-Torres, "Lou Reed: The Prince of Darkness Lightens Up," *GQ,* September 1986.

309 "I can't live in an ivory tower like people would like me to": Roy Trakin, "Lou Reed: New York State of Mind," *Hits,* February 6, 1989.

309 "ad people play fair with you": Matt Creamer and Sonya Chudgar, "The Famously Grouchy Lou Reed Had Good Words for Adland," *Advertising Age,* October 28, 2013.

311 "Lou kept going, 'My amp's fucked up!'" and following: Author interview, John Mellencamp.

314 "What's interesting is that after I wrote the song 'Mistrial'" and following: Vic Garbarini, "Lou Reed: Waiting for the Muse," *Musician,* July 1, 1986.

317 "I wanted to do a rap song—my version": Rob Bowman, liner notes, *Between Thought and Expression: The Lou Reed Anthology* (RCA).

Chapter 17. *New York*

319 "I've become completely well-adjusted to being a cult figure": David Fricke, "Lou Reed: The *Rolling Stone* Interview," *Rolling Stone,* May 4, 1989.

320 "Lou obviously was a great artist and had great stature, but it wasn't like Seymour had signed a superstar" and following: Author interview, Steven Baker.

321 "Generally speaking, I have to say that with most of my albums, I've felt that I was behind myself": Jonathan Cott, "Lou Reed: A New York State of Mind," rollingstone.com, October 27, 2014, http://www.rollingstone.com/music/features/lou-reed -a-new-york-state-of-mind-20141027.

321 "I rattled off a list of the usual names" and following: Jim DeRogatis, "Fred Maher on Lou Reed," WBEZ Chicago, November 20, 2013.

322 "It sounds like it was produced by an eighth grader, but I like it": Bill Forman, "James McMurtry on Lou Reed, Gun Control, and Why Leonard Cohen Must Die," *Colorado Springs Independent*, February 13, 2013.

323 "Faulkner had the South, Joyce had Dublin. I've got New York—and its environs": Fricke, "Lou Reed: The *Rolling Stone* Interview."

324 "We had tried to put the songs in order, to tell the story moodwise and emotionally": "The 100 Best Albums of the Eighties," *Rolling Stone,* November 16, 1989.

324 "For a while, I felt a little self-impelled to write Lou Reed kind of songs": Fricke, "Lou Reed: The *Rolling Stone* Interview."

324 "In *New York,* the Lou Reed image doesn't exist, as far as I'm concerned" and following: Cott, "Lou Reed: A New York State of Mind."

325 "We're in this terrible morass of people absolutely not giving a shit about anybody but themselves" and following: David Fricke, "Lou Reed: Back on the Streets," *Rolling Stone,* March 9, 1989.

326 "What is this, some sort of Velvet Underground reunion?": DeRogatis, "Fred Maher on Lou Reed."

327 "I saw the speech Jesse made about 'common ground,' and it was amazing, emotionally moving": Roy Trakin, "Lou Reed: New York State of Mind," *Hits,* February 6, 1989.

327 "He could take a conservative stance on the pro-Israel side": Author interview, Sylvia Morales.

329 "I was watching Marty Scorsese on *Nightline*": Fricke, "Lou Reed: The *Rolling Stone* Interview."

329 "sounds like the best thing Lou Reed's ever done": Bill Flanagan, "The Velvet Interview: White Light/White Heat," *Musician,* April 1989.

329 "In whatever future there is, whenever anyone wants to hear the sound of the eighties collapsing into the nineties in the city of dreams": Anthony DeCurtis, "Lou Reed's New York State of Mind," *Rolling Stone,* February 23, 1989.

329 "I'm not going to let that be my future": Fricke, "Lou Reed: The *Rolling Stone* Interview."

Chapter 18. *I Hate Lou Reed*

331 "No doctor looked in on him": Ronald Sullivan, "Care Faulted in the Death of Warhol," the *New York Times,* December 5, 1991.

332 "Mr. Warhol's keenest talents were for attracting publicity": Douglas C. McGill, "Andy Warhol, Pop Artist, Dies," the *New York Times,* February 23, 1987.

332 "Lou was always very wary of Andy, always a bit guarded": Author interview, Sylvia Morales.

332 "He may be *the* American artist—period": Author interview, Lou Reed.

333 "This day was, in many ways, Andy's masterpiece": Christophe von Hohenberg, "The Day the Factory Died: Andy Warhol's Memorial Service in Pictures," *The Telegraph,* July 11, 2011.

333 "a simple, humble, modest person, a child of God who in his own life cherished others" and following: Grace Glueck, "Warhol Is Remembered by Two Thousand at St. Patrick's," the *New York Times,* April 2, 1987.

334 "I noticed Lou was just standing alone, so I walked over to him": Author interview, Eric Andersen.

334 "He said, 'Look, you got to do something for Andy' ": Victor Bockris and John Cale, *What's Welsh for Zen: The Autobiography of John Cale* (Bloomsbury, 1999).

335 "three steps forward, two steps back" and following: Scott Isler, "The Velvet Overview: Bloodied but Unbowed," *Musician,* April 1989.

335 "First of all, we wanted to see if anyone anywhere had done a rock album that teaches you something about the life of whomever": Author interview, Lou Reed.

336 "a hundred percent collaboration. John and I just rented out a small rehearsal studio for three weeks and locked ourselves in": Bill Flanagan, "The Velvet Interview: White Light/White Heat," *Musician,* April 1989.

336 "I don't think Lou could have had a clue how I felt about Andy" and following: Bockris and Cale, *What's Welsh for Zen.*

336 "I watched Andy. I watched Andy, watching everybody. You've got to understand. I was never part of it. I was not a great friend of Andy's": David Fricke, "Lou Reed," *Rolling Stone,* November 5–December 10, 1987.

337 "*proud* of him. For once, finally he's himself, he's not copying anybody": *The Andy Warhol Diaries,* edited by Pat Hackett (Warner Books, 1989), p. 299.

337 "And oh, Lou's life is everything I want my life to be": *The Andy Warhol Diaries,* p. 386.

337 "a great present, a one-inch TV, and he was so adorable, so sober": *The Andy Warhol Diaries,* p. 398.

337 "They had a big reception and everything": *The Andy Warhol Diaries,* p. 883.

337 "She's nothing special": *The Andy Warhol Diaries,* p. 899.

337 "so glum, so peculiar": *The Andy Warhol Diaries,* pp. 1240–1.

338 "never even looked over. I don't understand Lou, why he doesn't talk to me now": *The Andy Warhol Diaries,* pp. 1408–9.

338 "I just don't understand why I have never gotten a penny from that first Velvet Underground record": *The Andy Warhol Diaries*, p. 1512.

338 "I hate Lou Reed more and more, I really do": *The Andy Warhol Diaries*, p. 1502.

338 "When John was doing the reading...I kept telling him that when we get to that line, 'I hate Lou,' you gotta say it like a kid": Mark Kemp, "John Cale/Lou Reed: Fifteen Minutes with You," *Option,* July 1990.

339 "Perhaps the two incidents that haunted Reed the most": Flanagan, "The Velvet Interview: White Light/White Heat."

339 "John's idea. He had said, 'Why don't we do a short story like "The Gift"?'": Kemp, "John Cale/Lou Reed: Fifteen Minutes with You."

339 "It's emotionally honest, which is something I've tried to be on all my records": Jim Sullivan, "Lou Reed: On the Wild Side," rocksbackpages.com, October 2013, https://www.rocksback pages.com/Library/Article/lou-reed-on-the-wild-side.

339 "Lou comes to terms with himself in songs": Isler, "The Velvet Overview: Bloodied but Unbowed."

340 "so that if I decided to take poetic license with certain facts": Kemp, "John Cale/Lou Reed: Fifteen Minutes with You."

340 "You'd have to be in Andy's shoes before casting the first stone": Kemp, "John Cale/Lou Reed: Fifteen Minutes with You."

341 "I was really excited by the amount of power just two people could do without needing drums": Flanagan, "The Velvet Interview: White Light/White Heat."

341 "In this particular show, we're throwing an amazing amount of information at you" and following: Flanagan, "The Velvet Interview: White Light/White Heat."

342 "Tell us something we don't know" and following: Kemp, "John Cale/Lou Reed: Fifteen Minutes with You."

342 "was a very powerful part of the thing" and following: Flanagan, "The Velvet Interview: White Light/White Heat."

343 "*Songs for Drella* is a collaboration": John Cale, liner notes, *Songs for Drella* (Sire Records, 1990).

343 "You can just say that John Cale was the easygoing one and Lou was the prick": Kemp, "John Cale/Lou Reed: Fifteen Minutes with You."

344 "a shining, tense merger of visions": Paul Evans, review of *Songs for Drella, Rolling Stone*, May 17, 1990.

Chapter 19. *Magic and Loss*

347 "By this I mean to say...the music, underground music" and following: Lou Reed, "To Do the Right Thing: Lou Reed Interviews Václav Havel," *Musician,* October 1990.

347 "I don't like it when the interview's so cleaned up that the interviewer and subject sound like the same person" and following: Simon Reynolds, "Lou Reed: Mourning Glory," *Pulse,* February 1992.

348 "It was definitely terrible...I could see why *Rolling Stone* rejected it": Author interview, Rob Bowman.

349 "It was hard to get clear answers to the most basic requests" and following: Reed, "To Do the Right Thing."

352 "I do consider myself even lucky to be here": Mark Cooper, "Lou Reed," *Q,* February 1992.

352 "Between two Aprils I lost two friends": Lou Reed, liner notes, *Magic and Loss* (Sire, 1992).

353 "I couldn't even believe your father knew who I was" and following: Author interview, Sharyn Felder.

355 "like a novel...at the head of each chapter a little phrase explaining what it is": Simon Reynolds, "Lou Reed: Alchemical Engineering," *The Wire,* February 1992.

356 "is the culmination of everything I've tried to achieve, all the mistakes I've made" and following: Cooper, "Lou Reed."

357 "I don't think of my records as disposable": Cooper, "Lou Reed."

357 "I'm not interested in 'Lou Reed' the character now" and following: Cooper, "Lou Reed."

358 "pose of cultivated cool, of someone who has not only seen it all but experienced it": Stephen Holden, "According to Lou Reed, Life Is a Fatal Journey," the *New York Times*, January 19, 1992.

Chapter 20. *Between Thought and Expression*

359 "He immediately gave me his phone number" and following: Author interview, Rob Bowman.

369 "If the box was going to be representative" and following: David Fricke, "Lou Reed: Beyond the Underground," *Rolling Stone*, April 2, 1992.

370 "It isn't a rock star's compilation": Max Bell, "Lou Reed: Read 'em and Weep," *Vox*, September 1992.

371 "Over the last few years I have done occasional 'poetry' readings, always using my lyrics as the basis": Lou Reed, introduction to *Between Thought and Expression: Selected Lyrics of Lou Reed* (Hyperion, 1991).

371 "drugs and liquor did not do me any good" and following: Mark Cooper, "Lou Reed," *Q*, February 1992.

372 "Lou built a real toughness around himself": Author interview, Bill Bentley.

Chapter 21. *Me Burger with I Sauce*

373 "The fact is, *New York* had great tracks and a strong first single in 'Dirty Blvd.'" and following: Author interview, Steven Baker.

374 "George Clinton used to have this expression": Author interview, Jeff Gold.

375 "was probably not that well versed in the mechanics of Warner Bros. Records at that point" and following: Author interview, Steven Baker.

375 "Whenever you would hear something from Sylvia" and following: Author interview, Jeff Gold.

378 "science of magic": Simon Reynolds, "Lou Reed: Alchemical Engineering," *The Wire*, February 1992.

378 "He never screamed at me": Author interview, Steven Baker.

381 "We're confronting the myth head-on": David Fricke, "Waiting for the Band," *Rolling Stone*, June 24, 1993.

381 "Should we stay in hiding just because a myth is loose in the land?": John Rockwell, "Older but Still Hip, the Velvet Underground Rocks Again," the *New York Times*, June 5, 1993.

381 "unique godhead status will begin to diminish almost from the moment they start their first number": David Sinclair, the *Times of London*, quoted in Rockwell, "Older but Still Hip, the Velvet Underground Rocks Again."

382 "did not produce a feeling of déjà vu, more an impression that, after twenty-five years, the rest of the world has only just caught up with them": David Sinclair, the *Times of London*, quoted in Rockwell, "Older but Still Hip, the Velvet Underground Rocks Again."

382 "We've got to go to the first show in Edinburgh, because there might not be a second one" and following: Author interview, Jeff Gold.

383 "You don't want me to do it? Okay" and following: Bill Flanagan, "Lou Reed," *Musician*, January 1994.

383 "I was in the middle of that whole situation" and following: Author interview, Steven Baker.

384 "draped in white towels, looking like an outpatient or an old-age pensioner": Victor Bockris and John Cale, *What's Welsh for Zen: The Autobiography of John Cale* (Bloomsbury, 1999).

Chapter 22. *Fourteenth Chance*

387 "Yes! Absolutely!" and following: Laurie Anderson, "For Twenty-One Years We Tangled Our Minds and Hearts Together," *Rolling Stone*, November 21, 2013.

388 "Lou grabbed my hand and started stroking it": Author interview, Suzanne Vega.

389 "We had been getting very close": Author interview, Erin Clermont.

390 "'the Ma and Pa Kettle' of the New York underground": Author interview, Bob Neuwirth.

391 "a house that was separate from our own places": Anderson, "For Twenty-One Years We Tangled Our Minds and Hearts Together."

392 "There's no explanation for relationships": Author interview, Jeff Gold.

392 "I was just so amazed that Lou and Laurie found each other": Author interview, Steven Baker.

393 "I wanted to make a record that would take you on a trip of passion" and following: Dan DeLuca, "Reed Talks Hoops, Happiness, and, Yes, Music," *Philadelphia Inquirer*, March 8, 1996.

397 "I was talking to Lou somewhat regularly on the phone at the time" and following: Author interview, Jeff Gold.

398 "I should have been dead a thousand times": Barney Hoskyns, "A Dark Prince at Twilight: Lou Reed," *Mojo*, March 1996.

399 "extreme gauntness of his once-muscular physique": Lou Reed, "The Lives They Lived: Sterling Morrison," the *New York Times Magazine*, December 31, 1995.

399 "I'd like to thank all the people who worked so hard to get us in" and following: Velvet Underground Rock and Roll Hall of Fame induction, January 17, 1996, https://www.youtube .com/watch?v=MXI3bFTgtSc.

Chapter 23. *Sadly Listening*

402 "with straightforward rock songs backing brief, abstract scenes, *Time Rocker* bumps into unexpected competition: music video": Jon Pareles, "Echoes of H. G. Wells, Rhythms of Lou Reed," the *New York Times*, November 14, 1997.

405 "Every night, when the recording sessions were over and everybody would leave the studio" and following: Max Dax, "From the

Vaults: An Interview with Lou Reed," electricbeats.net, October 28, 2013 (originally published in German in *Die Woche,* 2000), http://www.electronicbeats.net/from-the-vaults-an -interview-with-lou-reed/.

406 "To this day, I have never worked harder on a record,": Author interview, Hal Willner.

409 "Incinerated flesh repelling" and following: Lou Reed, "Laurie Sadly Listening," the *New York Times Magazine,* November 11, 2001.

411 "Obsessions, paranoia, willful acts of self-destruction surround us constantly": Lou Reed, liner notes, *The Raven* (Sire/Reprise, 2002).

412 "I saw it as a can't-win situation" and following: Jon Pareles, "Lou Reed, The Telltale Rocker," the *New York Times,* November 25, 2001.

Chapter 24. *This Is Today*

414 "He combines the very beautiful form, the great control, the focus, and a really, truly remarkable *fajing*" and following: Martha Burr, "A Walk on the Wild Side of Tai Chi," kungfu magazine.com, May/June 2003.

414 "I had made it for myself": Bob Beninoff, "Lou Reed and I Talk Tai Chi and Knees," digitalwkshop.com, 2007, http://www.digitalwkshop.com/bob4.htm.

415 "He's just wonderful and I love him": Mick Brown, "Lou Reed: Iron Glove, Velvet Fist," *The Telegraph,* October 27, 2013 (originally published May 26, 2007).

416 "This record was the embodiment of love's dark sisters: jealousy, rage, and loss": Ben Sisario, "Revisiting a Bleak Album to Plumb Its Dark Riches," the *New York Times,* December 13, 2006.

416 "I couldn't imagine that anyone would want to do it": Ed Pilkington, "The Day the Wall Came Down," *The Guardian,* June 5, 2007.

417 "*Rolling Stone*? Who cares?": Pilkington, "The Day the Wall Came Down."

417 "It was just another of my albums that didn't sell": Sisario, "Revisiting a Bleak Album to Plumb Its Dark Riches."

417 "I go out and I was like, 'Turn your cell phones off, please, and no flash photography'": Author interview, Hal Willner.

420 "I'd never listened to the Velvet Underground" and following: Author interview, Sarth Calhoun.

420 "We didn't play live that often": Author interview, Paul Chuffo.

421 "was very complimentary about the band" and following: Author interview, Sarth Calhoun.

424 "venture into deep acoustic space, drawing on new music, free jazz, avant-rock, noise, and ambient": Ulrich Krieger, "Lou Reed 1942–2013: Ulrich Krieger: Unclassifiable," *The Wire*, November 2013, http://www.thewire.co.uk/in-writing/essays/lou-reed -1942-2013_ulrich-krieger_unclassifiable.

424 "I think initially Ulrich was like, 'Why are you bringing some random dude into this?'" and following: Author interview, Sarth Calhoun.

424 "Krieger's saxophone was heavily processed into rich, electronic, glacial sweeps" and following: Jeffrey Overwood, "Review: Lou Reed/October 3, 2008, Los Angeles (REDCAT/CalArts Theater), *Billboard*, October 8, 2008, http://www.billboard.com/ articles/news/1043833/lou-reed-oct-3-2008-los-angeles-red catcalarts-theater.

Chapter 25. *Metallica*

427 "I can clearly draw a line from Ray and Lou to what we're doing now": David Fricke and Brian Hiatt, "Inside the Rock and Roll Hall of Fame Twenty-Fifth Anniversary Concert," *Rolling Stone*, November 26, 2009.

427 "We're your backing band. We can go this way. We can go that way. Tell us what you would like" and following: David

Fricke, "When Metallica Met Lou Reed," *Rolling Stone,* September 30, 2011.

428 "It says a lot about the Hall of Fame that in 2009 there's a place for what we represent at this kind of party": Fricke and Hiatt, "Inside the Rock and Roll Hall of Fame Twenty-Fifth Anniversary Concert."

428 "If you watch the Rock and Roll Hall of Fame thing, 'Sweet Jane,' it's off": Author interview, Hal Willner.

428 "We knew from then that we were made for each other" and following: David Fricke, "Metallica and Lou Reed Join Forces on New Album," *Rolling Stone,* June 15, 2011.

429 "It was extremely difficult for the live band to interpret the material, and it was unworkable just to play back the recordings" and following: Author interview, Sarth Calhoun.

430 "Lars and I listened to the stuff...and it was like, 'Wow, this is very different'": Fricke, "Metallica and Lou Reed Join Forces on New Album."

430 "He was defensive, ready to roll his eyes" and following: Fricke, "When Metallica Met Lou Reed."

431 "It was crazy" and following: Author interview, Sarth Calhoun.

432 "I think Lou and Metallica met equally": Author interview, Lenny Kaye.

432 "You gotta mean it" and following: Fricke, "When Metallica Met Lou Reed."

433 "One time, I had to point something out to him": Jon Wiederhorn, "Tough Questions for Lars Ulrich," *Spin,* May/June 2012.

433 "Things just kept falling into place": Author interview, Sarth Calhoun.

434 "After that...anything Lou wanted, he had me. I'd play it": Fricke, "When Metallica Met Lou Reed."

435 "The record got bad reviews before it was even recorded": Author interview, Hal Willner.

435 "It was more spiteful than anyone was prepared for" and following: Wiederhorn, "Tough Questions for Lars Ulrich."

435 "I played the record for my kids yesterday in the car, and it sounded as relevant and more intense than ever": Lars Ulrich, "Metallica's Lars Ulrich on Lou Reed's Rock and Roll Poetry," *The Guardian,* October 30, 2013.

436 "Maybe that would have served the material better": Author interview, Sarth Calhoun.

436 "David Bowie made a big point of saying to me": Laurie Anderson, Rock and Roll Hall of Fame acceptance speech for Lou Reed, April 18, 2015.

Chapter 26. *The Measure of a Man*

437 "I never learned German... I never studied physics, I never got married" and following: Laurie Anderson, "For Twenty-One Years We Tangled Our Minds and Hearts Together," *Rolling Stone,* November 21, 2013.

439 "It was intense hanging out with them every day": Author interview, Sarth Calhoun.

440 "Some people marry themselves": Author interview, Hal Willner.

440 "To a certain extent, I wasn't surprised" and following: Author interview, Suzanne Vega.

441 "the appeal of wanting to do something in the live arts in New York" and following: Author interview, Michael Dorf.

442 "'Jewish soul.' Rabbi Weiman-Kelman also described how, during their first meeting, he and Reed had 'quite a long, complicated discussion about the origins of circumcision'": David Brinn, "Jerusalem Rabbi Recalls Lou Reed's 'Jewish Soul,'" the *Jerusalem Post,* October 29, 2013.

443 "This was an act of love... I realized if I didn't do this, a connection of a lot of things would be lost forever. So there was a great impetus to do this": Nicolas Rapold, "Lou Reed's 101-Year-Old Story," the *Wall Street Journal,* January 11, 2011.

443 "had one of the best Burgundy collections in the world" and following: Author interview, Michael Dorf.

444 "All the Secret Service folks were about to draw their weapons": Michael Dorf, "Lou Reed: The Wise Child," the *New York Jewish Week,* October 28, 2013.

445 "If you had as much fun as I did just now, you should give President Havel all the credit" and following: Roxanne Roberts and Libby Ingrid Copeland, "International Velvet," the *Washington Post,* September 17, 1998.

446 "Laurie was super engaging": Author interview, Suzanne Vega.

447 "so much and so fast that it was like having locusts in the house" and following: Suzanne Vega, draft version of "Suzanne Vega Remembers Her Friend Lou Reed," the *Times of London,* November 2, 2013.

447 "He would complain about other people's diva behavior": Author interview, Suzanne Vega.

447 "We have an alchemist in our company tonight": Rob Enslin, "Doin' the Things That He Wants To: Lou Reed '64 Honored for Achievements in Music, Writing, and Artistic Expression," throughthejungle.com, 2014, http://www.throughthejungle .com/clients/art-sci/loureed.html.

448 "Who would've believed this one?": Author interview, Merrill Weiner.

448 "I will always love the university for giving me the opportunity to study with him": Enslin, "Doin' the Things That He Wants To."

448 "I look back on *Lulu* pretty favorably, except Lou was ill and I couldn't really tell the Metallica guys that": Author interview, Hal Willner.

448 "I didn't understand why he canceled the Coachella tour, and he canceled a tour before that": Author interview, Sarth Calhoun.

449 "She took care of him, and she canceled everything": Author interview, Hal Willner.

449 "It's as serious as it gets. He was dying. You don't get it for fun": Tim Teeman, "Laurie Anderson on the Avant-Garde and Life with Lou Reed," the *Times of London*, June 1, 2013.

449 "I figured that covered the spectrum with Lou, as it did with me": Paul Simon, Lou Reed memorial at the Apollo Theater, New York, December 17, 2013.

450 "You send out two planes—one for the donor, one for the recipient—at the same time" and following: Teeman, "Laurie Anderson on the Avant-Garde and Life with Lou Reed."

450 "This operation takes the measure of a man, and Lou measured up in every way and more": Dr. Charles Miller, Lou Reed memorial at the Apollo Theater.

450 "I would like to thank the Cleveland Clinic and all of you around the world who have lifted me with prayer and wishes of love": Lou Reed, loureed.com, June 2013.

451 "Lou is in the best physical shape in years—strong and energetic": "A Message from Laurie Anderson," loureed.com, June 2013.

451 "What people often don't get about Lou is his love of life": Author interview, Hal Willner.

451 "I had to help him up on the stage": Author interview, Michael Dorf.

452 "It's really hard to get along with Lou": "New Liver Complains of Difficulty Working with Lou Reed," *The Onion*, June 3, 2013, http://www.theonion.com/article/new-liver-complains-of -difficulty-working-with-lou-32669.

452 "I have trouble seeing in the dark" and following: Author interview, Suzanne Vega.

452 "rock and roll is a young man's game": Vega, draft version of "Suzanne Vega Remembers Her Friend Lou Reed."

452 "Oh, those are interview sunglasses" and following: Author interview, Suzanne Vega.

453 "When we first thought about who we wanted to give our Inspiration award to, there was only one name we spoke of: Lou Reed": Stuart McGurk, "When *GQ* Honored Lou Reed," *British GQ*, October 28, 2013, http://www.gq-magazine.co .uk/article/lou-reed-gq-men-of-the-year-2013-tribute.

453 "the bedrock beneath my feet and a beacon shining through the black night of crap": "Iggy Pop Pays Tribute to Lou Reed," *British GQ*, October 28, 2013, http://www.gq-magazine.co .uk/article/inspiration-lou-reed.

454 "There's only one great occupation that can change the world: that's real rock and roll": McGurk, "When *GQ* Honored Lou Reed."

455 "Beautiful book, Mick…and beautiful price" and following: Author interview, Mick Rock.

Chapter 27. *The Afterlife*

456 "We all agreed that we did everything we could": Dr. Charles Miller, Lou Reed memorial at the Apollo Theater, New York, December 17, 2013.

457 "I was with Lou the morning he died, and he knew exactly what was happening": Laurie Anderson, Lou Reed memorial at the Apollo Theater.

457 "Jenni and I were just lying on the floor with him": Author interview, Hal Willner.

457 "I have never seen an expression as full of wonder as Lou's as he died" and following: Laurie Anderson, "For Twenty-One Years We Tangled Our Minds and Hearts Together," *Rolling Stone,* November 21, 2013.

458 "We were in the swimming pool and I was holding him in my arms": Julian Schnabel, Lou Reed memorial at the Apollo Theater.

458 "My father didn't give me shit": "Lou Reed's Last Words: Watch His Final Interview," rollingstone.com, November 8, 2013,

http://www.rollingstone.com/music/videos/lou-reeds
-last-words-watch-his-final-interview-20131108.

459 "had a major influence on generations of rock musicians":
Ben Ratliff, "Outsider Whose Dark, Lyrical Vision Helped
Shape Rock and Roll," the *New York Times,* October 27,
2013.

459 "Johnny Cash of New York rock: he was always the man in
black": Mick Jagger, "Remembering Lou," *Rolling Stone,* November 21, 2013.

459 "a still figure in the eye of a metallic hurricane": Bono, "A
Perfect Noise," *Rolling Stone,* November 21, 2013.

459 "work and that of the Velvets was a big reason I moved to New
York": "David Byrne Remembers the 'Brave' Lou Reed," roll-
ingstone.com, October 28, 2013, http://www.rollingstone
.com/music/news/david-byrne-remembers-the-brave-lou
-reed-20131028.

459 "no words to express the sadness at the death of Lou Reed":
Morrissey statement on the death of Lou Reed via true-to-you
.net, October 27, 2013, http://true-to-you.net/morrissey_news
_131027_01.

459 "Lou Reed": Ryan Adams, Twitter, October 27, 2013.

459 "The world has lost a fine songwriter and poet": John Cale,
Facebook, October 27, 2013.

460 "Unlike so many others with similar stories": John Cale statement on the death of Lou Reed, October 27, 2013.

460 "Lou and I had a special friendship": Harry Siegel, "Moe
Tucker's Tribute to Velvet Underground Bandmate Lou
Reed," the *Daily Beast,* October 29, 2013.

460 "a master": David Bowie, Facebook.

460 "noooooooooo nottttttttt LOU REED": Miley Cyrus, Twitter, October 27, 2013.

460 "RIP Lou Reed. One of the greatest artists of our time":
Ricky Gervais, Twitter, October 27, 2013.

460 "We love you Lou. We love you Laurie": Lena Dunham, Twitter, October 27, 2013.

460 "I still can't believe Lou Reed passed away": Cyndi Lauper, Twitter, October 27, 2013.

460 "R.I.P. Lou Reed…The music of my generation": Samuel L. Jackson, Twitter, October 27, 2013.

460 "NY lost one of its originals with Lou Reed's passing": Susan Sarandon, Twitter, October 27, 2013.

460 "Deepest gratitude Lou Reed. Peace": Mia Farrow, Twitter, October 27, 2013.

460 "I thought I was someone else, someone good": Sarah Silverman, Twitter, October 27, 2013.

460 "so sad with the loss of Lou Reed": Kesha, Twitter, October 27, 2013.

461 "a gathering open to the public": Lou Reed Facebook page, November 2013.

462 "while 'White Light' played, some odd homeless dude with Down's syndrome": Attendee of Lou Reed celebration at Lincoln Center, November 14, 2013.

462 "The event didn't feature any large signs": David Chiu, "Lou Reed's Memorial Lets the Music Speak for Itself," rollingstone .com, November 14, 2013, http://www.rollingstone.com/music/ news/lou-reeds-memorial-lets-the-music-speak-for-itself -20131114.

462 "I think at first I was like, 'Oh, well, that's not really a shock'": "Dean Wareham on Lou Reed," salon.com, October 28, 2013, http://www.salon.com/2013/10/28/dean_wareham _on_lou_reed_velvet_underground_seemed_to_appear _fully_formed_beyond_influence/.

463 "I was tired of mourning him": Joseph Arthur, liner notes, *Lou: The Songs of Lou Reed* (Vanguard, 2014).

463 "It was fucking huge. Lou would never have believed it": Author interview, Eric Andersen.

464 "to set in motion the forty-nine days of prayers of *powa*" and following: Laurie Anderson, Lou Reed memorial at the Apollo Theater.

466 "I don't think anyone was ready for her speeches": Author interview, Richard Barone.

466 "It later came to light that Reed's estate": Julia Marsh, "Lou Reed Left Behind $30 Million Fortune," the *New York Post,* June 30, 2014.

466 "I wasn't really ready for this" and following: Laurie Anderson, Lou Reed memorial at the Apollo Theater.

468 "At the moment, I have only the greatest happiness": Anderson, "For Twenty-One Years We Tangled Our Minds and Hearts Together."

469 "'Cremation' could stand as your elegy": Bill Flanagan, "Lou Reed," *Musician,* February 1992.

ABOUT THE AUTHOR

ANTHONY DECURTIS is a contributing editor for *Rolling Stone*, where his work has appeared for more than thirty-five years, and a distinguished lecturer in the creative writing program at the University of Pennsylvania. He is the author of *In Other Words* and *Rocking My Life Away*, and the coauthor of Clive Davis's autobiography, *The Soundtrack of My Life*, a *New York Times* bestseller. DeCurtis is a Grammy Award winner and has served as a member of the Rock and Roll Hall of Fame nominating committee for twenty-five years. He holds a PhD in American literature and lives in New York City.